Information Systems for Sustainable Development

Lorenz M. Hilty
EMPA, Switzerland

Eberhard K. Seifert
Wuppertal Institute, Germany

René Treibert
Hochschule Niederrhein, Germany

IGP
IDEA GROUP PUBLISHING
Hershey • London • Melbourne • Singapore

Acquisitions Editor: Mehdi Khosrow-Pour
Senior Managing Editor: Jan Travers
Managing Editor: Amanda Appicello
Development Editor: Michele Rossi
Copy Editor: Ingrid Widitz
Typesetter: Jennifer Wetzel
Cover Design: Lisa Tosheff
Printed at: Yurchak Printing Inc.

Published in the United States of America by
Idea Group Publishing (an imprint of Idea Group Inc.)
701 E. Chocolate Avenue, Suite 200
Hershey PA 17033
Tel: 717-533-8845
Fax: 717-533-8661
E-mail: cust@idea-group.com
Web site: http://www.idea-group.com

and in the United Kingdom by
Idea Group Publishing (an imprint of Idea Group Inc.)
3 Henrietta Street
Covent Garden
London WC2E 8LU
Tel: 44 20 7240 0856
Fax: 44 20 7379 3313
Web site: http://www.eurospan.co.uk

Library of Congress Cataloging-in-Publication Data

Information systems for sustainable development / Lorenz M. Hilty, editor, Eberhard K. Seifert, editor, Rene Treibert, editor.
p. cm.
Includes bibliographical references.
ISBN 1-59140-342-1 (hardcover) -- ISBN 1-59140-343-X (pbk.) -- ISBN 1-59140-344-8 (e-book)
1. Sustainable development. 2. Information technology. I. Hilty, Lorenz M. II. Seifert, E. K. (Eberhard K.) III. Treibert, René.
HC79.E5I5148 2004
338.9'27'0285--dc22

2004003746

British Cataloguing in Publication Data
A Cataloguing in Publication record for this book is available from the British Library.

Information Systems for Sustainable Development

Table of Contents

Section II: Supporting Change Toward Sustainability

Section III: Risk Management

Preface

Information and Communication Technologies (ICT) bring about new opportunities as well as new risks for the goal of sustainable development. This book focuses mainly on the opportunities that show how information systems can help society to approach sustainable development, that is, to reach a kind of economic activity that is compatible over the long run with human and social welfare, and with nature.

Even after the first UN World Summit on the Information Society in Geneva 2003, the relationship between issues of the global information society and of sustainable development is not being discussed adequately. It seems that the interdisciplinary and international research in this field is just beginning.

However, there have been large projects to develop information systems that contribute to sustainable development in recent years, most of them on a national level in European countries. This book gives an overview of the background and the current state of these efforts in presenting the basic principles of such information systems and giving practical examples.

Sustainable Development and the Information Society

The most widely cited definition of sustainable development was given by the World Commission on Environment and Development in 1987: In order to be considered sustainable, a pattern of development has to ensure "that it meets the needs of the present without compromising the ability of future generations to meet their own needs" (WCED, 1987).

The world summits on environment and development in Rio de Janeiro in 1992 and in Johannesburg 2002 have shown that the goal of attaining sustainable development has become a predominant issue in international environmental and development policy. It is widely accepted that sustainability has an environmental, a social and an economic dimension. A number of national and international research programmes and activities have been set up in order to refine the scientific basis for the sustainability concept.

But while these issues are being discussed, the world is rapidly changing under the growing influence of ICT and globalization, which are mutually reinforcing factors. This process, which is transforming our industrial society into an information society, has the potential to substitute information and knowledge for material products to some extent. But besides this so-called dematerialization, the change process also entails a progressive globalization of the economy that has thus far boosted goods production, freight volume and passenger transport. Finally, the information society also means acceleration of innovation processes, and thus an ever faster devaluation of the existing by the new, whether hardware or software, technical products or human skills and knowledge.

The rate at which the information society is coming about is determined by Moore's Law, which says that the performance of ICT doubles about every 18 months. The result is that people can take advantage of more and more computing power and data transfer without requiring more space, energy or cost, thus giving rise to new services based on this technical infrastructure almost daily, services which are penetrating more and more areas of our lives.

In this introduction, we want to classify the relationships that exist between the goal of attaining sustainability and the transition to an information society.

Environmental Information Processing

Computer-based systems for processing environmental information have been in use for more than three decades now. A broad range of applications is covered by these systems, including monitoring and control, information management, data analysis, as well as planning and decision support. Some of these systems comprise so-called "micro-macro linkages" between corporate and regional or national information systems (Krcmar, 2000; Seifert, 2002). The generic name for this type of system is *Environmental Information System (EIS)* (Rautenstrauch & Patig, 2001).

Progress in informatics has made an invaluable contribution to our ability to analyze the biological, chemical and physical processes taking place in the environment. Inversely, the complex nature of problems occurring in environmental contexts is a great challenge to informatics. From this process of mutual stimulation, a special discipline has emerged known as *Environmental Informatics.* It combines computer science topics such as database systems, geographic information systems, modelling and simulation, knowledge based systems and neural networks, with respect to their application to environmental problems (Avouris & Page, 1995).

The environmental informatics community maintains an international annual conference series that started in 1986. The 15th conference in 2001 opened the scope of environmental informatics to the broader perspective of ICT and sustainable development (Hilty & Gilgen, 2001). The 2004 conference continues this process in focusing on sharing information and technologies, in particular between the global North and South (Susini & Minier, 2004).

The categories of applications described in the following sections show the type of work being done in environmental informatics. Examples can be found in this volume and in the proceedings of the regular environmental informatics conferences.

Applications in the Public Sector

Computer applications for processing information related to the natural environment have been under development in the public sector since the early days of computing. For instance, simulation models were in use in water supply already in the 50s. Today, most developed countries operate environmental *monitoring systems* that regularly provide up-to-date information about the state of the environment. One part of the data is gathered by fully automated telemetry networks that are used to monitor air quality, water quality and radioactivity. Telemetry means that automated sensor systems are placed in the medium (e.g., air, water) and transmit data to a central control office, usually operated by a municipal, regional or national environmental agency. Another part of environmental data is obtained by increasingly powerful remote sensing techniques based on processing aerial or satellite images in combination with geographical information.

EIS in the public sector fulfill at least the following three important functions:

Public awareness: Agencies in many countries are legally compelled to publish data from environmental monitoring. When such data are published, the public becomes more aware of the condition of public goods (such as the atmosphere or recreation areas), which would otherwise not be the case because public goods, having no price by definition, cannot create awareness by means of price signals. Furthermore, publishing environmental data has other important effects such as enabling citizens to judge for themselves the success or failure of the government's environmental policy.

Decision support: Environmental information is an indispensable basis for making political decisions that have effects on the natural environment or inversely are dependent on the condition of the environment. Decision support consists not only of providing information about the status quo, but also about making predictions (e.g., short-range forecasts on ozone-related summer smog) and in considering the effects of various available alternatives (scenarios, *what if* questions). Informatics makes an important contribution to decision support by providing methods and tools for modelling and simulation.

Executing environmental policy: Environmental policy instruments can only be implemented effectively when accurate and up-to-date information is provided continuously. EIS aid in checking for violations of regulations (such as tracing illegal emissions back to their *source*), help to monitor the success of measures taken, and provide the information needed for immediate action in case of crises and disasters.

Applications in the Private Sector

EIS were used mostly in the public sector until a decade ago. However, recently a market has come about for software systems that support environmental management in companies (Krcmar et al., 2000); these are known as *Environmental Management Information Systems (EMIS)* (Hilty & Rautenstrauch, 1997). EMIS can be viewed as the ICT infrastructure of Environmental Management Systems (EMS). Most EMIS today fulfill the following functions:

Legal compliance: For one thing, EMIS help to comply with laws and regulations by providing insight into *complex legal frameworks* (cf. Riekert & Kadric, 1997), for example on information retrieval networks for environmental regulations. Secondly, the information systems aid top managers in *discovering and understanding developments in their own company* relevant to environmental regulations. Examples of the second type of application are systems for company-internal emissions monitoring and systems for modelling material flows.

Environmental reporting: EMIS also enable a company to fulfill its many *reporting requirements* to stakeholders (government agencies, banks, insurers, suppliers and customers, employees, neighbours, and the general public) as regards its environmental impact and risks. There has been a trend in recent years to make environmental reporting software suitable for use on intranets to share data among subsidiaries and employees, and to publish a subset of the data to wider circles of interested stakeholders such as suppliers. Such HTML-based solutions then can automatically sift out the subset of the data public enough for publishing on the Internet. Applied properly, this efficiency could give a further boost to reporting.

Eco-efficiency: EMIS help to improve *ecological efficiency* (or *eco-efficiency* for short). In order to determine at which stage of the value-added chain eco-efficiency can be improved, Life Cycle Assessments (LCAs) are done, which investigate the life of a product or service "from cradle to grave" – starting with extracting natural resources from the environment, running through all production and use phases and ending with disposal of the waste – and evaluate its ecological impacts. Product life cycles, production processes and thus whole companies can be viewed as *material flow systems* that can be optimized for eco-efficiency. Such *material flow* management can be done on different levels, from the most strategic to the most operative level, and may include, for example:

- building up strategic corporate networks (especially recycling networks),
- using LCAs to rank product or process alternatives when making or buying products or parts,
- "Design For the Environment" (DFE) with the goal of reducing the life-cycle-wide material flows and environmental hazards caused by the future product,
- real-time process control for minimizing emissions or increasing energy efficiency.

Material Intensity and ICT

With regard to sustainability, a crucial aspect of ICT is how they could help to reduce the *material intensity* of economic processes (including production, consumption, and disposal, as well as the connecting logistical processes such as transportation and storing). The goal of reducing material intensity has been debated for about a decade under the heading "Factor X" discussion (Weizsäcker et al., 1995). An important project on the role of ICT in "Factor X" dematerialization was the *Digital Europe* project (Alakeson et al., 2003; Kuhndt et al., 2003).

As is common in discussions on this topic, we use the term "material intensity" in a very broad sense. It includes every transformation of mass or energy involved in providing a product or service. The spread of information society technologies affects the material intensity of an economy directly and indirectly, classified as follows (see also Forum for the Future, 2002):

- *directly* through the production, use and disposal of the ICT hardware itself (first order effects),
- *indirectly* by the impact of their application (*second order effects*) and by the changes in structure and behavior that their application causes in the long term (*third order effects*).

The *first-order effects* have been discussed widely in recent years under the aspect of how ICT industry could change its products and services in order to make them more environmentally compatible (Park & Roome, 2002).

According to a widely accepted scheme, the *second-order* effects of ICT can be classified under the following three types:

- Substitution effects
- Optimization effects
- Induction effects

Let us demonstrate this scheme using paper consumption as an example. The PC as the modern form of a typewriter and in particular the PC used as a medium to access e-mail, WWW and other Internet services do in fact have the potential to reduce paper consumption. Plenty of textual and graphical information can be received directly from the screen, which in fact is *substituted* for paper in many cases. There is also an *optimization* effect, since for instance many errors can now be corrected before a text or picture is printed for the first time. However, as the reader may know from everyday experience, the *induction* effect offsets the other effects by far, because today's PC and printer technology enables the user to print out hundreds of pages with just a few mouse clicks. Therefore, all in all, ICT contributes to the same general trend for paper that has been observed for the past 60 years.

The counter-intuitive trend that can be observed in paper consumption is an example of the most typical third-order effect, known as the *rebound effect.* This concept refers to a potential created by efficiency gains that is balanced off or even overcompensated for by quantitative growth (Binswanger, 2001; Radermacher, 1996). Every substitution or optimization effect achieved by ICT creates new degrees of freedom which tend be used for quantitative growth. This should be kept in mind in order not to promote purely technical solutions for attaining sustainability, but rather to analyze the problems and possible solutions to them from a broader, more comprehensive perspective.

A recent prospective study assessed potential first-, second- and third-order effects of ICT on environmental sustainability by modelling three scenarios for the European Union in the year 2020 (Hilty et al., 2004). This project was carried out by the Institute for Futures Studies and Technology Assessment (IZT), Berlin, the Forum for the Future, London, the International Institute for Industrial Environmental Economics at Lund University (IIIEE) and EMPA, St.Gallen.

Organization of Book

This book is organized in three parts, each of which consists of several chapters which cover the topical spectrum ranging from theory to practice. Each part starts with chapters devoted to background knowledge and basic principles, and ends with chapters describing application examples.

Section I focuses on the "classical" approach to support the environmental efficiency of companies, their production processes and products by systematically providing information on material and energy flows. This includes methods such as Life Cycle Assessment and other elements of environmental management that depend on the availability of accurate information.

Section II reports on approaches that explicitly address and support processes of change towards sustainability, involving social processes such as mediated discussion processes, institutional innovation, the creation of virtual communities, and new types of producer and consumer networks. All change processes mentioned can be supported by information systems.

Section III, finally, shows how the safety and risk issue, which has been underestimated for some time in the sustainability discourse, can be integrated in management systems, and how risk monitoring and management can be supported by information systems.

Chapter I opens the first part with an introduction into the ISO standardization process for environmental performance evaluation. The ISO14000 series defines basic principles of environmental management along whose lines many environmental information systems have been built.

Chapter II describes how national strategies for sustainable development, integrated product policies and product life cycle assessment are connected. These strategies and policies largely depend on the availability of high-quality life cycle inventory data.

Chapter III shows an example of providing such data by building a harmonized life cycle inventory database with clearly defined data quality standards, using the case of the Swiss national database "ecoinvent".

Chapter IV reports on the research project OPUS, which provides solutions for the organization of product development and production processes in and between companies. The goal is to support production-integrated environmental protection.

Chapter V describes how a system supporting industrial ecology can be successfully integrated in the workplace IT environment. The core idea is to provide the formerly missing link between material flow management and the working environment in companies.

Chapter VI presents a methodology with similar goals, but takes a different approach. Here, existing business management software such as an enterprise resource planning (ERP) system is used to match the requirements of consistent material flow management, called flow cost accounting.

Chapter VII introduces a middleware system, developed in the ARION project, to support the search and retrieval of scientific information. The system has been used for ocean wave statistics as well as for the inter- and inner-organizational workflow management in scientific organizations.

Chapter VIII shows how a software tool for modeling material flow networks can be methodologically and technically linked to economic optimization and simulation approaches. This approach has been applied to transport optimization as well as discrete-event production and inventory simulation.

Chapter IX closes the first part by applying environmental information processing to the ICT sector itself, in particular to the Internet. The impacts of this technology on resource consumption and environmental pollution must be taken into account to create a complete view of the effects of ICT in the context of sustainable development.

Chapter X opens the second part by introducing a social context model for the analysis of discussion processes. This model can be used to construct information tools that enable more effective discussions.

Chapter XI explores the link between ICT and organizational and institutional patterns, which are crucial for sustainable development. A normative framework is proposed for judging the sustainability effects of organizational designs and supports the creation of "e-organizations" contributing to sustainable development.

Chapter XII gives an introduction to state-of-the-art corporate sustainability reporting supported by the Internet. Companies are shown how to develop from early environmental reporting stages towards the more comprehensive sustainability reporting, while exploiting the Internet's specific capabilities.

Chapter XIII describes the principles of "ecoradar," a Web portal that creates knowledge communities of small and medium-sized enterprises cooperating in environmental management. The system provides the users with low-threshold introductions to environmental management, lists of common mistakes to be avoided, checklists and benchmarks for comparison with other enterprises.

Chapter XIV shows how recycling networks of industrial companies can evolve to sustainability networks, and how this process can be supported by information systems. As an example, the case of the sustainability network in the Eisenerz region in Austria is described.

Chapters XV and XVI both show examples of how a change toward sustainable consumption can be organized by the use of Web-based information systems, the first one in the field of organic food, the second one in carpooling.

Chapters XVII and XVIII discuss examples of information systems that contribute to environmental awareness by making environmental information available, in the first case by the dissemination of high-quality information via multiple channels, in the second case by creating a national portal for public sector environmental information.

Chapters XIX and XX open the last part of the book by describing how safety and risk management can be integrated in other management and information systems, including in-plant monitoring data in the second case.

Chapter XXI shows an example of a risk-oriented information system, providing remote monitoring of nuclear power plants.

Chapter XXII closes the third part by describing a GIS-based decision support tool for technological risk management, which is able to process remote sensing data.

References

Alakeson, V., Aldrich, T., Goodman, J., & Jorgensen, B. (2003). *Making the Net work: Sustainable development in a digital society.* Xeris.

Avouris, N., & Page, B. (eds.) (1995). *Environmental informatics – Methodology and applications of environmental information processing.* Dordrecht: Kluwer Academic Publishers.

Binswanger, M. (2001). Technological progress and sustainable development: Different perspectives on the rebound effect. Technological progress and sustainable development: What about the rebound effect? *Ecological Economics, 36*(2001), 119-132.

Forum for the Future. (2002). The impact of ICT on sustainable development. In A.M. Frankfurt (Ed.), *EITO – European Information Technology Observatory 2002* (pp. 250-283, 10th ed.). European Observatory Interest Grouping (EEIG).

Hilty, L., & Gilgen, P.W. (eds.). (2001). Sustainability in the information society. *Proceedings of the 15th International Symposium Informatics for Environmental Protection,* ETH Zürich, Marburg.

Hilty, L.M., & Rautenstrauch, C. (1997). *Environmental information systems for production and recycling.* Keynote lecture at the 2nd International Symposium on Environmental Software Systems (ISESS), Whistler (Canada) (pp. 21-29). New York: Chapman & Hall.

Hilty, L.M., Wäger, P., Lehmann, M., Hischier, R., Ruddy, T., & Binswanger, M. (2004). *The future impact of ICT on environmental sustainability.* Fourth Interim Report. Refinement and Quantification. Report to the Institute of Prospective Technological Studies (IPTS) of the European Commission, Sevilla.

Krcmar, H. (2000). *Informationssysteme für das Umweltmanagement. Das Referenzmodell ECO-Integral.* München and Wien: Oldenbourg Verlag.

Kuhndt, M., Geibler, J.V., Türk, V., Moll, S., Schallaböck, K.O., & Steger, S. (2003). *Digital Europe: Virtual dematerialisation: eBusiness and factor X.* Report to the European Community. Wuppertal.

Park, J., & Roome, N. (2002). *The ecology of the new economy – Sustainable transformation of global information, communications and electronics industries.* Greenleaf Publishing.

Radermacher, F.J. (1996). Die Informationsgesellschaft: Langfristige Potentiale für eine Nachhaltige Entwicklung und die Zukunft der Arbeit. *Oracle Welt – Die Globale Informationsgesellschaft als Chance, 3,* 36-39.

Rautenstrauch, C., & Patig, S. (eds.) (2001). *Environmental information systems in industry and public administration.* Hershey, PA: Idea Group Publishing.

Riekert, W.F., & Kadric, L. (1997). A hypertext-based information retrieval network for environmental protection regulations. *Proceedings of the 11th Symposium on Environmental Informatics,* Straßburg. Marburg: Metropolis-Verlag.

Seifert, E.K. (2002). Zum Stand der Diskussion von micro-macro-linkages in der NI-System-Entwicklung – Kompatibilitäten zwischen Unternehmens- und Regionalberichterstattungen. In U.A. Wittel (Ed.), *Nachhaltig keitsindikatoren und Partizipation* (pp. 67-84). Hamburg: Hamburg University Press. *http://www.hup.rrz.uni-hamburg.de.*

Susini, A., & Minier, P. (2004). Sharing. *Proceedings of the 19th International Symposium on Environmental Informatics,* EnviroInfo 2004, CERN, Geneva.

WCED – World Commission on Environment and Development. (1987). *Our common future.* Oxford: Oxford University Press.

Weizsäcker von, E.U., Lovins, A.B., & Lovins, L.H. (1995). *Factor four. Doubling wealth, halving resource use.* London: Earthscan.

Acknowledgments

The editors would like to acknowledge the support provided by Thomas Ruddy, EMPA, who commented on many of the chapters and contributed to this book by extensive discussions with authors and the editors. Therese Bracher and Daniela Hofstetter at EMPA managed the whole process of collecting and editing the book chapters and solved the huge amount of small problems that regularly occur in a large publication project.

Special thanks go to all the authors who provided their chapters early considering the long time it takes to assemble a book of this size. The reviewers provided substantially to the quality of this book by commenting on early drafts.

We also wish to thank the publishing team at Idea Group Inc. In particular to Mehdi Khosrow-Pour, Amanda Phillips, Michele Rossi, Jennifer Sundstrom, and Jan Travers, without whose support the book could not have been satisfactorily completed.

Lorenz M. Hilty
Eberhard K. Seifert
René Treibert
St. Gallen and Wuppertal
January 2004

Section I

Environmental Performance and Eco-Efficiency

Chapter I

EPE According to ISO 14031: Concept, Experience, and Revision Issues

Eberhard K. Seifert, Wuppertal Institute, Germany

Abstract

ISO 14031 on "Environmental Performance Evaluation" (EPE) was released in late 1999 and published in Germany by DIN in early 2000 also as DIN EN ISO 14031 in two languages (German and English) as the last standard of the original ISO-14000 family started in 1993 as a follow-up to the UN world summit in Rio 1992. But even before 1999/2000 users had already begun gathering experience with this new instrument for measuring performance, which had proven the standard to be an effective instrument especially for small-to-medium-sized enterprises (SMEs) both for continual improvement processes in operative environmental protection and as a basis for lean reporting to external stakeholders. Once again it was the ecological pioneer KUNERT AG which became the first mover to practically apply and test the standard with a view to improving it in view of the first revision process of the standard planned for 2004.

Historical Development

"Environmental Performance Evaluation" (EPE) was one of the original five main areas for a ISO 14000 series which had been set up by ISO Geneva in connection with the Rio Summit in 1992 as a measure to "strengthen the role of business" in the Agenda 21 process (Seifert 1998a, p. 27): A Subcommittee 4 (SC4) was set up to develop an EPE standard in 1993 in addition to standards for environmental management systems, corresponding auditing procedures, product labeling and Life Cycle Analysis (LCA). The USA got the chair and secretary of SC 4 along with convenorship of one of the two working groups (WG) on an "EPE of the management area". A second WG convenorship on an "EPE of the operational area" was given to Norway, which was especially active in the time thereafter in important stations of the development of ISO 14031 (Seifert, 1998b).

Dividing the management of the standardization process into these two areas indicates differences in the philosophy applied to the ISO process, which have been referred to as the Anglo-Saxon versus the Rhine model (as discussed further below), and comprises one of the reasons that the development of this new standard took around six years, whereas the flagship of the whole series, ISO 14001, took only half as long. The international drafters of this new standard had to try a new approach to get to a first draft with official status. From 1993 to the beginning of 1996 drafting committees consisting of SC4 members needed a total of four working drafts (WDs) before the SC head laid the foundation with two other WDs it had come up with for the next stage consisting of two subsequent committee drafts (up to the end of 1997), which attained preliminary official status: an English version can be obtained from national standard institutions and one can work with it. It took another two years for ISO 14031 to accomplish the next two main stages, that is, becoming a DIS (draft international standard) and an FDIS (final DIS), and to obtain final approval and publication – thus reflecting the pioneering task of this ISO subcommittee.

Philosophy and a Few Main Points on ISO 14031

As mentioned above, ISO 14031 represents a significant change in philosophy compared to the flagship 14000 series: Whereas the definition of environmental performance in ISO 14001 primarily has to do with improving the environmental management system, the consciously different definition of SC4 aims at the "results of an organization's management of its environmental aspects" – that is, not at the environmental management system itself, but rather primarily at the results of environmental management, at the real environmental performance of an organization. Despite an application from SC4 to make the two definitions compatible with one another, this difference has remained an apparent contradiction in the series of standards that has yet to be dealt with.

The 14031 standard was not initially planned to become a basis for certification like that under ISO 14001, or objectives or limits to environmental performance. Accordingly the text of this guideline does not have any prescriptive character, and is kept in the tone of recommendations.

Furthermore, unlike the site orientation of EMAS I, a concept of organization applies throughout the 14000 series which extends from trades and businesses to organizations of all sizes, types and degrees of complexity, which intend to do environmental management. In general EPE is characterized as a management instrument "to provide management with reliable and verifiable information on an ongoing basis to determine whether an organization's environmental performance is meeting the criteria set by the management of the organization". Thus the continual EPE is distinguished from periodic audits, the objective of which is to represent conformity with defined requirements.

The definition of EPE is "a process to select indicators and to measure, analyze, assess, report and communicate an organization's environmental performance against its environmental performance criteria" – with the main focus on the organizational activities, products and services, over which the organization has (the main) influence. However there is an appeal to take into account local, regional, national and even global issues as well (see more on this below).

The explicit recommendation to systematically incorporate concerns of interested parties (stakeholders) and the inclusion of corresponding guidance in the annex are also philosophical components to be emphasized in ISO 14031, as are the complementary recommendations and guidances on reporting and communication.

The EPE process is structured analogously to the plan-do-check-act (PDCA) scheme known from the ISO management series, in order to evoke a familiar "a-ha" effect for the continual improvement processes in environmental management as well.

In the end, after long consultations, some of which were controversial, the 14031 document was subdivided into a main body text and an extensive annex, which despite its innocent sounding generic type contains essential details and recommendations; examples are:

1. on interested stakeholders,
2. on selecting indicators,

3. on recommendations for Management Performance Indicators (MPIs),
4. on recommendations for Operational Performance Indicators (OPIs),
5. on recommendations for Environmental Condition Indicators (ECIs).

The fact that one differentiates between MPIs and OPIs reflects the above-mentioned philosophical difference between the Anglo-Saxon and Rhine approaches: whereas MPIs are environmental performance indicators that are supposed to give information on the activities of management to improve the environmental performance of an organization, OPIs provide information on the environmental performance in the operative area of an organization. Some delegates, mainly European ones, have regarded it as a success that OPIs are based on a definite input-output table structure, thus providing the operative processes with an explicit physical framework.

Environmental Condition Indicators and Micro-Macro Linkages

In addition to the above two "shop-floor" types of indicators, ISO 14031 also contains a type of indicator that was truly new to the whole ISO 14000 family, namely "environmental condition indicators" (ECIs), that were the subject of debates for a long time until they were recognized as a relevant innovation in an environmental management standard. They are by definition *"specific variables that represent information about the local, regional, national and global condition of the environment."* The main body of ISO 14031 explains that *"the condition of the environment may change with time and/or in particular cases. Although environmental condition indicators are not a measure of environmental effects, changes in the environmental condition indicators supply useful information regarding the relation between the condition of the environment and the activities, products and services of an organization"* (p. 16). There follows a list of aspects that provide an organization with the environmental framework to help with the following:

1. determination and management of its significant environmental aspects,
2. evaluation of appropriate environmental performance criteria,
3. selection of environmental performance indicators (MPIs and OPIs),
4. determination of a reference point on the basis of which changes can be measured,

5. determination of environmental changes over time in connection with a current environmental program,
6. investigation of possible relationships between the condition of the environment and the activities, products and services of an organization,
7. determination of a need for action.

The text goes on to the effect that *"the development and use of environmental performance indicators are usually task of local, regional, national or international government offices, nongovernmental organizations or scientific and research institutions than it is of an individual company. Organizations, however, which determine a relationship between their activities and the condition of the environment may determine their own environmental condition indicators to help with their evaluation of environmental performance in keeping with their possibilities, interests and needs"* (p. 17). There is a practical help box giving two examples intended to illustrate the following sentence: "An organization which determines that a specific environmental condition is being caused directly by its own activities, products and services might like to select management performance indicators and operative performance indicators which establish a connection between the management activities and operative performance with changes in the environmental condition" (p. 18, retranslated here into English).

Such links between "shop floor" indicators and environmental condition indicators are also dealt with more generally in an earlier section of the standard at the end of the section titled, "Selection of Indicators for Environmental Performance Evaluation" and in the section preceding the remarks on selecting indicators: *"regional, national or global indicators referring to environmental performance or sustainable development are being developed by government offices, nongovernmental organizations and scientific research institutions. When selecting indicators for the environmental performance evaluation and data collection, organizations will wish to rely on indicators that have already been developed by such institutions, and they should, whenever possible, make sure that their data are compatible with those supplied by such institutions"* (p. 14). These "micro-macro linkages" were an innovation (introduced initially by the author in his capacity as INEM delegate at that time) in international consultations of experts, coming from mainly corporate backgrounds; they have been controversially discussed for a long time now as regards both their feasibility and their purpose. We will surely need a greater range of applications before the benefits of such a form of "linked" data generation and presentation will become evident and be used.

ISO TR 14032 and German EPE Pilot Project with SMEs

Together with the IPU Munich, the author submitted a research project proposal to apply ISO 14031 in SMEs to the Deutsche Bundesstiftung Umwelt (German Federal Environment Foundation) in Osnabrück, in order to obtain practical experience in applying environmental performance evaluation and general experience with the CD version. At the same time SC4 had decided after long debates to gather practical experience with environmental indicators and EPE processes as regards a few controversial aspects in the standard draft. SC4 therefore set up a new working group 3, whose job it was to select practical examples for Technical Report (TR) ISO 14032 to be submitted through national delegations/standards institutes available anywhere in the world. Then those examples that had been proposed were presented according to the ISO 104031 structure (in particular the "p-d-c-a" model); however it was not a requirement that they be done based on the draft EPE standard. Only the above-mentioned German pilot project with six SMEs was able to present explicit application experience according to the draft standard in three of them. Therefore these three SMEs were accepted for indicator identification in this ISO 14032 TR together with one other German example from an earlier project on an "Indicator Guideline" from the German Environment Protection Agency (EPA) project (UBA, 1997). All in all, this TR contains 17 reports from 10 countries: four from Germany, three from Argentina, two each from the USA and Denmark, and one each from Malaysia, Japan, the Czech Republic, Norway, Sweden and England. The organizational size of them ranges from the two small German companies with 11 (the Schmidt Lumberyard from the EPA project) and 33 (the Haerle Brewery from the EPE project) employees to the UK multinational ICI with almost 70,000 employees. The USA submitted two examples of indicator development on the regional level from the city of Seattle and Silicon Valley. Only the three (preliminary) German EPE pilot project reports (Haerle, Hipp Baby Food and Immenstadt Clinic) were based on an ISO cd 14031 application, whereas the others had been done "only" on the basis of proprietary methods or, in the case of the example with the German EPA's example, were done according to its indicator guideline developed earlier. That is one of the reasons that the German mirror committee decided not to accompany the (English) publication of TR 14032 with a German translation; these three preliminary reports by the German SMEs still can only be read in the English TR, as there has not yet been any overall (English) publication on three project findings (only a final internal German report is available from the author). However, one of the participating companies, the GEALAN Co., did published its environmental report for the year 1999 including the ISO 14031 application and presented its experience during a corresponding SC4 EPE workshop at the ISO annual meeting in 2000 in Sweden (any presentations at SC4 workshops on ISO 14031 applications in 1999, 2000 and 2001 or at future workshops will be documented on the ISO Web site, *http://www.iso.org*).

The main findings from the German EPE pilot project with six SMEs – the Thermopal Co. (decorative tiles) and the Eberl Co. (printing and newspaper printing) in addition to those named above – were encouraging especially for SMEs, since all involved had been able to carry out the EPE process producing some impressive benefits using only comparatively "lean" external consultant support. The main findings on the issue of "what makes the standard interesting for companies" can be summarized as follows:

1. the standard leaves considerable freedom for individual design and application while providing a clear structure,
2. less important data can be put off for now,
3. orientation around the ecological issues placed on the company while at the same time establishing who is being addressed by the report,
4. providing a "lean" way of getting involved in the establishment of a systematic environmental management and reporting system,
5. focusing on information, data and indicators that are of prime importance,
6. controlling corporate flows with the aid of indicators has many advantages,
7. a way to compare a series of indicators over several years,
8. a transparent presentation of environmental performance,
9. environmental indicators can be integrated into other indicator systems,
10. reports can be produced with lean means and combined with other management or annual reports.

KUNERT Tests: "Lean" Performance Evaluation and Reporting

Some of the persons (including the author) involved in the SME applications described above also closely cooperated with the KUNERT AG, which in the year 1998 broke with its many years of worldwide respected tradition of issuing environmental reports (for instance, in 1995 it was given an award by the UN for the worldwide best report, the only English one ever): it then shifted from doing reports over 60 pages long to a lean report, the world's first environmental performance report according to ISO 14031 – without any substantial loss of information! This historical break with previous reports that had been getting longer and longer in the past in favour of lean ones, so exemplary for SMEs, was then continued with the annual reports for 1999 and the 10th anniversary year 2000 with environmental performance reports from KUNERT according to ISO 14031. With such continual improvements, this medium-sized enterprise demonstrates its continual proactive approach to reporting internationally: KUNERT restructured its third environmental performance report for the year 2000 into a new "architecture," which was designed together with the author and presented by him at the ISO SC4 workshop on EPE applications in July 2001 (for a detailed description of these three worldwide first "Environmental Performance Reports according to ISO 14031" see the author's contribution, 2002a).

One of its most essential innovations – in addition to various further improvements in detail – was the restructuring of the indicator architecture: whereas the ISO 14031 guideline seems to suggest a sequence of identifying indicators leading from MPIs to OPIs and finally to ECIs, this 3rd report gets right to the environmental condition indicators at the Immenstadt site, the original site of KUNERT AG, after the traditional input/output comparison, which it has been doing continually for almost a full decade now (as the only one in the world). This innovation entails identifying indicators for four main areas: air quality, protective forest, water quality and waste water quality. Let me also mention the company's close cooperation with the Local Agenda process in the city of Immenstadt, which presented its first sustainability report under a charming title in the local Swabian dialect. The KUNERT report "will in future incorporate the indicators of the sustainability report of the City of Immenstadt into its own environmental management as important environmental condition indicators" (p. 9, 2000).

The Kunert OPIs refer to these Immenstadt condition indicators as they are determined for energy/emissions, water/waste water, dyes and chemical/products and waste, in order to be able to determine corresponding MPIs with a view to monitoring and improving the entire environmental program and its objectives, measures as well as deadlines and responsibility. If this process logic is expanded, it would not only correspond to the same succession in the practical examples that is given in the help boxes of ISO 14031 as quite logical, but also would satisfy the requirements of Local Agenda processes to include more "micro-macro linkages" in indicator development (as, for instance, has been started in Immenstadt). Thus, the presentation by KUNERT in the ISO-EPE workshop in 2001 was recognized with a lot of interest and was discussed further for developing integration of ECI in an operative environmental performance evaluation in the working group that followed during the EPE workshop. KUNERT's pioneer experiences demand more examples. Such examples could come from the experiences of companies that are testing a new guideline from the German EPA on "The Environmental Impacts of Companies," and how such data are gathered and evaluated in the framework of environmental management

(UBA, 1999). Or it could be activities of companies that have started an EPE process, as in a northern German pilot project on implementation experience with ISO 14031 in the dairy industry – not to mention here experiences in other countries, including for example China, indicating that an international survey of real applications is the desideratum upon which to base the forthcoming review in 2004.

For the new links between the shop floor and condition indicators, the final results of the German EPA research on companies' environmental impacts on the municipal or local level will be very interesting, where the environmental information systems have only begun to be used, but have the potential to supply plenty of material for ways to improve "micro-macro linkages" (Bartelmus & Seifert, 2003; LDS, 2001; Seifert, 2002b).

Critique of Standard and Future Issues in Performance Measurement

Implementation experience provides the best basis for "testing" the first global environmental performance standard, and provides at the same time a starting point for critique and future improvements of the standard and for farther reaching issues such as sustainability performance evaluation and reporting.

ISO standards have to be reviewed at the latest after every five years – ISO 14001 for instance as issued in September of 1996 has been placed under review and still can boast a dynamically growing number of worldwide certifications: by the end of 2000 the annual ISO survey showed around 23,000 14001 certifications in a total of 98 countries. With ISO 9000, already 10 years older, quality management certifications numbered around 409,000 certificates in 158 countries by the end of 2000. Japan has many more ISO 14000 certifications with its 5,500 than Great Britain with its 2,500; Sweden had 1370 and Germany "only" 1260, although one must take into account the fact that there is another environmental management system practiced in Germany too that additionally can be seen as a trove of experience with formal environmental management systems and environmental reporting equivalent to the Japanese experiences, namely EMAS (I and II) with its almost 3,000 additional environmental reports (not to mention various environmental practices lacking formal certifications or validations altogether).

According to ISO's last published 12th cycle, which ended in December 2002, more than 611,000 quality or environmental management systems conforming to ISO standards are being implemented by organizations large and small, in public and private sectors, in some 160 countries. Concerning ISO 14000 certification, about 49,462 have been recorded in 118 countries (a growth of 12,697 against 2001).

Before criticizing the first EPE standard then, considering such figures, we should hope that the still relatively unknown ISO 14031 with its explicit performance orientation would come into broader use.

With regard to the performance requirements of EMAS I and II, for instance, it may be beneficial (especially for SMEs) to have a preliminary EPE phase without any certification or cost pressures, so that an efficient and systematic entry into an performance indicator based environmental management system might be had (as shown above in the German EPE project findings).

Furthermore, weaknesses in the standard itself that become apparent in practical applications have to be identified and documented for a future revision; at least two weaknesses of the standard are already known to SC4: the "assessment gap" and the insufficient guidance on reporting and communication.

Anyone reading the mere 10 lines regarding "assessing information" (section 3.3.4, p. 20) would hardly guess that long debates were held in SC4 on this topic, and even initiatives taken on the part of the Swedish delegation considering setting up a separate work project on this topic. They were not pursued any further due to tough resistance from a few delegations, and were ultimately abandoned for ISO 14031 due to resistance from a few; however there are starting points for the above mentioned testing in the collection of practical examples in TR 14032 and elsewhere. One must concede, however, that it was not possible to close the evident assessment gap in the final document version, thus leaving an urgent item requiring decisions for future reviews. Perhaps impulses would help us along further here, which have been presented in the German debate by Stahlmann and Clausen (2000), as one of the two main points of their treatment (although it was based on an earlier draft) of ISO 14031: "The examples of management performance indicators cited are very quantification oriented and drop off sharply from the status of evaluation provided by complex environmental management systems; the product indicators used focus a lot on material products, like those that are used in the legislation on recycling; they fail, though, for instance, for the most part when used on groceries. ... Established methods of evaluating the quality of management systems such as those preferred in EFQM (a process explained in the Stahlmann and Clausen book, the Author) take a completely different approach" [288]). However well justified complaints about the inappropriate quantification of qualities may be, the consequences that both authors draw do not appear to apply to the standard at all, when they summarize: "the same pattern can be found throughout. ... things are quantified everywhere and added up, the significance of which can differ considerably" (ibid.). Such adding up, though, of apples and pears is by no means an intention of the ISO 14031 standard and is not suggested anywhere.

Perhaps a basic misunderstanding is the reason for the second main point criticized, that of the "excessively heavy orientation around material design products" (p. 289). The critics do praise the inclusion of products in the indicator system; the catalogue suggested in the standard (annex) however appears confusing to them. "The strong orientation on (only, the Author) one product type leaves a number of other product types without any treatment" (ibid.). In reality, the missing "product nexus" criticized rightfully in the EPE standard (as was acknowledged in SC4 itself) is not too strongly oriented around one type of product; it is not developed at all! Instead, the production oriented, input-output approach for organization/sites dominates, as all of ISO 14031 is counted as a standard of this type rather than one taking the product-oriented approach as in LCA and labeling (Schmincke & Seifert, 1998).

The text says in the introduction to ISO 14031 *expressis verbis* in reference to its position within the ISO 14000 family: "Whereas the environmental performance evaluation aims at the description of the environmental performance of an organization, a life cycle assessment (LCA) is a process to evaluate the environmental aspects and potential effects of product and service systems. Further information on LCAs can be found in ISO 14040, ISO 14041, ISO 14042 and ISO 14043... Relevant information derived from these and other data sources can support the implementation of the environmental performance evaluation and other environmental management instruments" (p. 3).

Therefore the correct criticism might sooner be that product orientation is lacking in ISO 14031 altogether than to say product orientation is "one-sided". The ISO SC4 responsible was conscious of this (temporary) deficit, referring to the other product oriented standards, knowing full well that products and services may have essential environmental impacts, as conceded right in the first sentence of the introduction. Therefore it would be a justified and necessary ISO task in the future to aim more towards the issues and problems involved with better integration of these aspects, once all individual standards are available – as has already been started with the integration of quality and environmental auditing standards into the common standard ISO 19001.

The second above-mentioned deficit that SC4 recognizes in ISO 14031 referred to reporting and communication of environmental performance evaluations. In this case, however, initiatives came out of SC4, which led to a New Working Item Proposal (NWIP) through a much respected reporting workshop at ISO's annual meeting in 2000 in Stockholm. This proposal was first developed by Sweden, and then voted on internationally and positively after being brought into agreement with a counterproposal from the USA. The ISO 2001 annual meeting started work on a new and forthcoming ISO standard 14063, "Environmental Communications," which should be concluded within a maximum of three years (according to new ISO rules for standardization processes). The author is involved in this ongoing work nationally as well as internationally and may be contacted for further information.

A third topic that has hardly been dealt with, even in SC4, is an internationally discussed area where there is a lot of German experience: inclusion of a proactive environmental cost management standard in the ISO 14000 family (Diffenhard et al., 1998), as included in the "future visions" paper of the ISO TC 207 task force, and approved by the TC plenary at the annual conference in 2003.

These and other examples of new work items (such as "ecological product design" in the already released ISO 14062 or the forthcoming standards ISO 14063 on "communication" and 14064 on "climate change") show that the original 14000 series is not only subjected to periodic revision, but also that new and future oriented topics might get included in the standard family. It will therefore be very interesting to see whether and, if so, to what degree, a follow-up task force to the one on 'future visions' set up expressly for this task at the annual conference in 2003 under the title "strategic planning group" (SPG) will promote new proposals that go beyond the original program of TC207. Such topics may grow in importance, as integrating standard work (for instance, with quality standards) and sustainability issues come up that go beyond environmental aspects. Then performance evaluation and reporting approaches that are restricted to the environment might be, of course, too short-sighted, to whatever degree they may have assimilated justified criticism. That cannot be applied as criticism to ISO 14031, but does indicate that there are other initiatives outside ISO TC 207 (some of them from NGOs), such as the Global Reporting Initiative (GRI), pursuing quasi standardizations, in this case sustainability reporting, with success. Thus there is a fruitful competition of ideas and initiatives, about which a decision will yet be made as to which is the most sustainable form of performance evaluation and reporting. ISO 14031, though – perhaps for the very reason of its original appearance, which did deserve criticism, may well represent an indispensable yardstick for theoretical/conceptional and practical improvements of what sustainability oriented performance evaluation and corresponding eco-integrated information and reporting systems (Krcmar, 2000; Treibert, 2001) in sustainable enterprises of the 21st century (Seifert, 1999) can achieve.

Anyway, the EU-Commission has only recently released a recommendation concerning EMAS II (summer of 2003), calling for environmental performance indicators in support of this performance oriented European scheme, referring explicitly to the ISO 14031 EPE standard.

The recent call (January 2004) for an international vote on a revision process for ISO 14031 shows the international interest in an improvement of this unique global performance standard, which could benefit from some conceptional discussions and based on some remarkable application experience gained with it worldwide (illustrated here by German ones) since its release at the turn of 1999/2000.

References

Bartelmus, P, & Seifert, E.K. (eds.) (2003). *Green accounting, A reader in the international library of environmental economics and policy.* Ashgate, UK.

Diffenhard, V., Kreeb, M., Seifert, E., & Wucherer, C. (1998). Kostenwirkung Betrieblicher Umweltschutzmassnahmen. In G. Winter (Ed.), *Das Umweltorientierte Unternehmen* (6th ed., p. 129). Munich.

DIN EN ISO 14031. (2000). *Umweltmanagement – Umweltleistungsbewertung. Leitlinien.* Berlin: Beuth Verlag.

ISO: ISO/TR 14032. (1999) *Technical report – Environmental Management – Examples of environmental performance evaluation* (EPE) (first ed.). ISO-Geneva.

Krcmar, H., Dold, G., Fischer, H., Strobel, M., & Seifert, E. (Eds.) (2000). *Informationssysteme für das Umweltmanagement. Das Referenzmodell ECO-integral.* München and Wien: Oldenbourg Verlag.

KUNERT AG. (2000). *Umweltleistungsbericht nach der DIN EN ISO 14031.* Immenstadt (1998-2000).

LDS – Landesamt für Datenverarbeitung und Statistik NRW. (2001). StatistisAhe analysen und Studien NRW. Tagungsband Workshop, *Regionalisierung der Umwelt-ökonomischen Gesamtrechnungen* (2nd ed).

Schmincke, E., & Seifert, E.K. (1998). Bewertung von Umweltorientierten Leistungen und Deren Norenkonzepte. In G. Winter (Ed.), *Das Umweltorientierte Unternehmen* (6th ed., p. 455). Munich.

Seifert, E.K. (1998a). Nachhaltig Entwicklung und Agenda 21 – Herausforderungen für Wissenschaft, Politik und Wirtschaft. In G. Winter (Ed.), *Das Umweltorientierte Unternehmen* (6th ed., p. 21). Munich.

Seifert, E.K. (1998b). Kennzahlen zur Umweltleistungsbewertung – Der Internationale ISO 14031-Standard im Kontext Einer Zukunftsfähigen Umweltberichterstattung. In Seidel, Clausen & Seifert (Eds.), *Umweltkennzahlen* (p. 71). Munich: Vahlen Verlag.

Seifert, E.K. (1999). Sustainable Enterprise – Wie Alles Anfing. In E.K. Seidel (Ed.), *Betriebliches Umweltmanagement im 21. Jahrhundert* (p. 167). Berlin: Springer Verlag.

Seifert, E.K. (2002a). Umweltberichterstattung und Umweltleistungsbewertung bei der Kunert AG. *UWF-Umweltwirtschaftsforum, 10*(3), 64-70.

Seifert, E.K. (2002b). Zum stand der Diskussion von Micro-Macro-Linkages in der NI-System-Entwicklung: Kompatibilitäten Zwischen Regional- und Unternehmensberichterstattung. In S. Witteck (Eds.), *Nachhaltig keitsindikatoren und Partizipation* (pp. 67-84). Hamburg: University Press.

Stahlmann, V., & Clausen, J. (2000). *Umweltleistung von Unternehmen. Von der Öko-Effizienz zur Öko-Effektivität.* Wiesbaden: Gabler Verlag.

Treibert, R.H. (ed.). (2001). *Betriebliche Informationssysteme für Umwelt, Qualität und Sicherheit.* Marburg: Metropolis.

Umweltbundesamt. (1997). *Leitfaden Betriebliche Umweltkennzahlen.* Bonn.

Umweltbundesamt. (1999). *Leitfaden Betriebliche Umweltauswirkungen – Ihre Erfassung und Bewertung im Rahmen des Umweltmanagements.* Berlin.

Chapter II

Life Cycle Assessment Databases as Part of Sustainable Development Strategies: The Example of Ecoinvent

Roland Hischier, Swiss Federal Laboratories for Materials Testing & Research, Switzerland

Paul W. Gilgen, Swiss Federal Laboratories for Materials Testing & Research, Switzerland

Abstract

This article describes the importance of standardized, comprehensive and up-to-date life cycle inventory (LCI) databases for implementing policies that point towards sustainable development (SD). Taking present-day Swiss politics as an example, this article shows the interrelations among SD, an integrated product-policy (IPP) and a comprehensive LCI database. For this reason, the Swiss government states in its report on SD that IPP is one of the measures that will be put into practice as new instruments for fiscal policy. As it is essential to be able to calculate real existing value-added chains to arrive at a real application of the IPP concept, the creation of a

Swiss competence centre for LCI data is one of the different measures foreseen for the application of IPP. Therefore several LCA institutes within the ETH domain of engineering institutions along with the Swiss Federal Research Station of Agroecology and Agriculture and several Swiss offices/ agencies founded the Swiss Centre for Life-Cycle Inventories called ecoinvent.

Introduction

One can discern several successive stages over the development of environmental politics. Environmental thinking had a heyday in the 1960s with the appearance of the first ecological NGOs – regarded by industry mainly as people that disturb their work, and thus people to be rejected for their ideas and convictions. Therefore this epoch is nowadays looked back on as the age of "confrontation". In the '70s, when the recession hit industry, ecological thinking was mainly seen as a constraint that costs a lot, but returns a little, and therefore, in an ecological sense as well as in economic history this period can be associated with "recession". This often unfounded impression of ecology as an additional cost factor did not change until the end of the '80s/the beginning of the '90s – and there especially at the summit in Rio in 1992, where the word "sustainability" started to be used instead of "ecology". This change in terminology reflected a shift in industry from a stance of rejecting everything that detracts from the main goal (i.e., earning money) to a broader, more cooperative form of politics, for example, in relation to one's neighbourhood, and one's government at its various levels (from the municipal up to the federal) and to NGOs.

Principles of Sustainable Development

Looking back in history shows that the principle of sustainable development is much older than Rio '92. Conceptually, it was developed in the early 18th century, when population growth and industrialization had increased pressure on the resource wood to an extent that threatened further supply. Hans Carl Carlowitz claimed in 1713 in *Sylvicultura Oeconomica* that *"(...) man mit dem Holtz pfleglich umgehe, und wie eine sothane Conservation und Anbau des Holtzes anzustellen, dass es eine continuirliche, beständige und nachhaltende Nutzung gebe"* (Carlowitz, 1713, quoted in Grober, 1999). Actually, sustainable development has a much broader meaning, including and bringing into balance not only ecology, but also sociology and economics. In the famous "Brundtland Report" (WCED 1987), sustainable development is described as being a development that is able to meet the needs of the present generation without resulting in restrictions that would keep future generations from meeting their respective needs. In fact, this description shows the most important aspect of the whole philosophy behind the expression "sustainable development" – the inter-temporal contract between successive generations.

Such a lofty political goal should not go undocumented; it should be recorded at a more realistic level – the level of the constitution. The Swiss population agreed in 1999 on a completely revised and updated constitution – put into force on January 1, 2000 – where right in Article 2 it is written that:

Article 2 *Aims*

1. The Swiss Confederation shall protect the liberty and rights of people and safeguard the independence and security of the country.
2. It shall promote the common welfare, the sustainable development, the internal cohesion and the cultural diversity of the country.
3. It shall seek to guarantee the greatest possible equality of opportunity.
4. It shall commit itself to supporting the long-term preservation of natural resources and in favour of a just and peaceful international order. (Swiss Constitution 1999, English edition, see *www.admin.ch*)

Further on in the new Swiss constitution, it is written in the part about environment and spatial planning:

Article 73 Sustainable Development

The Confederation and the Cantons shall work to establish a lasting equilibrium with nature, in particular enhancing both its capacity to renew itself and the way it is used by man. (Swiss Constitution 1999, English edition, see www.admin.ch)

Looking beyond Switzerland to neighbouring countries, one sees that the principle of "sustainability" is anchored for example in the German constitution (Art. 20), although not in such a central position as in the Swiss constitution.

In Switzerland, the government started to act within the principle of a sustainable development culminating with the report of the Swiss government entitled "The

Sustainable Development Strategy 2002" (Swiss Federal Council, 2002). The guiding idea of this report is that the Swiss government recognized sustainable development as a political field that deals entirely with guaranteeing future development, and therefore takes on ecological, economic and social challenges, and implements them in equal parts. Based on this, the main characteristics or cornerstones of this strategy of the Swiss government can be summarized as follows:

- An emphasis on an equilibrium among the three pillars of sustainable development (economy, society, environment)
- A fundamentally wide-ranging strategy – not confined to just a few very specific policy areas
- Practical and result-oriented measures, in the sense of a specific plan of action
- The involvement of cantons, municipalities, civil society as well as the private sector

In order to put theory into practice, the report referred to 22 different measures in 10 different fields of application – these fields were: economic policy and public services/financial policy/education, research and technology/social cohesion/ health/environment and natural resources/spatial and settlement development/mobility/development cooperation and the promotion of peace/methods and instruments.

One of the most important instruments planned for in the total of 22 measures is Measure #4 in the field of "financial policy": the introduction of an integrated product policy (IPP).

Principles of Integrated Product Policy

Toward the end of the 1980s/beginning of the '90s, the OECD and other organizations started to realize that the product had to be a central part of environmental policy. But not until 1997 did integrated product policy (IPP) appear as an expression used by the European commission. IPP stands for a policy that deals in a comprehensive manner with products (both goods and services). Thus, IPP takes into consideration the whole life cycle of a product – planning, production, use and disposal – and integrates economic, social and ecological aspects across the whole cycle. In Figure 1, the different elements of an IPP are represented. To put it simply, IPP is the application of the principles of sustainable development to a product-oriented policy.

Figure 1. Different elements of an integrated product policy IPP

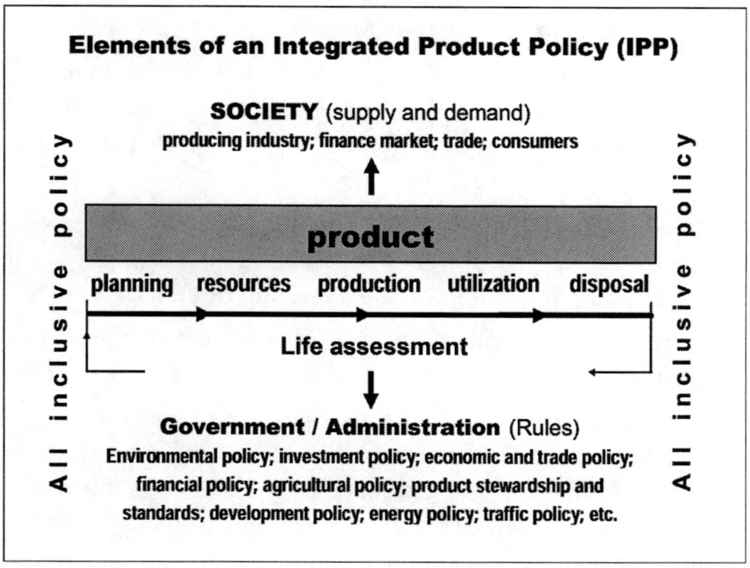

Source: Gilgen, 2002

Since 1999, IPP has been recognized as an essential concept for the implementation of sustainable development, and in 2000 the Swiss EPA published a first status report on the integration of IPP into Swiss policy.

Within the sustainable development strategy of the Swiss government, IPP is just one of the instruments chosen to ensure that the principles of sustainability are put into practice for goods and services, for example, by establishing a framework based on the principles of sustainable development, the Swiss authorities would like to guide the demand side (public and private) in the direction of goods that meet high environmental, economic and social standards. This means that products or services have to comply with such high standards throughout all phases of their life – from their planning, to production and use, until their final disposal. Therefore the principles of IPP have to be implemented into all stages of policies related to products. Thus, criteria or instruments have to be developed for all different areas that are relevant to the implementation of IPP that will make measurement possible, representing all three dimensions of sustainability and therefore will support such implementation.

In the present version of the technical documentation of the strategy paper (IDARio, 2002), seven different measures are defined for successful implementation of IPP in Swiss policy:

1. *Law on parliamentary business/administration internal rules* – adding ecological aspects to the already existing policies and rules.

2. *Research* – Further development of the methodological know-how as well as the instruments for the development and the application of IPP. Evaluation of already existing instruments.
3. *Centre of Competence for Life Cycle Assessment* – making available ecological data of high quality for establishing quantitative life-cycle analyses and respective assessments. Creation of basis for calculation of external costs, grey energy or product LCA.
4. *Public procurement* – integration of ecological and social aspects into all processes of public procurement by creating for example the legislative basis and establishing adequate tools and instruments.
5. *Agriculture* – LCA of food production, in combination with economic data and examination of the ecological and economic aspects of sustainability.
6. *Product stewardship* – establishing a system along with a catalogue of measures concerning an extended stewardship of producers covering not only production and disposal (extended producer responsibility) but also the preliminary supply chain (supply chain responsibility).
7. *Controlling* – Development and introduction of a controlling system – starting with recommendations concerning sustainable construction.

The importance of the above-mentioned Measure #4, "Public procurement function," for example can be represented by the annual expenses incurred by the Swiss confederation, cantons and municipalities on the order of CHF 40,000 million – for CHF 12,000 million of which the confederation is responsible itself. Thus, the potential for green procurement is really important. Examples of other measures can be found as well – for example for Measure #2, "Research," with the "Augsburg Material declaration" (Strizker, 2002), which is just one example of the inclusion of the principles of sustainable development by IPP.

In other words, this means that for a real application of IPP, it is essential to be able to calculate completely and in a conclusive manner real existing (not just typical) value-added chains by the use of complete and reliable data, all of which have been subjected to quality control. Otherwise, it is not possible to create the indispensable basis for a credible integrated product policy (IPP). Thus, Measure #3, "Centre of competence for life cycle assessment," is really a crucial factor within a successful start of the principle of IPP. And just such a centre has been established in Switzerland in the form of the "Swiss Centre for Life Cycle Inventories" chaired by EMPA.

Swiss Centre for Life Cycle Inventories and Its Database Ecoinvent

Toward the end of the 1990s, several LCA institutes in the ETH domain (the Swiss Federal Institutes of Technology (ETH) Zürich and Lausanne, the Swiss Federal Laboratories for Materials Testing and Research (EMPA) St. Gallen and Dübendorf, the Paul Scherrer Institute (PSI) Villigen, and the Swiss Federal Institute for Environmental Science and Technology (EAWAG)) as well as the LCA Department of the Swiss Federal Research Station for Agroecology and Agriculture (FAL) in Zürich agreed on a close cooperation. Together with the Swiss Agency for the Environment, Forests and Landscape (SAEFL or BUWAL in German), the Swiss Agency for Energy (BFE) and other agencies jointly founded the Swiss Centre for Life Cycle Inventories. Its steering committee, chaired by Dr. X. Edelmann, a member of the board of EMPA, launched the ECOINVENT 2000 project, which aims to establish a harmonized, revised and updated Swiss national LCI database – the database ecoinvent.

The database ecoinvent consists of average life cycle inventory data for a huge number of materials, energy systems, transport systems, waste disposal systems, and so forth. Due to the fact that most value-added chains do not stop at the frontiers of a country, such a life cycle inventory database cannot be limited to one's own country – that is, the database ecoinvent will contain specific electricity mixes for almost all European countries. Likewise, the world needs an internationally accepted standard for databases, containing national and international compatible database content in a uniform presentation.

Ecoinvent: Information System for the LCA Community

But ecoinvent is much more than just a collection of life cycle inventory data for the Swiss user of this instrument – it is actually a whole information system for the LCA community. Thus, ecoinvent means also a clearly defined and comprehensive data exchange format for the exchange of LCI and LCA information among different users or systems. This format has been established in XML technology, making it platform independent and flexible for further development, and so forth. The central database has an architecture allowing for very fast calculation of several thousands of datasets by matrix inversion. And lastly, the user does not need any special software – access to the database is through a Web interface, and thus a simple Web browser is sufficient.

Further information about the technology and content of this database can be found in the next chapter of this book.

Similar Activities Abroad

Outside Switzerland as well, similar activities are going on. Therefore, bearing in mind the great importance of IPP as one part of the plan to put the principle of sustainable development into practice, the European commission proposed the following in October 2002 (ENDS, 2002):

> *"The European Commission should propose a new framework directive outlining minimum requirements for environmental product (type III) declarations or EPDs, an extensive report ordered by the EU executive has recommended. EPDs are product profiles that use life cycle analysis to provide an environmental assessment of individual goods. They offer an alternative to other forms of ecolabelling in assisting green procurement practices.*
>
> *The Commission should also support the creation of a "harmonised European life cycle analysis database". This would supply data for product declarations, possibly joining up with the UN environmental programme, which is already involved in this area. (...) In addition, the EU executive could stimulate demand for EPDs by including details of these in guidelines on European public procurement."*

Tapping into its contacts outside Switzerland, the newly created Swiss Centre for Life-Cycle Inventories is sharing the experience it has gained from the ecoinvent 2000 project with several national initiatives (e.g., in Germany or the United States of America) as well as with international initiatives (e.g., the COST Action 530, the UNEP-SETAC Life-Cycle Initiative, or the recent efforts of the European Joint Research Centre in Ispra (Italy)). Furthermore, the Swiss Centre for Life-Cycle Inventories is a project partner in several proposals of the 6th Framework Programme of the European Commission. The goal of all these activities is, first of all, to take part in the international harmonization efforts in the area of life cycle assessment. Currently, the main weakness preventing wider application of this instrument is the present state of the art – a state that still contains several areas where no clear standard has yet been established (e.g., data exchange format, dataset content, the impact assessment method, etc.).

Figure 2. Interrelations among sustainable development, integrated product policy and life cycle inventories

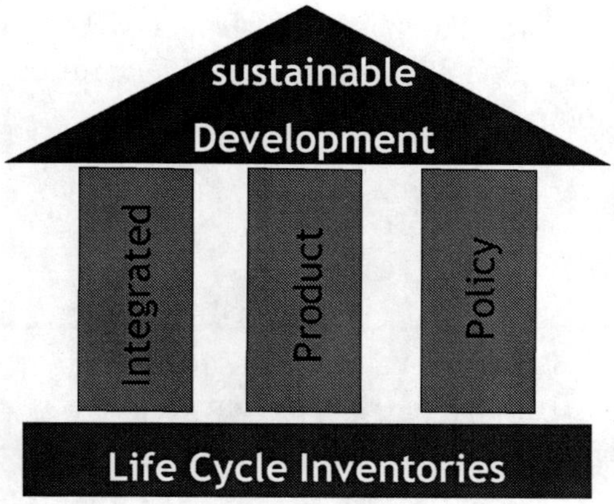

Besides these more methodical efforts, several members of the Swiss Centre for Life-Cycle Inventories are involved in ongoing/planned LCI data collection projects of specific sectors or future technologies within a sector. These projects will make updating and expansion of the data content of the ecoinvent database possible in the future.

Conclusions

If our society is interested in making sustainable development more than a mere theoretical concept, and it is to be applied in the form of an integrated product policy (IPP) in political decisions, then all actors in this framework require reliable facts and figures as the indispensable basis for their actions – because the motto applies in this domain as well that "what is not measurable is not manageable". This means nothing else than what has been shown in Figure 2 – life cycle inventories, IPP and sustainable development are interconnected from the bottom up as well as from the top down.

Out of this infusible linkage of sustainable development, integrated product policy and life cycle inventories the high strategic relevance of the latter can be deduced: Without life-cycle inventories there will be no sustainable development.

Acknowledgment

The authors would like to thank Thomas Ruddy from EMPA for proofreading this chapter as well as Dr. Christoph Rentsch from BUWAL for his valuable support in establishing this chapter.

References

ENDS (2002, October 10). *Europe's Environmental News Service, 1305.* Online information system at: *www.environmentdaily.com.*

Gilgen, P.W. (2002, November 18-19). *Ökoinventare und deren strategische Bedeutung.* Presentation at the workshop "Qualitätssicherung und Nutzerorientiere Bereitstellung von Lebenszyklusdaten – Ergebnisse und Perspektiven der BMBF-geförderten Vorstudie," Forschungszentrum Karlsruhe (Germany), (*only in German*).

Grober, U. (1999). Der Erfinder der Nachhaltigkeit. *Die Zeit, 1999*(48), 98 (*only in German*).

IDARio (Interdepartementaler Ausschuss Rio). (2002, December 18). *Strategie Nachhaltige Entwicklung 2002 – Technischer Teil: Massnahmenblätter.* Federal Office for Spatial Development (ARE), Bern (Switzerland). Online version at: *www.are.admin.ch* (*only in German*).

Stritzker, B., & Reller, A. (eds.). (2002). The Augsburg materials declaration. Retrieved March 19, 2003, from: *http://www.amu-augsburg.de/matforum/augsburg_materials_declaration.pdf.*

Swiss Federal Council. (2002, March). *Sustainable development strategy 2002.* Federal Office for Spatial Development (ARE), Bern (Switzerland). Online version at: *www.are.admin.ch.*

WCED (World Commission on Environment and Development). (1987). *Our common future.* Oxford, UK: Oxford Press.

Chapter III

Ecoinvent Database: Quality Control and User Interfaces for a Web-Based Life Cycle Assessment Database

Rolf Frischknecht, Centre for Life Cycle Inventories, Switzerland

Abstract

In late 2000 the project ecoinvent 2000 was officially launched. Several Swiss Federal Offices and research institutes of the ETH domain agreed on a joint effort to harmonise and update life cycle inventory (LCI) data for its use in life cycle assessment (LCA). Life cycle assessment is a technique for assessing the environmental aspects and potential impacts associated with a product or service from resource extraction, manufacturing and use to final disposal.

Introduction

In order to accommodate LCI data a central database has been developed building on past experiences with a large network-based LCI database built up at ETH Zürich. The ecoinvent database comprises LCI data from the energy, transport, building materials, wood, chemicals, paper and pulp, waste treatment and agricultural sector. Furthermore, several actual and widespread impact assessment methods such as the Danish EDIP 1998, the Dutch Eco-indicator 99 and the CML characterisation scheme 2001, the Swedish EPS 2000 or the Swiss ecological scarcity 1997 are implemented.

Quality guidelines are established in order to ensure a coherent data acquisition and reporting across the various institutes involved. Aspects that require a harmonised procedure comprise the reporting of pollutants (e.g., heavy metals), the modelling of electricity consumption, the system boundary definitions, the reporting and quantification of data uncertainty, the treatment of transport service requirements, the naming of processes and elementary flows and so forth.

The content of the database is publicly available via the Internet (*www.ecoinvent.ch*). Processes as well as impact assessment methods are documented with the help of meta- information and flow data (unit process raw data and LCI results). The structure of the data format takes pattern from the ISO/TS 14048 data documentation format. The Web interface allows for an easy as well as a sophisticated search for processes, elementary flows and impact assessment methods. Meta-information and flow data can easily be downloaded and imported into commercial LCA software. Data exchange between project partner institutes and between the database and its clients is based on XML technology.

Motivation and Problem Setting

Up to now, several public Life Cycle Assessment (LCA) databases exist in Switzerland, partly covering the same economic sectors (Frischknecht et al., 1994, 1996; Gaillard et al., 1997; Habersatter et al., 1996, 1998; Künniger & Richter, 1995). However, life cycle inventory data for a particular material or process available from the databases often do not coincide and therefore the outcome of an LCA is (also) dependent on the institute working on it. Furthermore the efforts required to maintain and update comprehensive and high quality LCA-databases are beyond the capacity of any individual institute.

At the same time, LCA gets more and more attention by industry and authorities as one important tool for example, integrated product policy, technology assessment or design for the environment (see Chapter IV). In parallel with this increasing trend in LCA applications the demand for high-quality, reliable, transparent and consistent LCA data increased as well. Only a few publicly available LCI databases fulfil these criteria and most of them were published in the '90s.

Goal of Ecoinvent 2000 Project

That is why LCA institutes in the ETH domain (Swiss federal Institutes of Technology (ETH) Zürich and Lausanne, Swiss Federal Laboratories for Materials Testing and Research (EMPA) St. Gallen and Dübendorf, Paul Scherrer Institute (PSI) Villigen, and the Swiss Federal Institute for Environmental Science and Technology (EAWAG)) as well as the LCA department of the Swiss Federal Research Station for Agroecology and Agriculture (FAL) in Zürich agreed on a close cooperation. Together with the Swiss Agency for the Environment, Forests and Landscape (SAEFL or BUWAL), the Swiss Agency for Energy (BFE) and other agencies and Swiss federal offices, they founded the Swiss Centre for Life Cycle Inventories initiated by Prof. Dr. K. Hungerbühler, ETH Zürich. Its steering committee, chaired by Dr. Xaver Edelmann, member of the board of directors of EMPA, launched the project ecoinvent 2000, which aims for a harmonised, revised and updated Swiss national LCI database. The database will comprise LCI data from the energy, transport, building materials, chemicals, paper and pulp, waste treatment and agricultural sectors. The tasks are distributed according to the expert knowledge of the partners (Table 1).

Table 1. Database content, responsible institutes and their partners in LCI data compilation

Database content	Responsible Institute	Partners
Energy Supply - Fuels - Heat production - Electricity production	PSI	ESU-services
Plastics Paper and Board Basic Chemicals Detergents Waste treatment services	EMPA SG	Doka Ökobilanzen, Öko-science
Metals Wood Building materials Basic chemicals	EMPA Dü	
Transport services	ETHZ UNS	
Basic chemicals	ETHZ ICB	
Agricultural products and processes	FAL / FAT	

A large, network-based database and efficient calculation routines are required for handling, storage, calculation and presentation of data and are developed in the course of the project. These components partly take pattern from preceding work performed at ETH Zürich (Frischknecht & Kolm, 1995).

The Basic Structure of the Ecoinvent Database System

The ecoinvent database system consists of the following components (Figure 1):

1. central database,
2. calculation routines,
3. editor,
4. administration tool,
5. query tool,
6. data (exchange) format, and
7. local databases.

Ad 1. The central database contains life cycle inventory data on energy systems, transport systems, waste treatment systems, chemicals, building materials, and so forth, and life cycle impact assessment methods such as the Swiss Ecological Scarcity 1997, Eco-indicator 99 or the CML characterisation scheme 2001. The database is located on a server and accessible via the Internet.

Ad 2. Data will be supplied by the partner institutes as non-terminated unit processes. The computation of cumulative inventory results is performed with powerful calculation routines related to the central database. Unit process raw data as well as LCI results will include (cumulative) uncertainty ranges.

Ad 3. The local administrators use the editor to create new datasets and to change, complete or delete existing datasets. The editor administrates the dataset names (via a direct link to the central database, where the index of dataset names is placed), ensures the use of the actual list of names when compiling new inventories and includes a unit converter. The editor acts as the interface between the local administrator and the central database and generates files in the ecoinvent data format (named EcoSpold, see below).

Ad 4. The administration tool supports the integration of datasets delivered by the cooperating institutes into the central database. It helps to verify the

Figure 1. Basic structure of ecoinvent 2000 database system

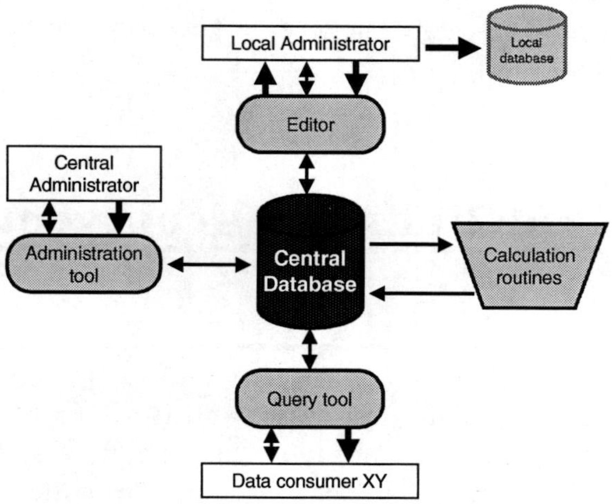

completeness of datasets, calculates inventories and (normalised and weighted) category indicator results and ensures the accessibility for clients respecting the users' rights.

Ad 5. The Query tool is used to interrogate the database and to download datasets from the central database. It enables the search for individual processes, for processes of a certain economic sector (e.g., transport or energy sector) or for data from a certain institute. General information (so-called meta-information) about the processes (technology, age, geographic coverage, etc.) is accessible to everybody whereas the quantitative LCI data are only accessible for registered ecoinvent members (clients).

Ad 6. The data exchange format lists all data fields that need to be completed when data are imported into the central database. It has evolved from the international SPOLD data exchange format (Weidema, 1999) and takes pattern from the committee draft of the international technical specification ISO/TS 14048 (International Organization for Standardization (ISO), 2001). Some of the data fields are mandatory; that is, information must be provided. Among other features, the data exchange format allows for specifying upper and lower estimates (or the 95% standard deviation) as well as the probability distribution (e.g., lognormal).

Ad 7. Commercially available LCA software such as Emis, Gabi, KCL-eco, SimaPro, Regis, Team and Umberto are used as local databases. These local databases are suited for an implementation and use of ecoinvent data v1.0. The ecoinvent data (exchange) format is recommended for that purpose.

In the next two sections two aspects of the ecoinvent 2000 database system are highlighted. One covers the quality guidelines for life cycle inventory analysis performed within ecoinvent 2000. The other one describes certain aspects of the Web interface (Query tool).

Quality Guidelines for Ecoinvent Data

Introduction

The creation of one central life cycle assessment database requires a high degree of coordination and harmonisation. In the following section several harmonisation issues are listed and described. Besides structural aspects and naming conventions, content-related aspects have been discussed and unified. This guarantees a maximum degree of consistency of process data available in the database.

Structural Aspects and Naming Conventions

The inventory of a unit process is divided into its investment (including dismantling) and the operation phase. Thereby the entire investment necessary to run for instance a fuel cell combined heat and power unit is evenly spread over the expected lifetime production. For instance, "1 kWh electricity, at fuel" cell requires a tiny share of "1 unit fuel cell, 1.5kW$_e$".

Co-production processes such as the above-mentioned fuel cell, which delivers electricity and heat, are stored as such in the database (i.e., before allocating inputs and outputs to their co-products). In order to be able to attribute a certain share of requirements and burdens to each of the co-products, allocation factors are defined and stored additionally. This procedure allows for a flexible and easy handling (and change, if necessary) of allocation factors.

Any process is defined by the four data fields "name," "unit," "location" and whether it is an "infrastructure process" or not. For infrastructure processes, the investment (and dismantling) requirements and emissions are reported, contrary to the other processes where only operational requirements (including a demand for a share of the infrastructure process) are reported. The process name is created according to the following scheme (see also Table 2):

1. Name of the product/service; production process or processed product; level of treatment

Table 2. Examples of process names used in ecoinvent data v1.0

Name	Location	Unit	Infrastructure-Process
heat, natural gas, at industrial furnace >100kW	RER	MJ	no
gypsum, at plant	CH	kg	no
electricity, low voltage, production UCTE, at grid	UCTE	kWh	no
disposal, newspaper, 14.7% water, to municipal incineration	CH	kg	no
transport, airplane, freight	GLO	tkm	no
nuclear power plant, pressure water reactor 1000MW	DE	unit	yes

2. Additional description (if available), separated by comma and in the following fixed order: sum formula; site (or place of origin); company; imports included or not, and so forth.
3. Level of value chain (e.g., "at plant," "at regional storehouse") or destination (especially for wastes, e.g., "to waste incineration," "to landfill").

For an unequivocal identification of elementary flows there are required slightly different data fields, namely: name, unit, category and subcategory. The names of elementary flows take pattern from the structure developed in the SETAC working group on data quality and data availability (Hischier et al., 2001). Category and subcategory are used to describe the compartment (air, water, soil and resources) and its specification (e.g., for air: stratosphere, high population density, low population density, protected area and unspecified). Additionally, long-term emissions are distinguished for processes that are likely to emit during several thousands of years (such as landfill sites, nuclear waste depositories and overburdens at mining and milling sites).

Pollutants are reported only once and on the level of detail of the information source. This avoids double counting and maintains the detailedness of information. For instance, benzene, reported to be emitted to air in a highly populated area is registered under "benzene, air, high population density" but not under "hydrocarbons, aromatic," nor under "NMVOC, non-methane volatile organic compounds, unspecified origin," nor under "VOC, volatile organic compounds, unspecified origin".

Content-Related Aspects

While structural aspects and naming rules are in many cases controllable by the software, a consistent application of content-related rules is less straightforward. Nevertheless, clear rules are required in order to minimise differences caused by individual, unsystematic choices of the LCI practitioners involved.

System boundaries are drawn based on expert knowledge and not based on fixed rules such as mass or energy shares. If the emission of a pollutant must be expected but no data are available, estimates are used in order to identify whether or not this pollutant may be environmentally relevant.

Electricity is supplied on high, medium and low voltage with increasing losses and investment requirements. Hence electricity demand of processes must be linked to the correct (or most likely) voltage. The supply mix (as well as the export mix) is calculated based on the domestic production plus the imports. In cases where the electricity mix actually purchased deviates from the average supply mix of a nation (or region), such specific mixes (or particular power plant technologies) are used.

Standard transport distances are applied for materials such as steel, cement, basic chemicals and so forth in case the exact distances are unknown. A similar approach is chosen for waste treatment processes. If no particular information is available, standard waste treatment processes defined per material are applied. It is supposed that inert materials go to landfill, plastics and paper are incinerated and metals are recycled.

Allocation is a ubiquitous issue that calls for a harmonised approach. A cutoff approach is used for recycled materials and for by-products (outputs with no economic value that are not sent to waste treatment but are used in other processes). No burdens and no requirements of a preceding process chain and of a process are allocated to the recycled materials and by-products, respectively. On the other hand no benefits are granted for any subsequent use of recycled material or by-product. No fixed prescriptions are made for joint product allocation (co-products) except that system expansion (especially the "avoided burden" concept) is not recommended.

Fossil and renewable carbon are distinguished for CO_2-, CH_4- and CO-emissions. For renewable energy sources and materials an equal amount of CO_2 is registered as a resource consumption according to the binding capacity of the corresponding crops. Carbon that is emitted as CO is considered when calculating CO_2-emissions. On the other hand, CO will get a global warming potential assuming its subsequent conversion to CO_2.

Uncertainty of flow data is quantified on the level of unit processes. If uncertainty is not known (because not stated in the sources used or because not known by the company providing the data) a standardised procedure is used for estimations. A data quality matrix has been developed that takes pattern from the pedigree matrix published by (Pedersen Weidema & Wesnaes, 1996). Scores from 1 to 5 are given for reliability, completeness, temporal correlation, geographical correlation, further technological correlation and sample size. Fixed uncertainty factors are attributed to each of the scores and an additional basic uncertainty is attributed to categories of exchanges (such as electricity and thermal energy consumption, groups of combustion emissions, waste treatment requirements and the like). In most cases a lognormal distribution is assumed. With the help of these standardised uncertainty factors, the geovariance is determined for each individual exchange in the unit processes.

Web Interface for the Ecoinvent Database

Introduction

The content of the ecoinvent database is publicly available via the Internet. For that purpose a Web site is created that allows for efficient searching in the database. Guests will be able to explore all meta-information of all unit processes stored in the database. Members will additionally have the opportunity to check flow data of all unit processes (unit process raw data as well as LCI and impact assessment results), and to download process data and characterisation and weighting factors of several impact assessment methods.

Database Search

The search for processes, elementary flows (resources and emissions) and impact assessment methods can either be performed in an easy way or in an advanced search (see Figures 2 and 3). The easy search checks the data fields' name (English and German), and synonyms.

Furthermore the database structure can be explored directly by listing categories and, subsequently, subcategories and processes, elementary flows and (parts of) impact assessment methods.

The advanced search allows for a stepwise procedure by selecting one (or several) categories, one (or several subcategories) and finally one (or more) unit processes. Processes may as well be searched with the help of the CAS number,

Figure 2. Search mask for an easy search in the ecoinvent database

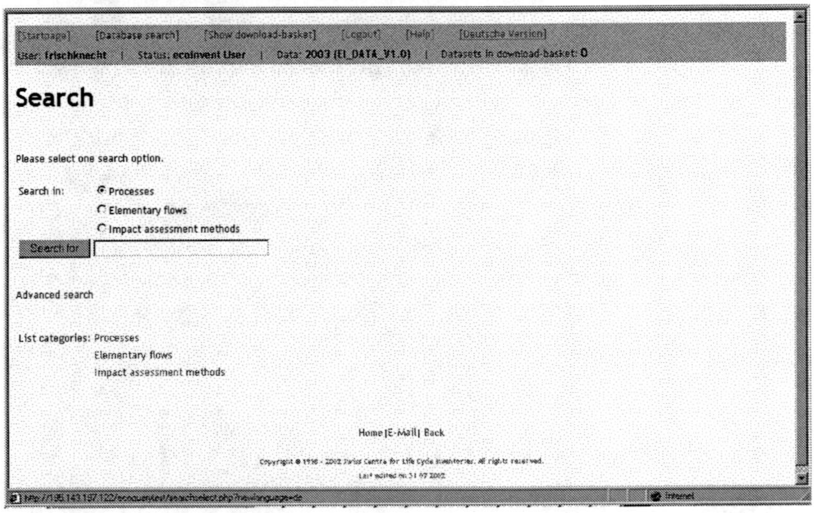

Figure 3. Search mask for the advanced search in the ecoinvent database

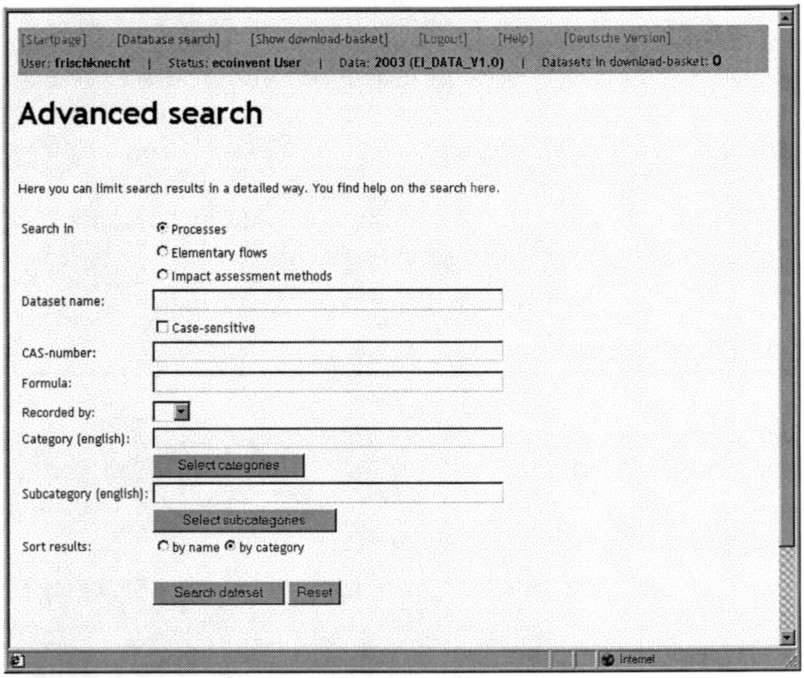

via a chemical formula or via the organisation that generated the dataset. Processes found may then be ordered by process name or by category.

Dataset Documentation

A process, its products and its life cycle inventory data are documented using the ecoinvent data format (EcoSpold) with the following structure:

Meta information

Process

Area ReferenceFunction, defining the product or service output to which all emissions and requirements are referred.

Area TimePeriod, defining the temporal validity of the dataset.

Area Geography, defining the geographical validity of the dataset.

Area Technology, describing the technology(ies) of the process.

Area DataSetInformation, defining the kind of process or product system, and the version number of the dataset.

Modelling and validation

Area Representativeness, defining the representativeness of the data used.

Area Sources, listing the literature and publications used.

Area Validations, listing the reviewers and their comments.

Administrative information

Area DataEntryBy, documenting the person in charge of implementing the dataset in the database.

Area DataGeneratorAndPublication, documenting the originator and the published source of the dataset.

Area Persons, listing complete addresses of all persons mentioned in a dataset.

Flow data

Area Exchanges, quantifying all flows from technical systems and nature to the process and from the process to nature and to other technical systems

Area Allocations, describing and quantifying allocation procedures and factors, respectively, required for multi-function processes.

Clients have the possibility to check the content of processes online (see excerpt in Figure 4). This helps to judge whether or not the process is of interest and whether or not it is worthwhile to download the corresponding dataset. Links within the html-documents facilitate the navigation.

Once a dataset is chosen for download, one or several datasets are converted to one XML-file (XML: Extended Markup Language) and saved on the local computer. XML schemes facilitate data exchange between different LCA databases and software. It can easily be extended by LCA software-specific requirements and upwards and downwards compatibilities pose no major problems.

Figure 4. Excerpt of online dataset documentation in ecoinvent data format

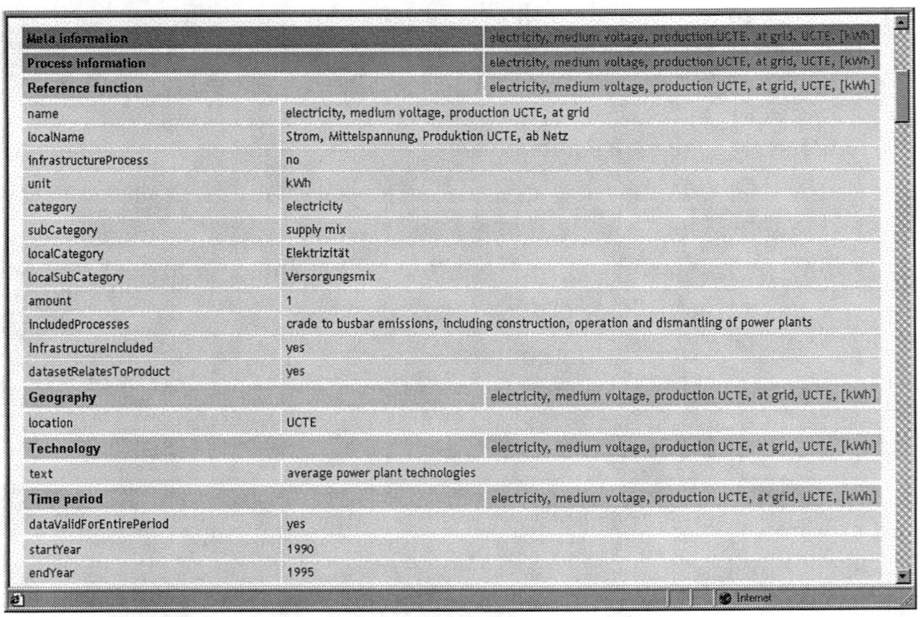

Meta information	electricity, medium voltage, production UCTE, at grid, UCTE, [kWh]
Process information	electricity, medium voltage, production UCTE, at grid, UCTE, [kWh]
Reference function	electricity, medium voltage, production UCTE, at grid, UCTE, [kWh]
name	electricity, medium voltage, production UCTE, at grid
localName	Strom, Mittelspannung, Produktion UCTE, ab Netz
infrastructureProcess	no
unit	kWh
category	electricity
subCategory	supply mix
localCategory	Elektrizität
localSubCategory	Versorgungsmix
amount	1
includedProcesses	crade to busbar emissions, including construction, operation and dismantling of power plants
infrastructureIncluded	yes
datasetRelatesToProduct	yes
Geography	electricity, medium voltage, production UCTE, at grid, UCTE, [kWh]
location	UCTE
Technology	electricity, medium voltage, production UCTE, at grid, UCTE, [kWh]
text	average power plant technologies
Time period	electricity, medium voltage, production UCTE, at grid, UCTE, [kWh]
dataValidForEntirePeriod	yes
startYear	1990
endYear	1995

Outlook

The software system presented in this chapter was completed in spring 2002. LCI datasets and life cycle impact assessment methods were imported until end of 2003. First experience, especially concerning decentralised LCI data acquisition using common quality guidelines and their feeding into a central database, has been gained with very promising results.

The size of the economic part of the matrix (more than 2'500 unit processes) poses a real challenge for the project team in terms of database response, computation time as well as harmonisation of naming and methodology and co-ordination of work.

The online interface of the database facilitates the compilation of LCI data for specific studies and projects. LCA practitioners may search for appropriate datasets with the help of online meta-information available for each individual dataset. They may as well download datasets they are interested in. The use of XML technology for dataset documentation facilitates the import of data into commercial LCA software tools and the data exchange between the ecoinvent institutes. Variations of the data exchange format are possible thanks to the flexibility of the XML technology. This should further enhance the acceptability of this format in the LCA community.

Quality-controlled LCI data with the reference year 2000 are available on the Internet since late 2003. They can be used for many basic commodities and services (such as energy supply, transportation and waste treatment services, building materials, wood products, chemicals and agricultural products) that are part of most LCI process networks.

References

Frischknecht, R., & Kolm, P. (1995). Modellansatz und Algorithmus zur Berechnung von Ökobilanzen im Rahmen der Datenbank Ecoinvent. In M. Schmidt & A. Schorb (Eds.), *Stoffstromanalysen in Ökobilanzen und Öko-audits* (pp. 79-95). Berlin Heidelberg: Springer-Verlag.

Frischknecht, R., Bollens, U., Bosshart, S., Ciot, M., Ciseri, L., Doka, G., Dones, R., Gantner, U., Hischier, R., & Martin, A. (1996). Ökoinventare von Energiesystemen: Grundlagen für den Ökologischen Vergleich von Energiesystemen und den Einbezug von Energiesystemen in Ökobilanzen für die Schweiz. *Vol. 3, Gruppe Energie - Stoffe - Umwelt (ESU), Eidgenössische Technische Hochschule Zürich und Sektion*

Ganzheitliche Systemanalysen, Paul Scherrer Institut, Villigen, Bundesamt für Energie (Eds.), Bern. *www.energieforschung.ch.*

Frischknecht, R., Hofstetter, P., Knoepfel, I., Dones, R., & Zollinger, E. (1994). Ökoinventare für Energiesysteme. Grundlagen für den Ökologischen Vergleich von Energiesystemen und den Einbezug von Energiesystemen in Ökobilanzen für die Schweiz. *Vol. No. 1, Gruppe Energie - Stoffe - Umwelt (ESU), Eidgenössische Technische Hochschule Zürich und Sektion Ganzheitliche Systemanalysen,* Paul Scherrer Institut Villigen, Bundesamt für Energie (Eds), Bern.

Gaillard, G., Crettaz, P., & Hausheer, J. (1997). Umweltinventar der Landwirtschaftlichen Inputs im Pflanzenbau. *FAT-Schriftenreihe No. 46,* Eidg. Forschungsanstalt für Agrarwirtschaft und Landtechnik (FAT), Tänikon.

Habersatter, K., Fecker, I., Dall'Acqua, S., Fawer, M., Fallscheer, F., Förster, R., Maillefer, C., Ménard, M., Reusser, L., & Som, C. (1996). Ökoinventare für Verpackungen. *Schriftenreihe Umwelt No. 250.* Bern: Bundesamt für Umwelt, Wald und Landschaft.

Habersatter, K., Fecker, I., Dall'Acqua, S., Fawer, M., Fallscheer, F., Förster, R., Maillefer, C., Ménard, M., Reusser, L., & Som, C. (1998). Ökoinventare für Verpackungen. *Schriftenreihe Umwelt No. 250, 2.* Bern: Bundesamt für Umwelt, Wald und Landschaft.

Hischier, R., Baitz, M., Bretz, R., Frischknecht, R., Jungbluth, N., Marheineke, T., McKeown, P., Oele, M., Osset, P., Renner, I., Skone, T., Wessman, H., & de Beaufort, A.S.H. (2001). Guidelines for consistent reporting of exchanges from/to nature within life cycle inventories (LCI). *Int. J. LCA, 6* (4), 192-198. Landsberg.

International Organization for Standardization (ISO). (2001). *Environmental management - life cycle assessment - Data documentation format.* Technical Specification ISO/DTS 14048 Geneva.

Künniger, T., & Richter, K. (1995). *Ökologischer Vergleich von Freileitungsmasten aus Imprägniertem Holz, Armiertem Beton und Korrosionsgeschütztem Stahl.* Dübendorf: EMPA.

Pedersen Weidema, B., & Wesnaes, M.S. (1996). Data quality management for life cycle inventories - An example of using data quality indicators. *Journal of Cleaner Production, 4*(3-4), 167-174.

Weidema, B.K. (1999). SPOLD '99 format - An electronic data format for exchange of LCI data (1999.06.24). *www.spold.org.*

Chapter IV

Organisation Models and Information Systems for Production-Integrated Environmental Protection (OPUS)

Hans-Dietrich Haasis, Institute of Shipping Economics and Logistics, Germany

Gunnar Jürgens, Continental Teves AG & Co. oHG, Germany

Torsten Kriwald, Institute of Shipping Economics and Logistics, Germany

Abstract

Environmental protection in companies gains higher importance as the demand for information on environmental performance is rewarded by society, market and policy makers. Additive environmental technologies encounter increasing ecological and economical borders. Production-integrated measures for environmental protection are much more efficient and sustainable. Such measures extend over inner enterprise and enterprise spanning order processing and value chains. They open up numerous possibilities for product and process innovation by combining ecological and economical potentials. The research project OPUS provides solutions for the organization of product-development and production-processes in and between companies under environmental aspects. Parts of those solutions are information technologies and information systems that support the processes within a company and over the entire logistical network. The development of methods, models and prototypes within the project is based on the processes of construction, process planning, production planning and control, production scheduling, balancing and controlling and intercompany environmental management. Results were applied, evaluated and optimised in different companies out of the branches of machine building, aircraft building, chemical industry, electronic industry and software development for industrial fields of application.

General Structure of the Project

The purpose of the OPUS project is to develop concepts of IT and information management with the objective of integrating environmental protection into the business processes of enterprises. The business processes cover the whole range of the company-related order processing (Figure 1).

The examined topics were supplemented by intercompany aspects of integrated environmental protection external to the enterprise, in particular with regard to the management of material flows.

The research work was carried out in close collaboration of the following institutes:

- Institute for Technology Management (IAT), University of Stuttgart (project coordination),
- Fraunhofer Institute for Industrial Engineering (IAO), Stuttgart,
- Research Institute for Rationalisation (FIR) at the RWTH Aachen,
- Fraunhofer Institute for Production Technology (IPT), Aachen,
- Department of Production Management, University of Bremen,
- Laboratory for Machine Tools and Production Engineering (WZL) at the RWTH Aachen.

The integrated approach to support environmental protection needs to address aspects of organization and information. Due to this, a parallel examination of the fields of organization and information was chosen as a central approach of the project work.

Figure 1. Order processing in enterprises

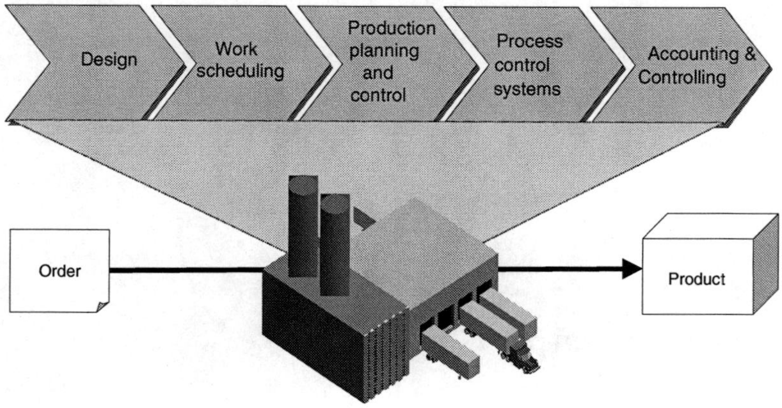

In the *organization field* the main purpose of the investigation was to determine precisely which changes in the organization of order processing must be established in order to achieve the integration of measures designed to protect the environment. It was decided to place the focus on issues of process organization.

The *information field* focused on the environmentally relevant information that has to be gathered and then exchanged between the individual business processes in order to ensure that due regard is taken of potential impacts on the environment during the processing of orders.

The project work was targeted at a modular approach in the formulation of solutions. One advantage was that the results obtained are suitable for integrating environmental protection into individual business processes. Another advantage was that the concepts that were developed could also be combined freely with each other.

Integration of the concepts was achieved by the development of an integrated organization and information model. This model depicts a coherent overview of all the steps involved in decision-making and implementation of order processing that takes environmental issues into account as well as the information that has to be exchanged. The modular structure of the project results is depicted in Figure 2.

The concepts developed within the OPUS project for an integration of environmental protection into order processing within enterprises have since been tested and optimised in industrial practice, involving the following companies:

Figure 2. Modular approach in OPUS on the basis of an integrated organisation and information model

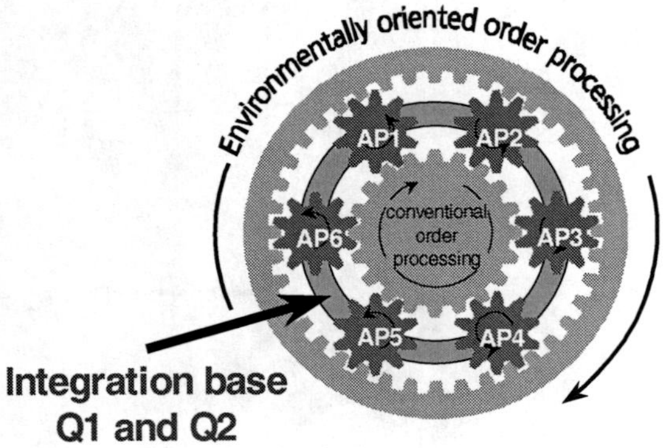

- Battenfeld GmbH, Meinerzhagen,
- Deutsche Castrol Industrieöl GmbH, Hamburg,
- DaimlerChrysler Aerospace Airbus GmbH, Bremen,
- infor business solutions AG, Karlsruhe,
- Philips GmbH Bildröhrenfabrik u. Glasfabrik, Aachen,
- SCHOTT GLAS, Mainz,
- STAWAG Stadtwerke Aachen AG, Aachen,
- TRUMPF GmbH & Co. KG., Ditzingen.

Conception of Work Packages

In accordance with the prescribed goals with regard to a holistic and integrated approach that are applicable to all links in the chain of order processing, the main issues in OPUS comprise the following work packages (cf. Figure 2):

- *Intercompany environmental management (AP1):* The subject of this work package is the development of methods and instruments that enable the identification of system boundaries and interrelationships in the logistical chain and the creation of corresponding models as well as enabling mechanisms of environmentally-oriented intercompany collaboration to be identified and put into effect.

- *Design (AP2):* This work package consists of concepts and mechanisms for the systematic design of resource-saving products.
- *Work scheduling (AP3):* The task involved here is the development of tools to support the environmentally oriented generation of work plan.
- *Production planning and control (AP4):* The subject of this work package is the creation of an architecture for environmentally oriented production planning and control systems in connection with procedures and methods for the environmentally efficient synchronisation and planning of internal and intercompany flows of materials and energy as well as the corresponding expansion of existing system approaches.
- *Production and process control systems (AP5):* This work package deals with procedures which make it possible to coordinate material and energy flows on the shop-floor level in such a way that, taking due consideration of the technical operational parameters of the different stages of production both upstream and downstream, the available resources are utilised to the optimum extent. Thereby all kinds of emissions resulting from the production process are, if technically feasible, either avoided or reduced.
- *Accounting and controlling (AP6):* The task in this context is the development of instruments for the generation and integration of environmentally oriented accounting and indicators along the value-added chain.

In OPUS the following overlapping themes also contribute to the development of solutions:

- The conception of an environmentally oriented *organization model* (Q1) with the aim of arriving at reference models - consisting of task and process models – for the implementation of environmentally-oriented processes of order processing as well as processes involved in product development and manufacturing.
- The development of an *infrastructure of communication and information technology* (Q2) with the aim of arriving at an integrative system platform and formulating the definition and design of internal and intercompany communication channels.

Overview of Results

The first stage in the conception of innovative techniques in intercompany environmental management was to determine precisely where the potential for the introduction of intercompany environmental management lies with respect to individual business functions (design, work scheduling, production planning and control as well as accounting and controlling) and which changes would subsequently have to be made in the internal organization structure in order to harness this potential. Parallel to this, aspects of intercompany environmental management were analyzed with regard to possible forms of collaboration. The results of these investigations were combined in the form of a Web-based handbook.

In the field of *design,* existing methods were analyzed with regard to their ecological impact on product design and their suitability for adaptation to form the basis for methods leading to the systematic design of resource-saving products. The result of this analysis is the choice of VDI Guideline 2221 as an operation plan for a systematic procedure. The individual phases were expanded to include environmental aspects. A generic reference model consisting of the product model, resources model and life cycle model was developed as the basis for the compilation and provision of technical, economic and ecological information covering the entire product life cycle. Targeted access to the information depicted in the reference model is by means of an extension and adaptation of the operations schedule in accordance with VDI 2221.

On conclusion of the specifications analysis, the field *work scheduling* went on to identify functions and attributes which serve as basis for the subsequent implementation of function patterns based on the object model for work scheduling that must be drawn up. These were embedded in an already existing object-oriented environment and expanded by the necessary environmentally relevant functionalities. Parallel to this, the interfaces to the fields of design and PPC were designed accordingly. The determining factors for environmentally oriented work scheduling were thus identified and order-specific planning parameters were derived from them. A concept of operations organization for environmentally oriented work scheduling was drawn up. In addition, a special IT object library for work scheduling was specified and modelled. This represented the basis for the subsequent development and implementation of function patterns of the essential elements of environmentally oriented work scheduling.

The field production planning and control had two goals:

- The development of an environmentally-oriented PPC system for the planning and control of production processes as well as inclusion of environmentally relevant restrictions and goals in existing standard systems of PPC.

In both cases approaches were developed which create links between processes both upstream and downstream of the production process. Initial results of an environmentally oriented eco-PPC system were obtained by the development of a material-flow model. Using Petri nets as a modelling approach it was possible to develop a three-layer information model which makes it possible to gain a broadened understanding of the materials involved (waste, recycles, emissions, energy consumption, etc.) as well as a planning and control of their flows, taking into account aspects of quantity and scheduling. The expansion of individual business processes with environmentally relevant aspects is based on the Aachen PPC model.

In the field of *production and process control systems,* systems were developed which make it possible to integrate environmental protection into the synchronization of flows of materials and energy. The potential for the implementation of these systems in daily production operations was assessed. Their task is in particular the scheduling of production, selection of the production techniques to be employed, as well as determination of the operating modus of the individual machinery under due consideration of economic aspects and environmental protection. In contrast to a central production control, the decentralized concept offers benefits, particularly with regard to a customer-friendly, schedule-oriented production. Moreover, it can be seen that the integration of goals oriented to environmental protection (e.g., the creation of materials cycles, an increase in the potential for recycling, a reduction of waste transport, waste amounts and emissions) does not necessarily bring about an increase in costs, or impair the efficiency of production. Methodologically, the concept of production systems oriented to protection of the environment is based on a corresponding expansion of the approach of a load-oriented manufacturing control in combination with advanced procedures in information and control technology, such as fuzzyfied knowledge-based systems.

With a view to the integration of ecological considerations in financial controlling the field *accounting and controlling* formulated a resource-oriented process model. With the assistance of this model it is possible to introduce into the enterprise a resource-oriented form of management accounting. In addition to this, assessment criteria and benchmarks were developed by means of which it was possible to implement a resource-oriented description and evaluation of processes. For manufacturing companies there are the following advantages:

- Concepts to make it possible to plan, implement and control ecological improvement measures,
- Random depiction of business areas or process chains as well as support for resource-oriented analysis of weak spots, and

- The compilation of a process catalogue as a prerequisite for a systematic substitution of resource-intensive processes (e.g., specific to the enterprise, specific to the sector).

All in all, the modules developed provide a comprehensive concept for the implementation of an environmentally oriented chain of order processing. Their applicability and acceptance were evaluated by the test partners named above.

The report entitled "*Auftragsabwicklung Optimieren nach Umwelt- und Kostenzielen,*" containing a detailed account of the results, has been published by Springer-Verlag. The report is accompanied by a CD-ROM containing prototypes of the IT systems developed throughout the project.

References

Bullinger, H.-J. (ed.). (1997). Anforderungen an Methoden und Systeme für Eine Umweltorientierte Auftragsabwicklung. *Project Report OPUS – Organisationsmodelle und Informationssysteme für Einen Produktionsintegrierten Umweltschutz.* Stuttgart: Fraunhofer IRB Verlag.

Bullinger, H.-J., Eversheim, W., Haasis, H.-D., & Klocke, F. (eds.). (2000). *Auftragsabwicklung Optimieren Nach Umwelt und Kostenzielen.* Berlin: Springer.

Chapter V

Integration of Material Flow Management Tools in Workplace Environments

Jan Hedemann, ifu Institut für Umweltinformatik Hamburg GmbH, Germany

Andreas Möller, University of Lüneburg, Germany

Peter Müller-Beilschmidt,
ifu Institut für Umweltinformatik Hamburg GmbH, Germany

Dirk Rohdemann, SAP AG, Germany

Mario Schmidt, Fachhochschule Pforzheim, Germany

Bernd Schmitt, SAP AG, Germany

Abstract

This chapter describes how information technology (IT) support for industrial ecology can be integrated in a workplace environment, providing a homogeneous user interface and role-based access to information. The term "industrial ecology" comprises all activities of a company in regard

to the natural environment. These can be, among others: operative tasks (e.g., handling of hazardous materials), compliance tasks (e.g., preparing declarations to be submitted to authorities), as well tasks involved in building up an environmental management system. It may also include innovative new approaches, such as "Design for Environment" or recycling oriented design. Other terms with a similar connotation are "cycle-oriented industry" or "integrated production". To the user it is not really relevant which application furnishes the data he or she accesses. Rather, the user wants the data to be served in a harmonized way and adapted to his or her specific work context; the user wishes to use it in material flow models and he or she needs to utilize the data in cooperative work processes. Computer support and data aggregation are therefore only one aspect. Additionally it is required to work with adequate tools for creating and using material flow models as well as for supporting communication in business processes. The result is a "Business Package for Industrial Ecology".

Orientation

When discussing IT support for industrial ecology tasks and integration of tools into an existing information system environment, the focus of discussion is mostly on technical aspects of integration. The central question is how software systems for material flow management can access and make use of data administered in business software, such as Enterprise Resource Planning (ERP) systems (see Figure 1, Focus 1). This way of thinking is dominated by the paradigm, that *data* handled in existing application systems in the company actually represent *information* (i.e., that they are an actual image of business reality) relevant to IT support of environmental activities. Systems and system boundaries in this case are discussed based on the assumption that multiple overlapping data requirements exist (Lehner et al., 1995, p. 289).

However, this perspective leads to conclusions that fall short of reality in several ways: Firstly, the vast concept of computer support is reduced to a mechanism of mere data handling by a machine. Secondly, using data is focused mainly on available and actual data, not considering adequately the very important aspect of software support for planning tasks and decision making, which are characterized by future-directed data requirements. Thirdly, the fact that environmental activities of a company have to be considered cooperative tasks is often neglected.

Another perspective emerges when we approach these questions from the point of view of the user or of different user groups. The requirements are then defined

Figure 1. Architecture for IT support of workplaces for environmental activities of a company

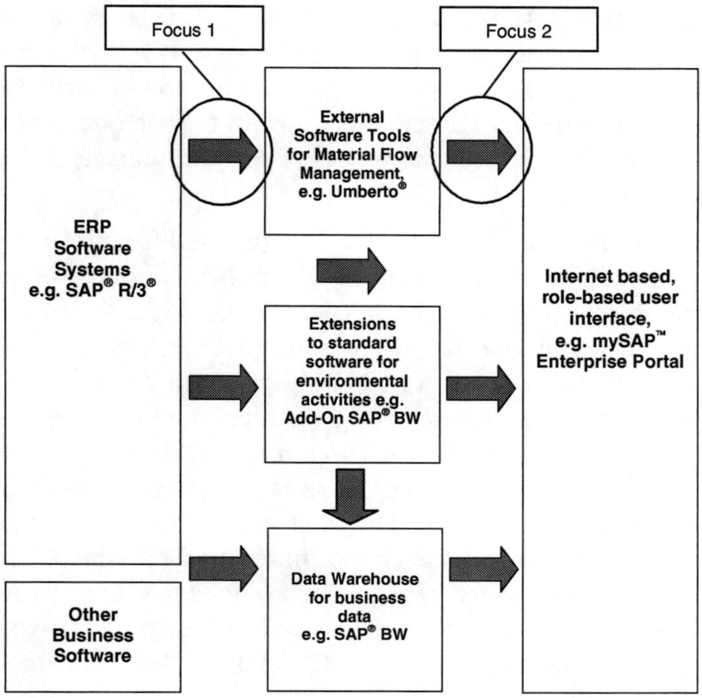

by the various tasks they face. One approach is to provide a uniform and well-structured graphical workplace, which uses Web-based technologies and whose contents can be personalized individually ("Single Point of Access"). This type of support can have the following characteristics:

- Material and energy flow data or figures derived from flow data, such as eco-efficiency indicators, can be combined with other relevant information and can be presented adequately in the workplace. In this case the IT focus is rather strong, especially with regard to the computing of actual data. The material flow management system can be considered a business environmental information system (Kraus et al., 1995, p. 99; Rautenstrauch, 1999, p. 12).
- Taking advantage of the possibilities of role-based user interfaces, the aspect of planning support is stressed. A variety of future-directed planning instruments can be offered, which, for example, make it possible to conduct scenario analyses or risk-benefit-analyses. It is likely that such an instrument at the same time supports certain systematic methods of proceeding

within the framework of strategic planning such as Product Lifecycle Management (Eisert et al., 2001; Möller & Rolf, 2001), Supply Chain Management (Bartsch & Bickenbach, 2002), Life Cycle Assessment or SWOT analyses (Boseman & Phatak, 1989, p. 23). These instruments all have the characteristics of tools (Möller, 2000, p. 45): Models are created, calculated and assessed interactively. When used in material flow based environmental activities (Brandt, 2000, p. 50) these models can represent possible measures and serve to assess ecological impacts and economic figures.

- The role-based user interface, on top of being used for information access or as a modelling tool for the decision-maker, has another advantage: it can be interpreted as an active medium (Schelhowe, 1997, p. 182), especially when joining it with Internet technologies (Preece, 2000). In the simplest case, an e-mail client is integrated into the workplace. But, in contrast to other media, messages are not only transmitted to another person, they also can serve as the base technology to support activities of collaborative work. Goal-oriented acting of different persons in a common social context is supported and leads to the exchange of procedural knowledge between actors (Coy, 1993, p. 50). For example, the expert for production simulation can develop models, which can then be provided to others, by integrating them into their computer workplace environment. The co-workers can easily configure and adapt these models and use them as tools.

Based on these various types of support, it will be pointed out in the following how software solutions for industrial ecology can be integrated as components into a role-based user interface. The mySAP™ Enterprise Portal might serve as a starting point and orientation.

User Interface "mySAP™ Enterprise Portal"

SAP AG has developed the mySAP™ Enterprise Portal, a role-based and individually configurable user interface. It is based on Internet technologies, making it accessible through common browser tools (see Figure 2). The applicability and suitability of such a user interface for industrial ecology activities has been shown in a demonstration project ("showcase") for the role of a plant manager. All relevant information and tools to serve his or her needs

Figure 2. Integration of various components in a workplace for operational environmental tasks

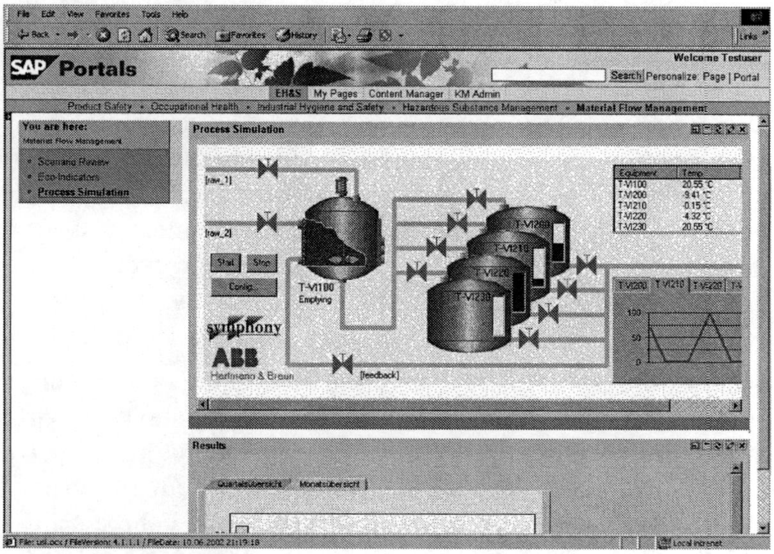

in fulfilling the tasks involved in environmental protection activities (Arndt et al., 1999, p. 248) were united in the mySAP™ user interface. For example, the responsible person can check any time which transports of hazardous materials are scheduled in the near future, which quantities of various types of waste have been stored on site, which legal compliance requirements result from that, and so forth. To provide this information, the data contained in the SAP® R/3® system itself (e.g., in the SAP® EH&S® software module) are used. The plant manager also has direct access to tools for process simulation, process analysis and others.

The content provided uses so-called iViews, which provide a well-structured and comprehensible access to business information within the mySAP™ Enterprise Portal. Content from various sources can be included.

If we keep in mind that iViews not only present data, but also deliver procedural knowledge by providing configurable models, it is justified to consider them as modular components: The user interface can be individually assembled from a pool of components ("Business Packages") for each user role. SAP provides numerous components, which are pre-configured and oriented at certain frameworks, such as mySAP™ PLM or mySAP™ SCM (Bartsch & Bickenbach, 2002; Eisert et al., 2001). Components for industrial ecology can also be obtained from specialized third party sources.

Components for Providing Relevant Information for Industrial Ecology Activities

Components for providing information relevant to environmental activities are useful for companies that actively pursue an environmental policy and have committed themselves to strive for a more sustainable way of producing (Dyckhoff, 2000, p. 20). Protection of the natural environment has been formally declared a goal in these companies. Process-oriented and cycle-oriented methods and procedures thus can be applied to bring life to the company's environmental strategy (Dyckhoff, 2000, p. 27).

These businesses are at first mainly interested in obtaining relevant information. What should be considered relevant information in the context of environmental protection activities? For example, life cycle data or environmental performance indicators, possibly linked with data from other sources, edited and presented in a Sustainability Balanced Scorecard (BMU, BDI, 2002; Fahrbach et al., 2000; Schaltegger & Burritt, 2000, p. 151). To lay the basis for mid- or long-term planning, the decision-maker in the company should have access to material flow information served in an adequate way and aggregated in the form of environmental performance indicators. However, to keep the indicators understandable, their calculation must remain transparent and one must be able to break down the values to the actual material and energy flow level.

As mentioned above, various software tools that serve the information needs for industrial ecology activities do exist, but these solutions have to tackle the problem of not being fully integrated into ERP systems (see Figure 1, Focus 1). With this new approach, the data provided by these solutions are treated in such a way that they can be presented as content through the mySAP™ Enterprise Portal (Figure 1, Focus 2).

Key Figures: Link between Material Flow Management System and Working Environment

The policies and goals of the company should constitute the framework for integration of components in a working environment. Especially the goals in regard to the environmental protection have to be analysed. Then the actual information needs have to be investigated. Key figures – considered to be an important information instrument (Küpper, 1997, p. 320) – are used to meet such needs. The character of the key figures, being a "purposeful condensation of complex reality" (Weber, 1999, p. 217) with regard to a specific context of decision-making and acting, makes them the most important link between material flow management systems and the working environment (Fahrbach et al., 2000, p. 85). The set of environmental performance indicators of the material flow management systems is combined with the iView component concept: iViews visualize the key figures that are relevant in a specific work context.

In the showcase mentioned above the role of a plant manager has been selected. His or her decision-making and acting within his/her work situation relies on the comprehensibly structured information provided in the iViews (Rautenstrauch, 1999, p. 8). Selected key figures are visualized, for example, as a bar chart, indicating the development of the value and the degree of performance with regard to the target value. In case several different key figures are used to meet the information need and to give a more complete picture, they can be combined in various ways to constitute a set of indicators (key figure system). To understand how the values of the performance indicators were produced, it is required to be able to trace their way back to the original data, the values used for their calculation. In other words: it has to be possible to access the inventory data, present the figures therein with individual views or display selected data on the mass and energy flow level, for example by using Sankey diagrams. This requirement is referred to as the transparency of material flows.

Similar to key figures in conventional accounting, sets of key figures have been suggested for material flow management. These suggestions can be used as a basis or structure when building individual tailor-made systems of performance indicators. Furthermore they can also serve for benchmarking of companies. One such system has been proposed by the World Business Council for Sustainable Development (WBCSD, 2000). It contains, for example, absolute indicator figures for energy consumption and carbon dioxide equivalents for the emission of a variety of greenhouse gases. Also, we find ideas for relative key indicators, such as the ratio of sales revenue and energy consumption. The proposal of the WBCSD has been used as an example throughout the demonstration project to calculate environmental performance indicators based on material flow systems for the plant manager.

The WBCSD concept should be regarded as a first approach and can serve as a basis. But it has to be adapted for each company and must be customized for the individual user roles. As a result, cost-center specific environmental performance indicators become available locally to the decision-maker, which are, at the same time, elements within a comprehensive environmental performance indicator system.

Material Flow Modelling and Information Needs

According to the concept of material flow networks, a distinction has to be made in the material flow management system between modelling and analysis. The objective of modelling is to be able to conduct material flow analyses, whose results can be used in a variety of ways: input/output balances, life cycle assessments for products or cost accounting. The results of the analyses also provide a basis to calculate environmental performance indicators, by combining and aggregating the data. The practitioner regards the material flow management system as a workbench for modelling (Möller, 2000, p. 45).

Modelling and assessment are separated when providing the data in the mySAP™ Enterprise Portal, which is desirable from a software engineering point of view and which facilitates implementation of role-based software support: The modelling expert uses the modelling and calculation components of the software system to perform material flow analyses. He is also responsible for specifying the system of key indicators adequately to cover the information needs of the different user types (role-based channelling of information use). A high degree of modelling competence is expected from the modelling expert.

Such qualifications are not needed to simply access and assess material flow data in the context of decision-making or to use them in operative tasks. In fact,

Figure 3. Visualizing eco efficiency indicators with iViews

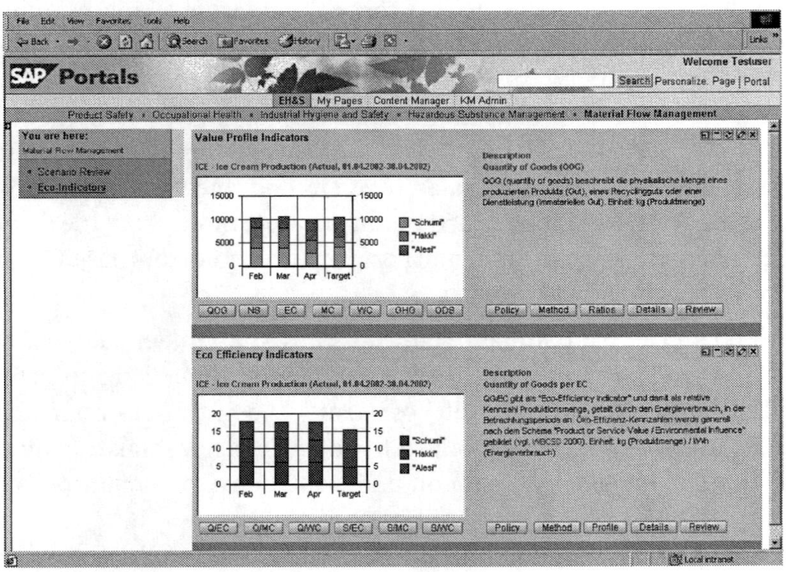

the data are served adequately and comprehensibly to the different users or user groups, enabling them to benefit the most from them. Above all, they do not have to know another software system and can continue to use their accustomed working environment.

The visualizations typical for iViews rely on a comprehensive data basis. Imagine, for example, that you wish to display energy consumption for the production of three products of a company separately for the last three months, and compare them to the target value (see Figure 3). Four different scenarios (actual values for three months, another for the target value) have to be considered for calculating the performance indicators. Each of them delivers the life cycle data for the three products, thus resulting in twelve different totals, which are calculated to create the desired diagram in a single-step operation for the user.

When analysing a problem, it might be required to access the data basis. Therefore it is not sufficient to just present eco-efficiency indicators in a bar chart. The diagrams can serve as an entry point for a more in-depth analysis of the material flow models, which were used to calculate the data (Schmidt, 2000, p. 134). Input/output inventories and life cycle assessments, as well as the key indicator systems and cost accounting data can be accessed in detail (Figure 4). And, of course, the material flow networks can be displayed as graphical models or as Sankey diagrams.

Figure 4. Inventory of a product (limited to the on-site section of the life-cycle, not considering pre- and post-chains)

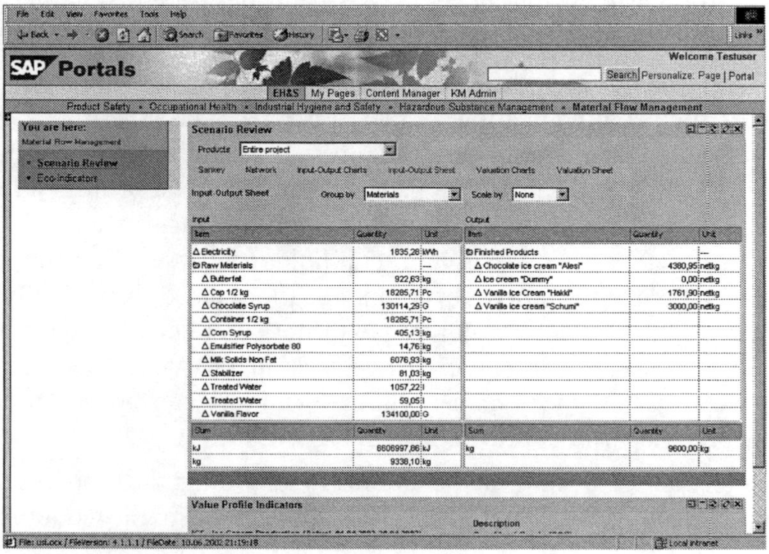

Using the Computer as a Tool and Medium

Starting with the tables and diagrams of the iView components and taking a closer look at the working situation, a step-by-step change in the way the computer is used can be observed: Closely linked to the problem analysis is the desire to improve the existing situation. This results in a new set of requirements, as the user wishes to get orientation and advice for acting; he or she wishes to develop alternatives and would like to compare them to find out the most suitable one, and so forth. The computer thus changes from its original role as a data furnisher, and is now being used as a modelling instrument: It turns into a tool that is used to handle and act on (data-) material. The material itself is being "moulded" and takes a new shape. The small embedded iViews may eventually turn out to be unsuitable for this operation and specialized systems might be regarded as more adequate.

However, a radical change of the work environment is not needed. If, in addition to the actual data served to the user through iViews, generalized models are provided, which can be parameterised, the user could experiment with these models within the common working environment and, in the broader sense of the term, perform simulations.

The perception of the computer as a data manipulating machine or as a tool to handle data material is based on the supposition that a single decision-maker exists who uses information and instruments for his or her decision-making process. However, it was pointed out many years ago that this idea is rather atypical for a business manager (Winograd & Flores, 1991, p. 151). Most of the activities of these decision-makers have been described as target-oriented communication. This should also have an impact on IT support (see Figure 5).

Looking closer at this hypothesis, we see it relates to the computer as a medium for interpersonal communication. In fact, this type of IT support has long been established, and consequently e-mail clients such as Outlook™ can be integrated into the mySAP™ Enterprise Portal. However, this type of utilization of the computer as a medium neglects one important aspect that distinguishes it from all other media: it is an *active* medium. This holds true in regard to the following three aspects: Firstly, the process of communication can be purposefully directed into certain distinct channels according to the target or goal. Next, the transmission of signals can be influenced in a systematic way. And, thirdly, the transmitted messages (seen as a string of symbols) can be interpreted by a computer; in other words, they represent algorithms.

The latter characteristic hints at the possibility of joining the tool-like character of the computer with its character and use as a medium. For the modelling expert

Figure 5. Community System CommSy

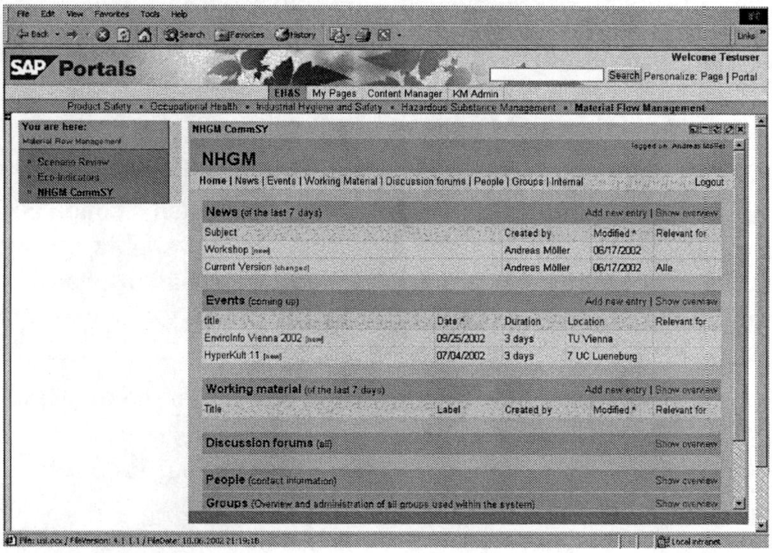

and the users of models the calculated material flow networks (i.e., models) become part of their communication and cooperative work through iViews. The modelling expert transmits a model that contains his or her expertise to other users, who can integrate it into their specific working environments and modify it by changing parameter values.

Components Supported by IT

To define the component-based architecture for a computer working environment for industrial ecology tasks, we rely on the following assumptions:

- The company has implemented and uses an ERP system, for example, SAP R/3. The system constitutes the technical backbone of the business information system.
- Several other external software systems are available for specialized requirements, such as optimisation tools for planning purposes (Bartsch & Bickenbach, 2002, p. 221), software for material flow management or tools for an active support of cooperative work.
- A Web browser is installed on the client computer at the workplace. It can be used to access the Web-based user interface, for example the mySAP™

Enterprise Portal. Selected iView components are delivered to the content section of the mySAP™ Enterprise Portals from different Web servers.

The following requirements with regard to the components and their interaction can be defined from the user's point of view:

- The ERP system ensures that the information the user obtains is based on consistent and complete data. All information that cannot be directly delivered by the ERP system should be made available by integrating external software systems (Figure 1, Focus 1). Such additional information required by the user could be, for example, the environmental life cycle assessments calculated in the company for past years.
- It must be possible to integrate and embed the various components into the mySAP™ Enterprise Portal. More specifically, this requires that the Web server is capable of creating an iView using special Web server components, thus establishing a link between the server and the components (Figure 1, Focus 2). To ensure a consistent design within the working environment, design guidelines have been developed for iViews. Components for industrial ecology have to comply with these guidelines. Software development environments such as the Portal Development Kit 4 Java™ provided by SAP facilitate the embedding of components into the portal.
- A user-specific adaptation of the data displayed is often required. This can be achieved either through customizing the back end system or through individual user settings for the iViews.
- It is desirable for the user to only identify him- or herself once when logging on to the portal, even if in fact he or she accesses and works with a number of different back end systems. In the mySAP™ Enterprise Portal this concept of "Single Sign-On" (SSO) is implemented by digital certificates, tickets or cookies exchanged between the portal and the embedded iView.
- Once a pool of various components for environmental activities of the company is being used, the question of interaction of the components among each other arises. This not only relates to the compatibility of the various information systems or software tools which provide data within a common framework, but also to the challenge of harmonizing the various manners of utilizing the computer models as procedural elements of cooperative work, that is, a community system which constitutes a mediation layer between modelling and assessing. It should therefore be possible to use a "Business Package for Industrial Ecology" in conjunction with "Packages for Collaboration".

It is possible to use specialized tools, integrated into a role-based user interface, to conveniently and efficiently support cooperative work and the division of labor according to various emphases and levels of information processing. The level of controlling constitutes an embracing bracket.

Summary and Vision

This chapter describes possibilities for a computer working environment for activities in industrial ecology. It is important for the person in the workplace that contents are served up, but in such a manner that the situation can be understood quickly and "without having to think much". This points to a close connection between the technical iView concept and the key performance indicators. The system of key indicators forms a framework that has to be filled with content, for example, with the eco-efficiency scheme of the WBCSD or with a Sustainability Balanced Scorecard. Such concepts represent a lot more than suggestions for the mere aggregation of data: they can be applied in companies to create a common view of the situation, ensuring that the data are interpreted in the same way and communicated to all parties involved.

This common view and the role-based perspective reveal quite clearly that providing the data is only part of the IT support needed. One also wishes to use the computer as a (modelling) tool and as an active medium. The question of integration therefore must be considered with regard to these different types of utilization of IT systems.

Computer based modelling tools provide good support for future-directed acting, thinking and planning: they help to create scenarios, they make it possible to verify these scenarios in comparison to the actual data, they support prognosis and forecasting, they help to assess risks and opportunities, and so forth. Their tool nature has the additional advantage that there is no pre-determined path for their use, no scheme layout in advance. Software systems can therefore even support creative and innovative activities. On the other hand, using any kind of tool requires a certain level of competence and skill.

The use of the computer as a medium gains special importance in industrial ecology activities, since sustainability and active environmental protection have to be considered as action-oriented approaches involving people. They can hardly be achieved with a top-down approach through directives and regulations, but rather have to be the crystallized result of cooperative activities and a communication process.

References

Arndt, H.-K., Fugmann, T., & Günther, O. (1999). Umweltmanagement-informationssysteme: Der Arbeitsplatz. In C. Rautenstrauch & M. Schenk (Hrsg.), *Umweltinformatik ´99 – Umweltinformatik zwischen Theorie und Industrieanwendung.* Marburg: Metropolis.

Bartsch, H., & Bickenbach, P. (2002). *Supply chain management mit SAP APO,* 2. Aufl. Bonn: Galileo Press.

BMU, BDI. (2002, Hrsg.). *Nachhaltigkeitsmanagement in Unternehmen – Konzepte und Instrumente zur Nachhaltigen Unternehmensentwicklung.* Berlin: Bundesministerium für Umwelt, Naturschutz und Reaktorsicherheit.

Bosemann, G., & Phatak, A. (1989). *Strategic management — Text and cases.* New York: John Wiley & Sons.

Box, D. (1998). *COM – Microsofts Technologie für Komponentenbasierte Softwareentwicklung.* Bonn: Addison Wesley.

Brandt, E. (2000). Interdisziplinarität in den Umweltwissenschaften. In E. Brand (Hrsg.), *Perspektiven der Umweltwissenschaften.* Baden-Baden: Nomos.

Dyckhoff, H. (2000). *Umweltmanagement.* Berlin: Springer.

Eisert, U. et al. (2001). *mySAP product lifecycle management.* Bonn: Galileo Press.

Fahrbach, M. et al. (2000). Strategisches Umweltcontrolling Mit Hilfe der Balanced Scorecard. In L.M. Hilty et al. (Hrsg.), *Strategische und Betriebsübergreifende Anwendungen Betrieblicher Umweltin formationssysteme.* Marburg: Metropolis.

Haasis, H.-D., Hilty, L.M., Kürzl, H., & Rautenstrauch, C. (1995). Anforderungen an Betriebliche Umweltinformationssysteme (BUIS) und Ansätze zur Realisierung. In Haasis et al. (Hrsg.), *Betriebliche Umweltinformationssysteme (BUIS) – Projekte und Perspektiven.* Marburg: Metropolis.

Hummel, J., Kytzia, S., & Siegenthaler, C. (1995). Umweltschutzrelevante Informationen in Unternehmen – Quellen und Auswertungsmethoden. In Haasis et al. (Hrsg.), *Betriebliche UmweltinformationsSysteme (BUIS) – Projekte und Perspektiven.* Marburg: Metropolis.

Kraus, M. et al. (1995). Computergestütztes Stoffstrommanagement-System zur Realisierung Produktionsintegrierter Umweltschutzstrategien. In H.-D. Haasis et al. (Hrsg.), *Umweltinformationssysteme in der Produktion.* Marburg: Metropolis.

Küpper, H.-U. (1997). *Controlling,* 2. Aufl. Stuttgart.

Lehner, F., Hildebrand, K., & Maier, R. (1995). *Wirtschaftsinformatik. Theoretische Grundlagen.* München, Wien: Hanser.

Möller, A. (2000). *Grundlagen Stoffstrombasierter Betrieblicher Umweltinformationssysteme.* Bochum: Projekt.

Möller, A. et al. (1997). *Öko-Controlling in Handelsunternehmen.* Berlin: Springer.

Möller, A., & Rolf, A. (2001). Eco product lifecycle management. In EcoDesign 2001 Secretariat (Eds.), *Proceedings Eco Design 2001.* Los Alamos: IEEE Press.

Preece, J. (2000). *Online communities: Designing usability, supporting sociability.* Chichester, UK: John Wiley & Sons.

Rautenstrauch, C. (1999). *Betriebliche Umweltinformationssysteme – Grundlagen, Konzepte und Systeme.* Berlin: Springer.

Schaltegger, S., & Burritt, R. (2000). *Contemporary environmental accounting — Issues, concepts and practice.* Sheffield: Greenleaf Publishing.

Schelhowe, H. (1997). *Das Medium aus der Maschine — Zur Metamorphose des Computers.* Frankfurt a.M., New York: Campus Fachbuch.

Schmidt, M. (2000). Betriebliches Stoffstrommanagement. In H. Dyckhoff (Ed.), *Umweltmanagement.* Berlin: Springer.

Weber, J. (1999). *Einführung in das Controlling,* 8. Aufl. Stuttgart: Schäffer-Poeschel.

Winograd, T., & Flores, F. (1991). *Understanding computers and cognition – A new foundation for design.* Reading, MA: Intellect Books.

World Business Council for Sustainable Development. (2000). *Measuring eco-efficiency: A guide to reporting company performance.* Conches-Geneva: World Business Council for Sustainable Development.

Chapter VI

Eco-Efficient Controlling of Material Flows with Flow Cost Accounting: ERP-Based Solutions of the ECO Rapid Project

Stefan Enzler, Institut für Management und Umwelt, Germany

Helmut Krcmar, Technische Universität München, Germany

Roland Pfennig, Green IT GmbH, Germany

Wolfgang Scheide, Green IT GmbH, Germany

Markus Strobel, Institut für Management und Umwelt, Germany

Abstract

The point of departure for ECO Rapid is the assumption that environmental management instruments have been perfected, but they will only be able to be used in practice to any extent worth mentioning if costs and benefits are in a favourable relationship to one another for companies. A key factor for achieving this goal is the question of how standard business management software can be used as instruments for solving the problems of company environmental management (environmental cost accounting, flow cost accounting, preparing an environmental balance sheet and environmental figures, etc.). This is the reason why we developed a method in the ECO Rapid project that puts companies and software retailers in a position to use and further develop enterprise resource planning systems (ERP systems) in a fashion that is orientated more towards material flows. We have used the reference model of ECO-Integral (Krcmar et al., 2000) to make it possible to take advantage of the database of ERP systems for a number of new evaluations on company material flows in quantities and values. This means that companies will be better able to use the ERP software they already have for the purposes of company environmental management while creating synergies to business management. We are publishing this method as a digital CD manual for small- and medium-sized companies and to a great extent it can be used independently of any particular software product. An important step along this route is pilot implementation in three companies. These hands-on projects are being followed up by imu augsburg (Augsburg, Germany) and Green IT GmbH (Konstanz, Germany). The chair for economic IT (at the Stuttgart-Hohenheim University) has the all-round responsibility for handling the project and IT support. And this chapter has the purpose of presenting the experience gathered in ECO Rapid.

Methodology of ECO Rapid

Flow Cost Accounting

The following report is limited to the implementation of flow cost accounting, as this tool was given highest priority by the pilot companies involved. The continuous linking of quantity and value data enables companies to systematically combine cost reduction and resource-saving measures. Flow cost accounting as a tool of modern cost accounting has been the subject of a number of publications and guidelines (among others, LfU/Ministerium für Umwelt and Verkehr Baden-Württemberg, 1999, Krcmar et al., 2000; Strobel, 2001). Essentially, flow cost accounting is a cost accounting method that aims at the quantitative and monetary valuation of a company's material flows on an accrual basis. The underlying concept of flow cost accounting is the material-flow-related distribution and calculation of a company's total manufacturing costs by allocating these costs to the individual material flows (Pojasek, 1997; US EPA, 2000). The material flows are considered to be the main cost drivers and therefore also serve as cost collectors (Figure 1).

Figure 1. Basic concept of flow cost accounting

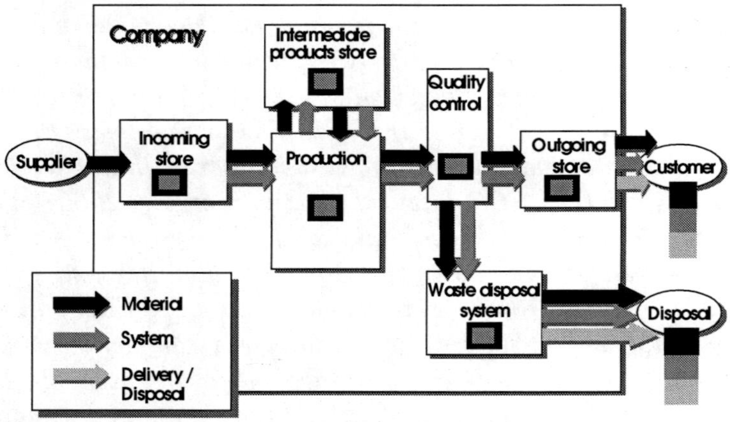

Source: Strobel, 2001

The calculation requires a comprehensive database and consists of a great number of individual arithmetic operations, leading to a variety of result and reporting formats. Flow cost accounting can therefore only be carried out utilising comprehensive EDP support. However, experience shows that the existing databases of companies (material control systems, production planning and control systems) already contain most of the data required. The costs associated with flow cost accounting are not so much generated by the ongoing acquisition of additional data, but rather by the one-off establishment of the calculation method.

Flow cost accounting distinguishes among the following main steps:

- Check for data consistency
- Calculation of inventory differences at all storage sites
- Calculation of these differences with regard to all production orders
- Calculation of material flows
- Merging of data to form user-specific reports

Database

Both the data flow and the sequence of flow cost calculation encompass the determination of the required database and computing elements as well as the individual result and reporting formats. On the other hand, specific requirements of the result or reporting format may necessitate adjustments to the computing elements or even the required database.

In principle, the approach to the practical implementation of flow cost accounting is based on the 3-level model used in the preliminary project, ECO-Integral (Krcmar et al., 2000). This involves, first of all, the examination of material flows on a physical level, followed by an analysis of the information system and the eco-management tools.

Procedure

It is absolutely necessary to have a systematic procedure to be able to use the existing database of an ERP system for the purposes of flow cost accounting. The procedure sketched out in Figure 3 has the purpose of achieving high data and report quality while limiting the expenditures for the flow account. We start off by surveying the benefit-to-cost potential for introducing the flow cost accounting in preliminary discussions (the step of analysing the potential). If a decision is made affirming the project, we establish a project structure and put together our team (the step of installing project management). Afterwards, we plan on eight consecutive phases that will be run through several times:

- The idea behind the **first phase (modelling)** is to map the essential aspects of the company with reference to material flow. This first phase forms the basis for further work in all of the following phases. First of all, work groups inspect the company to record material flows that are presented in a material flow model. They simultaneously map the structure of the terminal material postings in the ERP system in their own model. Then, the two individual models are matched against one another to draw conclusions as

Figure 2. Examination objects for implementation of flow cost accounting

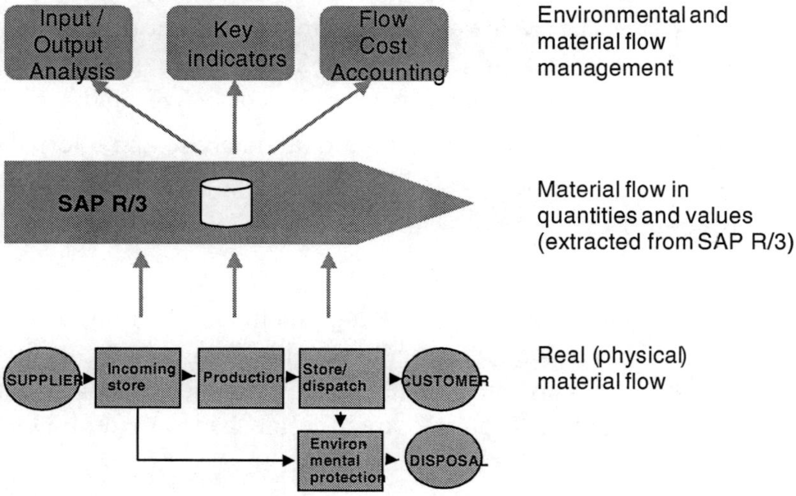

Figure 3. Model of the ECO rapid procedure

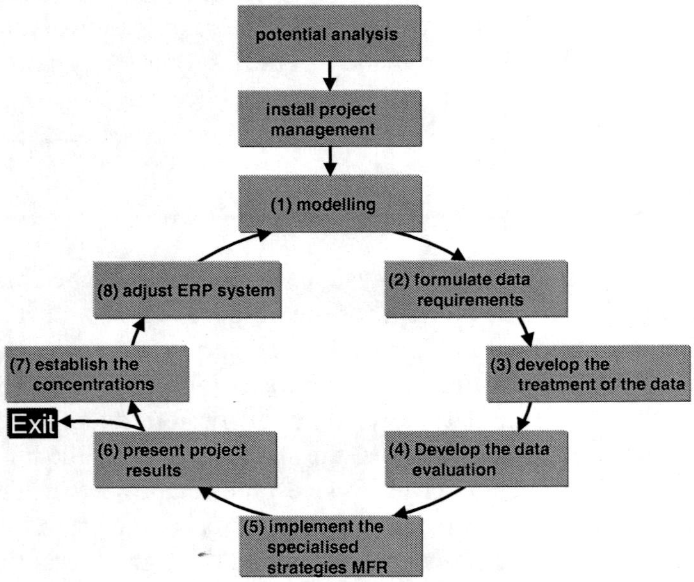

to where the real material flows and their image of them in the ERP system agree with or differ from one another.

- In **phase 2**, they can establish the data requirements for flow cost accounting with reference to the material flow based upon their knowledge of the posting structures in the ERP system. The basic structure of the data required is similar in all productive companies. Then they do fine-tuning based upon the data quality and functions of the ERP system. What is essentially required are material master data, parts lists, stocks and movement data. The precise data requirements will also depend upon which scenario of implementation is selected. Two scenarios have shown to be suitable and practical in the pilot companies of ECO Rapid:
  (a) evaluation with the aid of a relational database and interfaces to the ERP system
  (b) evaluations with a data warehouse.

- **Phase 3** (developing data processing) includes planning how data are supposed to be provided in accordance with the requirements formulated in advance. They may be flat files for a relational database (scenario of implementation a) or through extraction mechanisms (an ETL tool, flat files) loaded into a data warehouse (scenario of implementation b). Beyond this, several forms of processing have to be developed that do not represent material flows such as eliminating cancellation posting or automatically generated counter-postings. The objective is a specialised strategy that forms a basis for generating a data structure that can be evaluated for implementation (phase 5).

- The **fourth phase** of developing the data evaluation will produce two documents. The specialised strategy of "consistency check" describes how we can check the completeness and consistency of the data supplied. The repairable data requirements will be filtered in later implementation and the data relevant to evaluation will be separated.

  The specialised strategy for flow cost accounting contains the design of the customised reports on material flows and material losses. This should be designed to supply the persons in the company in charge with a new view of corporate processes based upon material flows. This view forms the basis of developing actions and organisational changes.

- **Phase 5** (implementing specialised strategies of material flow accounting) implements the data processing implementation strategies worked out in phases 3 and 4 in the real system landscape. This involves a great deal of work because inconsistencies in data and lacking material flow data in the ERP system make it difficult to directly evaluate the data and the additional repair requires a great deal of effort. Beyond this, it is necessary to build up the evaluation algorithm for the specific company when flow cost accounting is done for the first time.

- **Phase 6** (presenting the results of the project) processes the results of the flow cost accounting. The target group for the presentation is a committee of executive employees and members of the management that decide whether and in what departments it is necessary to have improvements in the material flow structure (for avoiding material losses), in the IT systems, cost accounting or in the organisation (Enzler/Strobel, 2001). The results flow cost accounting allow us to draw conclusions on where the ERP system has to be adjusted to map the material flow more completely.

- **Phase 7** (establishing concentrations) will work out the adjustments required in these concentrations. Some of the typical areas are improving the mapping of material flows with contract workers or improved information on returns.

- Adjustments will be made in the ERP system based upon these proposals for action in **phase 8**. This may be done with customising or the functionality has to be expanded.

This complete the first cycle. It is generally not possible to implement all of the proposals for improvement and reporting structures the first time the project is run through so that it can be run through again. Regularly adjusting the data structures and doing flow cost accounting on a periodical basis provides us with clearly improved material flow transparency. This means that all of the essential areas for improvement with reference to material efficiency can be taken advantage of one after another (cf. Strobel/Enzler, 2001).

Advantage of Flow Cost Accounting

The **main advantage** of flow cost accounting lies in the production of a very detailed and timely transparency of quantities, values and costs in connection with material flows. This new cost transparency applies to 50% to 90% of the total costs of the creation of services and goods. If the relevant staff is integrated in the reporting and if corresponding target and motivation systems are created and sufficient freedom for measure development and implementation is granted, this can lead to a significant efficiency increase and contribute to a surge of innovations. All this, however, will not only depend on flow cost accounting but on its organisational integration as well.

The measures developed on the basis of flow cost accounting will basically lead to a reduced use of material and therefore to cost reduction with environmental relief at the same time. In this context, the following basic points for actions concerning measure development can be distinguished:

- Material reductions during new developments or adaptation of products and packings (e.g., thinner container sides, reduction of packing components)
- Organisational measures for reducing material losses (e.g., extension of charge sizes, better machine adjustments, coordination of distribution and production planning, different material purchase, coordination with providers, coordination of storage and machine adaptation to recycling packing)
- Technical optimizing of existing production installations for the reduction of material losses (e.g., more precise channelling, controlling via solar cell, return of material losses to the installation)
- Investments in new production installations for the reduction of material losses

Apart from a few big measures there can be a couple of little measures to be taken over several years concerning a continuing process of improving, which will lead in sum to significant effects. The following scenario, which is confirmed in a great number of projects, shows how great the benefit of cost management based on flow cost accounting can be.

Cost / Benefit Scenario*

Data base

Annual turnover: 206 Mio. €
Profit: 8 Mio. € (profit-turnover ratio about 5%)
Costs for creation of
goods and services: 196 Mio. €
from with 131 Mio. € are material costs
(material losses of 14,5 % add up to 19 Mio. €)
from with 85 Mio. € are ending up in the product
from with 27 Mio. € are used for packaging
from with 44 Mio. € are system costs
from with 3 Mio. € are delivery- and disposal costs

Measures

1. Reduction of material losses up to 10% (1.9 Mio. €)
2. Reduction of the amount of material in the product by 0.5 % (4.25 Mio. €)
3. Reduction of the material quantity in the packing by 3% (0.81 Mio. €)

Thus, only few measures can lead to an annual decrease of material costs of up to 7 Mio. €
Based on the measures delivery and disposal costs can be cut by up to 0.3 Mio. €

Cost

The necessary investments to realize the measures amount to 10 Mio. €

Benefit

The costs for measures are amortized after one year and three months.
After this period the company's profit has nearly doubled.

*To simplify, taxes are not considered in this scenario.

A **further advantage** of flow cost accounting, which should not be underestimated, consists of the development of the ERP-system. On the one hand, the introduction of flow cost accounting and the adaptation of the ERP-system mean a great effort. In above-mentioned scenario, there could be for example costs of 0.15 Mio. • for applying flow cost accounting. The permanent use of flow cost accounting, however, does then not require a lot of work. On the contrary, the following benefit capacities result from improved data quality and a higher degree of detailing in the running operation:

- Reduction of the problems in operational applications (especially concerning material purchase and production controlling) because of an improved database. As an example, incorrect material inventory can lead to delays in material purchase and as a consequence to losses of production or additional tooling-up activities because of lack of material. The elimination of such controlling deficits can contribute to noticeable cost reductions.
- Reduction of the manual rework for elimination of a defective database (e.g., elimination of incorrect entries, adaptation of inventories) that results in a significant cost reduction for data base update.

- Reduction of redundant data input because of entry transparency, so that a cost reduction for data handling can be expected. With this, for example, it can be prevented that bills are booked twice from the financial accounting department and the material management.

Results and Conclusions from the Pilot Projects

Implementation Partners and Project Status

The development of implementation options is based both on a comprehensive analysis of the actual situation of the partner company and the development of target plans. The implementation of target plans within the operative ERP systems is carried out both by internal IT staff of the pilot companies and outsourcing partners.

The first pilot project of **J. Stehle + Söhne AG** in Esslingen, Germany, was completed in 2001. At 250,000 units, the production centres on the manufacture of electric drives for roller blinds and sun protection systems. In addition, Stehle is a supplier to the automotive industry. Stehle's manufacture can be classified as series production consisting primarily of the areas "mechanical production," "plastics production" and "assembly". With a staff of 165, the company achieved a turnover of DEM 40 million in 1999 and has enjoyed growth in turnover of approximately 15% over recent years. Various management systems were introduced over the past few years: eco-management in accordance with EMAS and ISO 14.001 as well as quality management in accordance with ISO 9001. In the area of IT, Stehle uses SAP R/3. Nearly all modules are being utilised (with the exception of PP). The operative system is operated by the company's outsourcing partner Hewlett-Packard. Stehle is a medium-size reference client of SAP AG and uses the results generated by ECO Rapid as input for the imminent SAP R/3 release change-over. In addition, the storage location and cost center structure was adapted to material flow, which will allow improved material flow tracking in the future. Apart from the posting structures, we also adjusted the existing parts lists to be able to make precise evaluations on material losses with adjusted gross and net parts lists. The new data landscape will allow detailed analyses with flow cost accounting in the coming years that will form the basis of improved material efficiency.

The second practice-related project was carried out at **Dr. Grandel**, a medium-size company having 200+ staff. The company's development, production and logistics centre is based in Augsburg, Germany, where cosmetics, food supplements and a range of different substances are produced. The company's operating procedures are characterised by modern production technologies, continuous laboratory tests and a standard of hygiene that is equal to that of pharmaceutical production. Dr. Grandel has introduced a quality management system based on the Total Quality Management concept and an eco-management in accordance with ISO 14.001. In the area of IT, Dr. Grandel uses an Oracle-based logistics system that integrates sales logistics, material control and production control. Dr. Grandel successfully ran through all phases of the project and is presently in the stage of implementing the results of the project. Executive management made the conclusions and decided on the necessary adjustments in the company at a workshop based upon the results of flow cost accounting. The activities for reducing material losses and simplifying processes may altogether be broken down into two concentrations:

1. Implementing immediate actions for adjusting the system
   - determining and posting the purchase value, incidental material costs and average price
   - handling contract production
   - handling destruction, cancellation and erroneous entries
   - handling contract production postings
   - implementing and documenting manual postings
   - reimbursing customers for products complained about
2. Introducing material flow controlling with flow cost accounting
   - preparing the calculation algorithms in Oracle for flow cost accounting
   - preparing a reporting system for the various company departments

When the activities slated are implemented, management hopes that they will provide possibilities for improving material efficiency, simplifications in the entire posting process and also more detailed and accurate data for existing company applications.

The third pilot project is performed at **Konrad Hornschuch AG** at the company's head office in Weißbach. Hornschuch is a well-established company that produces approximately 4,000 sales items whose primary components are raw materials for plastics. The company's product range includes design foils (e.g., d-c-fix) as well as footwear, bag-making and upholstery materials for fashion articles. In addition, Hornschuch produces components for the automotive industry (e.g., imitation leather) as well as laminates and special foils for the construction industry. In recent years, Hornschuch was faced with difficult market conditions (among others, the Asian crisis and the collapse of the Russian market). Nevertheless, the company was able to maintain its turnover level of just under • 105 million, which was generated by a total of 670 staff. In terms of technology, Hornschuch's manufacture must be classified as process production, based on formulas. However, within SAP R/3 the production is mapped as shop production in module PP. Konrad Hornschuch AG was chosen as a pilot company, as they have introduced the SAP AG data warehouse (SAP Business Warehouse) and flow cost accounting can therefore be implemented based on this tool.

Company Projects: Results To-Date

At present, the following conclusions may be drawn:

(a) Firstly, it has been demonstrated that, among the various eco-management tools, the participating pilot companies assign highest priority to flow cost accounting, followed by the environmental balance and the determination of key indicators. Other tools (such as ecological assessment or the micro/macro link (Krcmar et al., 2000)) have significantly lower priorities, as their benefit to the business is considered to be relatively small.

(b) Flow cost accounting can be carried out utilising the data basis of existing business ERP systems, proceeding in accordance with standardised steps. This statement has yet to be verified with regard to environmental balance tool. It is, however, likely that this statement would also apply here, as flow cost accounting is far more complex and difficult.

(c) Some business ERP systems contain considerable weaknesses in terms of data quality and the continuous presentation of material flows. This not only hampers flow cost accounting, but also creates problems with regard to business processes, for example in the areas of procurement, production planning or dispatch.

Therefore, all inconsistencies and implausibilities must, first of all, be eliminated from the database in order to track material flows uninterruptedly with regard to quantities and costs. Missing data must be added or computed for further evaluation. Erroneous data must be eliminated. Errors in parts lists, for example, result in incorrect material requirements planning for both procurement and production, and incorrectly used movement codes lead to discrepancies in material inventories and therefore to a significant increase in labour and costs when carrying out inventories.

The accounting structures and the underlying logic interact with the data quality. These structures may cause problems, as they are not always designed for exact material tracking. Errors occur when the accounting structure per se causes discontinuities in the mapping of the material flow. This may be the case where the SAP system has not been perfectly customised or the system design is too lean for consistent material tracking (but a lean system design is nevertheless useful for other reasons). However, errors may also be caused by staff who omit to acquire data or capture data incompletely. This may happen with the intention to simplify accounting procedures or out of ignorance of the existing interrelations. Also, in some cases the intention is to avoid material flow transparency.

However, users benefit from the implementation of suggestions of how to improve both the database and accounting structures in other ways than just having more transparent material tracking. In fact, better data quality also eliminates sources of error for other applications of the ERP system and serves as a basis for the decision-making process with regard to the benefits of data maintenance.

(d) Flow cost accounting on the basis of existing ERP systems is not only feasible, but also useful from a business management point of view. Using the project results, weaknesses in the material flow and the information system can be eliminated. The associated future material savings not only reduce costs, but also help save resources and reduce waste, thereby achieving the frequently demanded integration of economy and ecology.

The tables showing the results as well as the overviews of flow cost accounting provide information as to where material losses occur and for which materials, production areas and products. This information forms the basis of further plausibility checks for evaluation purposes and contributes to prioritising problem areas that must be addressed by implementing IT measures, operational measures and, eventually, process measures.

Digital Guideline for Disseminating and Flow Cost Accounting

We will be publishing this method of ECO Rapid worked out for implementing and utilising flow cost accounting based upon ERP in a digital multimedia manual in the second half of 2002. This manual will contain the following building blocks that allow companies to introduce and use flow cost accounting:

- the model of procedure for implementing flow cost accounting
- hands-on examples from the pilot companies on flow cost accounting

- the theoretical basis for explaining the method
- a collection of tools for supporting implementation in the company
- frequently asked questions
- short case studies about flow cost accounting

Our model for implementing flow cost accounting is structured so that managers can introduce flow cost accounting in their companies independently using the manual. This manual not only has general chapters that demonstrate the benefits to users with different backgrounds and provide a summary description of the procedure. Its core is also a model of how to proceed. Here, the project manager is picked up in the point of departure of his or her company and directed step for step on how to implement flow cost accounting. This digital manual allows the user to skip back and forth quickly between the chapters for implementation without losing his or her way in this complex topic. At the same time, they can use links to access the appropriate examples and aids to be used or also the theoretical foundation on the description of the procedure for each chapter on implementation.

The method for implementing and permanently utilising flow cost accounting is described independently of any particular software, so that it can be easily transferred to the ERP system used. This model for proceeding with implementation takes the various scenarios of using ERP in practice at companies into account and demonstrates several possibilities for analysing and preparing data although emphasis is placed upon evaluation in a data warehouse and in a relational database.

References

Enzler, S., Strauß, T., & van Riesen, S. (2003). Flusskostenrechnung bei der Freudenberg Hauhaltsprodukte Augsburg KG. *Controller Magazin 02/ 2003,* 168-171.

Enzler, S., & Strobel, M. (2001). Win-win-potenziale Organisieren – Wirtschaftlichkeit und Umweltentlastung Durch Flussmanagement. *Ökologisches Wirtschaften 2/2001,* 26-28.

Germann, E. & Strobel, M. (2003). Flusskostenrechnung auf der Basis Betrieblicher ERP-Systeme – Zum Stand der Umsetzung in der Praxis. In M. Kramer & P. Eiffler (Eds.), *Umwelt – und Kostenorientierte Unternehmensführung – Zur Identifikation von Win-win-potenzialen* (pp. 113-129). Wiesbaden: Deutscher Universitäts-Verlag.

Hessisches Ministerium für Wirtschaft, Verkehr and Landesentwicklung. (ed.). (1999). *Flusskostenmanagement. Kostensenkung und Öko-effizienz Durch Eine Materialflussorientierung in der Kostenrechnung.* (Leitfaden), Wiesbaden.

Krcmar, H., Dold, G., Fischer, H., Strobel, M., & Seifert, E. (2000). Informationssysteme für das Umweltmanagement. *Das Referenzmodell ECO-Integral München.* Wien: R.Oldenbourg Verlag.

LfU/Ministerium für Umwelt and Verkehr Baden-Württemberg. (ed.). (1999). *Betriebliches Material- und Energieflussmanagement. Öko-effizienz Durch Nachhaltige Reorganisation.* (Leitfaden), Karlsruhe.

Pojasek, R. (1997). *Materials Accounting and P2, Pollution Prevention Review,* Autumn, 95-103.

Scheide, W. (1999). *Die informationsversorgung für das Umweltcontrolling.* Stuttgart: Verlag Grauer.

Scheide, W., Enzler, S., & Dold, G. (2002). Efficient eco-management using ECO-integral – How to save costs and natural resources at the same time. In M. Bennet, J. Bouma & T. Wolters (Eds.), *Eco-efficiency in industry and science. Environmental management accounting: Informational and institutional Developments.* Dordrecht.

Strobel, M. (2001). *Systemisches Flussmanagement. Flussorientierte Kommunikation als Perspektive für eine Ökologische and Ökonomische Unternehmensentwicklung.* Augsburg: Ziel.

Strobel, M., & Enzler, S. (2001). Flussmanagement – Kostensenkung und Umweltentlastung durch einen Materialflussorientierten Managementansatz. *Umweltwirtschaftsforum 2/2001,* 54-60.

Strobel, M., & Müller, U. (2003). Flusskostenrechnung – Ein ERP-basiertes Instrument zur Systematischen Reduzierung des Materialeinsatzes. In M. Tschandl & A. Posch (Eds.), *Integriertes Umweltcontrolling – Von der Stoffstromanalyse zum Integrierten Bewertungs- und Informations-system* (pp. 119-136). Wiesbaden: Gabler Verlag.

Strobel, M., & Redmann, C. (2002). Flow cost accounting, an accounting approach based on the actual flows of materials. In M. Bennett, J. Bouma & T. Wolters (Eds.), *Eco-efficiency in industry and science. Environmental management accounting: Informational and institutional developments* (vol. 9, pp. 67-82). Doordrecht: Kluwer Academic Publishers.

US EPA Environmental Accounting Project. (2000, January). *The lean and green supply chain. A practical guide for materials managers and supply chain managers to reduce costs and improve environmental performance.* EPA 742-R-00-001. Washington D.C.

Chapter VII

Advanced Middleware for eScience Applied to Environmental Integrated Systems

Catherine Houstis, Institute of Computer Science, FORTH, Greece

Spyros Lalis, Institute of Computer Science, FORTH, Greece

Emmanuel Vavalis, Institute of Computer Science, FORTH, Greece

Marios Pitikakis, Institute of Computer Science, FORTH, Greece

George V. Vasilakis, Institute of Computer Science, FORTH, Greece

Abstract

An advanced eScience middleware system is designed and implemented (the middleware has been developed within the ARION project, IST-2000-25289, funded by EU 5th Framework Programme) to support search and retrieval of scientific information. It is capable of integrating collections of scientific datasets, including simulation models and associated tools for statistical analysis and dataset visualization. These collections represent application software in several scientific domains, they reside in geographically disperse organizations and constitute the system content. It also actively supports on-demand scientific data processing workflows. The system design makes use of two recently advancing technologies, the Semantic Web and the Grid, as well as state of the art distributed systems' technology. The systems' demonstration scenarios involve mainly environmental applications.

Introduction

Not so many years ago researchers relied solely on themselves to go through with their everyday activities or to achieve an important breakthrough in their discipline; and the only collaboration that used to exist was within institutional boundaries. Recently, however, more and more communication technologies are meeting widespread acceptance, enabling research as well as industrial communities to closely collaborate and share resources through a secure and scalable network infrastructure. These technologies come to realize a long awaited vision, introducing ways of sharing knowledge and of collaboration within distributed communities previously unheard of.

At the heart of this drive for ubiquitous collaboration lies the eScience initiative. There are two closely related technology trends that seem to be driving forward and promoting this initiative: the Semantic Web (W3C Semantic Web) and the Grid (Foster et al., 2001, 2002; Foster & Kesselman, 1998). Both these technologies are undergoing continuous development and have reached an acceptable level of maturity.

The ambition interwoven with the Semantic Web is of an environment where software agents are able to dynamically discover, interrogate and interoperate with resources, building and disbanding virtual problem solving environments, discovering new facts, and performing sophisticated tasks on behalf of humans (Hendler, 2001). On the other hand, the essence of the Grid is the power provided by large-scale integration of resources. The scale and automation of the Grid necessitates the universally accessible platform that allows data to be shared and processed by automated tools as well as by people. These last two sentences make apparent the close relationship between these two technologies and how each stands to benefit from the other.

It only makes sense, therefore, for middleware platforms involved in/dealing with information integration and management, sharing of resources and advanced collaboration to pay due attention to and embrace the afore mentioned technologies. As our approach towards eScience, we propose ARION as the middleware architecture that brings the best of these convergent visions, combining the concepts found in each.

ARION promotes semantic interoperability by making use of ontologies and associated Semantic Web technologies, such as RDF (Resource Description Framework) (Lassila & Swick, 1999) and RDFS (Resource Description Framework Schema) (Brickley & Guha, 1999), at the information modelling level, whereas with respect to the resource-sharing aspect of the system, a computational framework is defined. The main motivation for our work is the need to enhance *information-sensitive* systems with better mechanisms for eScience composition and integration. ARION is a service-based infrastructure designed to support search and retrieval of scientific objects, and capable of integrating collections of datasets and scientific applications including simulation models and associated tools for statistical analysis and dataset visualization. It also actively supports on-demand scientific data processing workflows, in both interactive and batch mode. The system's demonstration scenarios involve mainly environmental applications (offshore to near shore transformation of wave conditions, synthetic time series and monthly statistical parameters, coupled ocean-atmosphere models, etc.).

A Service Oriented View

In designing the system, a service oriented model has been adopted, supporting a high degree of automation and providing a flexible environment for large scale computations and resource retrieval. In a computing paradigm, a user might proceed by:

- **gaining** the necessary authentication credentials and access rights
- **querying** the information system to determine the existence of required datasets and view the corresponding metadata information
- **submitting** requests to initiate computations (workflows), move data, and so forth
- **monitoring** the progress of the various computations, notifying the user when all are completed, and detecting and responding to failure conditions
- **visualizing** the results of computational workflows

A service can simply be viewed as an abstract characterization and encapsulation of some content or processing capabilities. Thus, services can be related to the data, computational or knowledge grid. The data grid provides access (search and retrieval) to datasets stored in geographically distributed systems in various organizations. The computational grid deals with the way that computational resources are allocated, scheduled and executed and the way in which data are shipped between the various processing resources. The knowledge grid handles the way that information (i.e., metadata, ontology) is represented, stored, shared and maintained. Given its key role in many scientific activities, the Web is the obvious point of interest at this level. Here information is understood as data equipped with meaning.

All of the above give rise to the view of the eScience infrastructure as a set of services that are provided by particular individuals or institutions for consumption by others, under various forms of contract.

ARION System Architecture

ARION provides the means (Houstis & Lalis, 2000, 2001, 2002) for organizing geographically distributed and heterogeneous resources of scientific content, so that its disparate and varied parts are integrated into a coherent whole. Hence, ARION can be viewed as the middleware between *users*, the *data* being processed and the computational *resources* required for this processing.

Our architecture combines both a horizontal and a vertical integration (Figure 1). The horizontal integration is expressed by ontologies and the vertical by workflows (applications). These are the main mechanisms for recording expert knowledge, for information representation and navigation, and for expressing computation processes over a grid of resources.

ARION is composed of a set of distributed nodes containing data sets and programs (scientific collections). These nodes interoperate using an agent platform, and provide the basic infrastructure for workflow execution. Workflows typically rely on distributed and autonomous tasks and are controlled by a centralized server (the ARION main server in our case). Mobile agents installed on each node execute workflow tasks (mainly computations) and monitor the execution flow.

The architecture of our prototype consists of four subsystems and is shown in Figure 2. The *Search Engine* allows users to pose queries to the knowledge provided by ARION. It is mainly based upon RDFSuite (Alexaki et al., 2001), a suite of tools for RDF metadata management providing storage and querying for both RDF descriptions and schemas. It consists of three main components: a RDF validating parser (VRP), a RDF schema-specific storage database (RSSDB) and a query language (RQL). The RDF Query Language (RQL) (Karvounarakis

Figure 1. ARION horizontal and vertical integration

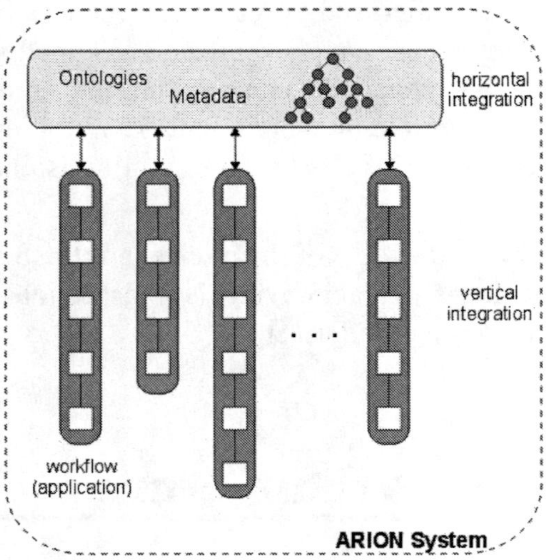

et al., 2002) is used to uniformly query RDF metadata information and RDF schemas (i.e., queries can be posed for either the metadata information or the concepts and properties of the ontology). Thus, we can exploit this ability to implement schema browsing, since large RDF schemas carry valuable information themselves due to class refinement.

The *Workflow Data Base System* contains the workflow specifications and handles the preparation of execution specifications to be sent to the workflow runtime. It consists of the following components: Workflow Editor, Workflow Storage System, Workflow Database Server and Statistical Database.

The *Workflow Runtime System* is responsible for the execution of workflows and the management of the information produced during this execution from the distributed nodes. It consists of two main components, namely the Workflow Manager and the User Monitoring System. For each workflow definition received from the *Workflow Data Base,* an execution environment is initialized and a Task Scheduler is created. The Task Scheduler makes decisions about the order of execution of tasks and assigns blocks of tasks to the Task Manager, which is responsible for the execution. The Task Manager cooperates with the Agent Management System where all the objects related with the agent platform are located, including the agent generation mechanism, the communication objects and the proxies to Grasshopper objects. We used Grasshopper (Grasshopper 2 Agent Platform) for the prototype that we have developed.

The *User Authentication & Authorization System* is responsible for all security and access control issues in our prototype. The authentication process is

Figure 2. ARION architecture

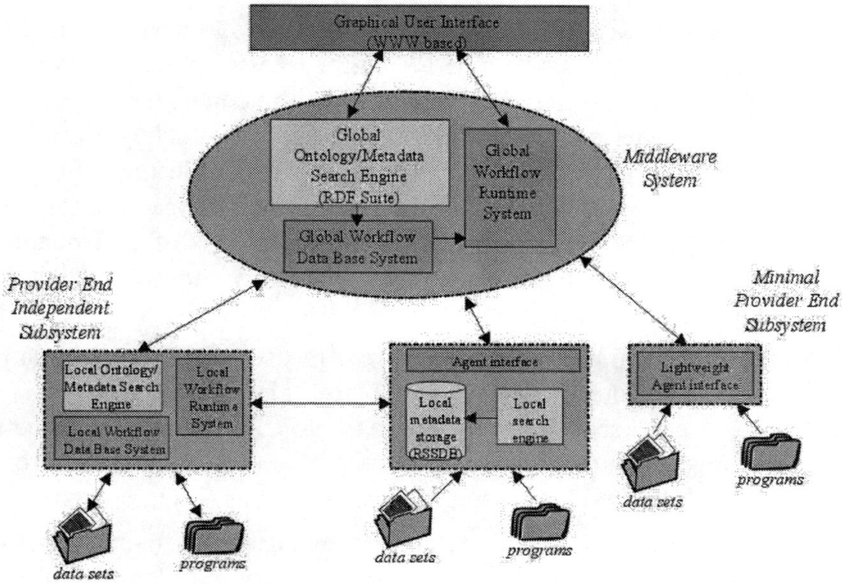

implemented via a miniLDAP authorization mechanism (downscaled implementation of the Lightweight Directory Access Protocol), which grants or denies permission to access a digital object (data or resource). In order to define these permissions, we have adopted a role-based access control mechanism to handle the users and objects. These roles are shared inside the distributed system by using a hierarchical structure, based on trust domains. Authorization is achieved by validating resource access, signed with certificates that were issued by the ARION system.

Ontology Based Scientific Resource Representation

Ontologies are a useful mechanism to classify metadata of various resources. However, such annotations would be of limited value to automated processes unless they share a common understanding as to their meaning of terms in a given domain. We usually attribute the notion of ontology to the "specification of a conceptualization" (Gruber, 1993) – that is, defined terms and relationships between them, usually in some formal and usually machine-readable manner –

which is either domain specific or generalizes or reconciles domains and can be communicated across people and applications.

An ontology contains a set of classes and each class has an associated set of properties. Each property has a range indicating a restriction on the values the property can take. An ontology relates more specific concepts to more general ones (from which generic information can be inherited). Such links are used to organize concepts into a hierarchy or some other partial ordering, which is used for storing information at appropriate levels of generality and automatically making it available to more specific concepts by means of a mechanism of inheritance. The notion of ontological concepts is very similar to the notion of classes in object-oriented programming.

Ontologies provide common semantics that can be used to improve communication between either humans or computers. Ontologies may be grouped into the following three areas, according to their role: to assist in communication between people, to achieve interoperability among computer systems, or to improve the process and/or quality of engineering software systems (Uschold et al., 1998).

The general approach to semantic integration has been to map terms and concepts onto a shared ontology. A shared scientific ontology ensures total integration, though constructing such an ontology may be costly and time-consuming.

In ARION, we are interested in the semantics of scientific collections. We have designed an environmental ontology comprising of different facets. Facets may describe data sets, production methods including mathematical modelling, parameters used, and so forth. This way we can provide modularization of a potentially large monolithic ontology. In addition, facets capture the elementary knowledge that users want to explore during query formulation. A facet-based engineering of an ontology scales well with large scientific ontologies. New information may be appended in accordance to user/provider needs. The ontology definition contains an "is-a" hierarchy of relevant domain concepts, relationships between concepts and properties of concepts. There are two main concepts in our ontology, consisting of two different facets describing the scientific data and scientific models respectively. The basic structure of our ontology is shown in Figure 3.

Considerable efforts are in progress to develop technologies for asserting facts about resources, and a common language for expressing metadata and knowledge embodied by ontologies for a shared understanding and a common vocabulary; notably RDFS (Brickley & Guha 1999), DAML+OIL (Horrocks, 2002) and OWL (OWL Web Ontology Language 1.0 Reference).

In our implementation, scientific collections are semantically described by concepts (classes) that are defined in an ontology constructed with RDFS, while

Figure 3. Structure of our environmental ontology

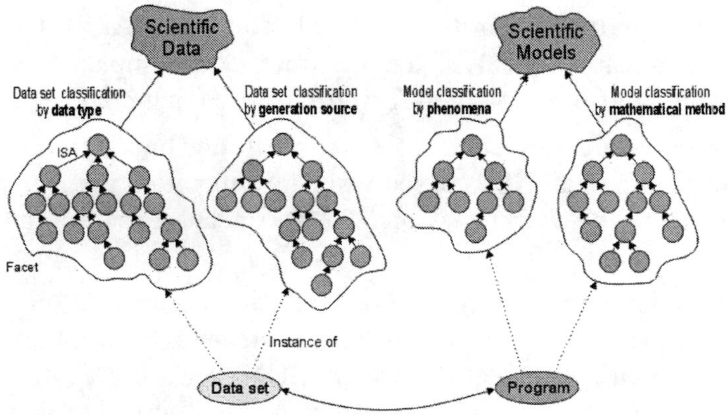

the representation of resource metadata is realized by RDF. Objects, classes, and properties can be described using a standardized syntax (XML) and a standard set of modelling primitives like instance-of and subclass-of relationships. The expressive capabilities of RDF and RDF Schema suffice for the purposes of ARION and are used as the basis for modelling our domain of knowledge. In particular, metadata description is ontology-driven, in the sense that the construction of the metadata information is carried out in a top-down fashion, by populating a given ontology, rather than in a bottom-up fashion. Every scientific object (data set or model) is described by a collection of attributes (properties), inherited from its parent-class or native to the specific object.

Information Integration

Most of the activities in a day-to-day scientific work involve many tasks that need to be executed in a specific order. The tasks involved in an activity may vary based on the results of the other tasks being executed. This dynamic sequence of execution of tasks to complete an activity leads to the notion of a workflow.

Scientists typically link resources by workflow orchestration, that is, by coordinating and chaining tasks using a systematic plan, which allows the representation of the e-scientist's experimental process explicitly. Both the results and the way they are obtained are highly valued. Where data came from, who created them, when, why and how they were derived is as important as the data themselves for the user and the service provider.

Scientific knowledge can be replicated and archived for safekeeping. It is essential to be able to recall a snapshot of the state of understanding at a point in time in order to justify a scientific view held at that time. As data collections and analytical applications evolve, keeping track of the impact of changes is difficult. Storing workflows is a step forward towards that goal.

The ARION middleware provides: (a) tools to create and publish computational workflows according to an XML based workflow specification, (b) a runtime platform to execute the workflows and (c) the means to store and retrieve workflows.

The manual creation and maintenance of metadata is generally problematic. People are not always in the best position to create it or produce accurate metadata, through circumstance or error. ARION workflow applications are also designed to include a mechanism to automate the creation and management of metadata.

Workflow Definition

The formal representation of a workflow is a fundamental issue concerning the development of mechanisms to support e-services. One approach is to use a declarative and structured specification language such as WSDL (Christensen et al., 2001) or XLANG (Thatte, 2001).

In ARION, workflows provide abstractions of natural process models. An important portion of a process model (workflow) is the definition of the process logic. Our workflow specification language is based on XRL (Exchangeable Routing Language) (Van der Aalst & Kumar, 2001), an XML-based routing language. XRL has large expressive power, can be mapped to Petri Nets (this provides formal semantics and availability of analysis techniques and tools) and a DTD (Document Type Definition) can be used to easily validate our workflow specifications.

Workflows, in our case, are considered as a kind of multi-agent cooperation, in the sense that software agents may be used to perform tasks (computational processes), and the workflow can be used to orchestrate or control the interactions between agents. To be more specific, we define a workflow specification by the following elements:

- activities to perform (tasks)
- sequence of activities (control flow)
- data sets (input, output)
- data flow

A workflow consists of several tasks and the relations among them are managed by the control flow. The runtime system enables the integration of each task's application-specific logic into a large application that combines the knowledge of separate tasks. The specification of a task contains a description of the required input (i.e., data sets and initialization parameters) as well as the produced output. It may also describe execution rights or privileges for users, groups of users, machines or computer programs. Tasks are usually executable programs installed on remote machines and therefore the definition of a task also includes information related to the remote host. The data flow describes how data sets are being transferred between different tasks. Examples of data sets are files of scientific content and database entries.

Example Use Cases

Within the ARION project, we cover three major use cases that can easily be turned into commercial e-services. The first one deals with the cooperation of a technical university (providing ocean wave models) with an oceanographic company (providing ocean data and measurements). The second use case involves the collaboration between two research institutes, using our system as a research environment for experimental inter-organizational scientific (computational) workflows. The third use case manages inner-organizational workflow executions, keeping track of relevant information concerning the workflows (number of executions, input files used, parameters used, etc.) and presenting final results to possible customers of this company.

Our approach has also the potential to become an interesting learning and educational tool. The user can take advantage of the expert knowledge encapsulated within our system and set up new experiments or computations.

The following sections describe a prototype implementation of two of the ARION scenarios.

Ocean Wave Statistics Scenario

The purpose of this scenario is the statistical processing of long-term time series of wave parameters on various geographical locations around Europe and the production of basic statistics, histograms and analytic PDFs (Probability Density Functions) for surface wave data. The statistical processing procedures and tools were developed by one project partner, while the calibrated long-term time series were provided by another partner.

Figure 4. Hyperbolic tree view of our ontology

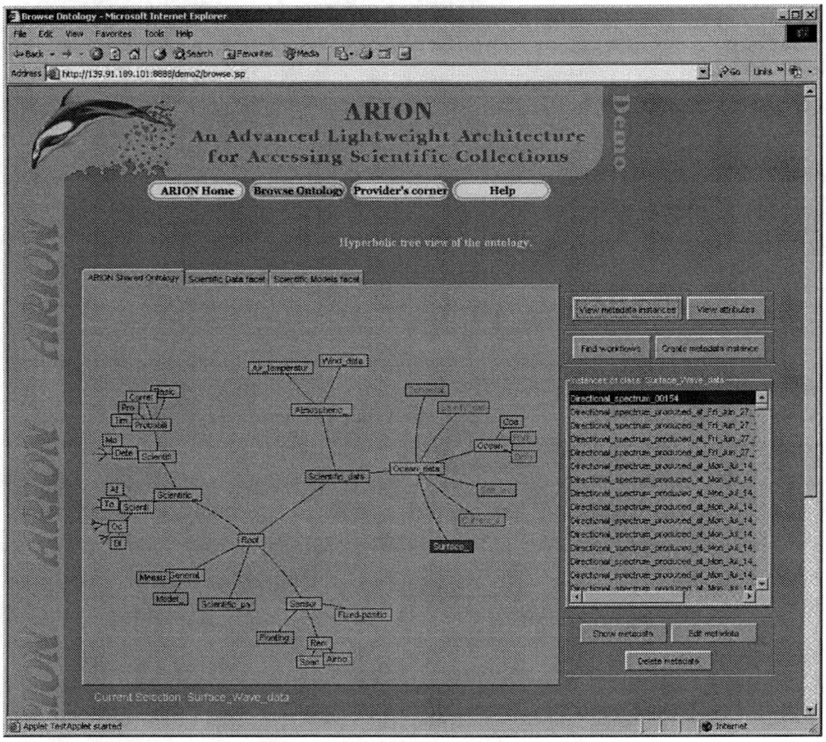

Initially, the user is prompted to choose a specific type of scientific data, by browsing a hyperbolic tree that contains our ontology. An applet (Figure 4) is loaded, providing a view of the entire ontology structure or even different facets of the ontology. By selecting a specific class (concept) in the schema, the user is able to see all instances (data sets) and attributes of the selected class, as well as metadata information regarding a specific instance of the class. It is also possible to create or edit metadata instances of a selected class.

After that, some predefined queries concerning the type of data chosen are presented to facilitate the user. At this point the search can be further refined by specifying more precise search criteria. Possible queries in this specific use case are:

- Search for wave data in a specific geographical region (e.g., Black sea, Baltic sea, Mediterranean sea, Atlantic ocean, etc.)
- Search for specific wave parameters (e.g., significant wave height, mean wave period, mean wave direction, etc.)

- Search for wave data in a specific time period
- Combination of the above

When a query is executed the matching data sets are returned as a set of references. By following such a reference, the user can view all the metadata information related to the selected data set. The query results can also be further refined by selecting one or more specific attributes to be shown. From the metadata, the user is able to access the raw data and/or visualize them.

In case no results are returned or the user is not satisfied with the existing data sets, the system is able to search for workflows that can produce the type of scientific data needed (performing the necessary computations).

The tasks performed during a workflow execution, shown in Figure 5, are described below:

- Selection of the geographical area of interest
- Visualization of the available data points and the corresponding geographical area, by means of a versatile geographic GUI
- Selection of a number of wave parameters and data points for which statistical information is requested
- Selection of the time period of interest
- Selection of the appropriate partition(s) for the calculation of histograms
- Retrieval of the appropriate time series on the corresponding wave parameters
- Statistical processing and production of the corresponding histograms (univariate, bivariate, etc.)
- Fitting of analytic (known) probability models
- Production and visualization of the results both in ASCII and graphic format

User interaction is required for the selection of the geographic location of interest, the selection of specific points and the specification of statistical parameters concerning the data requested. This interaction is accomplished through a map applet shown in Figure 6.

Some typical results of such a workflow execution (basic statistics, histograms and analytic PDFs for surface wave data) are shown in Figure 7. Metadata concerning these results are automatically stored into the system.

Figure 5. Workflow diagram

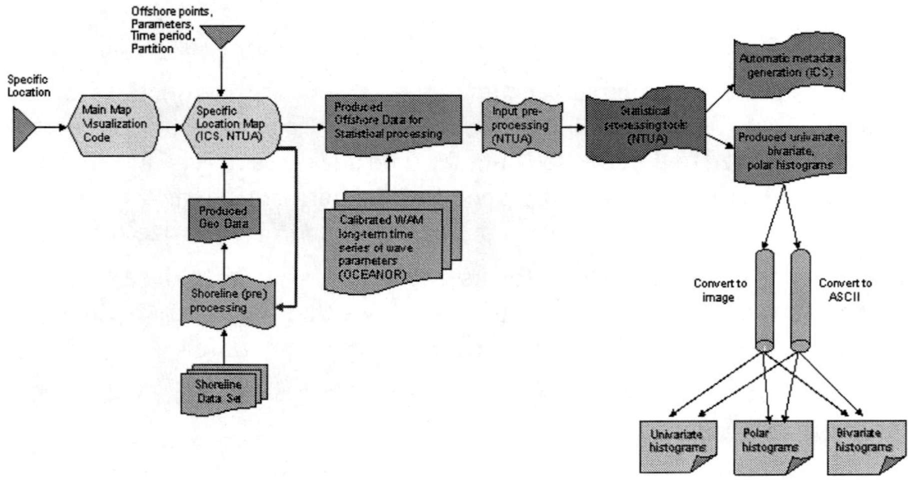

Figure 6. Map applet GUI for ocean wave statistics scenario

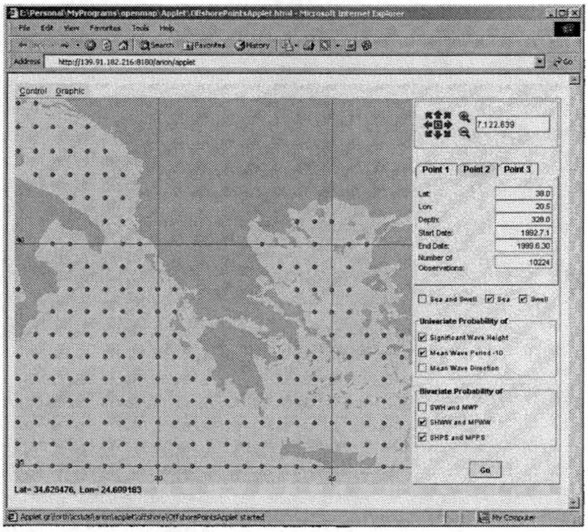

Simulation of the Adriatic Sea

The purpose of this scenario is to apply an oceanographic model for the Adriatic Sea to produce simulated fields of sea level, temperature, salinity and ocean currents.

Figure 7. Workflow execution and graphical results for the ocean wave statistics scenario

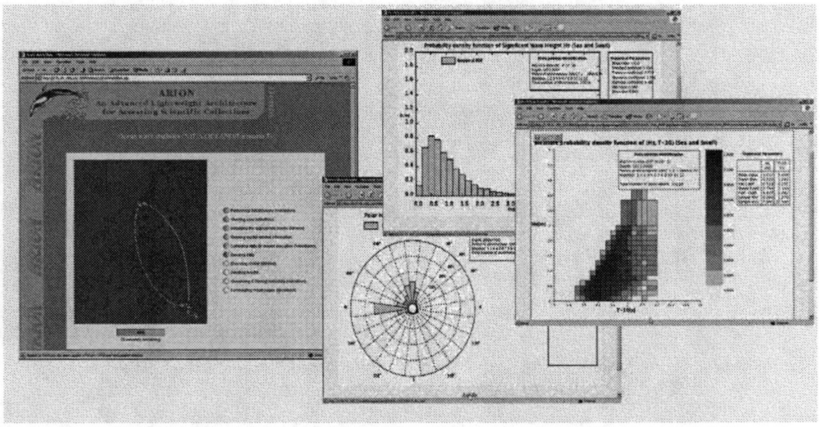

The user starts the scenario with the choice of a horizontal grid. A grid may be considered as a mesh covering a geographical area for which measurements exist in a database (see Figure 8). Grids differ depending on the horizontal resolution, number and resolution of vertical levels and the coverage of the specific sea – the denser a grid is, the more accurate the model simulation will be. Then, the user chooses the simulation starting time, the simulation duration and the frequency of the outputs. When the model simulation completes, the user can download the output fields or interactively plot them using a Web browser.

In the first task of the workflow, part of the input data submitted by the user (grid selection) is used to create the bottom topography for the model - for the specific sea. The new bottom topography with the rest of the input is transferred to the server where the model is located. The model is executed and the output is stored to a Web-accessible location where the user can either download the output or interactively plot the output fields.

The specific tasks performed during a workflow execution are described below in clearly separated steps:

- Visualization of the available grids and data sets through a geographic GUI
- Selection of a grid
- Selection of the starting date for the simulation
- Selection of the simulation duration period
- Selection of the frequency of the outputs

Figure 8. Map applet GUI for simulation of the Adriatic Sea

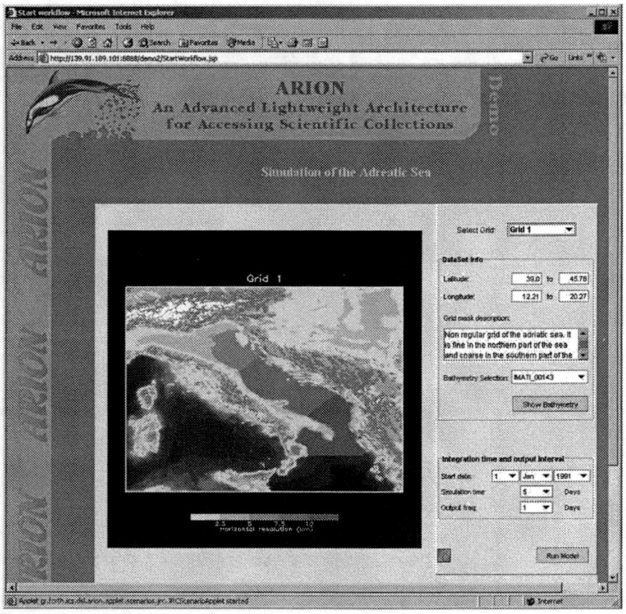

Figure 9. Workflow execution and graphical results for the simulation of the Adriatic Sea

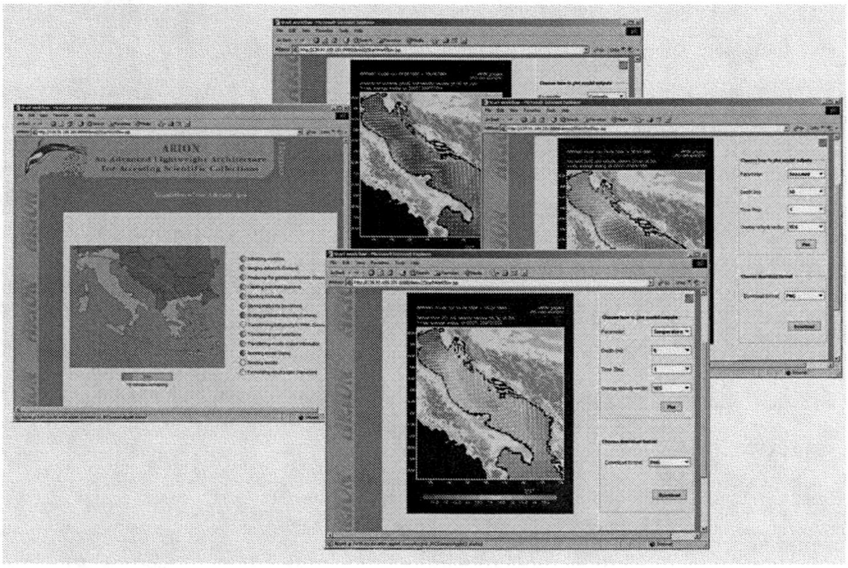

- Creation of the bottom topography for the model
- Model run and production of output fields
- Interactive plotting of the model output fields through a Web interface

Some typical results of such a workflow execution are shown in Figure 9.

Conclusions

The integration of agent technology and ontologies could significantly affect the use of e-services and the ability to extend programs to perform tasks for users more efficiently and with less human intervention. ARION provides a middleware architecture realizing eScience in the domain of environmental systems. Recent standards and their software implementations (RDF suite of tools, workflows and agent based associated runtime, etc.) have made this possible. More advanced e-services, which depend on the scientific content of the system, can be built upon this infrastructure, such as decision making and/or policy support using various information brokering techniques.

It is clear that as eScience technologies continue to evolve and mature, in the next few years, an increasing number of applications and large-scale systems harnessing the vast potential offered by these technologies will be brought forward.

Acknowledgments

This work is supported by the EU through the 5th Framework Programme, in particular the ARION project (IST-2000-25289). The authors wish to thank all their colleagues and partners in this project.

References

Alexaki, S., Christophides, V., Karvounarakis, G., Plexousakis, D., & Tolle, K. (2001). The ICS-FORTH RDFSuite: Managing voluminous RDF description bases. *Proc. of the Second International Workshop on the Semantic Web, WWW10.*

Brickley, D., & Guha, R.V. (1999). *Resource description framework (RDF) schema specification.* Technical report, W3C Proposed Recommendation. *http://www.w3.org/TR/PR-rdf-schema.*

Christensen, E., Curbera, F., Meredith, G., & Weerawarana, S. (2001). W3C, Web Services Description Language. *http://www.w3c.org/TR/wsdl.*

Foster, I., & Kesselman, C. (1997). Globus: A metacomputing infrastructure toolki.t. *Intl J. Supercomputer Applications, 11*(2), 115-128. *ftp://ftp.globus.org/pub/globus/papers/globus.pdf.*

Foster, I., & Kesselman, C. (eds.). (1998). *The grid: Blueprint for a new computing infrastructure.* Morgan Kaufmann.

Foster, I., Kesselman, C., & Tuecke, S. (2001). The anatomy of the grid: Enabling scalable virtual organizations. *International Journal of Supercomputer Applications, 15*(3).

Foster, I., Kesselman, C., Nick, J., & Tuecke, S. (2002, June 22). *The physiology of the grid: An open grid services architecture for distributed systems integration.* Open Grid Service Infrastructure WG, Global Grid Forum.

Grasshopper 2 Agent Platform. (n.d.). Retrieved October 2002, from: *http://www.grasshopper.de.*

Gruber, T.R. (1993). A translation approach to portable ontology specifications. *Knowledge Acquisition, 6*(2), 199-221.

Hendler, J. (2001, March/April). Agents and the Semantic Web. *IEEE Intelligent Systems Journal, 16*(2), 30-37.

Horrocks, I. (2002, March). DAML+OIL: A reasonable Web ontology language. *Proc. of EDBT 2002.*

Houstis, C., & Lalis, S. (2000). ARION: An advanced lightweight architecture for accessing scientific collections. *RTD Information Society Technologies,* III.1.4.

Houstis, C., & Lalis, S. (2001). ARION: A scalable architecture for a digital library of scientific Collections. *Proc. of 8th Panhellenic Conference on Informatics.*

Houstis, C., Lalis, S., Christophides, V., Plexousakis, D., Houstis, M., Pitikakis, M., Kritikos, K., Smardas, A., & Gikas, Ch. (2002, May 27-28). A service infrastructure for e-science: The case of the ARION system. *Proc. of E-Services and the Semantic Web workshop* (ESSW2002), 175-187, Toronto, Canada. Springer, LNCS 2512.

Karvounarakis, G., Alexaki, S., Christophides, V., Plexousakis, D., & Scholl, M. (2002, May 7-11). RQL: A declarative query language for RDF. *Proc. of*

Eleventh International World Wide Web Conference (WWW2002), 592-603, Honolulu, Hawaii, USA.

Lassila, O., & Swick, R.R. (1999). *Resource description framework (RDF) model and syntax specification.* Technical report, W3C Recommendation. *http://www.w3.org/TR/REC-rdf-syntax.*

Protégé-2000. (n.d.). Retrieved May 2002, from: *http://www.smi.stanford.edu/projects/protege/.*

OWL Web Ontology Language 1.0 Reference. (n.d.). Retrieved August 2003, from: *http://www.w3.org/2001/sw/WebOnt/.*

Thatte, S. (2001). XLANG: Web services for business process design. Microsoft, Inc.: *http://www.gotdotnet.com/team/xml_wsspecs/xlang-c/default.htm.*

Uschold, M., Healy, M., Willamson, K., Clark, P., & Woods, S. (1998). Ontology reuse and application. In N. Guarino (Ed.), *Formal ontology in information systems* (pp. 179-192). Trento, Italy.

Van der Aalst, W.M.P., & Kumar, A. (2001). *XML based schema definition for support of inter-organizational workflow.* University of Colorado and University of Eindhoven report.

W3C Semantic Web. (n.d.) Retrieved August 2003, from: *http://www.w3.org/2001/sw/.*

Chapter VIII

Linking Economic Optimisation and Simulation Models to Environmental Material Flow Networks for Ecoefficiency

Bernd Page, University of Hamburg, Germany

Volker Wohlgemuth, University of Hamburg, Germany

Abstract

This chapter outlines Material Flow Networks as a special modelling approach in the context of ecobalancing, that is, for modelling the environmental impacts of economic activities. This approach focuses on understanding the underlying material and energy transformations and the environmental impact of the resulting material and energy flows. The software tool Umberto® was the first product in the market for material flow analysis based on Material Flow Networks. This approach models the material and energy flows in production and distribution systems by means of Petri-Net notation with transitions (i.e., the material and energy transformation processes), places (i.e., inventories for material) and connecting arrows (i.e., energy and material flows). Using the Microsoft COM-technology, optimisation and discrete simulation models of economic processes can be embedded into ecologically oriented Material Flow Networks as complex external transitions. Three application examples (a transport optimisation model, a production and an inventory simulation model) are presented to demonstrate this useful approach of combining different modelling techniques in ecomanagement and its potential for ecoefficiency in resource and energy use.

Introduction: Material Flow Networks – Concepts and Software Support

Material Flow Networks describe the flow of materials and energy within a defined economic system. The representation and evaluation of these material flows and their impact on our environment caused by human economic activities has become one of the most important tasks of the so-called environmental management (Rautenstrauch, 1999). Material flow networks have their origins in several disciplines. The most important sources are the Petri-Net theory from computer science as well as double-entry bookkeeping and cost accounting from business administration. The Petri-Net approach is used to describe the structure of a material flow network. Material flow networks consist of three elements: transitions, places and arrows. Mathematically speaking, the structure of a Petri-Net is a 3-tupel $N = (T, S, F)$, $F \subseteq (S \times T \cup T \times S)$, with T being a set of transitions, S a set of places and F a set of arrows between transitions and places (Baumgarten, 1996). Thus, there are no direct connections between places or transitions.

In material flow networks the transitions, represented in diagrams by squares, stand for the location of material and energy transformations. Transitions play a vital role in material flow networks, because material and energy transformations are the source of material and energy flows. Another defining characteristic of material flow networks is their concept of place. Places separate different transitions. This allows a distinct analysis of every transition. Beyond that places can describe inventories for materials. Circles are used in diagrams to represent places. Arrows show the paths of material and energy flows between transitions and places. The diagram in Figure 1 illustrates a material flow network with several transitions and places connected by arrows.

The 3-tupel $N = (T, S, F)$ only describes the static structure of a Petri-Net. Another part specifies its dynamic behaviour. This part is necessary to model the

Figure 1. Structure of a simple material flow network

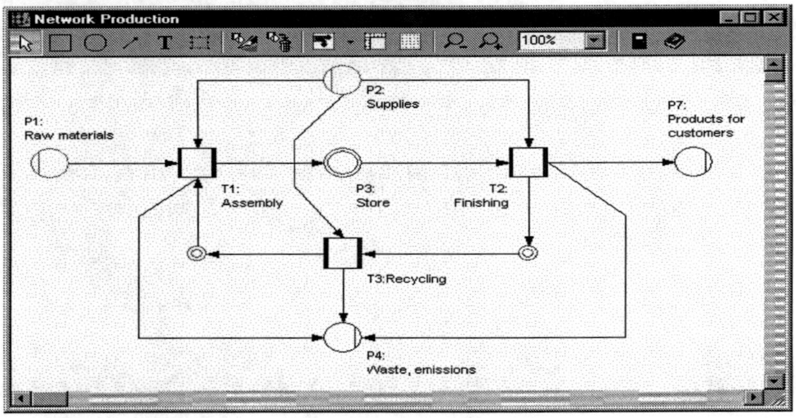

behaviour of computer systems, computer networks, or communication systems, where Petri-Nets are mostly applied. These objectives of Petri-Nets are not in line with those of material and energy flow analysis as described above. So in material flow networks the dynamic part of Petri-Nets is replaced by double-entry-bookkeeping techniques (Möller, 2000). The structure of material flow networks represents an accounting system for material and energy flows. An arrow can be interpreted as an account of material and energy flows. Places are used for taking stocks into account. The first step in collecting data is to specify the stocks at the beginning of the period of time (starting inventory); the second step is to determine all flows during the period. After that the stocks can be calculated in a final step at the end of the period (ending inventory). The result is a material and energy model, which may be evaluated in several ways.

However, the outstanding feature of the material flow network approach is that it combines the site-specific aspect of compiling input/output ecobalances for companies, plants or production processes with the analysis of material flows associated with a certain product or service in a seamless way. Therefore, material flow networks, originally developed at the University of Hamburg (Möller, 2000), may be interpreted as a bookkeeping technique based on graphical modelling in order to analyse distributed material and energy flow systems. Together with various concepts of calculation, material flow networks can be used as a starting point for a computer based support for environmental management.

It is obvious that a software supporting this approach has to fulfil a number of requirements. For instance, the software must be capable of modelling complex production processes from different application fields like chemistry or engineering and must provide flexibility in data management, in updating and extending the model and in offering different possibilities for interpretation and presentation purposes. The software system Umberto®, already introduced into the market as the first software product based on this material flow network approach a in the mid-nineties, tries to meet these demands. Umberto® was developed as a powerful and user-friendly tool for material flow analysis. It runs under Microsoft's WINDOWS family of operating systems and meets software ergonomic standards (Schmidt et al., 1997). Furthermore it provides several interfaces to other programs. An interface of relevance for this chapter refers to the transition specification. In connection with complex algorithms this interface allows for integrating submodels into material flow networks which are developed outside Umberto®.

Technical Implementation: Complex Transitions as COM-Objects in Material Flow Networks

Material flow networks provide a wide range of options for representing material flow systems and evaluating them efficiently for environmental management. Thus, many of the properties and much more of the scope resulting from the network approach can be used to gain a better insight into production, consumption, transport, waste treatment and many other processes with environmental impacts. In material flow networks these processes are represented by transitions as shown above. In this sense, a transition describes an activity: Materials, which are needed for a certain process, enter the transition, and new or modified materials leave the transition as output. Thus, transitions describe material transformations and stand for a link between consumption and production. As mentioned above, there are several ways to specify transitions.

An ambitious approach to specify a transition is to apply a complex algorithm within this transition. Since the release of version 3.2 of the software Umberto® this can be done technically by definition of a script, written in any scripting language that supports Microsoft's Active Scripting architecture. This means that the user can specify a transition without being limited to the default specification methods offered by Umberto®. For example, the user can specify a fuzzy-based model of dye works within a transition or implement a discrete event simulation model of a bottle filling process, which will be executed when the calculation algorithm within the material flow network reaches the transition representing the model in the network. An advantage of this approach is the fact that this kind of transition specification actually does not conflict with the

Figure 2. Active scripting and material flow networks (Möller et al., 2001)

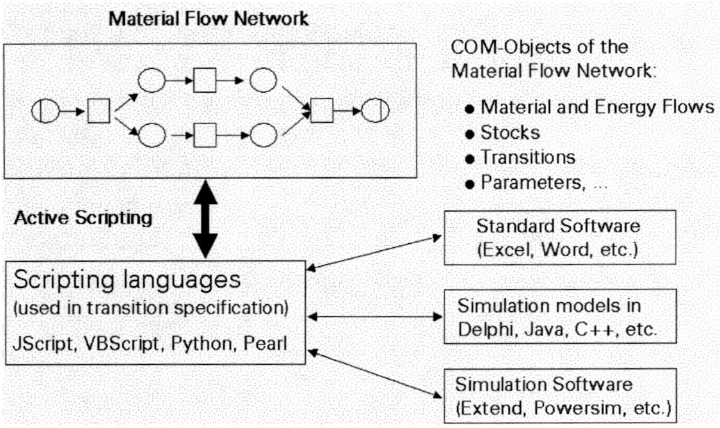

theoretical foundations of material flow networks. In this way, the scripting approach extends material flow networks in a powerful manner.

To activate the scripting mechanism in Umberto® for the specification of a certain transition the user has to set the transition's calculation attribute to "User defined". Then, the user can select one of the available scripting languages. During the calculation process the transition's attributes are checked and the stored script code is executed. The interpretation of the script is controlled by a scripting engine for the selected scripting language. Technically, the scripting engine is based on Microsoft's Active Scripting architecture and coordinates appropriate DLL calls for the scripting language used. Currently, Active Scripting interpreters are available for the languages VBScript, JScript, Pearl, Python and Rexx. However, to ensure an exchange of information between Umberto® and a script in a transition, a suitable interface is required to access and modify the elements of a material flow network. This interface is based on Microsoft's Component Object Model (COM). For all relevant material flows, stocks, or parameters of a material flow network that should be accessible from a script or in general from another application, suitable COM-Objects are defined by Umberto®, which are registered at the operation system (WINDOWS). These COM-Objects can easily be accessed and manipulated through its unique identifier. More information about the Component Object Model and its functionality can be obtained from Box (1998). Thus, calling the COM-Objects supplied by Umberto® within a script allows the user to access and modify all relevant information of a material flow network. In the same way it is possible to call COM-Objects, which are supplied by standard software like Word or Excel, so that an Excel Sheet serves as a data source for a transition specification. Furthermore, user specific objects like a library for discrete event simulation written in a programming language like Java or Delphi can be called from a material flow network, as long as these objects support COM. Figure 2 illustrates the scripting concept and the possibilities of accessing several applications from a material flow network.

Note that the script is only executed when the calculation process reaches the transition that contains the script. This means that the script execution is only carried out for the local context of the transition. Thus, functional dependencies between this transition and other transitions of a material flow network are not taken into consideration.

Applications

For illustration purposes of the coupling of material flow networks with other modelling components, or the use of the scripting mechanism in transition specifications, respectively, three application examples for jointly modelling environmental and economic impacts aiming for a higher ecoefficiency are given in this section. They deal with the embedding of a transport optimisation model, as well as the embedding of a discrete event production and inventory simulation model into a material flow network.

Coupling Material Flow Network with Optimisation Model

The first application example of the approach introduced above deals with a material flow analysis of a trading company (Möller et al., 1997) and demonstrates how scripting can be used in material flow networks. Here the emissions resulting from the company's distribution activities are of particular interest. The distribution sector handles the delivery of goods from a central store to the company's branches specified by a route plan. This route plan determines the composition of the tours using a certain means of transport (trucks) and the sequence of customers for delivery. Such a transport produces material and energy flows such as goods, fuel and pollutants emitted by the trucks. The first task of the material flow analysis performed is to register all relevant flows connected with the distribution. Therefore, all transport processes have to be modelled in a material flow network as place/transition/place-chains according to the actual route plan. As a result you get a material flow network as shown in the top area of Figure 3. Note that each way within a certain route has to be modelled separately and that the associated route plan has to be known before modelling. Furthermore, for each transition modelling a truck transport, data about the distance between the branches, the truck's load capacity and its utilisation, and so on, has to be provided by the user. Overall, this only possible way of modelling a distribution system could be very complex and time-consuming.

Thus, we developed the idea to use methods from the field of operations research to determine the tour and route planning and feed the optimisation results into the material flow network. Based on the existing data and further assumptions of our route planning problem we used a heuristic approach (savings- and sweep method) to calculate an optimised route plan with regard to a determined objective (i.e., cost or distance minimisation). In this step the structure of the route plan (clustering) is calculated. The saving and sweep algorithm usually supplies a route plan with a good evaluation, which, however, can be improved by using 2- or 3-opt algorithms (edge exchange methods). Therefore, based on the clustered route plan supplied by the savings or sweep method, we first applied the 2-opt algorithm to determine an optimised route plan for our problem. In this way an improvement of about 10% distance saving as compared to the composition of the route plan using rules of thumb could be achieved due to a more favourable supply order of the branches within the individual routes. According to our assumptions, this leads to a reduction in pollutant output of about the same value. For more details on the algorithms used, the implementation and the application of other restrictions (i.e., concerning the amount of allowed emissions or using alternative transportation devices) (Heffter, 1999).

To implement these optimisation algorithms in Umberto® with regard to our route planning problem means – from the modelling point of view – that the place/transition/place chains have to be replaced by one single transition as shown in the lower part of Figure 3. Therefore, the mass of transport processes and the mass of branches is modelled using a single transition in correspondence with the abstraction mechanism of Petri-Nets. This eases our modelling efforts significantly. This transition is specified by a Python script, which implements the algorithms mentioned above. For this purpose the user has to be familiar with the syntax of the Python programming language and should have programming skills. Note that our approach leads to an optimised route plan regarding cost or distance aspects, which has to be evaluated in relation to its environmental impact. Additionally, it should be pointed out in this context that we did not take time dependencies into consideration (i.e., time windows for delivery of branches, needed time for truck transports, etc.) in this (static) example model.

Figure 3. Transforming a material flow network for optimisation purposes

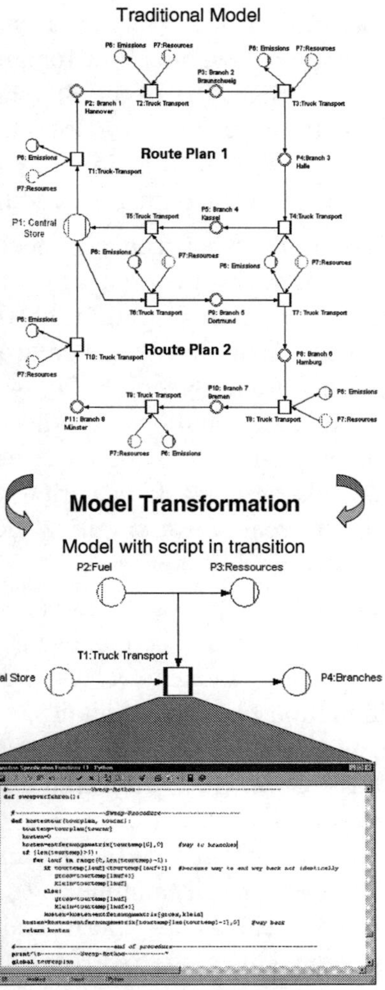

Embedding of Discrete Event Production Simulation Models into Material Flow Networks

One inherent limitation of material flow networks is the lack of information about how often a transition has been actually activated during an accounting period, because only the sums of all transition switches of the material and energy flows in a material flow network are monitored for an observation period. This complies with the main goal of this approach to generate a balance sheet in the context of ecobalancing. The time relationship of material flow analysis is always one period (e.g., one balance year). Linking the static material flow analysis with a discrete event modelling approach would allow for a more dynamical process and job-oriented view of production systems for planning purposes. In this way more information beyond material and energy flows could be derived for the modelled production system, for example providing economic parameters, such as mean waiting times, utilization, throughput, or deadline compliance.

The following example is outlining what such a connection could look like. We have developed a rather straightforward production simulation model for a cleaning, filling and packing process of a fictitious brewery. The beer bottles to be filled enter the filling station from the outside environment. The arrival rate as well as the mean service times for the cleaning, filling and packing stations are following stochastic exponential distributions. Another assumption is that 1% of the delivered bottles are damaged and have to be sorted out. Finally six filled beer bottles are packed into sixpacks at the packing station. Compared to the earlier example, we do not deal with real-world empirical data here, but with constructed data based on reasonable assumptions.

The implementation of the simulation model was carried out with the Delphi-Programming language version of a discrete event simulation framework developed at our working group (Lechler & Page, 1999). This framework provides the required simulation base functionality, such as random number generation, time control, event handling, and statistical reporting. Therefore the implementation effort for the given production simulation model was not very high. To monitor the material and energy flows for the technical processes mentioned above some extensions of the simulation framework were necessary. In particular the recording of the material handling and transformation processes at each machine by means of typical machine performance data like production quantity, machine hours, setup times, and so forth had to be implemented. Compared to material flow networks, this simulation approach takes a more production job-related view and monitors all material transformations per machine and production job.

Based on the COM-architecture a linkage of the simulation models with the material flow network is possible by providing the simulation model with a COM interface. This COM interface allows the setting of typical simulation parameters, such as simulation starting time and simulation run length, access to produced simulation results like throughput and mean service times, as well as access to computed material and energy flows. In order to call this simulation model from a material flow network, a transition has to be specified by a script using the COM interface (like in the upper example). Reaching this specified

Figure 4. Coupling of material flow network and simulation model by a script

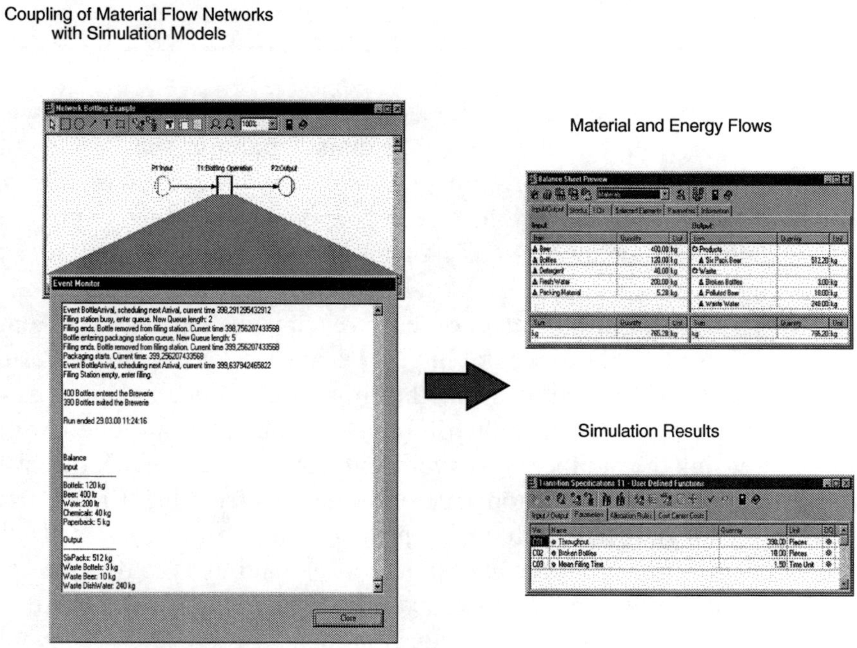

transition the computational algorithm of the material flow network transfers control to the Script Control, which in turn carries out the script (i.e., the discrete simulation model). In the script the simulation parameters are set by a COM call, the simulation results generated and the material flows for the simulation results computed. The script takes the results and passes them on to the calling material flow network by the COM-Interfaces of Umberto®. Thus, dynamical production-related economic performance measures can be added to environmental material and energy flows and additional analyses are provided. In this way an extension of material flow networks by an event-oriented view is realized through monitoring single events in the network. However, the simulation period has to be equivalent to the observation period of the material flow network. Beyond that, an event-oriented extension is only feasible for one transition without consideration of functional dependencies between several transitions in the network.

Finally we should mention that in the second example two applications are linked by the COM architecture, namely Umberto® and our simulation model. The script is used as a kind of "glue" between the two applications. What kind of application is controlled by the script is irrelevant. A data exchange between Umberto® and an Excel-Worksheet could have been realized in the very same way.

Linking a Discrete Event Inventory Simulation Model to a Material Flow Network

Inventory systems are of economic relevance in many industrial sectors and also have some environmental implications. The main economic goals of inventory systems are the minimisation of inventory costs and a high service level of supply. Mathematical methods of operations research, and because of the complex and mostly stochastic character of many inventory systems, even more so of computer simulation, are applied to find inventory strategies compromising between the two conflicting goals in order to reach a cost optimum. Inventory strategies have also an environmental impact because inventory orders result in product deliveries mainly by trucks with the known environmental burdens such as pollution and noise. Pollution reduction can be achieved by an adequate order logistics decreasing the number of deliveries, the transportation distances (e.g., with local suppliers) or the selection of environmentally friendlier transportation vehicles. In this way the selection of a proper ordering policy is a strategic business decision with economic as well as ecological impacts. It makes sense to link economic simulation models to material flow networks to provide also environmental material information beyond the economic indicators in inventory policy analysis. With the linkage of the two approaches typical questions can be answered, such as:

- Which emissions are caused by the current inventory strategy?
- Can the emissions be reduced by alternative strategies?
- How high is the cost increase or decrease, respectively?
- Can the service level of supply be kept up with a different inventory strategy?

In this application example an inventory simulation model is embedded as a component into a transition of an Umberto® material flow network. Only in this special transition an inventory simulation model is carried out, whereas the preceding and succeeding energy transformation processes are specified by the provided Umberto® methods. The simulation model deals with a fictitious clothing trading company offering trousers, shirts and shoes. The clothing orders come in by telephone and are delivered by a conveyance company. The clothing company gives their clients a delivery guarantee of one workday between order and delivery. Shirts and trousers are mainly sent by ship except for stock shortage situations, when an emergency delivery by plane is required to keep up the desired service level of supply. Shoes are sent by air freight with a reorder

Figure 5. Linking a discrete event inventory simulation model to a material flow network (Wohlgemuth et al., 2001)

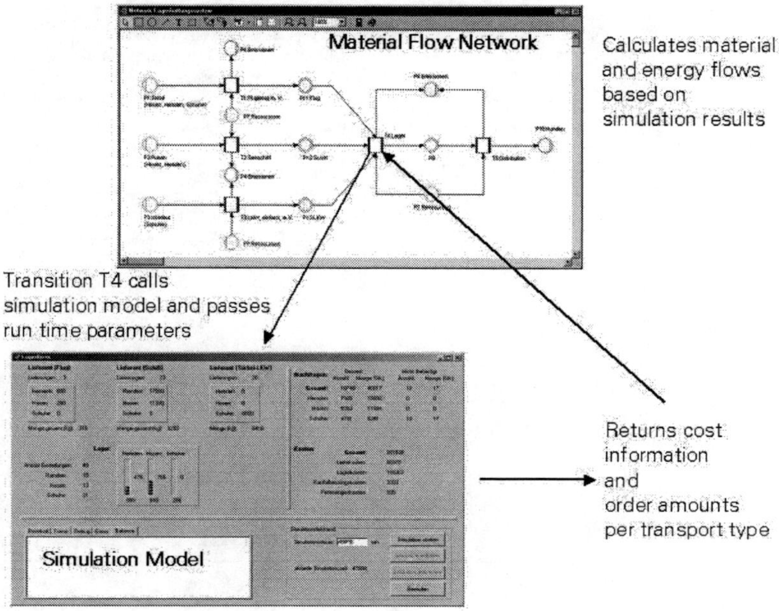

up to the maximal inventory level when a minimal stock is reached. Client demand is stochastic, following a normal distribution. The transportation times are also normally distributed. Cost data consist of inventory costs, indirect and direct order costs, shortage, and transportation costs. We have a standard scenario with a purely economic inventory policy and an alternative scenario also taking environmental aspects into account. The order logistics in this scenario are more ecoefficient in the sense that transportation distances are reduced and more environmentally friendly transportation modes selected without necessarily increasing inventory cost or decreasing service level of supply.

The problem statement addresses a typical challenge for a trading company looking for an environmentally friendly optimisation of its order logistics. For each scenario an inventory simulation model was implemented using the Delphi discrete event simulation framework mentioned above. The COM-Interface allows for the call of Umberto® functionality from the simulation framework as described in the last section. In this example the simulation model is activated when the Umberto® computational algorithm reaches Transition T4 in Figure 5.

Then relevant information (e.g., simulation run length = accounting period in the material flow network) is exchanged by the COM architecture and control is taken over by the simulation model. After completion of the simulation run, the collected information on the number of deliveries per transport means, the demanded and supplied number of products and on costs is returned to Umberto®

Table 1. Comparison of the results for the two simulation scenarios described

	Basic Scenario	Alternative Scenario (Substitution of flight transportation with truck transportation)
Costs	Total: 272147 MU	Total: 201520 MU
	Inventory costs: 99947 MU	Inventory costs: 116307 MU
	Delivery costs: 169260 MU	Delivery costs: 80975 MU
	Shortage costs: 0 MU	Shortage costs: 935 MU
Emissions	88024 kg (thereof 65326 kg CO2)	8685 kg (thereof 7596 kg CO2)
Resources	Crude Oil: 20420 kg	Crude Oil: 1505 kg
	Heavy Oil: 911 kg	Heavy Oil: 985 kg
Deliveries	Aircraft: 27 (7832 kg) Ship: 25 (8588 kg)	Aircraft: 3 (316 kg) Ship: 23 (9283 kg) Truck: 20 (6416 kg)
Service level	100 %	99.98 %

via the COM Interface for further processing. Based on this information Umberto® can compute the respective emissions from the transports. Thus we generate economic as well as ecological planning data on the order logistics connected to the inventory policy under study within a material flow network using Umberto®.

In Table 1 we have a comparison of the results for the two simulation scenarios. In both cases a service level of supply of almost 100% using a (S, s)-order strategy can be reached. The choice of a supplier for shoes located much closer to the clothing trading company with deliveries by trucks leads to lower total emission values as well as lower costs. Although inventory costs are higher, the lower delivery costs exceed this. Thus we have an example where the delivery substitution yields ecological as well as economic benefits.

Finally we should emphasise that a quantitative interpretation of the simulation results is limited due to the use of partially fictitious data. However, our main concern here is a technical feasibility study demonstrating the integration of different modelling methods and software products for a combined model based analysis of economical-ecological systems.

Conclusions

In this chapter we have shown how the more static view of material flow networks can be enhanced by dynamic simulation concepts. The COM architecture and its implementation in the ecobalancing software Umberto® is the technical framework for this integration. The three application examples introduced in Chapter III demonstrate how a more economic perspective can be introduced into the environmental modelling of material and energy flows and transformations. They show that ecoefficiency can also pay off economically.

From the technical point of view, using a scripting language requires a lot of programming skills and weakens the graphical concept of the material flow network approach. However, we argue that the scripting functionality is a useful feature to overcome the limitations that come with the material flow network software Umberto®. The users can now implement their own specification models within a transition. This is of particular importance with regard to the linking of external data sources to material flow networks. For example, it is also possible that a user can directly access relevant data from SAP's module PP within a material flow network. Furthermore, the user can build his or her own complex models for transformation processes within a transition if the specification methods that come with Umberto® do not fit his or her needs. Thus, users can make their own extensions while at the same time they can still use the existing features of Umberto® like creating balance sheets, applying evaluation systems or obtaining information about costs. These user specific models implemented in a scripting language can even be saved in the Umberto® library for reuse. This makes Umberto® an open tool for user specific extensions.

References

Baumgarten, B. (1996). *Petri-Netze. Grundlagen und Anwendungen.* Heidelberg: Spektrum Publ.

Box, D. (1998). *Essential COM.* Reading, MA: Addison-Wesley.

Heffter, J. (1999). *Konzepte und Realisierung Einer Einbettung von Tourenplanungsmodellen in Stoffstromnetze.* Diploma thesis. University of Hamburg, Department of Computer Science.

Lechler, T., & Page, B. (1999, October). *DESMO-J* – An object oriented discrete simulation framework in Java. In G. Horton & D. Möller (Eds.), *Simulation in Industry '99: The 11th European Simulation Symposium 1999,* 46-50, Erlangen, Germany. Delft (The Netherlands), SCS.

Möller, A. (2000). *Grundlagen Stoffstrombasierter Betrieblicher Umweltinformationssysteme.* Bochum: Projekt Publ.

Möller, A., Häuslein, A., & Rolf, A. (1997). *Öko-controlling in Handelsunternehmen: Ein Leitfaden für das Stoffstrommanagement.* Berlin: Springer Publ.

Möller, A., Page, B., Rolf, A., & Wohlgemuth, V. (2001). Foundations and applications of computer based material flow networks for environmental management. In C. Rautenstrauch (Ed.), *Environmental information systems in industry and public* (pp. 379-396). Hershey, PA: Idea Group Publishing.

Rautenstrauch, C. (1999). *Betriebliche Umweltinformationssysteme.* Berlin:Springer Publ.

Schmidt, M., Möller, A., Hedemann, J., & Müller-Beilschmidt, P. (1997). Environmental material flow analysis by network approach. In W. Geiger et al. (Eds.), *Umweltinformatik '97, 11th International Symposium of the German Society for Computer Science* (GI) (pp. 768-779). Strasbourg, France, Marburg: Metropolis Publ.

Wohlgemuth, V., Bruns, L., & Page, B. (2001). Simulation als Ansatz zur Ökologischen und Ökonomischen Planungsunterstützung im Kontext Betrieblicher Umweltinformationssysteme (BUIS). In L.M. Hilty & P.W. Gilgen (Eds.), *Sustainability in the information society. The 15th International Symposium for Environmental Protection,* 999-1008, Zurich.

Wohlgemuth, V., Page, B., & Heffter, J. (2000). Coupling a material flow network with an optimisation model. *Proc. Simulationstechnik* (pp. 389-394). Ghent: SCS European Publishing House.

Chapter IX

Virtual Networking without a Backpack? Resource Consumption of Information Technologies

Justus von Geibler, Wuppertal Institute, Germany

Michael Kuhndt, Wuppertal Institute, Germany

Volker Türk, Wuppertal Institute, Germany

Abstract

This chapter concentrates on the environmental impacts of the increasing use of the Internet. It highlights that the Internet and Internet applications are far from being purely virtual, but are clearly linked to the use of natural resources. With the growth of the Internet's infrastructure there is a seemingly inevitable increase in the resource consumption for the production of electronic equipment and its electricity consumption. A number of conclusions can be made regarding the minimisation of environmental risks and maximisation of ebusiness' potential to dematerialise. The presented findings are mainly based on findings derived from research within the Digital Europe project, which was conducted as the first pan-European study of the social and environmental impacts and opportunities of e-commerce and information communication technologies. Supported by the European Commission, the project has been led by the research organisations Fondazione Eni Enrico Mattei in Italy, Forum for the Future in UK and the Wuppertal Institute in Germany.

Introduction

The transition from an industrial society to a service society proceeding in many countries of the world is supported by information and communication technology (ICT) and ICT applications. The industrial society was primarily about large-scale production and distribution of goods. Within the service society, added value is increasingly generated from immaterial production factors such as information and know-how, and a large number of functional areas such as the economy, politics, legislation, culture or health depend to an increasing degree on knowledge. Adoption of this knowledge is supported by ICT. Thus ICT can be accounted as a key technology within the service society.

The diffusion of ICT within societies can be illustrated by the adoption of the Internet. Even if only experts knew the medium "Internet" at the beginning of the 90s, it became mass media in the middle of last decade. About 600 million people have gone online in the last 15 years – this is about 10% of the world population. And there are forecasts that there will be 710 million users of the Internet in the year 2004 (e.g., Cyber Atlas, 2003). On average, 81% of EU enterprises accessed the Internet in 2002, and a majority of them had their own Web site or homepage (European Commission, 2003). Even if the initial euphoria about the new technology is subsiding, every day we hear news about large ICT investments, technology innovation and new areas of ICT applications.

As ICT and ICT applications increasingly spread, so do also the ecological problems of this trend appear to become more relevant. For example, increasing Internet use is linked with increasing electricity use. However, ICT is generally not seen to be associated with significant environmental problems. In fact, the opinion predominates that new communication media are just as virtual as their contents. Sometimes it is even seen as an innovation, which would make possible a sustainable and resource-efficient way of life per se.

This chapter highlights the environmental impacts of the increasing use of the Internet. The following section provides insights into the physical elements of the ICT infrastructure with a specific focus on the Internet, and provides a classification of environmental effects caused by ICT. The subsequent sections discuss the direct and indirect effects as well as the systemic effects on the consumption of natural resources. Finally, conclusions are drawn on how to develop a more resource-efficient information society.

This book contribution is based mainly on findings derived from research within the Digital Europe project. The project was conducted as the first pan-European study of the social and environmental impacts and opportunities of e-commerce and information communication technologies. Supported by the European Commission, the project has been led by the research organisations Fondazione Eni

Enrico Mattei in Italy, Forum for the Future in UK and the Wuppertal Institute in Germany. Twelve corporate and regional partners have been involved: AOL Europe, Barclays Bank, EMI, Finmatica, the Global eSustainability Initiative (GeSI), Hewlett-Packard, Welsh Assembly Government, Netscalibur, Projekt Ruhr, Sun Microsystems, Vitaminic and Vodafone. Information on environmental effects of ICT are described by Kuhndt et al. (2003). Further information, for example, specific case study reports on mobile computing, digital music and e-banking can be found on *www.digital-eu.org*.

ICT Infrastructure and Environmental Effects

Electronic information processing (e.g., by computers) and telecommunication (telephone, radio, TV) have been separate technologies in the past. However, these two technologies have merged and spread increasingly by means of the digitalisation of previously analogue media (telephones, music, pictures, faxes, etc.) and an increase in digital communication. Among the different technologies connecting digital devices, the Internet is currently the main ICT infrastructure and seems likely to remain that throughout the near future (e.g., Office of Technology Assessment at the German Parliament, 2002). According to a survey by the Internet Software Consortium (2002), the number of Internet hosts grew worldwide from 30 million at the beginning of 1998 to over 172 million in January 2003, corresponding to a growth of more than 25 million per year.

The growth of the Internet goes hand in hand with an increase in ICT infrastructure, which can be illustrated by some examples. Worldwide more than 410 million people have access to the Internet through a personal computer at home (Cyber Atlas, 2003b). It is estimated that there were 117 million PCs in the EU in 2001, 31 per 100 inhabitants (European Commission, 2003). A study by Intel concluded that in 2001 only 4% of the servers were in place that will be needed in 2005 (VDI Nachrichten, 2001). Figure 1 illustrated the spread of "information appliances" in Western Europe, a trend highlighted by EITO as easy-to-use, low-cost tools to access the Internet (EITO, 2000).

The physical infrastructure forming the Internet can, with a certain level of abstraction and simplification, be broken down into four different categories:

- *Network access devices (client side)* are used by clients (users) to access the services provided by Internet service and content providers. These services are based on files and programmes stored on servers. PCs and laptops account for the overwhelming majority of devices used to access

Figure 1. Web access devices by type, installed base, Western Europe, 1997-2002 (EITO 2000)

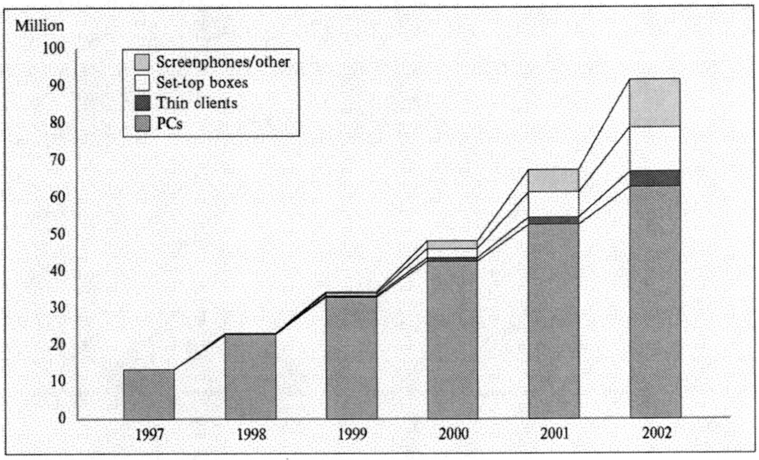

the Internet. A forecast for the near future sees many more devices such as mobiles, set-top boxes (located on top of a television set as interface between the home television and the cable TV company enabling Internet access, video-on-demand, video games, educational services, database searches, and home shopping), cars and household appliances as forthcoming connection devices.

- *Content providing devices:* This category basically covers servers. In general, a server is a computer programme that provides services to other programmes on the same or other computers. The computer on which a server programme runs is also frequently referred to as a server, though it may contain a number of servers and other programmes. Specific to the Web, a Web server is a programme (running on a computer) that serves the files that form Web pages, using the client-server model and the World Wide Web's HTTP protocol (Hypertext Transfer Protocol, defining the rules for transferring files on the World Wide Web). Several other types of servers exist, such as FTP servers, e-mail servers and news servers.
- *Intermediate devices* include several different devices that enable communication on the net. "Routers," "switches" or "gateways" switch or route traffic on the network – for example from a long-distance network to a local exchange point. "Bridges" connect different networks, "repeaters" receive, amplify and retransmit signals and "firewalls" are programmes located at network gateways or servers that protect the resources from other users and programmes. Until the mid-90s all national Internet traffic in Germany was routed via the US. In 1995 the Deutscher Commercial

Internet Exchange (DE-CIX) started operating and presently connects all but one major national and many international ISPs. 85% of German and 35% of European Internet traffic is routed over the DE-CIX. The advantage of such a centralised peering point is that traffic within Germany is routed within the country, leading to much faster and less costly data exchange (Deutscher Commercial Internet Exchange, 2001).

- *Data transfer media* are the "highways" (or sometimes just "country lanes") that transfer the data. Most common are "cables," traditionally made of copper; the newer and much faster ones are made of optic fibre. They range from old-style telephone networks with transfer rates up to 56,000 bps to intercontinental "backbones" with a bandwidth above 1 GBps. A backbone is a large transmission line that carries data gathered from lines that interconnect with it. The Internet is a wide area network (WAN) comprised of a number of backbones – regional networks that carry long-distance traffic. At the local level a backbone is a line or a set of lines that connects local area networks (LANs) to a WAN. On the national level, directional radio is used as well.

Looking more at the environmental effects of ICT, the associated resource consumption can be classified into direct, indirect and systemic effects (see Figure 2).

Figure 2. Environmental effects of ICT

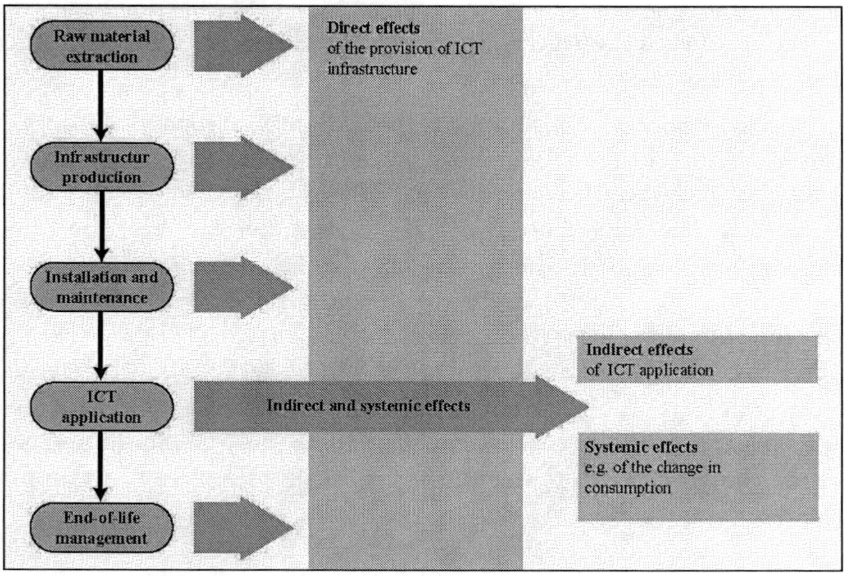

The direct effects refer to the effects caused by ICT infrastructure and equipment, for example the material consumption for producing PCs and Internet servers or from energy consumption. The reduced need for travelling or office space as a result of telework or the increase in just-in-time deliveries thanks to B2B applications are examples of indirect effects which are caused by the application of ICT. Indirect effects derive from existing desires or habits that are fulfilled through new, ICT-based applications. In contrast, systemic effects stem from new habits or consumption patterns that arise through the use of ICTs, such as the increase in transatlantic freight shipments as a result of online auctions in the US. This contribution highlights the fact that ICT infrastructure and the application of ICT are leading to both positive and negative environmental impacts and represent a recommendation of how to develop an information society which does not induce an increase in resource consumption.

Direct Effects of ICT Infrastructure on Resource Consumption

Backpack of ICT Production

While no studies quantifying the material intensity required to build the entire Internet system are known of, we do have some case study research within Digital Europe which highlighted specific components of the communication infrastructure (Geibler et al., 2003). Related studies are from Loerincik, Jolliet and Norris (2002) (on energy consumption and selected emissions) and from US EPA (2001), Atlantic Consulting (1998) or Behrendt et al. (1998) (for life cycle assessment of electronic products).

Regarding the resource consumption for the end appliances a comparative analysis of a handheld and a notebook's production has been conducted (Geibler et al., 2003). The analysis is based on the MIPS methodology (Schmidt-Bleek, 1995). MIPS provides indicators (e.g., abiotic raw material, biotic raw material and water consumption) to assess the systemwide resource consumption from the cradle to the grave taking in the total mass of material flows at all product stages, from raw material extraction to disposal. By associating the material fluxes connected to energy generation, the MIPS methodology integrates also the energy intensity. A traditional personal organiser has also been analysed to provide a base for comparison with non-electronic tools for mobile communication. The following table shows that the handheld's resource consumption lies between both other products.

Table 1. Results of material intensity analysis for production

Product	Components	Weight (kg)	Abiotic raw materials (kg)	Material intensity of component (kg/kg)
Notebook	Device	3.0	398	133
	Support items (cables, power adapter)	0.4	31	78
	Packaging	1.3	5	4
Handheld	Device (incl. modem)	0.2	58	290
	Support items (cables, power adapter)	0.6	19	32
	Packaging	0.7	5	7
Personal Organiser	Paper-based device	0.4	4	10

As these results show, the efficiency gains from the shift to the handheld are not proportional to the difference in weight. The handheld device (excluding packaging and support items) weighs 200 grams, but its production consumes 58 kg of abiotic, non-renewable raw materials. This yields a factor of 290. For the notebook, this factor is lower: at 133 comprising less than half of it. The high material intensity of the handheld device is a result of the large share of functional materials included in the handheld and the modem. These functional materials have intensive upstream processing demands for components such as PWBs, LCDs, chips and precious metals. Additionally, most of the materials in the electronic devices used arise from abiotic, non-renewable sources. Generally, it can be observed that the production of the paper-based personal organiser consumes by far the smallest amount of resources. The accumulative effects of these material-intensive appliances are visible at the macro-economic level.

A first and very rough estimate by the Wuppertal Institute of the material intensity necessary for producing just the servers installed in Germany came to about 1.7 million tons of abiotic raw materials or 0.2 kg if allocated per hour of Internet use. While this figure can only be regarded as an initial trace of what is to come, it might serve as an indication of the volume of resource flows still to be included if the entire infrastructure were considered.

Transporting ICT has Low Relevance

Transportation from ICT manufacturing to the consumer contributes little to the entire resource consumption caused within the device's life cycle. In the case study for the handheld it accounted for less than 1% of the abiotic raw materials. However, if the transport of components and subcomponents before assembly, possibly by air, were to be considered, transport's contribution to resource consumption would probably be higher. In addition, the consumer habits (transport mode and distance traveled to sales point) constitute an influential factor of the transport related effects.

More Electricity for the Net

In the use phase all Internet infrastructure parts are associated with energy demand, which is an important factor to include when calculating the overall resource consumption of the Internet. Researchers at the Wuppertal Institute and other researchers working on the electricity consumption of Internet infrastructure have highlighted its dimension.

The **electricity consumption of the end appliances** in the use phase contributes significantly to the resource consumption of the infrastructure (Loerincik, Jolliet & Norris, 2002; Türk, 2001; Türk et al., 2002). The electricity consumption of a single device is determined by the user behaviour (the time spent in active, standby, sleep and charging modes) as well as the device's and charger efficiency. Also the energy source (e.g., coal, oil, hydro, wind) and the technology used for electricity production determine the material use of the device. Within the Digital Europe case study (based on the European electricity mix and on specific assumptions regarding consumer behaviour) the use phase accounts for a resource consumption up to 1.5 times higher than the one of the production phase. The respective figures for a handheld are only a third or half; that is, the handheld is relatively energy efficient in the use phase. Regarding the service of "mobile information processing" that both products provide, there are differences in the convenience and handling of the information processing. There are mainly "mobility-related" advantages on the handheld's side, whereas there are "information processing-related" advantages for the notebook. But still, as the users of mobile computing devices do not need (and cannot use) all the functions at one time, the concept of a shared use of the electronic equipment is coming into the picture as an interesting improvement option. Regarding shared use of electronic devices, the question is what raw material savings could be achieved if for example a company provided handhelds to all of its salespeople and promoted sharing of notebooks. This could be compared to a situation where each employee uses an individual notebook (see Figure 3).

The shared use of notebooks and individual use of handheld devices can increase overall efficiency. Starting from the material intensity analysis of the notebook and its assumptions, the use intensities of the notebooks and the handhelds would increase with each increase in the number of persons sharing a notebook. However, with respect to the related use of abiotic raw materials, the saving attained with notebooks (and paper based personal organisers) is offset by the increasing use intensities illustrated in the figure.

Figure 3. Abiotic raw material intensity for sharing notebooks and additional use of handhelds

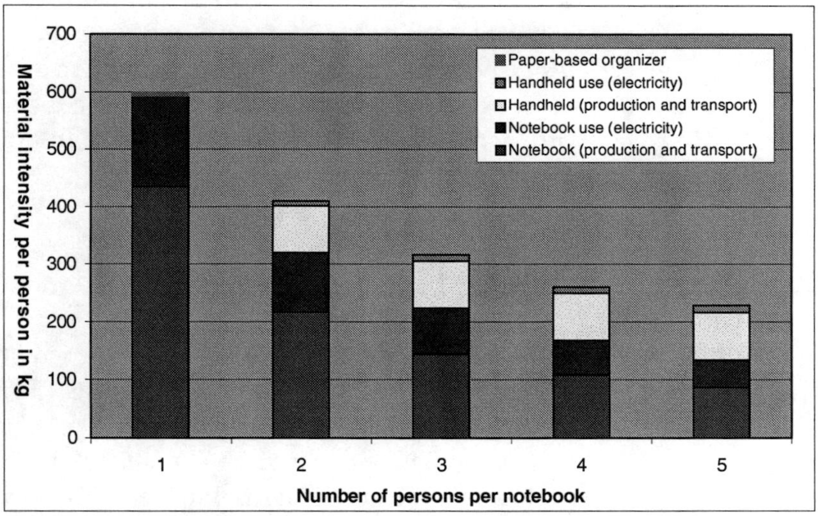

These savings seem to be high. However in practice there are a number of obstacles to the shared use of notebooks and related material saving. For example, in a company where salespeople share electronic equipment, some salespeople will need a notebook when they are travelling. The shared use of notebooks might force other salespeople to come back to the workplace when they need the notebook's processing capacities. Also, there are a number of changes needed to create shared working places (e.g., additional office equipment), which might be related to additional material intensities. As most of the handhelds are currently used in combination with notebooks, the handheld today is more an add-on device than a substitution for the notebook. As long as consumers demand a notebook or a PC in addition to the handheld, no increase in resource efficiency can take place. But still, the concept of sharing seems to be an opportunity for increased resource efficiency.

On the national level the Internet's electricity consumption is considerable. For example, in Germany the life cycle electricity consumption of the entire Internet infrastructure is estimated to account for almost 2% of national electricity consumption (Thomas, 2002). The future energy demand of the Internet is most likely to increase. Initial estimates of future energy consumption indicate that the electricity demand from the Internet in Germany could increase to 5% of total electricity consumption by 2010. Also, research conducted by Romm in the US and by Aebischer and Huser in Switzerland points to an increase in the demand for energy caused by the entire Internet infrastructure, despite the energy efficiency improvements of individual Internet-enabled activities (Aebischer & Huser, 2000; Thomas, 2002).

The resource consumption associated with the Internet's energy use depends on how the electricity is produced, as shown by research done at the Wuppertal Institute (e.g., by Liedtke et al., 1998 or Manstein, 1996). It is the specific energy mix of a country that determines the associated resource consumption. In Germany, the material flows associated with electricity consumption during the use phase currently account for about 0.5% of nationwide material consumption (Türk, 2001). However, with increasing electricity demand by the Internet, the related resource consumption is most likely to rise.

End-of-Life Aspects of ICT

In the year 1998, 6 million tons of electronic waste had to be disposed of at the European level. The growth rate is at least 3% to 5% per year (European Commission, 2000). In Germany more than 2 million used computers, printers and so forth accumulate every year. These cause large amounts of waste to be processed, which will be tripled over the middle term. If the electronic waste is disposed of in domestic waste, either it will end up untreated on a dumpsite (thus ensuring that contaminated waste will develop in the future), or will be fed into a "thermal utilization" type of waste incineration plant, the cleaning technologies of which are not designed for this kind of contaminated waste, or they will be transported to developing countries.

Considering the large amount of resources used to produce individual end-user appliances, reuse and recycling as well as the extension of the use phase are important improvement options from a life-cycle perspective. However, the actual number of recycled devices is low. The basis of an efficient recycling scheme includes both a good motivation for the end-user to return products and efficient logistics (take-back and recycling). As the material value of smaller products is reduced and the smaller size of devices allows them to be discarded with household waste, the take-back and recycling systems face major challenges. It is not yet clear what impact the WEEE directive will have on this matter. More practical data and research are needed for reliable evaluation of recycling schemes.

Indirect and Systemic Effects of Internet Applications on Resource Consumption

As highlighted in Figure 2, Internet applications have indirect effects as well as systemic effects. Both need to be considered for evaluation of the environmental effects of the broad system of the Internet. This section will highlight the resource consumption with a focus on the e-commerce applications of online banking and the digital provision of music.

Online = Virtual?

The analysis of the **indirect environmental effects** of e-commerce within the Digital Europe project highlights that the object of the economic transaction (the product or service) is an influential factor for the overall dematerialisation potential of e-commerce. This means that the material intensity of the transaction's object as such determines substantially the influence that e-commerce has on resource efficiency. Thus, e-commerce activities can be divided into product-based and information-based e-commerce, depending on the amount of physical material used to provide the specific service delivered by the product.

Information-based e-commerce, as one important application of ICT, can – under specific circumstances – provide significant resource efficiency potentials. Information-based e-commerce is not based on a physical product forming the object of the economic transaction. Online banking is one example where resource efficiency gains can be achieved by e-business, as illustrated in Figure 4 (Türk et al., 2003).

Based on the assumptions made in the online banking case study, a traditional payment causes resource flows in the order of 2.7 kg abiotic raw materials, whereas online payment only for 1.1 kg. Comparing these amounts with the amounts of raw materials needed to produce, e.g., beverage cans, we see that the traditional payment uses as much raw materials as the production of 10 cans requires. If the payment is conducted online, the equivalent of only four cans is needed. Assuming that from all 20 million online accounts in Germany (estimations of the number of online accounts are given for example by NUA Internet

Figure 4. Abiotic resource consumption of banking: Comparing a traditional payment with an online payment

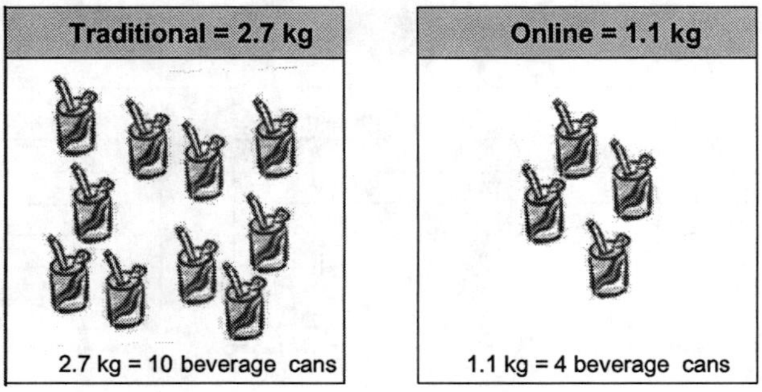

Surveys (2003)) annually 20 previously traditional payments would be replaced by online transactions, this would account for annual savings of 640 thousand tons of abiotic raw materials, that is, non-renewable resources.

Another example of information-based e-commerce is a music server that can provide a tremendous number of song units to many consumers (see Digital Europe case study on digital music by Türk et al., 2003b). The case study showed that downloading 56 minutes of music over the Internet is more than two and a half times less resource intensive than buying a CD with an equivalent amount of music at a shop. Savings are made at different stages in the process. For a start, a physical CD is replaced by a digital file. The resources needed to produce a CD are associated with an ecological backpack seven times their actual weight. Additionally, resource flows associated with the production and retail infrastructure as well as with transportation are made redundant. Moreover, resource savings associated with the reduced need for building infrastructure appear to be relevant. Other examples of dematerialised products are centralised voice mailing servers (Reichling & Otto, 2002) or news servers (Reichart et al., 2000).

With virtual products and services, consumers have a far greater influence on life-cycle-wide resource intensity because material intensity is no longer concentrated on the production and delivery phase of the product life cycle. Figure 5 shows how the overall material intensity is distributed among the producer, retailer and consumer when a CD is purchased in a music store (physical shopping), online (online shopping) or an equivalent number of compressed music files are downloaded over the Internet (digital distribution). There is a clear sign of a shift in material intensity down the value chain, making consumers the guardians of the environmental potential of virtual products and services.

In the case of product-based e-commerce, the physical production and delivery of a product takes place in a way similar to traditional shopping. Thus, the related resource consumption can be only partly influenced by ICT, as the production of the product and most of the logistical efforts remain. The resource savings due to e-commerce for products that have a high resource intensity during production

Figure 5. Environmental potential of virtual products and services in the case of digital music

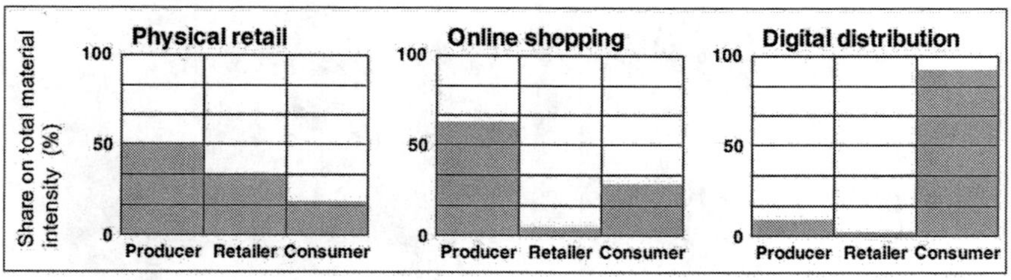

are small anyway, since production will likely dominate the material intensity along the life cycle. Additionally, there is an important difference compared to digitised products: digitised products can be shared by an unlimited number of users if not restricted by any kind of software protection. This means that one "product" can serve many users, adding a functionality that does not exist for traditional products even if they are sold by e-commerce.

Taking a Broader Perspective

Regarding **systemic effects**, influential factors for the resource consumption are the businesses and consumer habits or rebound effects. As with many other technical applications and services, these factors are important to consider in order to evaluate the full picture of the environmental effects of ICT and e-business. While on a case study level they might not turn out to be of relevance, on a macro level they are likely to be. A few examples are:

- The Internet will reframe markets, enabling companies and consumers to buy globally, which potentially increases transport demand;
- Flat rate internet access might reduce the (economic) incentives for Web users to disconnect from the Internet between sessions, resulting in an increasing energy demand, even if the PC itself is in sleep mode;
- Fast Internet connections might change consumer behaviour and increase overall material intensity, as consumers with a fast Internet connection are more likely to stay online or to download more files.
- Consumers tend to re-materialise digital information. Examples are music files burned on CDs or the tendency to print out most digital documents.

In particular, people's habit to re-materialise is a good illustration of how consumer habits can be rooted in a non-digital world. Information stored only on a remote server or hard-drive is burned onto a CD or printed out on a regular basis. The reasons for this can be manifold, including issues such as trust (Is the information safe? Is a back-up needed?), traditions (important information needs to be filed as a printout) or habits (working with long documents requires a printout). The case study on digital music has highlighted the fact that this habit might offset the savings obtained from digital distribution.

In summary, information-based e-commerce has the potential to decouple economic growth from resource consumption. However, larger savings on a macro scale are not expected at the present situation or in the near future for various reasons (Kuhndt et al., 2003). First, e-commerce is a sales channel built up and maintained in parallel with traditional channels. Second, the number of products that can be reduced to an "informational core" seems to be limited. In the resource intensive sectors such as building, food, clothing and community as well as large parts of health and leisure there are a number of products that are not likely to be digitised. This leaves a fraction of total material consumption in which information-based e-commerce could potentially contribute to a decoupling. Third, under the current framework influencing resource consumption, consumer habits and rebound effects might have a counterbalancing influence. Whether with changed framework conditions the benefits could outweigh the risks remains an open question.

Conclusions

The Internet and Internet applications are far from being purely virtual, but are clearly linked to the use of natural resources. It seems that a seemingly inevitable increase in the resource consumption for the production of electronic equipment and its electricity consumption comes with the growth of the Internet's infrastructure. Based on existing research, a number of conclusions can be made regarding the minimisation of environmental risks and maximisation of e-business' potential to dematerialise.

Monitoring Environmental Impacts of Internet and Internet Applications

The quantification of environmental effects caused by ICT technologies is still a major challenge. Having knowledge about environmental effects along the entire product chain is a necessary precondition for the identification of efficient improvement options. Efforts are required to improve macro-level statistical classification systems for ICT infrastructure and applications to provide adequate statistical information. At the company level, opportunities can be the combination of cost accounting systems with internal material flow data (material flow accounting) as well as improved supply chain communication covering the ecological costs of preliminary production and transport.

Greening ICT Hardware

The research within Digital Europe pointed out the importance of ICT infrastructure as a main factor for resource consumption of e-business and e-government. Often, the early manufacturing stages and the use phase are neglected within evaluations. However, these turn out to be of high relevance for a large share of ICT products and services. Improvement opportunities can be derived from the extension of ICT's lifetime, the promotion of the shared use of ICT equipment, extended warranties or design for environment, as initiated by proactive ICT companies.

Shifting to e-Services

E-commerce can – under specific circumstances – provide significant resource efficiency potentials, especially if physical products are shifted to e-services. Public administration and businesses can be a forerunner in offering e-services as part of their e-government strategies. As well as being a provider of e-services (push-strategy), these organisations could request services instead of products from their suppliers wherever possible (pull-strategy). Societal and technological framework conditions can be enhanced for the uptake of e-service applications. Fast, affordable and reliable Internet connections are a prerequisite, as is the trust in the confidentiality of data transferred via the Net. Besides this, large parts of the population still lack basic e-society literacy. Empowering these groups is a key for a wider uptake of e-services. Scientific assessments should be carried out to determine in which sectors of traditional industry with high resource consumption the use of ICT could enable a dematerialisation noticeable at the macro scale. Such an assessment could help to answer the question as to where it is worthwhile to promote e-services on a larger scale.

Raising Awareness and Changing Habits

The habits of ICT users and their awareness are to an increasing extent decisive for total material intensity. Efficiency gains may even be offset. Examples are re-materialisation of digitised information or building up of e-channels without reducing traditional ones. E-society literacy is needed, allowing users to handle digital information without re-materialisation. While the younger generation will hopefully grow up with a mindset allowing them to deal with this, training and empowerment might be needed for other population groups. A better understanding of the size and potential impact of rebound effects is urgently needed. Of particular importance is the early integration of information on potential rebound effects in the design phase of products and services, as the main effects are determined there. With the growth of the Internet, global and national framework conditions become more important as a means of limiting undesired rebound effects, such as additional resource or energy consumption.

References

Aebischer, B., & Huser, A. (2000). *Vernetzung im Haushalt, Auswirkungen Auf Den Stromverbrauch.* Bern: Swiss Federal Office of Energy.

Atlantic Consulting, IPU. (1998). *LCA Report: EU Ecolabel for personal computers.* Third report from study of the product group personal computers in the EU Ecolabel scheme for DG XI of the European Commission.

Berehndt, S., Kreibich, R., Lundie, S., Pfitzner, R., & Scharp, M. (1998). *Ökobilanzierung Komplexer Elektronischer Produkte.* Berlin: ITZ.

Commission Proposal COM. (2000). 347 final. *Proposal for a Directive of the European Parliament and of the Council on waste electrical and electronic equipment.*

Cyber Atlas. (2003, August). Global usage. *http://cyberatlas.internet.com.*

Cyber Atlas (2003b). The world's online population, 2003. *http://cyberatlas.internet.com.*

Deutscher Commercial Internet Exchange. (2001). *http://www.decix.org.*

European Commission (2003). Statistics on the information society. *Europe. Statistics in focus. Industry, trade and services.* Theme 4-38.

European Information Technology Observatory (EITO). (2000). Frankfurt: European Information Technology Observatory (Germany).

Geibler, J.v., Kuhndt, M., & Türk, V. (2002). Umweltauswirkungen von e-Commerce: Betrachtungen am Fallbeispiel Online-banking. [Environmental effects of e-commerce: Investigating the case study on line banking]. *Ökologisches Wirtschaften, 3-4.*

Geibler, J.v., Kuhndt, M., Türk. V., & Ritthoff, M. (2003). *Environmental impacts of mobile computing.* A case study with Hewlett Packard. Report to the European Community. Wuppertal Institute (Germany).

Greenspan, R. (2002). EU B2B Expected to Explode. *http://cyberatlas.internet.com.*

Hilty, L.M., & Gilgen, P. W. (eds.). (2001). *Sustainability in the information society.* Marburg: Metropolis-Verlag.

Internet Software Consortium. Internet Domain Survey. *www.isc.org.*

Kuhndt, M., Geibler, J.v., Türk, V., Moll, S., Schallaböck, K.O., & Steger, S. (2003). *Digital Europe: Virtual dematerialisation: ebusiness and factor X.* Report to the European Community. Wuppertal Institute (Germany).

Liedtke, C., Rohn, H., Kuhndt, M., & Nickel, R. (1998). Applying material flow accounting: Eco-auditing and resource management at the Kambium Furniture Workshop. *Journal of Industrial Ecology, 2*(3). MIT Press.

Loerincik, Y., Jolliet, O., & Norris, G. (2002, November 6-8). Life cycle environmental impacts of Internet. *Proceedings of the Fifth International Conference on EcoBalance. Practical tools and thoughtful principles for sustainability*, 121-123, Epochal Tsukuba, Japan.

Manstein, Ch. (1996). *Das Elektrizitätsmodul im MIPS-konzept* [Electricity module for the MIPS concept]. Wuppertal Papers, No. 51, Wuppertal Institute for Climate, Environment, Energy, Germany.

NUA Internet Surveys. (2003). Online banking on the rise in Germany. [Online] Quelle: *http://www.nua.com/surveys/?f=VS&art_id=905358742&rel=true.*

Office of Technology Assessment at the German Parliament (TAB). (2002). *Innovationsbedingungen des E-commerce – Die Technischen Kommunikationsinfrastrukturen für den Elektronischen Handel.* [Innovation conditions of e-commerce: The technical communication infrastructure for electronic commerce]. Background paper No. 7. TAB.

Reichart, I., Hischler, R., Schefer, H., & Zurkirch, M. (2000). *Umweltbelastung durch Internet-surfer, Fernsehzuschauer und Zeitungsleser.* [Environmental impacts of surfing the Internet, watching TV and reading a newspaper]. St. Gallen: Eidgenössische Materialprüfungs- und Forschungsanstalt, Switzerland.

Reichling, M., & Otto, T. (2002). Environmental impact of the new economy. In J. Park & N. Roome (Eds.), *Ecology of the new economy.* Greenleaf.

Romm, J. (1999). *The Internet economy and global warming.* The Centre for Energy and Climate Solutions.

Schmidt-Bleek, F. (1995). *Increasing resource productivity on the way to sustainability.* UNEP Industry and Environment, October-December, p. 10.

Socolof, M.L., Overly, J.G., Kincaid, L.E., & Geibig, J.R. (2001). *US EPA desktop computer displays: A life-cycle assessment.* US Environmental Protection Agency, 1.

Thomas, S. (2002, February 21-22). www.internet.co2? *GHG emissions of the Internet in Germany.* Presentation at the IEA Workshop: Information and Communication Technology: the Next Challenge for Energy Systems? Paris. Information is based on unpublished results by Stephan Thomas and Dr. Claus Barthel, Wuppertal Institute, Germany.

Türk, V. (2001). *Assessing the resource intensity of the Internet infrastructure: Data analysis for a material-flow oriented approach and first results on electricity consumption.* MSc thesis at the Lund University, Sweden. Retrieved July 17, 2002, from: *http://www.iiiee.lu.se/.*

Türk, V., Kuhndt, M., Alakeson, V., Aldrich, T., & von Geibler, J. (2003b). The environmental and social impacts of ebanking. A case study with Barclays PLC. Case study within the project *Digital Europe: Ebusiness and sustainable development. http://www.digital-eu.org/.*

Türk, V., Kuhndt, M., Ritthoff, M., & Alakeson, V. (2003). The environmental and social impacts of digital music. A case study with EMI. Case study within the project *Digital Europe: Ebusiness and sustainable development. http://www.digital-eu.org/.*

Türk, V., Ritthoff, M., Geibler, J. Von, & Kuhndt, M. (2002). Internet: Virtuell = umweltfreundlich? [Internet: virtual = environmentally sound?] In G. Altner, B. Mettler-von Meibom, U. Simonis & E.U. von Weizsäcker (Eds.), *Jahrbuch okologie 2003,* 110-123. Beck, München.

VDI Nachrichten. (2001, March 30). *Netzknoten Sind Wahre Stromfresser.* [Internet nodes are extreme electricity consumers]. VDI-Verlag, Düsseldorf, Germany.

White, A.L., Stoughton, M., & Fend, L. (1999, December 1-3). Servicizing: The quite transition to EPR. Tellus Institute, Boston, MA, USA. OECD Workshop. *Extended and Shared Responsibility for Products: Economic Efficiency/Environmental Effectiveness.* Washington, D.C.

Section II

Supporting Change Toward Sustainability

Chapter X

A Social Context Model for Discussion Process Analysis

Aldo de Moor, Tilburg University, The Netherlands

Rolf Kleef, AIDEnvironment, The Netherlands

Abstract

Computer-mediated discussion processes play an important role in achieving sustainable development. However, when part of authoring complex documents, these discussions have so far not been very effective. One reason is that in the design and application of the information tools supporting discussion, the social context is not sufficiently taken into account. We outline a social context model for discussion process analysis. The GRASS tool for group report authoring and the freeText tool for document review are authoring tools in which the social context of discussions is given explicit attention. Analyzing GRASS and freeText, we show how the model could be used to construct information tools that enable more effective discussions.

Introduction

Globalization leads to an increasing number of complex societal problems related to sustainable development. Their solution requires the involvement of ever more stakeholders, with often strongly opposing interests. Discussion processes play an important role in public debates, the development of alternatives, and political decision making. Many types of electronic discussion tools already exist, such as newsgroups, mailing lists and various Web tools. However, so far, computer-mediated discussions have not been very effective in consistently fostering societal change. One important reason is that in the design and application of many tools, the social context in which the discussion processes are carried out is not sufficiently taken into account. This is especially important when the tools are used not only for discussing the pros and cons of issues, but also for the authoring of structured documents. We therefore define authoring tools as those discussion tools that are tailored to the effective authoring of structured documents.

In this chapter, we aim to chart the social context of discussion processes, and investigate how it can be used in order to help in the development of discussion tools that are more effective for authoring. We start with an analysis of two tools used to support the authoring of group documents: GRASS and freeText. Next, we analyze related work on discussion theory and tools. We present our social context model for discussion process analysis in the following section. We then use this model to analyze and compare the functionality and application of GRASS and freeText. We conclude the chapter by indicating some future research on how the model could be used to construct information tools that help foster more effective societal discussions.

Authoring as an Effective Discussion Process

Many social, environmental, and developmental issues are examples of "wicked problems". These problems are very hard to formulate and solve, as their resolution requires input from many stakeholders and disciplines (De Moor, 1998). Co-authoring documents like policies and regulations is an essential activity in resolving wicked problems and thus making society more sustainable. Authoring is a good example of a goal-oriented communication process, in which multiple authors collaborate on a joint work. In complex discussions, editorial unity needs to be achieved, while at the same time a wide variety of author perspectives need to be preserved (Harasim & Walls, 1993).

Many tools exist that support discussion processes. These tools are increasingly Web-based and thus accessible to many, having great potential for achieving sustainability purposes. One typical example is The Fence (*http://www.thefence.com*), which allows people to launch and participate in debates on myriads of topics, often counting hundreds, sometimes over a thousand contributions. However, although these tools are useful to have stimulating exchanges and help in the formation of individual opinions, they are not very effective when it comes to systematically producing well-defined outputs, such as structured documents. One important reason is that the social context of the discussion is not much taken into account. If this context is neglected in the design of discourse norms, procedures, and tools, it is likely that participants will not adopt the design or not apply it towards intended uses (Aakhus, 1999). In this chapter, we present a model that can be used in the analysis of the role that discussion tools play in focused communication processes like authoring. By clarifying the social context of these tools-in-use, the authoring processes they support can be made more effective.

We next present two typical examples of discussion tools for authoring purposes, in which the social context of the discussion processes they enable plays an important role: the GRASS tool for group report authoring, and the freeText tool for document review.

Group Report Authoring: GRASS

In 1993, the Global Research Network on Sustainable Development (GRNSD) was formed. One of the groups it spawned was the B.C. Forests and Forestry Group (BCFOR; *http://infolab.uvt.nl/grnsd/bcfor*). This computer-mediated group consisted of Canadian and international members, ranging from timber industry consultants to environmentalists. The group aimed to produce group reports in which forestry policies in the Canadian province of British Columbia could be critically analyzed, by systematically presenting and contrasting all points of view.

Such a group report is an example of a truly *dialogic text,* in which not one, but many authorial voices are heard. These texts are not written with a single monotonic *group voice,* but instead reflect many different perspectives in the same document, while possessing enough structure to be comprehensible (Harrison & Stephen, 1992).

Not only the *structure* of the group report, but also the authoring *process* has complex requirements. Such a process should conform to what Habermas in his theory of discourse ethics calls the ideal speech situation, in which practical rules of discourse guarantee discursive equality, freedom, and fair play (Chambers,

1996). However, operationalizing these ideals into conversation support that actually works is not trivial.

Producing structured reports while still using only simple mailing list functionality turned out to be unsuccessful in BCFOR. Although a topic for the report was successfully chosen using an extensive voting process with significant group participation, the subsequent authoring process was never concluded.

To overcome the complex technical and organizational hurdles, the ongoing GRASS (**G**roup **R**eport **A**uthoring **S**upport **S**ystem) project was initiated (*http://grass-arena.net*). GRASS is to provide a balanced mix of information tool functionality and organizational procedures. The overall objective is to help produce concise group reports that answer specific questions. Much attention is paid to the group report structure, which consists of three main parts: a research problem, several sections, and a conclusion. Within the sections, positions can be taken on issues and addressed in argument threads. Different authoring roles are distinguished, such as report and section editors, authors, and readers. Not only the writing of the report itself, but also the dissemination of the results to societal stakeholders, such as the general public and various organizations, is supported. Furthermore, social constraints should be satisfied, like the neutrality of the document and the transparency of the authoring process (De Moor & Weigand, 1996).

Document Review: freeText

As a second example, we look at freeText (*http://www.drostan.org/projects/fafo*), an online tool for the review process of a draft report. It was developed for the Programme for International Co-operation and Conflict Resolution (PICCR) of the FAFO Institute for Applied Social Science in Norway. In 2001, FAFO and the Norwegian Institute of International Affairs (NUPI) organized a forum on gender and decision making in post-conflict transitions, having over 30 participants from international organizations, governments, NGOs, universities, and research institutes.

The forum did not intend to build consensus, but rather to explore the complexity of the issue. The report produced therefore had to represent the various views of the participants as expressed during the forum. Initially, a draft report was sent out by e-mail and on paper, soliciting individual comments. The editors faced the task of collecting all feedback and then tracing it back to the relevant parts of the document.

Using the freeText tool, however, participants could directly comment on report elements, thus substantially alleviating the editorial process. Furthermore, using the tool, participants were able to view and reply to each other's comments, thus engaging in dialogue. This all allowed the editors to have better access to the participants as a group, ensuring the report captures the views expressed most accurately.

Having presented two authoring tools in their context of use, we now continue with an overview of theory and tools relevant to our development of a social context model.

Discussion Theory and Tools

The term *discussion* has different meanings. One interpretation is that it is the consideration of a question in open and usually informal debate; another one that it is a formal treatment of a topic in speech or writing (Merriam-Webster). Central is that there is some issue or topic being addressed in a process of argumentation between different participants. The formality of this conversation may differ, however. This is important, as it affects the degree of structure that can or should be provided by supporting tools. Also, the argumentation process needs to be well-understood, not only at the basic level of discussing for or against a point, but also regarding its pragmatics, meaning what social effects it has. To ensure that discussion contributes to the common good, and does not become pathological, its social context needs to be clearly understood. After all, public discourse is about *making* an argument for a point of view, not *having* an argument (Tannen, 1998).

A classic model of argumentation is that of Toulmin (1958). His model is based on three principal elements: claims, evidence for those claims, and warrants linking these elements. Although useful to conceptualize the way people argue, the model – and many other more sophisticated discussion and argumentation theories – do not answer the question of how to design tools that provide argumentation *support*. In the rest of this section, we examine the functionality of some well-known discussion tools.

Discussion Tool Functionality

One step on the way to the design of effective discussion support tools is the idea of issue-based information systems (IBIS). Issues act as organizing principles for collaborative work, transcending individual conversations (Hartfield & Graves, 1991). An IBIS allows its users to identify questions and develop the scope of positions in response to them, and assists in creating discussions (Kunz & Rittel, 1970). Using an IBIS, stakeholders can conduct conversations about complex or "wicked" problems, by structuring the creation and handling of "issue nets" (Conklin & Begemann, 1988). Issue nets have three main types of nodes: *issues, positions,* and *arguments.* Many refinements of nodes and the types of links between them have been created in the applications developed. Some IBIS are generic and domain-independent; others are tailored to the needs of a particular domain. Examples of early generic IBIS-tools are gIBIS and HyperIBIS. gIBIS is a graphical hypertext system with as its main interface elements a browser and a structured node index (Conklin & Begemann, 1988). HyperIBIS is a simple text version of an IBIS, which can distinguish between deontic issues (should?), factual issues (what?), instrumental issues (how?), explanatory issues (why?) and conceptual issues (definitions) (Isenmann, 1993). One domain-specific IBIS especially designed for research purposes is the Scientific Collaboration System (Kim et al., 1993). SCS pays much attention to representing knowledge. It uses an ordinary database to store this knowledge and make it accessible to its users. Types defined include *hypothesis, claim,* and *argument.* It allows research fields to be modelled as object classes, and organizes these fields in a class hierarchy. Issue nets are then mapped to one or more of these hierarchies. Queries on this knowledge base enable, for example, interdisciplinary viewpoints on the same problem to be obtained.

These early IBIS systems focused much attention on developing and using often complex representations. There was still little attention for the way in which these systems were to be *used,* let alone how they could be made effective. This is changing, as modern IBIS become more sensitive to their context of use. Zeno, for instance, is a second-generation, Web-based IBIS tool (Gordon et al., 1996), which helps to mediate in conflicts. One purported application is that it can be used to democratize public policy making processes. A human mediator indexes documents according to the underlying argumentation model. By allowing for the preferences and value judgments expressed in messages to be modelled, and by using a reason maintenance procedure, the tool can indicate which of the alternative solutions proposed meet selected proof standards or decision criteria. Although still using complex representation and reasoning schemes, Zeno pays much more attention to usability issues than the earlier generation of IBIS tools. It meets several practical design requirements: widely available across platforms, inexpensive access, and a very intuitive user interface.

Zeno is a sophisticated tool with a clear purpose of supporting planning processes. In contrast, D3E (http://d3e.open.ac.uk) is a whole *kit* of functionalities that allows users to build their own document authoring tools. It supports the creation of sites that can be used to publish Web-based documents, and that have integrated discourse facilities and interactive components (Sumner & Shum, 1998). In this way, new forms of online publication processes are possible, which, for instance, involve authors and readers much more interactively in the review process.

Summarizing, ever more advanced functionalities are becoming available in the newer generations of discussion tools. However, the need for and application of these functionalities are still unclear. In order to use these functionalities more effectively, a systematic analysis of their social context of use is needed. We next provide our social context model that can be used to this purpose.

A Social Context Model for Discussion Process Analysis

The case descriptions of the GRASS and freeText tools demonstrate the complexity of the role of discussion processes in complex applications such as authoring.

Our goal is to increase the effectiveness of discussion processes, so that authoring can result in documents that contribute to the goals of the community of authors, like societal conflict resolution. It is important to realize that these documents are no longer merely a paper-based transport mechanism for preformed ideas, but rather a medium for negotiation within communities, with multiple and complex links between document and discourse (Brown & Duguid, 1996). Such collective document negotiation or interpretation can reduce complexity by helping participants to tackle an ill-structured problem systematically. It does so by focusing attention on a subset of issues and by providing a vocabulary in which to conduct the joint interpretive discourse (Shum & Selvin, 2000). Furthermore, experience shows that such document-driven discourse structuring can only work if practices are appropriately co-evolved with technologies and representations, requiring clearly defined socio-technical strategies for their deployment (Shum & Selvin, 2000). Thus, authoring entails much more than just starting and supporting some discussion threads, such as envisaged in the basic IBIS paradigm.

Building on the theory and tool analysis of the previous section, and generalizing from the cases, we now outline our social context model for discussion process analysis. In our model, we focus on discussion being a complex communication process. The model has two dimensions: a communication process *context* and a communication process *structure*. The first dimension focuses attention on the context of the discussion process, and is expressed in terms of the type and level of the communication process in which the discussion is embedded. The communication process structure dimension describes the configuration of the particular elements needed to make up the communication process.

Communication Process Context

Communication processes do not simply concern the stating of and replying to messages. They ultimately serve higher process goals. For example, one basic discussion process may be used to explore territory, another one to search for alternatives, and a third one to discuss difficult issues (Antunes & Ho, 1999). Journalists may cross-examine the authors of the group report, and so forth. We therefore distinguish different levels of communication processes, from basic discussion to complex societal communication processes.

Our model consists of four layers of communication processes, with each higher-level process providing a context that embeds the lower-level processes. From high to low-level processes, these are: collaboration, authoring, support, and discussion processes:

- **Collaboration processes** *give purpose* to the authoring activities and documents.
- **Authoring processes** *produce* the structured document.
- **Support processes** focus on the *organization* of the discussions between the participants, ensuring that they contribute to the document creation and interpretation.
- **Discussion processes** are the actual interactions in which the argumentation between participants takes place.

By embedding the basic discussion process in three top layers, a systematic context analysis can be performed.

Next, we briefly explain each layer in greater detail.

Collaboration Processes

The collaborative layer provides the ultimate context and rationale for the discussion processes, stimulates adherence to community norms, and increases commitment to the collaboration objectives. It is here that the overall "rules of engagement" in collaboration and argumentation are defined, for instance, derived from a courtroom setting, parliamentary rules of order, and so forth (Aakhus, 1999; Cannon, 1992). At the collaborative level, the online environment has to provide ways to cater to these broader goals. For example, given that the rules of order can be sufficiently and flexibly defined, partial automated mediation support may sometimes be provided (Prakken & Gordon, 1999).

It is crucial that at this level – and in the lower layers – core community values such as the need for neutrality and transparency are designed into the processes and supporting tools (De Moor & Weigand, 1996). There may be a need, for instance, for transparency of the goals to all stakeholders, and transparency of the way in which all contributions are presented or produced. The environment may have to provide tools to "break the ice" between participants, to allow the facilitator to have a good overview of what is happening in the group, and to occasionally invite external participants from outside the group. Finally, the collaboration process may have to be divided in several more or less detailed stages, and deliverables may be necessary that help check progress against the goals (Antunes & Ho, 1999).

Authoring Processes

Documents should help accomplish the objectives of the collaboration processes. The authoring processes include writing, reviewing, and editing. The final output of these processes is a structured document, although contributing authoring processes may focus on specific document parts like abstracts or issue positions. The form of this document can range from the traditional linear report formats to increasingly sophisticated network designs like the one Ted Nelson, who coined the term *hypertext,* has been developing in his Xanadu project (*http://www.xanadu.com*). Notification processes are important to indicate document evolution to the authoring participants.

Documents are not to be seen as isolated artefacts, but may contain live links to embedded discussions, consisting of support processes regulating discussion processes. There can be specific places for discussion of annotations and comments. These conversations may even continue after the final version (if there is one) of the document has been produced. Thus, the definition of the links between text and conversations needs careful attention, much more than has traditionally been the case (Taylor, 1993).

Furthermore, different authoring roles have to be specified (author, editor, reviewer, for example), as well as clear authorizations for these roles and procedures for role assignment.

Support Processes

The interactions making up the actual discussion processes need to be organized in order to achieve sufficient participation, as well as to keep all members in the discussion focused and informed about the progress in the discussion. Support processes thus set the direct context for the interaction processes making up the discussion, initialize the discussion, focus it, and ensure that the results are made available to the authoring processes. These functions are thus to be used in the context of writing (part of) a document.

The support layer includes for instance discussant registration, moderation, and facilitation processes (see e.g., Preece, 2000; Surman & Wershler-Henry, 2001 for many examples of support processes). Support functions can also include notification services for new messages, or digest versions. Also, a discussion moderator may have the option to summarize discussions, or even cut off discussions or conversations. In the support layer, there can also be rules to appoint discussion moderators. Furthermore, scheduling and file sharing may enhance the interaction between participants.

Note that the concept of facilitation is often used in different meanings. Sometimes, it means stakeholder facilitation so that they can find common ground and become productive. We consider this form of facilitation a collaboration process. Often, however, there is a much more restricted, technical interpretation of facilitation, such as the technical facilitator role in the well-known GroupSystems tool (*http://www.ventana.com*). This facilitation role properly belongs in the support process layer.

Discussion Processes

Basic interaction processes have not changed much over the history of the Internet. E-mail, online message boards, and chat rooms still support the majority of interactions. There is mostly only limited variety in the appearance of messages, and the organization is usually merely linear (based on the time sent) or hierarchical (based on threads of replies to specific messages).

Many discussion tools only allow for the support of discussion threads consisting of posts and nested replies, like Web-based newsgroups. More sophisticated tools also allow for issues to be defined and arguments to be constructed. These are all examples of *discussion processes*. However, although they are at the heart of the communication process model, we have argued that these processes should not exist in a vacuum. Thus, environments like D3E are promising, as they can be used to construct tools that classify and couple discussion processes to clearly defined document structures and other social context elements.

Communication Process Structure

Each communication process, whether it is a discussion process or one of its embedding context processes, has a structure comprised of certain process entities. First, we distinguish *process elements* (the elements the process itself is made of). Second, there are the processes constructed out of these elements. These we subdivide into *actions* (which constitute the actual communication process) and *change processes* (meta-processes in which the communication process can be adapted).

Process Elements

There are, at least, three types of process elements that play a role in the communication process actions and change processes: goals, roles, and objects.

Communication process *goals* define what the outputs of these processes should be focused on. The higher-level processes more closely reflect the societal purpose of the discourse. For example, a collaboration goal may be to reach a certain degree of resolution of an environmental conflict. A (low-level) discussion process goal, on the other hand, might be to reach a conclusion in a diverging discussion thread.

A second type of structural element is the different kinds of discussion *roles* that participants play. At the basic discussion level, participants simply are issue definers, argument defenders or attackers, and so on. However, at higher levels, people can be facilitators or mediators. Even more specific, domain-dependent roles also exist, from the editors, authors, and reviewers in electronic journals, to the case managers, experts, referees and judges of the law-inspired "Science Court" (Aakhus, 1999).

Third, we distinguish the *objects* that are the inputs and outputs of the communication processes. At the basic discussion process level, objects include arguments pro and con. At the higher context levels, however, these elements could consist of process logs, various document elements (sections, meta-information), the outlets in which these documents are published, and so forth.

Actions

Actions describe the dynamics of the communication processes. They define the workflows of the community and are composed of configurations of process elements. In actions, more complex objects are generated as outputs from simpler objects by the participants playing process roles. For example, in a discussion process, the action of replying can consist of a discussant producing a reply to a post. In an edit action, a section editor could create a final report section out of a draft section.

Change Processes

Change processes describe how the evolution of the socio-technical system takes place. Given that the complex context of most discussion processes continuously evolves, a static communication process structure will not suffice. To ensure that communication processes and their supporting functionality co-evolve adequately, the processes in which they are changed need to be explicitly defined. For instance, in the GRASS case, the mailing list members decided that they wanted to go beyond merely discussing the pros and cons of forestry policies and start authoring group reports together. This triggered a cascade of change processes to their socio-technical system, including their communication processes.

Action and Change Norms

An important process element for both the actions and change processes are the *norms* that apply. These norms describe the acceptable behavior in the community, by defining the authorizations of the participants in the process roles that they play. Norms prescribe what actions and change processes participants may, must, or may not be involved in. All communities have such norms, some explicitly laid down in charters and by-laws, and others only implicitly defined,

Table 1. Social context model for discussion process analysis

	Process Elements *Actor goals, roles, objects*	**Actions** *Actions* *(production, intervention process)*	**Change Processes** *Definition of socio-technical system* *(structure and actions)*
Collaboration processes *(Why is* the discussion taking place?)	- Collaborative roles (facilitator, judge, expert, keynote speaker) - Stakeholder profiles - Policy reports - Conflict resolution priorities	- Facilitation - Mediation - Conflict resolution - Debating - Political inquiry	- Define goals of collaboration - Define rules of engagement - Set social norms for roles
Authoring processes *(What* is produced in the discussion?)	- Authoring roles (editor, author, reviewer) - Document structure elements (section, position, case, argument)	- Editing - Authoring - Reviewing - Publishing - Notification	- Change authoring roles - Change authoring norms - Change authorizations - Adapt document structure
Support processes *(How* is the discussion *organized?)*	- Support roles (moderator, technical facilitator) - Discussant profiles - Message digests - Discussion summaries - Archives	- Inviting - Reminding - Registration - Agenda-setting - Moderation	- Set communication policy - Agree upon discussion planning - Change digest parameters
Discussion processes *(How* is the discussion *conducted?)*	- Interaction roles (discussant, attacker, defender) - Discussion elements (posts, replies, item labels) - Discussion objectives	- Raising issues - Replying - Creating a position - Playing devil's advocate - Position taking	- Assign attackers, defenders of position - Define discussion rules

but no less strong in impact (Preece, 2000; Surman & Wershler-Henry, 2001). Having clear and relevant communicative norms is essential for argumentation to become effective (Aakhus, 1999).

Examples of action norms are that an editor must discuss the submission with an author. An author, on the other hand, is not permitted to review his or her own article. An example of a change norm would be that only the editor is allowed to redefine the discussion process in which articles are reviewed.

As the structural dimension merely orders the elements of the communication processes introduced in the context dimension, we do not give a more detailed treatment here. Instead, in Table 1, we give examples of structural elements in the different cells of the social context model. This is not an exhaustive list, but should be considered a good illustration of how the model can be used to organize the complexity of discussion processes in their context.

Applying the Social Context Model to Authoring Tool Analysis

In this section, we illustrate potential uses of the model. The model can be used to determine *desired* and *actual* characteristics of discussion tools-in-context. We have used the social context model to compare the GRASS and freeText tool. The assumption is that for effective societal discourse, all cells of the model need to be addressed to some extent. What this extent is depends on the characteristics of the particular authoring community, and requires future research. Space does not permit a full analysis of all elements and processes here. To illustrate, we only briefly examine some key differences in support for the communication *roles* provided by the two tools as experienced by their users.

Applying the Model to GRASS

Roles are collections of processes that can be conducted by a person in a particular capacity. Each communication process level has its own roles. GRASS focuses on defining communication roles on the authoring process level: roles such as report and section editors, authors, and readers. In the action view, much stress is on the social norms that define the privileges and prohibitions attached to these authoring roles. In the change process view, strict procedures have been defined on how actors can change the roles they play. For example, editorial roles can be played by any author interested in doing so by simply

Table 2. Social context analysis of strongly supported GRASS roles

	Elements	Action	Change
Collaboration			
Authoring			
Support			
Discussion			

registering within a particular timeframe at the start of the report. Despite its strong focus on authoring roles, the roles at the other levels are less developed. Not much attention has yet been paid to collaborative roles (one possible link would be between *journalist* roles (collaborative level) that can be *readers* of the reports (authoring level)). No support-level roles exist yet, while discussion interaction level roles only consist of issue, position and argument creators and repliers, without much attention for how to adopt or change these roles (Table 2).

Applying the Model to freeText

FreeText focuses on roles for the collaboration, support, and interaction layers. Its original purpose was to streamline a review process for an existing document, with limited need for an elaborate document structure definition. The focus was therefore mainly on providing an easy way for group members to participate in the review process. Therefore, there is an important role for the facilitator.

A *facilitator* is a collaboration level role that keeps the social process of a document review going. No specific facilitation process functionality is provided yet (action view). On the other hand, freeText is quite adaptable, resulting in quite an important role for change (configuration) in the tool, especially at the collaboration level. One freeText (change) norm says that one person may take different roles, for instance.

A *moderator* is a support process role, guiding discussion contributions. There is basic, but adequate support for commenting and discussing at the discussion interaction level; although more refined discussion functionality could be included in the future. An (action) norm says that a moderator may remove discussion flames. Also, it is easy for different people to take on these moderator roles.

Table 3. Social context analysis of strongly supported freeText roles

	Elements	Action	Change
Collaboration	■		■
Authoring			
Support	■	■	
Discussion	■	■	

Like in GRASS, some basic discussion support is available.

Again using our Social Context Model, we can mark the relatively strong points of the first version (Table 3).

In a second version of freeText, we blended in several features from GRASS, making it technically easier to vary the definition of document structures, and to have more freedom in specifying roles and authorizations, thus strengthening its authoring layer. Discussions within the document are still limited. In our experience, the application of the context model by comparing freeText with GRASS has helped in identifying these issues.

This analysis is still only rudimentary. In future research, we intend to create more detailed reference models that can be used to define desired properties of tools in use, and to provide a checklist for the actual context in which they operate. Patterns could then be defined for very specific context features, and tools quickly compared on the basis of the degree to which they conform to these patterns, thus making effective tool selection and information system evolution much easier.

Conclusions

Much valuable work has been done on discussion process support, such as the issue nets creation and use in issue-based information systems (Conklin & Begemann, 1988). Other applications like the Digital Document Discourse Environment (D3E) provide support that is more directly tailored to the authoring of structured documents. However, we contend that if discussions are to lead to effective collaboration, a systematic analysis of the context of the discussion processes supported by such tools and environments is essential. In this chapter, we have presented a social context model with which we analyzed two authoring tools, GRASS and freeText.

In future research, we intend to use our model to analyze more discussion tools in their context of use. We predict that many patterns in the various communication levels are similar, but that combining them in different ways can lead to substantially different pragmatic effects. The results of these analyses could be used to (1) devise typologies of environmental discussion processes and tools; (2) create tool environments in which a *set* of tools is used for particular purposes (for example, an environment consisting of a mailing list for free-style discussions, and an authoring tool such as GRASS for structuring discussion results); and (3) generate specifications for the development of new authoring tools. By analyzing contextualized discussion tool functionality in this way, more adequate support for complex sustainability authoring processes can be provided, catalyzing much needed global change.

References

Aakhus, M. (1999). Science court: A case study in designing discourse to manage policy controversy. *Knowledge, Technology & Policy, 12*(2), 20-37.

Antunes, P., & Ho, T. (1999, December). Facilitation tool: A tool to assist facilitators managing group decision support systems. *Proceedings of the 9th Workshop on Information Technologies and Systems* (WITS'99), Charlotte, NC.

Brown, J.S., & Duguid, P. (1996). The social life of documents. *First Monday, 1. http://www.firstmonday.dk/issues/issue1/documents/.*

Cannon, H. (1992). *Cannon's concise guide to rules of order.* Boston, MA: Houghton Mifflin.

Chambers, S. (1996). *Reasonable democracy: Jürgen Habermas and the politics of discourse.* Ithaca, NY: Cornell University Press.

Conklin, J., & Begemann, M. (1988). gIBIS: A hypertext tool for exploratory policy discussion. *ACM Transactions on Office Information Systems, 6*(4), 303-331.

De Moor, A. (1998). Information tools for sustainable development: Enabling distributed human intelligence. *Journal of Failure & Lessons Learned in Information Technology Management, 2*(1), 21-31.

De Moor, A., & Weigand, H. (1996, *November 4-7*). The role of social constraints in the design of research network information systems. Proceedings of Eco-Informa '96, Global Networks for Environmental Information, *Orlando,* 672-677.

Gordon, T.F., Karacapilidis, N., & Voss, H. (1996, February 7-9). Zeno: A mediation system for spatial planning. *Proceedings of the ERCIM Workshop on CSCW and the Web,* Sankt Augustin, Germany.

Harasim, L., & Walls, J. (1993). The global authoring network. In L. Harasim (Ed.), *Global networks: Computers and international communication* (pp. 343-355). Cambridge, MA: MIT Press.

Harrison, T., & Stephen, T. (1992). On-line disciplines: Computer-mediated scholarship in the humanities and the social sciences. *Computers and the Humanities, 26,* 181-193.

Hartfield, B., & Graves, M. (1991). Issue-centered design for collaborative work. In R. Stamper, P. Kerola, R. Lee & K. Lytinen (Eds.), *Collaborative work, social communications and information systems.* IFIP.

Heng, M., & de Moor, A. (2003). From Habermas's communicative theory to practice on the Internet. *Information Systems Journal, 13*(4), 331-352.

Isenmann, S. (1993). How to deal with wicked problems using a new type of information system. In F. Stowell & D. West (Eds.), *Systems science: Addressing global issues* (pp. 367-372). New York: Plenum.

Kim, W., Suh, Y., & Whinston, A. (1993). An IBIS and object-oriented approach to scientific research data management. *Journal of Systems and Software, 23,* 183-197.

Kunz, W., & Rittel, H. (1970). *Issues as elements of information systems.* Techn.Rep. 131, Insitute of Urban and Regional Development, University of California.

Prakken, H. & Gordon, T.F. (1999). Rules of order for electronic group decision making: A formalization methodology. In J.A. Padget (Ed.), *Collaboration between human and artificial societies: Coordination and agent-based distributed computing.* LNAI 1624. Berlin: Springer.

Preece, J. (2000). *Online communities: Designing usability, supporting sociability,* Chichester, UK: Wiley.

Shum, S., & Selvin, A. (2000, September 19-20). Structuring discourse for collective interpretation. *Proceedings of Distributed Collective Practices 2000: Conference on Collective Cognition and Memory Practices,* Paris.

Sumner, T., & Shum, S. (1998, April 18-23). From documents to discourse: Shifting conceptions of scholarly publishing. *Proceedings of CHI'98: Human Factors in Computing Systems,* Los Angeles.New York: ACM Press.

Surman, M., & Wershler-Henry, D. (2001). *Commonspace: Beyond virtual community.* Pearson: FT.com.

Tannen, D. (1998). *The argument culture: Changing the way we argue and debate.* London: Virago Press.

Taylor, J.R. (1993). *Rethinking the theory of organizational communication.* NJ: Ablex.

Toulmin, S. (1958). *The uses of argument.* Cambridge: University Press.

Chapter XI

E-Organization and the Sustainable Information Society

Uwe Schneidewind, University of Oldenburg, Germany

Abstract

Information and Communication Technologies (ICT) have direct and indirect effects on sustainability. The direct effects are linked to the material and energy flows caused by the application of ICT. Indirect effects are caused by organizational and institutional changes driven by the new technologies. These latter changes can be summarized using the term "e-organization". E-organization describes organizational and institutional patterns enabled by ICT. Important examples are new forms of network coordination between firms (also between NGOs), virtual factories or virtual communities. This chapter proposes a normative framework for judging the sustainability effects of these organizational designs and makes suggestions on how to create e-organizations capable of offering a sustainability contribution.

Introduction: Two Perspectives on ICT and Sustainability

Information and Communication Technologies (ICT) mentioned in this chapter refer specifically to Internet-based technologies and communication services. A glance at ICT and sustainability reveals two relevant levels of sustainability effects:

1. Information and communication devices produce direct ecological (sustainability) effects during their product life cycle (production, use, disposal); that is, energy use, resource consumption, pollutants and electronic smog, and electronic waste.
2. Information and communication devices cause indirect effects due to organizational changes caused by ICT. These changes affect use and consumption patterns (first order structural effects) as well as organizational and institutional designs in business and society (second order structural effects).

The strong interaction between information infrastructure on the one hand and cultural phenomena on the other is already on the discussion agenda regarding a sustainable information society. Allenby (2001) makes clear that (concerning the organizational effects of ICT), "our ability to understand the environmental and social dimension of information systems begins to diminish rapidly, in part because of the increasing importance of the cultural dimension" (Allenby, 2001, p. 32).

It seems worthwhile to focus on these "cultural" indirect effects to determine the sustainability effects of new organizational designs. The empirical evidence of previous years supports the hypothesis that these indirect effects are of much larger importance than the direct effects of ICT. Three questions comprise the following chapter's arguments:

1. What are the new forms of organization caused by ICT? How can these types of e-organization be classified?
2. What must we understand about sustainable development in order to determine a normative framework helping us to judge different organizational and institutional designs from a sustainability perspective?
3. What guidelines exist for designing sustainable forms of e-organizations?

Figure 1. Three levels of interaction between ICT and sustainability

Effect		Examples
Indirect Effects		
	2nd order structural effects "institutional innovation" (new e-organization patterns)	▪ new forms of ICT-supported political participation ▪ eco-e-commerce (internet based marketing/selling of eco-products) ▪ internet based ecological and social reporting of companies
	1st order structural effects "substitution" and "rebound" (substitution and growth effects by ICT)	▪ PC/mobile phone diffusion through reduced prices ▪ more traveling through ICT-efficiency ▪ globalized supply chains and their ecological effects through ICT
Direct Effects		▪ emissions and resource consumption of ICT-production ▪ computer energy use ▪ electronic "smog" ▪ electronic waste

E-Organization

What are the new forms of organization caused by ICT? How can these types of e-organization be classified?

Organization means the coordination of individual and collective actors. To understand how ICT changes this coordination, it is necessary to look at the different kinds of interaction between relevant actors. ICT interconnects *different types of partners* and it allows *new qualities* of interaction.

New Quality of Interaction

The new information and communication technologies offer a new quality of interaction and communication between partners. Important aspects are:

- Independence from *time and space restrictions:* ICT reduces transaction costs, and allows more partners worldwide to exchange more information in a shorter period of time. This eases participatory and self-organization processes. Our further arguments will demonstrate its importance for a sustainable development.
- The possibility of *hyperlinked information:* ICT allows faster access to correlated and context information (including judgements/assessments of products and information). This eases the process of more quickly getting a "big picture" of aspects, and enhances the "reflexivity" of action – also an important sustainability element (demonstrated later).

- The possibility of more *structured communication:* ICT can support structured argumentation by using multimedia effects (e.g., visualization of arguments/aspects, and using background information) and reach better decisions in "political" processes (Wesselmann, 2002, p. 174).

ICT and Interconnection of Different Types of Partners

Figure 2 differentiates four types of actors interconnected by ICT: Business, Consumer, Administration and Stakeholder. These are the most important actor groups in the debate about sustainable development. Figure 2 shows that linkages between these groups are supported by ICT (see fields 1-10 in Figure 2).

1. Inner business applications of ICT are dominant in the e-organization debate: "virtual organizations," "electronic markets," or "ICT-based knowledge management" allow more flexible and efficient forms of coordination within and between companies (Field 1 in Figure 2).
2. ICT interconnects business and consumers in a more intense manner: Consumers are better informed during the whole "buying cycle" (i.e., the process of information collecting, decision making, buying and after-sales service of buying/selling a product or service). They get more information about products and can be better cared for in the after-sales period (e.g., by Internet-based technical support platforms). (2)
3. The link between business and administration is strengthened. For example, ICT can provide better and direct access to corporate environmental data for public authorities. On the other hand, ICT allows complex regulation to be more feasible and transparent, especially for small and medium-sized enterprises. (3)
4. A more relevant, ICT-based business link is the one to stakeholders. Firms are linked to many and very different stakeholders. The information channels to reach these stakeholders and their specific information needs were traditionally very time and cost intensive. ICT allows cheap and fast diffusion of specific and disaggregated information as well as the possibility of easy feedback from firm stakeholders. This can give business an early impression of relevant stakeholder issues. (4)
5. Besides business-related interconnection, new links between other actor groups are relevant: With ICT arose a new dimension of inner-consumer connections. The most important examples are evaluation platforms like Epinions (*www.epionions.com*) or Dooyoo (*www.dooyoo.com*) that allow unbiased "from consumers, for consumers" information about products and have a strong impact on consumer decisions. (5)

Figure 2. Partners interconnected by ICT

	Business	Consumer	Administration	Stakeholder
Stakeholder	4 • Stakeholder integration (e.g., environmental reporting, virtual neighborhood councils)	7 • Consumer awareness	9 • Data-access for NGOs (freedom of information) • Access of administrations to NGOdata	10 • NGO networks
Administration	3 • Access to corporate environmental data by administration • Transparency of legislation	6 • Civil participation	8 • Knowledge management in administration	
Consumer	2 • More and better information about products • Product/service-platforms (after- sales service)	5 • Evaluation/ informed buying platforms (e.g., Epinions.com)		
Business	1 • Virtual organizations • Company knowledge management • Electronic markets			
	Business	**Consumer**	**Administration**	**Stakeholder**

6. Administration-consumer links fall into the category of e-government and e-administration, and describe new forms of public participation in administrative and political processes (see Märker et al., 2001). (6)
7. ICT also creates a stronger link between stakeholders and consumers. This is particularly relevant for stakeholders like consumer, environmental or social activist organizations. These groups are able to inform consumers about products in a broader way regarding their environmental and social side effects than is usually done by product producers. (7)
8. Inner-administration linkages are of importance in complex administrative fields like environmental protection. Here, many different authorities must work together. ICT can help make their work more effective and efficient. (8)
9. *ICT-based administration:* NGO links can help both partners make better-informed decisions. Ready access to official environmental data (for example the Toxic Release Inventory (TRI) in the United States) eases the campaign work of environmental organizations. On the other hand, information gathered by NGOs can help public authorities control companies more efficiently (especially in the environmental protection field). (9)
10. ICT-supported NGO/stakeholder networks illustrated their power especially in the globalization debate. The effective work of anti-globalization networks such as "Attac" is explained by their efficient global Internet communication networking. (10)

A glance at these interlinkages shows that ICT can:

- provide more information,
- allow a more efficient coordination of partners,
- give a new dimension to the cooperation of only loosely-coupled partners.

Institutional Approach to Sustainability

ICT affects an institutional or "cultural" (Allenby, 2001) level. This is acknowledged by many authors in the field. But at the same time, difficulties become clear on how to properly measure the sustainability effects of these changes. Allenby states that we "now get to the point where engineering methodologies such as DFE (Design for Environment) are out of their depth, and use of tools such as scenarios becomes a more useful way to identify issues" (of sustainability). He develops seven scenarios for creating an impression of the sustainability effects of cultural changes caused by ICT (Allenby, 2001, p. 33). Cohen (2001, p. 50) defines 10 "steps" for the greening of online practices in e-commerce. All approaches remain on a heuristic level.

It is worthwhile to look for a normative framework helping us to judge the sustainability effects of new organizational designs in a more comprehensive way. For this, it is important to take a social science approach to sustainability:

One main characteristic of modern societies is their "differentiation" or "functional specialization" (Luhmann, 1995): Complex societies undergo a process of inner diversification to cope with their environment and inner complexity. Societal subsystems like the economic, political, legal, media or science system evolve. They are governed by subsystem specific "codes" helping the subsystems to differentiate from their environment and increase their productivity and rationality, but only at the price that the global system becomes more irrational. As a result, subsystem coordination becomes more and more difficult. We live in an "age of side effects" (Beck). The meaningful acting within the subsystem codes (e.g., the maximization of profits in the economic system or the creation of "truth" in the scientific system) creates unwanted side effects outside the subsystem (e.g., ecological problems or societal challenges of genetic research) that can no longer be dealt with.

From this point of view, the question of "sustainability" is not the sum of isolated ecological, social and economic challenges. It is in its heart an institutional crisis of modern societies that are less and less able to cope with the side effects of their highly productive societal subsystems. This is the basic message of an institutional or societal understanding of "sustainable development" (for this argument and the institutional strategies of sustainability see Minsch et al., 1998; for application of this argument in a sustainable information society see Schneidewind, 2000).

Sustainability becomes a "regulative idea" (Kant) like "freedom" or "justice," implying a notion of future societal development that cannot be described in concrete ecological or social standards, but a notion nevertheless helping modern societies undertake development in a desired direction. The analysis of modern societies can help systematize ways of an "institutional sustainability". "Institutional sustainability" is the search for institutional designs that are able to deal with ecological, social and economic side effects of modern societies. It classifies these problems into four categories (Minsch et al., 1998) to get a better understanding of "institutional sustainability":

All four categories are described in more detail in the following paragraphs and are illustrated by examples of "informed and organized sustainability".

Lack of Actors/Partners for Sustainability Strategies in Societal Subsystems: Self Organization/Participation Strategies

Because of its differentiation into societal subsystems, this category has at its disposal very specific roles for fulfilling subsystem goals (e.g., specific economic roles in markets or political roles in the political system). In general there is a lack of roles with an integrative perspective on economic, social and ecological issues. To fulfill the integration tasks of sustainability, new actors and coalitions

Figure 3. Problems of societal organization in modern societies and institutional coping strategies (Minsch et al., 1998)

Problem	Coping Strategy
Lack of actors/partners for sustainability strategies within societal subsystems	**Self-Organization/Participation**
Lack of knowledge and values for a sustainability change	**Reflexivity**
Lack of resources and incentives to overcome sustainability conflicts	**Power-Balance/Conflict Resolution**
Lack of technical or social options to solve sustainability problems	**Innovation**

must arise. Economic theory of political processes shows that the organization of such integrated interests can be very difficult. Strategies of self-organization and participation help strengthen the organization of such interests. Important examples of self-organization strategies are voluntary agreements of industries or local agenda processes on a regional level. They support an institutionalized integration of sustainability issues in economic and political processes.

Box 1 gives an ICT-based example of a self-organization strategy:

Box 1: Eco-e-commerce: Self-organization in the marketing of ecological food
The self-organization potential offered by ICT can be well illustrated by the marketing of ecological food. Eco-food still has problems establishing itself in traditional food distribution channels. Buying ecological products is often related to enormous transaction costs (for the identification and transport of appropriate products). The Internet offers a way to reduce these costs in a relevant manner. Ecological food producers recognized the Internet's potential to reorganize their product marketing (for successful examples see: Nachtmann/Kolibius/Schneidewind, 1999).

Lack of Knowledge and Values for a Sustainability Change: Reflexivity Strategies

Between the different societal subsystems (e.g., the political, economical, legal, and science system) exist communication barriers. In any of these systems, knowledge is produced and processed in a very selective way. Economic, social or ecological side effects occurring in one of the other systems are hardly recognized. A way to cope with this problem is to enhance the capacities in any societal subsystem to better perceive economical, social and ecological side effects of action in the own subsystem. This capacity can be described as *reflexivity* (Böhret, 1990). Reflexivity has the function of enhancing the knowledge about side effects through the actions of different actor groups such as managers, politicians, environmentalists and journalists. Reflexivity promotes a long-term perspective in political and economic processes. Concrete ways to put reflexivity strategies into practice are reporting systems (e.g., sustainability reports of companies or ministries) or the introduction of specific reflexivity councils (e.g., sustainability councils for national or regional governments). One example for an ICT-based reflexivity strategy is given in Box 2.

Box 2: Internet-based communication of sustainability by companies: An example for a reflexivity strategy in the information society

Today's multinational corporations (MNC) cause many ecological and social side effects. The reporting strategies of these MNCs have developed from pure PR brochures to a differentiated, focus group-oriented communication. The Internet plays an important role in this change of communication. It gives different stakeholders (employees, social and environmental organizations, rating agencies) ways to acquire information about the ecological, social and economic performance of a company on the exact aggregation level needed by the stakeholder. This enormously enhances the transparency of the ecological and social side effects of corporate activity and is an active contribution to reflexivity. The power of an Internet-based provision of environmental information about companies is illustrated by the American Toxic Release Inventory (TRI), which provides information of the most important pollutants issued by American companies. These data are regularly used by environmental groups to publicize dangerous corporate practices and create public pressure for corporate environmental improvement.

Lack of Resources and Incentives to Overcome Sustainability Conflicts: Power Balancing/Conflict Resolution Strategies

Sustainability problems are not only the result of coordination (self-organization) and information (reflexivity) deficits. They are also due to interest conflicts. Within the social subsystems, specific interests of interest groups arise. Societal institutions define the potential for enforcing the interests of different groups. In many fields today, it is easier to enforce economic rather than social or ecological interests. For further sustainability, a rebalancing of power and resources in the game of interest enforcement is required. Important resources in this process are expertise, financial resources and legal enforcement methods (e.g., the right of legal action for environmentalist organizations to protect the environment). Strategies of power balancing and conflict resolution aim in this direction.

Examples are advocacy institutions (e.g., a government sustainability council with veto rights), participation and decision rights for NGOs (Non-Governmental Organizations) in political processes or measures to strengthen the resource base of NGOs (i.e., better access to information or financial resources).

Box 3 illustrates how ICT can strengthen the participation power of civil society:

Box 3: Civil participation and the Internet: A new form of power balancing and conflict resolution?
With the change from representative democratic to direct and participatory forms of politics, the Internet is taking on a new importance for NGOs in the organization of countervailing power in political processes. The Internet makes social and ecological offences (e.g., those of multinationals in third world countries) globally oriented and (at times) visible. NGOs like the Clean Clothes Campaign (an international NGO fighting for social minimum standards in textile production) use these new opportunities to create public and political pressure on large textile producers and retailers whose production is based in third world countries having poor social and employment standards. Clean Clothes Campaign's power lies in its global, Internet-linked network of local activists all over the world who report abuses in textile production (*www.cleanclothes.org*).
For conflict resolution, Internet-based mediation platforms are gaining importance. They allow participation processes to be moderated via the Internet (for an example see the platform Zeno II, developed by the Fraunhofer Institute Autonomous Intelligent Systems (Märker et al., 2001)).

Lack of Technical or Social Options to Solve Sustainability Problems: Innovation Strategies

Sustainability strategies need technical and organizational alternatives of action. Such innovations must link different societal subsystems, because very often innovations in one subsystem (e.g., a technical innovation in the science system such as solar power) fail due to incompatible incentives in the economic system. For the success of such a technical innovation, for example a political innovation such as an ecological tax reform is needed. Sustainable innovation strategies link the different social subsystems.

Box 4: Internet-based innovation strategies in ecological product development

The Internet makes it possible for the customer and stakeholder to get involved in product development processes at an earlier stage and more easily. Ecological and social problems with future products as well as interesting ecological or social product alternatives can also be more easily identified. The first successful business-to-business-platforms like *www.texweb.de* illustrate the potential of such an approach. It is quite interesting to enlarge this approach to the use phase of products. The use of products very often causes the most severe ecological effects (e.g., the fuel consumption of cars or the power consumption of computers). Product users are experts in product use patterns. The creation of Web-based user communities can make this knowledge accessible to the manufacturer of the product and can introduce new ideas for product development.

Sustainable Designs of E-Organization

What can we learn from this procedural understanding of sustainability? It helps us judge organizational designs by their ability to cope with sustainability requirements:

> *Sustainable e-organizations are forms of Information and Communication Technology- (ICT) supported organizational designs that enhance the reflexivity, participation, power balance or conflict resolution and integrated innovation processes in modern societies.*

General Criteria for Sustainable E-Organizations

This definition allows us to develop a list for a sustainability check of e-organizations. Such a list helps define guidelines for the design of sustainable e-organizations. Figure 3 defines such criteria.

Figure 4: Criteria list for sustainable e-organizations

Dimension	Criteria for a Sustainable E-Organization
Reflexivity	• Is a discussion on ecological, social and economic side effects of the e-organization occurring? • Do ecological or social reporting mechanisms exist? • Do institutionalized evaluation bodies (e.g., a sustainability council) exist?
Participation/ Self-Organization	• Does the e-organization have a bottom-up structure (easy ways of participation for every member)? • Does the e-organization facilitate an easy integration of new partners?
Conflict Resolution	• Does the e-organization deal with ecological and social stakes in a fair manner? • Does the e-organization allow a powerful integration of critical points of view? • Does the e-organization have open discussion forums?
Innovation	• Is the organization a producer of new ideas? • Do innovations in organizational forms of the e-organization (continuous implementation of new organizational designs) exist?

E-Organization Sustainability Profiles—Three Examples

To illustrate how a sustainability check can work, we shall give an example of three different types of e-organizations. These examples have the function of illustrating a possible application of the criteria listed above. The applied "e-organization sustainability profiles" have a communication function of discussing the e-organization potential among organizers, members and stakeholders of an e-organization. Procedural dimensions such as "reflexivity" or "conflict resolution" cannot be operationalized on an independent 1 to 100 scale. But in specific contexts, it is nevertheless possible to define criteria for "more" or "less" of this dimension between participants. This potential shall be illustrated by the following three examples:

We have chosen three different types of e-organizations:

- E-Bay (*www.ebay.com*), the Internet auction house, one of the world's largest and most successful marketplaces in the consumer realm,
- Dooyoo (*www.dooyoo.com*) as a consumer-to-consumer product evaluation platform where user and buyers of products can evaluate any kind of product from toothpaste to university professors, and
- The Clean Clothes Campaign (www.cleanclothes.org) as an NGO network fighting for better social working conditions in the global textile chain.

The application of the e-organization sustainability profiles to the three cases does not deliver a comprehensive description of the three platforms. Instead, it focuses on the aspects relevant to the sustainability assessment.

Figure 5. e-Organization sustainability check for the E-Bay market place

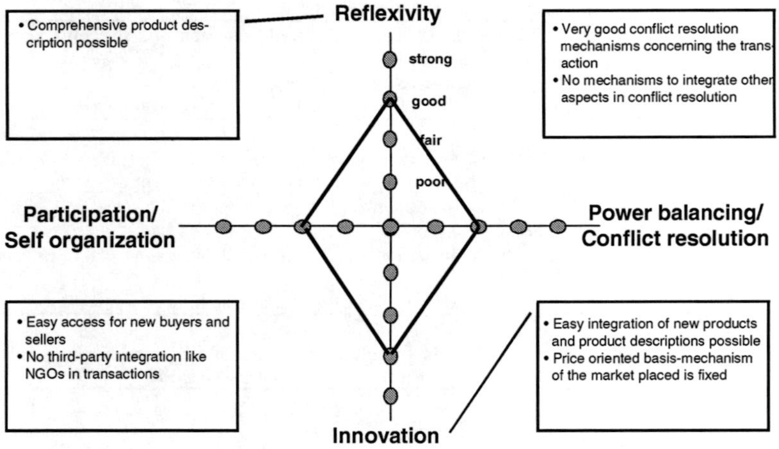

E-Bay

E-Bay (*www.ebay.com*) is basically a huge consumer-to-consumer marketplace where people can offer all kinds of new and used articles to sell through an auctioning process. Several hundred million transactions in thousands of product categories are handled on this platform every year. It is one of the few early New Economy business models that (still today) actually produces profits for its organizers.

Is E-Bay a sustainable e-organization? Figure 5 illustrates this question by applying the four dimensions of a procedural sustainability to E-Bay; that is, using a qualitative four-section scale which describes the performance in each of the four dimensions as "poor," "fair," "good" or "strong." The authors' subjective judgments are only validated by plausible arguments listed in the text boxes next to the four dimensions; the main function of this application is an illustrative one (see the argument above).

What does Figure 5 tell us about E-Bay? E-Bay implements a good standard of *reflexivity* because it offers a lot of information of any desired kind about the offered product in written, hyperlinked or picture form to interested buyers. Furthermore, a direct e-mail contact to the seller is offered to learn more about the product. But the information is only as good as the seller's own information. Here, the only fair *participatory* potential of the platform becomes relevant: In spite of the easy integration of new buyers and sellers, it hardly possible for third parties like NGOs to be integrated in the platform, for example as information suppliers for social and ecological aspects of offered products or possible means of product transportation. The same exclusivity can be perceived in the case of *power balancing and conflict resolution* mechanisms: These are very effective for buyers and sellers on the platform. They can judge the transaction performance of other platform members in very different ways and react according to received evaluations. But a real integration of social and ecological interests/parties in the performed transactions is not possible. The *innovative potential* of the platform is again of high quality. The platform offers the possibility of integrating continuously new products and comprehensive product descriptions. Therefore, it would be no problem to sell and buy ecological and social sound products on the platform in much greater quantities than is done today. Nevertheless, the auctioning mechanism behind the platform stays price-driven. The integration of additional criteria would affect the basic design of the platform and is not realistic.

Dooyoo

Dooyoo (www.dooyoo.com) is the European adaptation of a business model first implemented in the US (www.epinion.com). It is a huge evaluation platform and gives its members ways to evaluate any kind of product (from toothpaste to university professors; the products to be judged are organized into hundreds of product categories) by writing test and experience reports. Consumers help other consumers make better informed buying decisions through these evaluations.

Based upon its basic idea, Dooyoo is a highly *reflexive* e-organization. It helps its users learn more about products, their attributes, as well as wanted and unwanted side effects. The integration of ecological and social qualities of the products can be easily integrated into the product judgements - even if this is not done for many products today. Dooyoo also performs well as regards the *participation and self-organization* dimension. The integration of new and members of any kind is executed without problems. Also, NGO (such as environmental organizations) can access Dooyoo and for example contribute ecological product assessments of various products. The *power balancing and conflict resolution* mechanisms fall behind the two other categories. The platform only gives an overview of the different evaluations contributed by various members. No real conflict resolution or open discussion mechanism about the judgments is foreseen. Members only have the possibility of addressing other members on a bilateral basis to comment on evaluations provided by another member. The *innovative* effect of the platform is quite good, because product producers get interesting information for their product development processes as a result of the evaluations. Although new products are not integrated in Dooyoo by the members themselves, they can nevertheless initiate such integration through the community provider.

Figure 6. e-Organization sustainability check for the Dooyoo evaluation platform

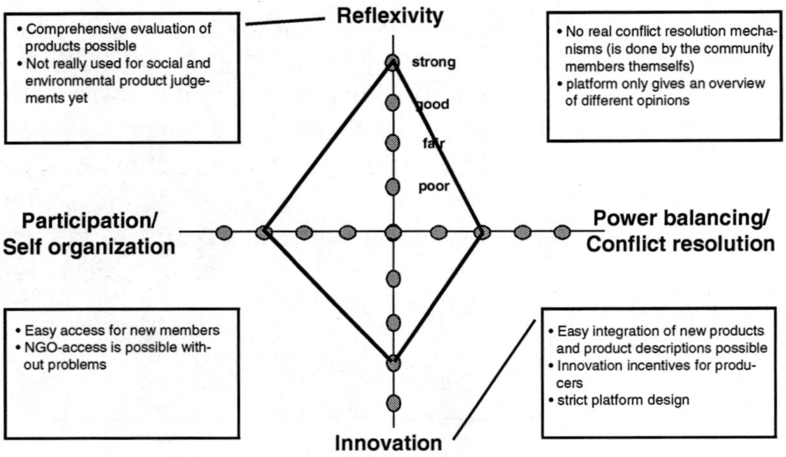

Clean Clothes

The Clean Clothes Campaign (CCC) has already been described in Box 3. It differs in many aspects from the other two platforms, E-Bay and Dooyoo. Behind www.cleanclothes.org is a real, globally active NGO that uses cleanclothes.org for better coordination of its organization and a greater expansion of its activities.

Cleanclothes.org gives an overview about the partners, goals, activities and program of the Clean Clothes Campaign. An important part is the company-oriented section where social offenses of multinational textile producers and retailers such as Levi's, Adidas and Nike are presented and discussed.

Cleanclothes.org is an e-organization platform in the heart of the sustainability debate. Therefore, it has a high *reflexivity* potential because it makes the social side effects of global textile production transparent. Also, the *self-organization* potential is high, as the platform is an important contribution to the self-organization of the Clean Clothes Campaign. Nevertheless, the integration of new partners on the platform could be improved. In the field of *power balancing and conflict resolution* the platform is an important contribution towards strengthening the countervailing power of NGOs in global textile production, even if the platform itself offers no conflict resolution mechanisms. The *innovative* potential of the platform is also high: The platform creates important pressure on textile producers to improve the social standards of their production.

Figure 7. e-Organization sustainability check for the Cleanclothes.org platform (Clean Clothes Campaign)

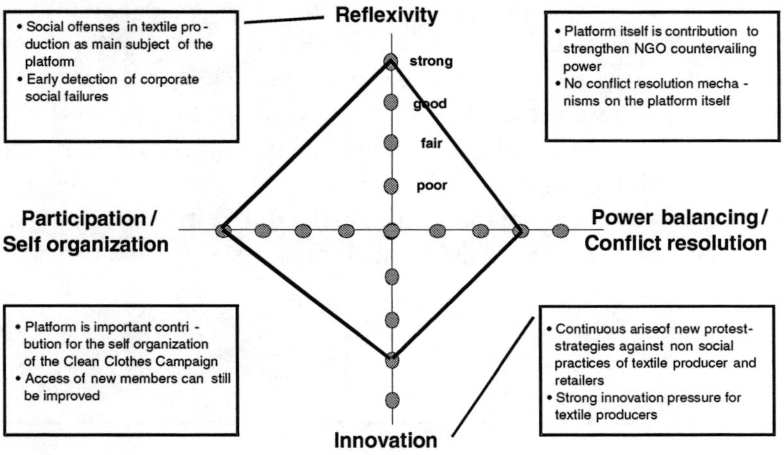

On the platform itself, new protest strategies regularly arise and create an atmosphere of institutional innovation.

Conclusions and Research Challenges

Using the theoretical argumentation and the three concrete examples, several hypotheses for an informed institutional sustainability conclude the article:

- New forms of e-organizations can be (if need be) a contribution to a sustainable information society
- Different forms of e-organization support different aspects of procedural sustainability
- Sustainable e-organizations ideally incorporate all four dimensions of procedural sustainability: They support reflexivity, participation, self-organization, conflict resolution and innovation. They try to continuously improve their performance in all of the four dimensions.
- The rise of such sustainable e-organizations is an ongoing process; only a few examples currently exist. Further development must be actively promoted.

What do these hypotheses mean for further research? It is interesting to apply the presented e-organization sustainability profiles to a broader set of e-organizations in order to see whether the profile is an adequate means of communicating the idea of procedural sustainability in the context of these e-organizations. Furthermore, appropriate ways for a continuous sustainability improvement in e-organizations must be developed. The examples of E-Bay and Dooyoo show that these kinds of platforms are designed for specific purposes and are used successfully. In spite of their interesting organizational sustainability potential (e.g., the integration of social and ecological evaluations in the Dooyoo platform) this potential has yet to be fully realized. We still must learn how such processes of "e-organizational change" in light of sustainability can be initiated.

References

Allenby, B. (2001). Culture, sustainability, and information infrastructure: A case study in earth systems engineering and management. In L. Hilty & P.W. Gilgen (Eds.), *Sustainability in the information society* (pp. 27-40). 15th International Symposium Informatics for Environmental Protection, Zurich 2001, Part 1: Impacts and Applications. Marburg: Metropolis.

Böhret, C. (1990). *Folgen – Nachweltschutz. Entwurf für eine Aktive Politik Gegen Schleichende Katastrophen.* Opladen, Germany: Westdeutscher Verlag.

Cohen, N. (2001). The environmental impacts of e-commerce. In L. Hilty & P.W. Gilgen (Eds.), *Sustainability in the information society* (pp. 41-52). The 15th International Symposium Informatics for Environmental Protection, Zurich 2001, Part 1: Impacts and Applications. Marburg: Metropolis.

Fichter, K. (2001). *Sustainable Business Strategies in the Internet Economy.* In: L. Hilty & P.W. Gilgen, (Eds.), *Sustainability in the Information Society*. The 15th International Symposium Informatics for Environmental Protection, Zurich 2001, Part 1: Impacts and Applications. Marburg: Metropolis, 109-118.

Luhmann, N. (1995). *Social systems.* Stanford: Stanford University Press.

Märker, O., Poppenborg, A., Trénel, M., & Voss, A. (2001). *Online mediation as a tool of public knowledge management for shaping a sustainable information society.* In L. Hilty & P.W. Gilgen (Eds.), *Sustainability in the information society* (pp. 167-172). The 15th International Symposium Informatics for Environmental Protection, Zurich 2001, Part 1: Impacts and Applications. Marburg: Metropolis.

Minsch, J., Feindt, P.H., Meister, H.-P., Schneidewind, U., & Schulz, T. (1998). *Institutionelle Reformen für Eine Politik der Nachhaltigkeit.* Berlin: Springer.

Nachtmann, M., Kolibius, M., & Schneidewind, U. (1999). Electronic commerce in environmental markets: Potentials and risks in biofood value chains. *Role and potential of IT, intranet and IT for advisory services* (vol. 4). Bonn: BMBF.

Schneidewind, U. (2000). Nachhaltige Informationsgesellschaft – Eine Institutionelle Annäherung. In U. Schneidewind, A. Truscheit, & G. Steingräber (Eds.), *Nachhaltige Informationsgesellschaft. Analyse und Gestaltungsempfehlungen aus Management- und Institutioneller Sicht* (pp. 15-35). Marburg: Metropolis.

Schneidewind, U., Müller, M., & Hübscher, M. (2002). Institutionelle Dimensionen Einer Nachhaltigen Informationsgesellschaft. In BMBF (Ed.), *Sozial-ökologische forschung* (pp. 239-260). München: GSF.

Wesselmann, C. (2002). *Internet und Partizipation in Kommunen. Analyse und Kriterien der Integration von Online-kommunikationsformen.* Wiesbaden: DUV.

Chapter XII

Corporate Sustainability Reporting: A Case for the Internet

Ralf Isenmann, University of Kaiserslautern, Germany

Abstract

Corporate environmental reporting using the Internet – especially the WWW – is a rapidly emerging and increasingly popular method. Today, online environmental reporting has become part of business practices and daily affairs for a number of companies, and thus many of the environmental communication vehicles provided for companies' target groups and other stakeholders (users) are available on the WWW: reports, brochures, leaflets, newsletters, press releases, slides, presentations, audio sequences, video clips and so forth are accessible via download and/or online, prepared for being pulled or automatically disseminated via e-mail or other current push technologies. Despite the considerable progress companies have made in recent years, however, it is not yet clear just how environmental reporting will advance to the next stage. In particular, the role of the Internet as an emerging computer-based medium and its unique capabilities in form and content need to be understood better. This chapter describes how to develop from early environmental reporting stages towards the more advanced sustainability reporting, while exploiting the Internet's specific capabilities properly. This path is illustrated as a progression in environmental reporting along three dimensions: integration of financial and social issues into environmental reporting, provision of reporting instruments on various media and fine tuning communication vehicles according to users' needs and preferences. These trends in terms of a more balanced reporting approach, cross media availability and customization seem to be converging to push the field towards sustainability reporting based on the Internet as a backbone for companies' underlying ICT infrastructure. Without support from ICT, progress in the field toward sustainability reporting is seen as quite difficult, as moving away from orthodox environmental reporting is a complex task. Hence, a framework on how to use the Internet and its associated technologies is proposed, including four conceptual components: stakeholder analysis, information requirement analysis, XML-based document engineering and ICT architecture of an Internet-based reporting system. When employing such an Internet-based approach, it is argued here, the company will be in a position to carry out its tasks of information management well, using its human and organizational resources more efficiently, and communicating on environmental and sustainability issues in a meaningful way; that is, facilitating stakeholder dialogue, interactivity, feedback possibilities and tailor-made reports that respond precisely to the requirements of certain reporting standards and guidelines, or exactly to the information needs of the target groups.

Introduction

Corporate environmental reporting using Internet technologies and Internet services – in particular the WWW – is a rapidly emerging and increasingly popular method. The rationale as to why more and more companies are making use of the Internet can be seen in its unique capabilities in form and content and other technical benefits, for example the opportunity to address multiple issues in flexible depth, ease of access, great potential to reach a wider audience or disseminate target group tailored vehicles to specific stakeholder groups, many facilities to effect two-way and even one-to-one communication, ease of updating, and – no less importantly – great potential for producing a number of customized, target group tailored, individualized or even personalized communication vehicles in an effective and cost-saving manner (cf. Isenmann & Lenz, 2001, 2002).

Compared with traditional methods on print media, Internet-based environmental reporting embraces a broader range of beneficial characteristics, for example combining text, still images and moving ones, sound, feedback, interaction, dialogue, integration of different contents and so forth. Because of its added value creating nature, the Internet is seen as an "indispensable tool" (Jones & Walton, 1999, p. 425; SustainAbility & UNEP 1999, pp. 20-21) for any forward-looking approach of corporate environmental reporting. At present, the Internet is already being used by some reporting companies and target groups as the pivotal platform to provide or to access, as the case may be, information on environmental performance and other related issues.

According to a recent article on corporate environmental reporting (Marshall & Brown, 2003), nowadays it is merely a question of *how* to report on environmental issues, and no longer a question of whether to report at all. Marshall and Brown argue that nowadays environmental reporting is becoming part of companies' daily affairs, even entering the business mainstream. Regardless of nationality or other differences in country results, this is not only true for environmental pioneers and sector leaders, but also for global players, multinationals and an increasing number of medium-sized companies whose activities either result directly in high environmental impacts or at least are suspected of causing them. Examples abound in the pharmaceuticals, chemicals, mining, transport, electronics and automotive sectors (Federal Environmental Agency, 2002; Kolk, Walhain & van de Wateringen, 2001, pp. 20-26; KPMG, 1999, 2002; Krut & Moretz, 2000, p. 85).

Within these industrial sectors, there is further empirical evidence that environmental reporting today has become of competitive relevance (Fichter, 1998) and strategic importance (Larsen, 2000). Companies realized that the "honeymoon period" (DTTI, IISD and SustainAbility 1993, p. 9) in which environmental reports received media and public attention just for existing rather than for what was disclosed in them is over. Today, the provision of "green glossy brochures" does not seem to be sufficient any longer; a substantial amount of information and quality in communication are required. Further, environmental reporting is only successful if the underlying management systems are appropriate and the associated processes are effective and operational. For example, goals have to be set, responsibilities have to be assigned to reach the goals, and outcomes must be assessed and used as the basis for forthcoming efforts.

Companies that have learned their lessons are clearly benefiting from environmental reports[1] used as "green management tools" (Kolk, 1999). This value added can be witnessed in decision making with internal and external value (Ernst, Young et al., 1999), especially in the fields of cost reduction (Merrick & Crookshanks, 2001), resource controlling, accounting, material and waste management (Steven, Schwarz & Letmathe, 1997), reputation (Berkeley, 2000) and compliance (ACCA, 2003). Together, Marshall and Brown's introductory note may answer, at least to a certain extent, one of the questions posed early in the field: "Will corporate environmental performance reporting be a 'passing fashion' such as social reporting some years ago, or will it increasingly enter the business mainstream?" (UNEP & Sustainability, 1994, p. 66).

Internet: Emerging Medium for Environmental Reporting

The question of how companies are reporting involves several aspects of ICT:

- Companies need to ponder the question of which media to use for managing environmental reporting, particularly along the reporting workflow and its underlying core processes, such as preparation, administration, distribution and presentation.
- Should these be predominantly print media or computer-based media such as Internet[2] and CD-ROM?
- Should reports available on the WWW be just duplicates of printed documents or should these WWW reports provide added value, for example through disclosing information with a higher level of quantity or detail?
- Via which channels should reports be distributed, and on what devices should these be available?
- Does the Internet and its associated technologies as the emerging eXtensible Markup Language (XML)[3] have any unique design and content capabilities that facilitate tailoring of reports according to different information needs and certain guidelines, and to reach the target groups addressed?
- How can reporters communicate environmental issues appropriately at present and in the near future?
- How could groups or individuals involved in or affected by environmental reporting truly benefit from Internet use, creating added value both internally for reporting companies and externally for target groups seen as the primary users?
- Finally, what is the role of ICT applications when moving away from outdated premature stages of providing simply "green glossy brochures" on print media towards a forward-looking approach, perhaps in the sense of "cybernetic reporting" (Wheeler & Elkington, 2001, p. 6)?

Companies should consider aspects of ICT carefully because they influence reporting capabilities. Furthermore, ICT aspects also determine what facilities can be used to design reporting instruments and other communication vehicles in form and content. No less importantly, they are to a large extent responsible both for the potential benefits and the total costs of corporate environmental reporting.

The cutting-edge approach in the rapidly developing field of environmental reporting seems to be Internet-based sustainability reporting (Isenmann, Lenz & Müller-Merbach, 2002; Line, Hawley & Krut, 2002; Scott & Jackson, 2002; Shephard, Abkowitz & Cohen, 2001; Weil & Winter-Watson, 2002). Recent studies suggest that the field is now entering a new phase of reporting, characterized by the emergence of sustainability reports and a growing trend of using the Internet. For example, in "The 2001 Benchmark Survey of the State of Global Environmental and Social Reporting" carried out by the CSR network (Line, Hawley & Krut, 2002, p. 71), Internet-based reporting and a more balanced reporting approach are seen as the top reporting priorities. Such a comprehensive and fully ICT-based reporting approach offers a variety of added-value creating features compared with early environmental reporting stages. For example, an Internet-based sustainability reporting system provides a set of:

- Important contents (environmental, financial, social issues and mutual interrelations) that comprise the core themes for corporate sustainability (Clausen et al., 2001; DTTI, IISD & SustainAbility, 1993; Morhardt, 2002; UNEP & Sustainability, 1994).
- Different media (print media, Internet, CD-ROM, etc.).
- Corresponding distribution principles (push, pull), and various presentation styles (media-specific, target group tailored).
- In technological terms, sustainability reporting is fully supported by an underlying ICT infrastructure that has its basis in using the Internet and employing XML.

In the following, an outline of how to develop from early environmental reporting towards sustainability reporting is given, while fully exploiting the benefits of an underlying ICT architecture based on using the Internet and employing XML. Without the direct link to ICT, progressing toward sustainability reporting is seen as quite difficult. According to this goal and scope this chapter is structured in four parts:

- First, major developments striving for sustainability and pushing companies to use the Internet are described. Integrated reporting, cross media availability and customized reports are three crucially important trends in the field.
- Based on these key trends, the unique capabilities of using the Internet and employing XML are arranged in a generic classification that is useful for

decision-making in terms of corporate reporting. Then, the array of potential benefits is grouped in a three-step strategy, highlighting the Internet-specific opportunities when moving away from orthodox reporting through an incremental approach towards sustainability reporting.

- Following this incremental approach of classification, a framework for advanced environmental and sustainability reporting based on the Internet is outlined in a more detailed fashion. Conceptually, the framework consists of four elements, discussed along a perspective moving from the outside to the inside: stakeholder analysis, analysis of stakeholder information requirements, XML-based document engineering and ICT architecture. Together, these four conceptual elements demonstrate Internet use for advanced reporting stages in a broader sense.
- In the concluding part Internet-specific opportunities and benefits of XML are discussed that present themselves when companies set out to improve their current reporting practices, for example when they decide to relaunch their Web sites and establish an Internet portal on environmental or sustainability matters (cf. Moore, 2003), when they ponder re-engineering the reporting workflow, when they refine reports that truly address stakeholder needs in content and form or exactly meeting requirements proposed by emerging guidelines, or when they just comply with technological trends and other tendencies users may expect in the near future.

From a research perspective, a more balanced approach leading to sustainability reporting based on the Internet as a backbone for companies' underlying ICT infrastructure is considered a forward-looking effort. As such, it may contribute to more conceptual clarity uncovering unique capabilities associated with the Internet, especially when progressing in the field of environmental and sustainability reporting. From a practitioner's point of view, helpful guidance is provided on how to employ the Internet productively and to make use of its associated technologies such as XML for applications in corporate reporting.

A more comprehensive and balanced approach of corporate reporting is likely to draw our attention immediately; it is intuitively appealing because it appears to spring from a company's wish for a broader presentation of its business, and a willingness to disclose its performance in a variety of dimensions. Additionally, the approach may also be rooted in target groups' demand for a new type of reporting which embraces financial, environmental and social issues as integral parts of a total, which discloses a company's integrative performance and perhaps overcomes traditional stand-alone reporting methods.

On the one hand, some may think that moving towards Internet-based sustainability reporting is an ambitious task, but one worth pursuing. On the other hand, others are skeptical as to whether such a reporting approach could be meaningful at all, for example because of its voluntary status, its definitional vagueness, its complexity and the growing number of competing frameworks, guidelines and scoring systems proposed (cf. Morhardt, 2002, pp. 161-169), the lack of generally accepted standards etc. (cf. Adams, Houldin & Slomp, 1999, p. 317; FEE 2002, pp. 13-14; Lange, von Ahsen & Daldrup, 2001, pp. 8-9).

The skeptical comments are well founded indeed. They reflect a similar issue with a skeptical note that marked the birth of environmental reporting: Will (Internet-based) sustainability reporting be just hype, or will it become good business practice? In response to the challenge raised by some critics against the concept of (Internet-based) sustainability reporting, there is an array of arguments that integrated reporting supported by the Internet is in fact acknowledged as a meaningful approach. Perhaps, when companies are asked why they are expanding the scope of reporting, they will answer that it works. Also, a number of target groups may say that they could reap benefits. Finally, despite some evidence of a deficient status quo (e.g., Gröner, 2000; Klaffke & Krick, 2003), current practice may itself not be an argument against a concept of (Internet-based) sustainability reporting.

Regardless of the perspective from which Internet-based sustainability reporting ultimately is seen, it can be described as a development path towards a concept of balanced reporting, technically based on the Internet and providing fine tuned reports on a variety of media[4]. As such, it could be seen as an improvement because it will create added value for reporting companies and target groups addressed.

Key Trends Pushing Companies Toward Sustainability Reporting Based on the Internet

Environmental reporting is a multifaceted, rapidly developing field, influencing a company's communication strategy and image profile as well as its organization, staff and particularly its ICT capabilities. Despite certain difficulties companies are struggling with at present, there are three crucial trends facing companies today and in the near future[5]:

- integration of financial and social issues into environmental reports,
- provision of reports on various media, and
- fine tuning reports according to users' needs and preferences.

Together, these key trends are setting the scene for any forward-looking approach in the field and thus they are taken as drivers to stimulate companies' efforts to improve their practices and push them towards sustainability reporting while using the Internet.

Trend 1: From Freestanding Environmental Reports Toward Integrated Reporting

At the early environmental reporting stages – in the late 1980s and early 1990s – environmental reports are initially thought of as the primary vehicles or core instruments for environmental communication, addressing a wide range of target groups, produced in many cases as single documents and issued for a certain period of time[6]. Companies used these documents for disclosing their environmental performance, often including the following topics: top management statement, management policy and system as well as input-output-inventory of environmental impacts of production processes and products (cf. Lober, 1997, p. 15; UNEP & SustainAbility, 1994, p. 11).

As the field matured, however, it then became apparent that a narrow perspective exclusively focused on communicating environmental performance ignores at its peril important interrelations with financial indicators and social aspects. In order to integrate these issues crucial for sustainability, many companies are in the process of broadening their communication strategy and thus the scope of reports' contents. This is still an ongoing process of gradual integration. For a number of companies expanding the scope of reporting it is a rather challenging task, requiring resources and expertise in the pursuit of a high quality standard.

For that reason, GRI (2002) proposed an incremental approach, illustrated by means of four simple models (Figure 1). These four models are useful for demonstrating the variety of communication strategies, from a stand-alone environmentally focused strategy (and thus producing an environmental report on its own) towards corporate reporting according to the triple bottom line.

The trend for expanding the scope of reporting has a number of reasons and is thus promoted by several drivers (cf. Kaptein & Wempe, 1999, pp. 42-49; Morhardt, 2002, pp. 3-26). The concept of sustainability is increasingly being recognized as a vital challenge and is being applied to the business of companies entering the 21st century:

- Many employees are environmentally and socially conscious and prefer working for a company that "feels" the way they do and "acts" accordingly. Integrated reporting helps to increase employees' job satisfaction and loyalty because well informed employees are less likely to change companies.

Figure 1. Communication strategies and corresponding reporting models according to GRI (2002, 73-75)

Communication continuum	Reporting model	Description and characteristics
Stand-alone and environmentally focused	"Environmental report"	Typical of a company just with experience in environmental reporting
↓	"Fragmented report"	Typical of a company providing the most data on environmental performance and the least on financial issues
	"Limited three-dimensional report"	Typical of a company that has just begun reporting and thus has embraced one or a few sustainability integration themes
Fully integrated and balanced	"Full adoption"	Full data gathering, triple bottom line reporting in accordance with GRI guidelines

- Further, there is a growing sensitivity in the public for the concept of sustainability taken as a whole. This increasing awareness closely linked with the demand for corporate transparency and credibility have compelled many companies to think hard about their "license to operate".
- A number of critical customers tend to discriminate against companies when the commitment expected for environmental and social responsibility is missing. Thus, reporting on such matters is at least a reasonable defensive action companies can take against being stigmatized as insensitive.
- Moreover, financial analysts, bankers and insurance agencies all want assurance that companies are doing their business well. For example, Dow Jones Sustainability Asset Management, Innovest and the Investor Responsibility Research Center are three of the major influential actors within the financial community that take companies' environmental and social performance explicitly into account, not just business indicators in monetary terms as this is usually done.
- Directly related to the above, institutional investors such as pension funds and ethically motivated organizations are increasingly expecting that companies disclose their environmental and social responsibility. Recently, Morley Fund Management (2001, p. 11) – one of UK's largest insurance and pension fund managers – has been urging large companies listed on the London stock exchange to publish environmental reports.
- In response to the growing demand, several companies, particularly in the food, beverage, communication, media and finance sectors think it cannot hurt to have a good sustainability reputation (cf. KPMG, 2002, p. 10) and

thus they provide additional information, for example on the protection of the biosphere, greenhouse gas emissions and ozone depleting gases, biodiversity and reduction of environmental health and safety risks to employees and communities.

- Leading edge companies, global players, multinationals and a growing number of sensitive middle-sized companies may need integrated reports nowadays. Because their range of influence extends across borders, their responsibilities also extend beyond basic compliance with national law and regulations and hence they are going to define their responsibilities on a global scale, often according to the triple bottom line approach.
- A number of governmental initiatives and other institutional programmes elevate sustainability reporting (cf. KPMG 2002, pp. 31-32; Morhardt, 2002, pp. 27-38), for example: the European Commission with its "green paper," promoting a European framework for corporate social responsibility (COM, 2001) and its communication concerning the business contribution to sustainable development (COM, 2002), the recommendations for communicating corporate social responsibility of CSR Europe (2000) as well as the framework and guidance on sustainable development reporting, recently proposed by the World Business Council for Sustainable Development (WBCSD, 2003).
- Probably the most forceful project is GRI, a non-governmental international organization that was launched in 1997 as a joint initiative of the Coalition for Environmentally Responsible Economics (CERES) and the United Nations Environment Programme (UNEP). The goal of GRI is to enhance the quality, rigor and utility of sustainability reporting, particularly by developing globally applicable guidelines. Despite its voluntary nature (GRI, 2002), GRI has a truly catalyzing role for stimulating the inclusion of social and financial performance in environmental reports and vice versa, perhaps finally converting them into sustainability reports. As Morhardt (2002, p. 32) has argued, "its guideline will become the *de facto* standard for sustainability reporting worldwide" and thus companies "almost cannot avoid meeting the GRI standard in any case" (Morhardt, 2002, p. 38).
- Taken as a whole, companies' movement towards integrated reporting is often not driven by altruism alone, but also by self-interest. Some are going to create a new type of *competitive advantage* and think of integrated reporting as a current way to differentiate themselves, enhancing their success in the marketplace (cf. Andrews, 2002, pp. 10-11; Clausen et al., 2001). Yet others are disappointed when their polished freestanding environmental reports receive little response today. One reason may be the phenomenon that reports are often poorly targeted to the needs target groups actually have (cf. Lober, 1997, p. 16). Another reason could be the

"plateau effect" (Wheeler & Elkington, 2001, p. 5), that is, the fact that single environmental reports will probably receive much less media attention and public perception than at the early stages because they have to a certain extent become business as usual. Hence, companies are thinking about appropriate ways to move from "additive reporting," frequently with limited success, towards integrated reporting, hopefully reaching a greater audience.

Summing up, we see that the early stages of environmental reporting have been focused primarily on companies' environmental issues. Now that more and more companies have committed to sustainability, the future focus will become more comprehensive, that is, gradually being supplemented with financial and social issues. This trend is increasingly referred to as sustainability reporting, and links environmental issues closely with financial and social ones. Sometimes, this integration is seen in terms of "making values count" (ACCA, 1998), "linking values with value" (KPMG, 2000) or just understood as a matter of combining shareholder value, eco-efficiency and corporate citizenship. In terms of corporate sustainability all efforts mentioned above recognize the recent rapid increase of interest in sustainability matters, and are also in response to demand from some of the companies' target groups. This will mean a need to move from freestanding environmental reports towards a more balanced approach, including environmental performance as well as financial and social aspects, and therefore a challenge.

Trend 2: From Reports Solely on Print Media Toward Cross Media Reporting

In the early years most companies prepared environmental reports in the form of documents solely available on print media (cf. CICA 1994, p. 40; SustainAbility & UNEP 1999, p. 7). More recently, however, the Internet has rapidly become a more popular reporting medium because of technological progress in ICT applications and Internet technologies in line with their overall penetration in corporate business as well as increasing access of the public (cf. Isenmann & Lenz 2001, 2002; Jones, Alabaster & Hetherington, 1999; Shephard, Abkowitz & Cohen, 2001).

Today many companies produce paper-based reports offering electronic versions available on the WWW as supplements – and in some cases replacements. Perhaps surprisingly, at present, print still dominates, whereas the Internet electronic versions are frequently viewed as a supplement – still.

Since environmental reporting has become business commonplace and hence more sophisticated, companies – especially some in environmentally sensitive industries – have been paying increasing attention to and experimenting with alternative reporting methods. One consequence of such behaviour is the increasing level of environmental reporting in its different forms. Thus companies are providing reports in different formats, presentation styles and on several media:

- For example, Beiersdorf produced its 1996 environmental protection and safety report in a hardcover edition.
- Likewise, AEG called its 2000 environmental report a "green paper," a tome with a huge collection of environmental statements according to EMAS of about 200 pages.
- Heidelberg provided its 1999/2000 environmental report in a fashionable hard cover folder with a spiral binding and hands-on index features.
- Daimler Benz produced its 1997 environmental report in the form of a newspaper, whereas EPCOR Group created its 1997 and 1998 environmental reports as small booklets.
- In addition to reports on print media, some companies provided CD-ROMs, for example Hoechst 1996 and Swissair 1995/1996.
- Unilever produced its 2000 environmental performance report as a digidisc, a smart CD-ROM in the form of a business card.
- Henkel's CD-ROM 2000 – which is called eco communication 5 – contains a considerable collection of publications, including milestones in eco-management and several other documents.
- As a supplement to its environmental report, Merck produced a more entertaining CD-ROM in 1999, providing a mix of infotainment, ecotainment and emotainment, available in two languages. The content can be updated via the Internet, including sound and hypermedia features.

It is true that some companies have produced environmental reports in different forms on print media, but the number of companies to have distributed electronic reports on CD-ROMs is small. Nonetheless, the rapidly emerging medium through which environmental reports are disclosed is the WWW. Confirming this trend, Jones and Walton (1999, pp. 416-417) have clearly made the point: "Whatever the nature of the current debate, it is evident that the Internet is becoming an increasingly popular medium for companies to communicate their environmental reports." Moreover, borrowed from SustainAbility and UNEP (1999, pp. 20-21; Jones & Walton, 1999, p. 425), the Internet is seen an "indispensable tool" to pass premature reporting stages providing environmental

Figure 2: Comparison of media and their beneficial nature used for environmental communication (after Jones & Walton, 1999, 414)

Capabilities / Medium	Text	Still image	Moving image	Sound	Interaction
Print	✓	✓			Simulated
Fax	✓	✓			Simulated
Audio/Tape				✓	Simulated
Phone				✓	✓
Video		✓	✓	✓	Simulated
Video conferencing		✓	✓	✓	✓
PC disk	✓	✓			Simulated
CD-ROM	✓	✓	✓	✓	Simulated
Internet	✓	✓	✓	✓	✓

reports solely on print media towards approaching an integrated reporting system, producing reports cross-media; that is, to make these available on different media, truly meeting users' needs and preferences for accessing information.

The rationale as to why more and more companies are using the Internet as a reporting "enabler" or "facilitator" can be seen in the unique capabilities provided by it (Figure 2). Compared with traditional media the Internet embraces a broader range of beneficial characteristics that are vital for current environmental communication.

In order to gain greater conceptual clarity on using the Internet, Isenmann and Lenz (2002) proposed a generic classification framework, arranging its overall usefulness in terms of reporting along four categories:

- first, benefits concerning the underlying purposes of reporting, for example disclosing performance, improving efficiency, polishing reputation, improving image and engaging employees;
- second, benefits concerning certain reporting processes, for example in terms of automation, efficient production and multiple-utilization of contents;
- third, benefits concerning the report contents, for example retrieval, tailored views, and personalized reports on demand;
- fourth, benefits concerning the report design, for example online/offline availability, navigation, hypermedia features, interactivity and dialogue.

Despite its unique capabilities (Figure 2) and the wide range of technical benefits mentioned, the Internet is often seen as yet another channel for dissemination (e.g., Lober, 1997, pp. 15, 17-18), frequently used as a platform with public access just for providing reports that are available as Portable Document Format (PDF) files[7]. Today, many environmental reports put on the Internet still have a clear print media focus, representing mere electronic duplicates of hard copy reports on print media. In the words of Elkington and Priddey (1997, p. 52), a number of companies "seem to have got stuck in the rut of thinking in terms of the printed page". In a number of cases, for example the 1996 environmental report of RheinLand Versicherungen, the 1999 environmental report of Bayerische Landesbank, the 2000 environmental statement of Badische Stahlwerke and the 1999 sustainability report of Dresdner Bank, one can see this print fixation in the note "printed on recycled paper". Further, a number of reports initially prepared for hard copy are then translated by external multimedia agencies or Internet services companies into HyperText Markup Language (HTML), the common formatting language used by the WWW, and then directly transferred to the Internet. This orthodox reporting practice is confirmed through empirical findings:

- Based on an exploratory survey, a total of 121 environmental reports available on the Internet in Germany 2000 were analyzed (Isenmann & Lenz, 2002). This survey was carried out by the Department of Business Information Systems and Operations Research at the University of Kaiserslautern, Germany. The goal was to evaluate environmental reports on the Internet according to its technical standards and concerned the extent to which its specific benefits have been exploited. In line with an underlying classification framework highlighting three methods prototypical for Internet use (Figure 3), it was found that most of the reports can be called "converted," that is, using the Internet merely for presentation; a number of reports can be considered "enriched," that is, using the Internet as an additional channel for distribution; of the reports analyzed, surprisingly no report could be called fully "integrated," that is, using the whole potential of this computer-based medium.
- Closely linked to the insights above, there is another empirical analysis of how the Internet is currently being used for environmental reporting, carried out by ACCA (2001). This analysis was based on two samples: first, 240 companies within the UK, EURO and Global FTSE 100 Indexes were surveyed; second, 42 UK FTSE 100 companies producing electronic reports in 2001 were analyzed. Three distinct ways of using the Internet were found. These are called "piggy-back," "integrated" and "stand-alone" (Figure 4).

Figure 3. Methods of Internet use prototypical for environmental reports (Isenmann & Lenz, 2002)

Method of Internet use	Report style	Description and characteristics
Medium just for presentation	"Converted"	Replica of a paper-based report, just converted in an electronic version, offline (PDF, RTF) or online (HTML)
↓	"Enriched"	Electronic version, but still with print media focus, translated into HTML with some nice multimedia features
Reporting facilitator	"Integrated"	Cross media focus, stored as XML-file, featured with multiple linking and complex hypertext structure

Figure 4. Methods of Internet use prototypical for environmental reports (ACCA, 2001)

Method of Internet use	Report style	Description and characteristics
Medium used for presentation	"Piggy-back"	Paper-based report, hosted on company's Website (PDF)
↓	"Integrated"	Two different implementations: – Short hard-copy summary report, with references to the URLs where further information can be found – "Piggy-back" approach, but its HTML version has some additional features incorporated
"Indispensable tool"	"Stand-alone"	No hard-copy report, solely on the Internet

To conclude, despite some diversity in detail and although the terms used are different, both analyses demonstrate that there are substantial differences between current environmental reports available on the Internet and some diversity as to how to make use of the Internet taken as a whole, whether it is used primarily a means for presentation, a channel for distribution or performing reporting processes. When analyzing such environmental reports on the Internet in the context of its technical benefits, it might be helpful to use such classifications, perhaps providing a basic tool: first, from a reporting company's perspective, for developing a clear strategy concerning Internet-based environmental reporting, probably for moving away from "converted" environmental reports towards "enriched" or fully "integrated" ones; second, from a benchmarking institution's point of view, for rating and ranking reports in terms of Internet-specific features.

On the basis of the insights above, one might ask if it is sufficient that environmental reports still be directly translated and uploaded to the Internet without creating more added value. An increasing number of target groups will probably no longer be satisfied when provided solely with reports on print media or mere electronic duplicates of them. Especially, professional users in the financial community such as financial analysts, investment consultants, brokers, private and institutional investors, banks, and insurance companies as well as ranking or rating organizations need updated and fine tuned environmental reports, preferably available online[8] and prepared for machine processing without any need to capture the data in an electronic form once again. Such a scenario may not be irrelevant. On the contrary, this could make good business and environmental sense for two main reasons: first, because environmental reporting is becoming increasingly relevant for decision making in this field (cf. Edwards & Andersen Consulting, 1998, Müller et al., 1996); and second, since multiple inquiries companies are receiving from a variety of target groups are a really time-consuming and costly exercise (Axelrod, 2000, pp. 4-5). Rather than endure these procedures, companies are recognizing the value in having a readily available tool for providing the information needed.

All in all, it is cross-media reporting that still seems to be needed, but particularly cross-media reporting based on the Internet[9]. Such an approach enables companies to provide environmental reports and other communication vehicles on a single source, be it a common database or another kind of repository. Consequently, the question should not be how to translate a hard copy report with its strict print media focus while expending great effort to adapt to other media. Instead, the question in fact should be how to create a cross-media reporting system containing relevant content to produce different reporting instruments on various media on demand.

In technical terms, such a system is called a (Web) content management system, appropriate to perform single source multiple media publishing (cf. Schoop & Gersdorf, 2001). A content management system allows content to be stored, retrieved, edited, updated, monitored and then output to cross media in a variety of ways. It usually includes a database along with workflow and editorial tools. Resulting from this, the report's content has to be structured in small modules or substantial entities – in terms of computer scientists these are called semantic components – and stored in a suitable data format, for example XML. XML has already proved its usefulness for providing fine tuned environmental reports on different devices and various media (cf. Lenz, Isenmann & Reitz, 2001). Borrowed from Jones and Walton (1999, p. 416), according to the second trend there is a need to define an environmental reporting system "that develops environmental disclosures in a holistic manner in all media".

In contrast to a monolithic recommendation either for print media or computer-based media, we argue for a cross-media reporting approach that relies on an underlying ICT infrastructure, instead of being based on the Internet and using the benefits of XML, finally supporting the whole reporting workflow. Such an approach keeps companies in a position to provide environmental reports and other communication vehicles on a variety of media, based on a single data source that serves as a shared publishing basis. Bearing this in mind, it is not going to be a case of either print media or computer-based media, or one of either paper-based reports or Internet-based ones, but of both (cf. Charter, 1998, p. 2; Isenmann & Lenz, 2001, p. 187).

Trend 3: From "One Size Fits All" Reports to Customized Reporting

In addition to the developments towards integrated and cross-media reporting dealt with above, the third trend is referred to as a movement away from "one size fits all" reports towards a more tailored approach. It is characteristic for customized environmental reporting to take into account the requirements of several standards, guidelines and the different needs of a number of users, and then to produce reports precisely meeting all these requirements and needs.

There is broad consensus that such customization or target group tailoring is vital for the success of environmental reporting (cf. Isenmann & Lenz, 2001; Skillius & Wennberg, 1998; Spencer-Cooke, 1995; van Dalen, 1997). Although that goal is often mentioned in reporting frameworks, concepts and guidelines, current practice reveals that there is still significant room for improvement, even for the best reporters. In total, customized reporting and the provision of fine-tuned environmental reports remain largely unrealized, still challenging companies in the near future but clearly lacking thus far.

Throwing more light onto methods of customized reporting is argued to be a real step forward on the way to sustainability reporting. Hence, customization should be seen as an integral part of companies' efforts to improve current practice and finally approach advanced reporting stages. Customization, however, is not as simple a process as it may appear at first glance. On the contrary, such an enterprise represents a challenging and multifaceted problem requiring both identification of relevant target groups and clarification of their particular needs, and also a pool of report content that companies are willing to disclose, preferably arranged in a specific structure appropriate for automated machine processing through ICT applications.

Analyses and empirical findings have shown that clear target group tailoring is usually still lacking in current practice. This is true for environmental reports on print media as well as on computer-based media (cf. KPMG 2002, p. 17; Lenz, Isenmann & Reitz, 2001). Of the majority of environmental reports available, usually a variety of target groups is addressed, but their specific information needs are heterogeneous and thus these needs cannot be fully satisfied through an orthodox practice or easily be met just by "business as usual" via one universal document (on print media), mostly produced as "one size fits all" report.

Employees, customers, suppliers, local authorities, legislators, neighbors, consultants, financial analysts, investors, insurance agents, media representatives, and members of rating and ranking organizations that are all identified as key addressees need more and more target group tailored, individualized or even personalized reporting instruments. This is also true for companies' top managers who hold an exceptional position, for local authorities who claim a specific right to know and also for banks and insurers who require confidential information. Moreover, distribution channels and design preferences may differ a lot from one another. Taken together, all the users above expect that companies' reports truly address their real needs.

For example, with growing general environmental awareness, employees are interested in the environmental performance of their employers and companies. They want to be informed about targets and activities related to the environmental management system. Further, they want to understand how companies are perceived by local community groups. Employees wish to see their company as a going concern, recognizing that environmental performance might have some influence on this.

In supply chains and other manufacturing networks, suppliers exchange information with participating business partners. Establishing partnerships implies extensive environmental communication along the whole supply chain or network (Lippman, 2001, p. 13). These groups need environmental information regarding resource efficiency, regulatory compliance, new product and service opportunities, especially in terms of extended product stewardship, and other environmental liabilities.

Investors, including institutional and private shareholders, financial analysts and investment consultants, are increasingly interested in environmental issues and their financial interrelations since these groups have noticed that environmental reports make good business and environmental sense (Blumberg, Korsvold & Blum, 2000). Many investors expect that environmental performance will influence financial performance and shareholder value (Kiernan, 2001; Schaltegger & Figge, 1997; VBDO, 1998). For example, in November 2000 a group of 39 financial investors, managing combined assets excess of $140 billion, sent a letter to CEOs of the 500 largest U.S. companies urging them to provide sustainability reports (Social Funds, 2000).

Publishing merely one (paper-based) environmental report – most often prepared as a "one size fits all" document – shows significant shortcomings in each case because it is rather difficult to meet heterogeneous information needs and individual preferences via a single uniform vehicle. As a result of this complexity, producing one (paper-based) environmental report actually means making compromises. A "report designed to appeal to everybody may end up serving nobody's real needs" (DTTI, IISD & SustainAbility, 1993, p. 6).

However, it is very laborious – and probably expensive as well – to produce a great number of tailored reports on print media through orthodox practice, because companies usually address a variety of target groups. The above-mentioned limits are closely linked with difficulties involved in using print media for communication for which they are often poorly suited. In the words of Mach: "An organization needs to send the right messages through the right distribution channels to the right audiences. To accomplish this, it may need a variety of communications vehicles – not just a single report. One size doesn't fit all in today's Internet world of mass customization." (Cited in MacLean & Gottfrid, 2000, p. 248; likewise Wheeler & Elkington, 2001, p. 2 claim that companies may provide the "right mix of information in the right format at the right time").

Approaching customization and providing fine-tuned environmental reports, companies may use the Internet as an excellent means while reaping the benefits of XML. These tools provide several unique capabilities, for example the benefits of employing push and pull technologies for efficient information supply, rapid and cost-saving distribution and provision of updated data and tailored information on demand: Initially, the Internet was designed as a pull technology, indicating that users "pull" the information they need from a company's Web site; that is, they "pull" a certain Web site from a server to their local client browser. Users "surfing" or "browsing" the Internet are then seen in an active role. The principle again illustrates that reporting companies "push" information to a wide audience through certain distribution channels, perhaps via e-mail, newsletters, the WWW and a number of newer technologies (cf. Isenmann & Lenz, 2001).

In a more detailed fashion, customized reporting based on the Internet could be implemented through three different approaches:

- The first approach is called stereotyping, a basic method of customization employing standard user profiles. These profiles record information needs that are thought of as characteristic of a specific group of users (e.g., illustrated in the columns in Figure 9). Stereotypes are usually based on an analysis of empirical studies and then refined for a certain company via questionnaires and interviews with its key target groups. Using stereotypes, a customized environmental reporting system provides different, but frequently static views of a report, perhaps dependent on a certain target group users are assigned to. For example, employees probably have a view of a report different from customers, and thus a company may prepare a set of tailored reports, particularly highlighting the information the company expects to meet the needs of the group primarily addressed. This is the way that a number of users may prefer: They are provided with a preselected report, probably meeting their needs and likely to suit their preferences.

- One step beyond, the second method of customization is described as individualization. Through this more sophisticated method, users are able to create their own reports, and they then become "reporters" themselves, selecting the information they need, either according to their current preferences or in line with a certain guideline. Individualization offers more interactivity. Tailored reports that users request, however, have to be produced dynamically through a (Web) content management system. In order to manage its administration well, it is helpful to employ user profiles. These profiles record users' preferences perhaps regarding their target groups (data view), density (status), media (kind of data), breadth (topical selection), depth (specification), time (timeliness and date of availability) and the form (style, layout, format) in which the report is to be prepared.
- The third method customization can be accomplished is personalization. Personalization is seen as the most sophisticated approach because it records personal data in addition to the users' preferences. Recording personal data, for example name, address and so forth however, is a sensitive issue that needs to be treated very carefully to prevent misuse. For that reason, any procedure of recording personal data should be voluntary, reversible and made transparent to the user. Furthermore, its employment should be strictly limited to fine-tuning communication vehicles. Implementing personalization mirrors an insight stated early in the field when environmental reporting was focused on reaching the target groups addressed (CICA, 1994, p. 40): "The choice of audience will directly affect the presentation of information, its tone, sophistication, emphasis, etc."

Indeed, customization seems to be very useful for reporting companies and the target groups addressed. From a company's perspective, customization is an opportunity to extend reporting success and multiply the number of target groups actually reached; from a target group's point of view, customization is seen as a requirement for truly meeting their needs and thus for tracking companies' performance over time. One approach of customized environmental reporting worth emulating may be BP's data desk[10]. It offers various ways to tailor access and fine-tune environmental information, also linked with financial and social issues within BP's Web sites. Users can take a specific view and create their Web site for their specific needs.

Another feature probably important for customized environmental reporting based on the Internet is its capability to gain deeper insights into users' information needs and preferences. This can be performed directly through online analyses or indirectly by observing users' pattern via Web mining tools. Today, such tools are standard features of current Web servers[11].

Summing up, we can say that the early incarnations described in terms of "one size fits all" reports served their purpose well in past years because they helped to communicate companies' environmental performance to a wide range of target groups. If reports are too detailed or too fragmented, requirements could have prevented interested companies from establishing environmental reporting as a common business practice. As they moved forward, however, further improvements and an increasing demand for different views will bring about true customization, not just piecemeal engineering if an advanced reporting stage is ever to be achieved. As such, it will require taking the different needs of different users into account and providing tailored, individualized or even personalized reports on demand. Customized environmental reporting, linked with a balanced integrated approach and cross-media availability will become crucial as more companies produce reports and claim to be providing useful information on environmental and sustainability issues for a variety of target groups.

Although environmental reporting serves a wide range of purposes and despite the fact that companies are targeting a diverse group of key users, most of them may emphasize the importance of three trends mentioned above; that is, first, providing a set of contents that target groups expect, including environmental issues as well as its financial and social counterparts, leading to a more integrated approach; second, cross-media reporting seen as producing vehicles on various media in order to reach target groups addressed through the channels they actually prefer; third, customized reporting understood as finding out ways that users want to see reports and what they expect to see in reports. Together, these key trends are taken as drivers to stimulate companies' efforts to improve their practice and push them towards sustainability reporting, rather than reporting merely through the Internet.

Media-Specific Benefits Using Internet and XML for Environmental and Sustainability Reporting

Within environmental reporting, reports available on the WWW have become one of the most fashionable topics since the inception of this field (cf. Butner, 1996; Charter, 1998; Elkington & Priddey, 1997; Isenmann & Lenz, 2001, 2002; Jones, Alabaster & Hetherington, 1999; Kerkhoven & Nelson, 1994; Ollier, 1996; SustainAbility & UNEP 1999; Wheeler & Elkington, 2001). The driving force that underlies this trend and promotes its use is the rapid development of Internet technologies and services and associated technologies. Together, these technical means offer unique capabilities that could be employed to improve environmental reporting (Isenmann & Lenz, 2001, 2002). In contrast to the many

Figure 5. Classification of Internet-specific benefits for environmental reporting

Technical benefits	Possible implementations				
Benefits concerning reporting purposes	Resource monitoring	Information disclosure	Dialogue, two-way communication	Engagement for transactions	...
Benefits concerning reporting processes	Rationale		Customization		...
	Easy administration of reporting elements	Efficient preparation of reports	Fast distribution of reports	Smart presentation of reports	...
Benefits concerning reporting contents	Reports		Additional information		...
	Customised selection (data view)	Topical selection, retrieval	Internal links: e.g. environmental division	External links: e.g. stock exchange, ranking	...
Benefits concerning reporting design	Online-, offline-availability	Navigation	Hypermedia	Enhanced communication	...

empirical studies and conceptual articles about successful Internet-based environmental reporting (SustainAbility, 2002; SustainAbility & UNEP, 1999; Weil & Winter-Watson, 2002), however, a detailed and structured underlying framework is missing. In pursuing greater conceptual clarity, a comprehensive classification of Internet-specific benefits is proposed and illustrated in the following extract (Figure 5).

This classification is based on a review of current approaches found in the literature dealing with Internet-based environmental reporting. Methodically, the classification rests on two heuristics, and has shown its usefulness in several empirical studies and other areas of corporate reporting, for example in financial reporting (Henseler, Isenmann & Müller-Merbach, 2004; Isenmann, Lenz & Müller-Merbach, 2001). The classification appears schematic, not photo-realistic. However, it constitutes a helpful scheme for surveying the impressive array of benefits the Internet could provide for environmental reporting in a broader sense. In addition, it may also be used to imagine ways to progress towards sustainability reporting.

For the latter purpose, a multitude of benefits could further be organized in terms of a three-step strategy:

- *Step 1:* The Internet facilitates the consolidation of complementary information that used to be contained in freestanding reports, for example the incorporation of financial and social issues into environmental reports.
- *Step 2:* The Internet provides skillful connection and smart cross-linking among stand-alone environmental, financial and social reports in the sense of a virtual compound document, featuring hyperlinks, perhaps pointing to

the company's environmental department, the stock exchange or rankings. These hyperlinks are employed to assist user navigation so that users always feel comfortable without "being lost in cyberspace" when browsing through such virtual reports.

- *Step 3:* The Internet can help to provide customized sustainability reports. Some target groups may wish to get a short divisional sustainability report. Some others may prefer a sustainability report in a more detailed fashion, just including two "dimensions," for example financial and environmental issues, while still others may be interested in an all-inclusive sustainability report with detailed disclosure of environmental, financial and social interrelations.

Computer scientists, ICT experts and a number of other reporting professionals recommend that employing XML helps to realize the Internet-specific benefits outlined above (Arndt & Günther, 2000). Due to the multitude of technologies associated with it, we understand XML to be a collective term that incorporates all the means shown below (Figure 6).

For example, XML has several advantages compared to HTML, and thus it is considered a preferred data format for environmental reporting. The suitability of XML is based on its characteristics of multiple-usability, exchangeability and the separation between contents (semantics), report structure (logical order) and representation (layout and style). XML is structure-oriented and appropriate for advanced Internet applications. XML documents consist of plain text, and they can be validated by machine processing. Furthermore, XML offers a number of opportunities to improve reporting workflow and helps to allocate human and

Figure 6. XML-based technologies, used for environmental reporting

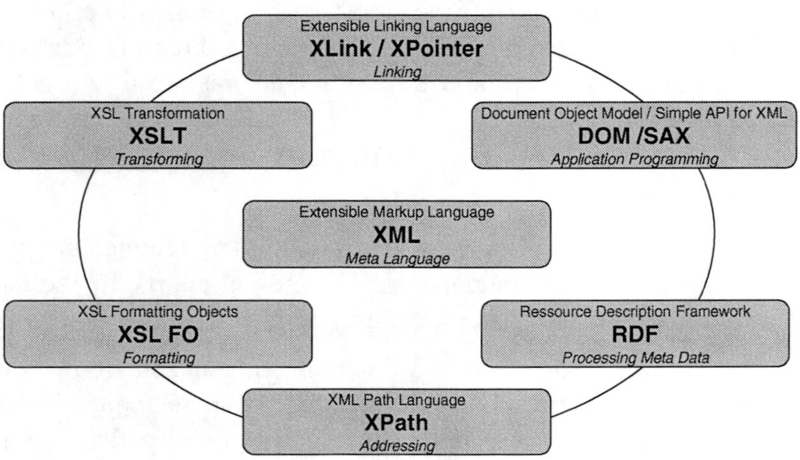

Figure 7. XML-specific benefits for environmental reporting

Core processes	ICT-specific challenges	XML-specific benefits	XML-technologies
Preparation	- Data stored in documents - Need for teamwork - Trend toward standardization	- Standardized document structure - Automated generation - Powerful hyperlinks	- DTD, schema - Xlink, XPointer, XPath - XML parser (DOM/SAX)
Administration	- Data stored in documents - Need for teamwork	- Clear data structure - Markup via metadata - Single source multiple media publishing	- XML database - RDF
Distribution	- Demand for customisation - Multitude of accessibility	- Integrated communication - Cross media distribution - Push and pull principle	- XSL FO - Data formats suitable for XML processing
Presentation	- Demand for customisation - Smart presentation	- Hypermedia features - Customised presentation - Presentation independent from structure and contents	- XSLT and XSL FO - XSL parser

organizational resources more efficiently, supporting all core processes ranging from automated preparation and effective administration to fast distribution and smart presentation, and also facilitates teamwork along the reporting procedures, inside and outside the company (Figure 7).

Framework for Advanced Environmental and Sustainability Reporting based on the Internet

The framework for Internet-based environmental reporting is illustrated along four elements, proceeding from the outside to the inside, or from inter-organizational aspects to corporate ones respectively:

- stakeholder analysis,
- analysis of stakeholder information requirements,
- XML-based document engineering, and
- ICT architecture.

This framework serves as a guideline on how to exploit the media-specific capabilities that the Internet and its associated technologies provide, bringing definite improvements in the areas of environmental communications, information management and organization, and perhaps smoothing the way to sustainability reporting.

Stakeholder Analysis

The starting point of any advanced Internet-based environmental reporting system is stakeholder analysis identifying the primary users and typically asking: Who are the relevant stakeholders (including the critical ones); that is, who are the key target groups inside and outside the company that require information via environmental reporting? Generally, there are two ways of identifying them; on the one hand, with a deductive approach or on the other with an inductive one.

According to the deductive approach, initially all stakeholders could be considered relevant or called a target group who are involved in or affected by a company's environmental impacts and activities. Perhaps, as certain stakeholders claim some exclusive information rights, they may be seen as specific users. For example, this is true for companies' top managers who hold ultimate liability, for local authorities who have a specific right to know and also for banks and insurers who require confidential information. Regardless of their particular information rights, it could be fruitful to address these users as groups anyway.

Despite its usefulness, the deductive approach should be combined with an inductive one for this task. Stakeholder analysis represents a company-specific task influenced by certain circumstances, for example size, industry, products, processes, location, environmental impacts, stakeholder relations, communication strategy, environmental management, strategic goals etc. Hence, an empirical analysis could validate the number of relevant stakeholders found through the deductive approach. Lenz (2003) provides a thorough stakeholder analysis. He reviewed a multitude of empirical studies that identified key target groups and primary users' needs in the field. Based on his in-depth survey he identified 12 key target groups, arranged in four groups (Figure 8):

- financial community, including investors, insurance agents and financial analysts;
- business partners, including employees, customers and suppliers;
- diffuse groups, including media representatives, neighbors and consultants; and
- normative groups, including local authorities, respective legislators, pressure groups and standard setting institutions.

The users within a certain target group can be identified by the fact that they have relatively homogeneous information needs, at least to a certain extent.

Figure 8. Target groups prototypical for environmental reporting

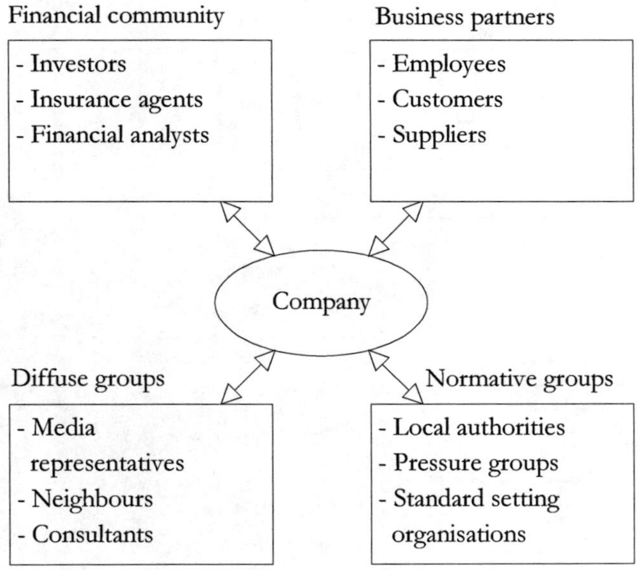

Analysis of Stakeholder Information Requirements

Following stakeholder analysis and the identification of primary users, a reporting organization should study the information needs and other preferences expected to be satisfied in report form and content. Such an analysis of stakeholder information requirements leads to the question: What are the relevant contents that target groups expect, and what are the preferences they want to be fulfilled regarding form, layout, design, media and distribution channel?

At present, little work has been done on conceptualizing users' information needs, especially as concerns distribution channels, presentation styles and the media favored. Hence, van Dalen (1997, p. 19) complains about a lack of more profound insights into users' information needs and preferences. Answering to this need, Lenz (2003) provides an analysis of stakeholder information requirements. He reviewed five major empirical studies that analyzed users' information needs (Figure 9), including the studies of DTTI, IISD and SustainAbility (1993), CICA (1994), Schulz (1995), Vollmer (1995) and Azzone et al. (1997).

Together, the analysis of stakeholder information requirements clearly demonstrates that employees, customers, suppliers, local authorities, legislators, neighbours, consultants, financial analysts, investors, insurance agents, media

Figure 9. Information needs of key target groups for environmental reporting (Lenz, 2003, p. 232)

	Employees	Customers	Suppliers	Local authorities	Neighbours	Env. pressure groups	Investors	Env. sensitive investors	Public/ media
Organization									
Commitment of top management	high priority	important	important	high priority	less important	high priority	less important	high priority	important
Overall structure and relationship between sites	less important	less important	less important	important	less important	important	important	high priority	important
Corporate culture, working climate, leadership	high priority	less important	less important	less important	less important	important	important	high priority	important
Compliance	high priority	high priority	important	high priority	high priority	high priority	important	high priority	high priority
Logistics and traffic (products and employees)	important	high priority	less important	important	high priority	important	less important	important	less important
Deposits of waste	high priority	less important	less important	important	less important	high priority	high priority	high priority	important
Complaints/legal proceedings/judgements	less important	less important	less important	important	important	high priority	important	important	high priority
Production process									
General information/survey	high priority	less important	important	important	important	less important	high priority	high priority	important
Current state of environmental technology	important	important	important	important	high priority	important	important	high priority	important
Environmental pollution (noise etc.)	high priority	important	less important	high priority	high priority	high priority	important	high priority	high priority
Environmental activities	important	less important	less important	important	important	high priority	less important	important	important
Emissions/waste/recycling	important	important	less important	high priority	high priority	high priority	less important	high priority	high priority
Consumption of energy and resources	important	less important	important	high priority	important	high priority	less important	high priority	high priority
Health and safety	high priority	high priority	important	high priority	high priority	high priority	important	high priority	high priority
Plants	important	less important	important	important	important	high priority	less important	important	important
Environmental risks	important	important	less important	high priority	high priority	high priority	less important	important	high priority
Prevention of accidents/risk management	high priority	important	important	high priority	high priority	high priority	high priority	high priority	high priority
Products									
General information/survey	important	high priority	high priority	important	less important	less important	high priority	important	important
Environmental impacts	important	high priority	important	high priority	less important	high priority	important	high priority	high priority
Impacts on human health	less important	high priority	important	important	important	high priority	important	high priority	high priority
Life cycle design/product stewardship	less important	high priority	high priority	important	important	high priority	less important	high priority	high priority
Research & development	important	high priority	high priority	important	less important	less important	important	high priority	important
New environmentally sound products	important	high priority	important	important	important	important	high priority	high priority	important
Environmental management system									
Environmental policy	high priority	important	important	high priority	high priority	high priority	important	high priority	high priority
Environmental goals	high priority	important	high priority	high priority	high priority	high priority	important	important	high priority
Organization/responsibilities/responsive persons	high priority	less important	less important	less important	important	high priority	less important	important	high priority
World wide standards	less important	important	less important	less important	less important	high priority	less important	high priority	high priority
Participation/training/motivation of employees	high priority	important	less important	important	less important	important	less important	important	important
Environmental instruments and programmes	important	important	important	important	important	important	important	high priority	high priority
Continuous improvement/performance	high priority	important	important	high priority	important	high priority	important	high priority	important
Eco balancing	important	less important	important	high priority	less important	important	important	high priority	less important
Environmental auditing	important	important	less important	high priority	high priority	important	important	high priority	high priority
External verification	important	important	less important	high priority	high priority	high priority	important	high priority	high priority
Stakeholder communication									
Promotion of environmental reports	important	less important	less important	high priority	high priority	high priority	important	high priority	high priority
Dialogue with the public	high priority	important	less important	important	high priority	high priority	important	important	high priority
Dialogue with local authorities	important	less important	less important	high priority	high priority	important	important	important	important
Cooperation with suppliers and business partners	important	high priority	high priority	important	important	important	high priority	high priority	important
Financial indicators									
Environmental expenditure	important	less important	less important	important	important	important	high priority	important	important
Cost savings	important	less important	important	important	important	less important	high priority	high priority	important
Environmental investment	important	less important	important	important	important	important	high priority	high priority	important
Environmental reserves	important	less important	less important	important	important	less important	high priority	high priority	less important
Penalties, damages, legal proceedings	important	important	important	important	important	important	high priority	high priority	important
Environmental accounting	less important	less important	important	important	less important	high priority	less important	less important	less important
Financial-environmental interrelations									
Financial risks (amount, probability, insurance)	important	important	important	important	important	less important	high priority	high priority	important
Opportunities (new processes, products)	important	less important	high priority	less important	important	important	important	high priority	less important

representatives and members of rating and ranking organizations have heterogeneous information needs. These different needs cannot be fully satisfied or easily met just by "reporting as usual" through orthodox practice, via one universal document (on print media), mostly produced as a one size fits all report. Users are increasingly expecting target group tailored, individualized or even personalized reporting instruments. Thus it is crucial to find out what target groups want, to identify their needs and preferences.

The results of the two analyses discussed above lend themselves to the creation of specific user profiles. For each of the core target groups, a profile of their information needs will be established that addresses content requirements, preferences as to the reporting form and secondary requirements such as distribution channel and so forth.

XML-Based Document Engineering

The results of stakeholder analysis and deeper insights into stakeholder information requirements have been used for XML-based document engineering, indicating the ICT-laden area where contents, structures, procedures and the design of reporting instruments and other communication vehicles are defined. This leads to the questions: What should an environmental report prepared as an XML document look like? What contents should be included? Who should be addressed? On what devices should the report be available? Which standards or guidelines need to be adhered to? Here, certain aspects of report structure, contents and layout are explicitly considered.

The core of XML-based document engineering is to develop a document type definition (DTD) – or a so-called scheme – that is essential for any XML-based application, and for Web content management systems. Such a DTD defines the overall pool of contents in a basic structure for a certain group of documents, for example for environmental reports. From this pool of structured contents, a number of customized reports can be prepared in an automated fashion by machine processing. In terms of document engineering, a DTD consists of several elements representing the contents and their corresponding attributes, specifying and indicating the elements. Consequently, a DTD determines what elements can be used within a XML document. Further, a DTD describes how elements can be arranged, and which attributes certain elements may carry.

The development of an XML-based DTD for environmental reporting is a sophisticated work because a number of different requirements have to be taken into account (Figure 10). Methodically, its development rests on a comprehen-

Figure 10. Process-oriented model to develop an XML-based DTD (Lenz, 2003, p. 235)

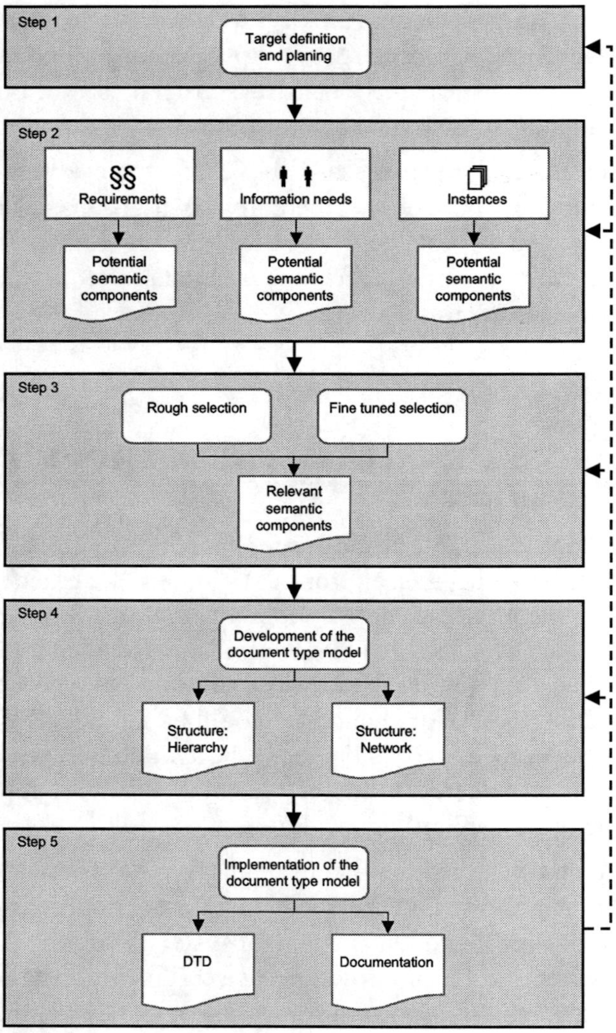

sive process-oriented model proposed by Schraml (1997) and then adapted by Lenz (2003):

- *Definition of the main target (step 1):* The target was to develop a DTD for XML-based environmental reports. The DTD had to simultaneously incorporate a variety of issues on sustainability, and the requirements of relevant regulations, standards, guidelines and manuals, especially at the European level.

- *Identification of possible semantic components (step 2)*: According to the target defined above, a multitude of resources were analyzed (e.g., ACCA, 1997; CEN, 1999; DIN, 1997; EC, 2001; future and IÖW, 1994; GRI, 2000; UNEP, 1994) to extract possible contents from relevant regulations, standards, guidelines, already available reports and users' needs and preferences. This task identified the pool of possible semantic components the DTD should contain.
- *Selection of relevant semantic components (step 3)*: From the pool of possible semantic components, a catalogue of relevant contents was developed through a verification procedure. The result was a total of 115 semantic components (Figure 11). Every component was classified as "must be" (required) or "might be" (optional) incorporated into the report and on which resource the component was rooted.
- *Design of the document type model (step 4)*: Based on the preceding catalogue, a document type model was designed. Therefore, all selected components were organized in a hierarchy typical of XML documents (Figure 12).

Figure 11. Catalogue of 115 relevant semantic components, extract (Isenmann et al., 2001, p. 825)

ID	Description			r/o	Source	Generic Identity
1	foreword			o	future 6.1, II	foreword
2	organization			r	EMAS II, A III, 3.2	organization
3		organization description		o	instances	orgDescription
4			corporate culture	o	users	corporateCulture
5			relationship to parent organization	o	EMAS II, A III, 3.2	parentOrg
6			sites	o	future 6.1, I	sites
...	...	...	...	...	...	...
98		economic-environmental interdependencies		o	users	econEnvInterdep
99			financial risks	o	users	financialRisks
100			financial chances	o	users	financialopportunities
101	formalities			r	EMAS II, A III, 3.2	formalities
102		imprint		o	instances	imprint
103			publisher/author/originator	o	DIN 33922, 5.6, instances	authorOriginator
104			publication date	o	instances	publicationDate
105			reporting period	o	DIN 33922, 5.6	temporalCoverage
106			date of next report	o	future 6.1, X	nextReport
107			responsibility and participation in env. rep.	o	future 6.1, III	reportTeam
108			contact	o	DIN 33922, 5.6	contact
109		verification		o	UNO 5, I, 11	verification
110			verifier name	r	EMAS II, A III, 3.2	verifierName
111			verifier accreditation number	r	EMAS II, A III, 3.2	verifierAccredNo
112			verifier address	o	DIN 33922, 5.6	verifierAddress
113			verifier statement	o	future 6.1, X	verifierStatement
114			verification date	r	EMAS II, A III, 3.2	verificationDate
115		additional information		o	future 6.1, X	additionalInfo

Figure 12. Document type model of an XML-based environmental report, illustrated (Isenmann et al., 2001, p. 825)

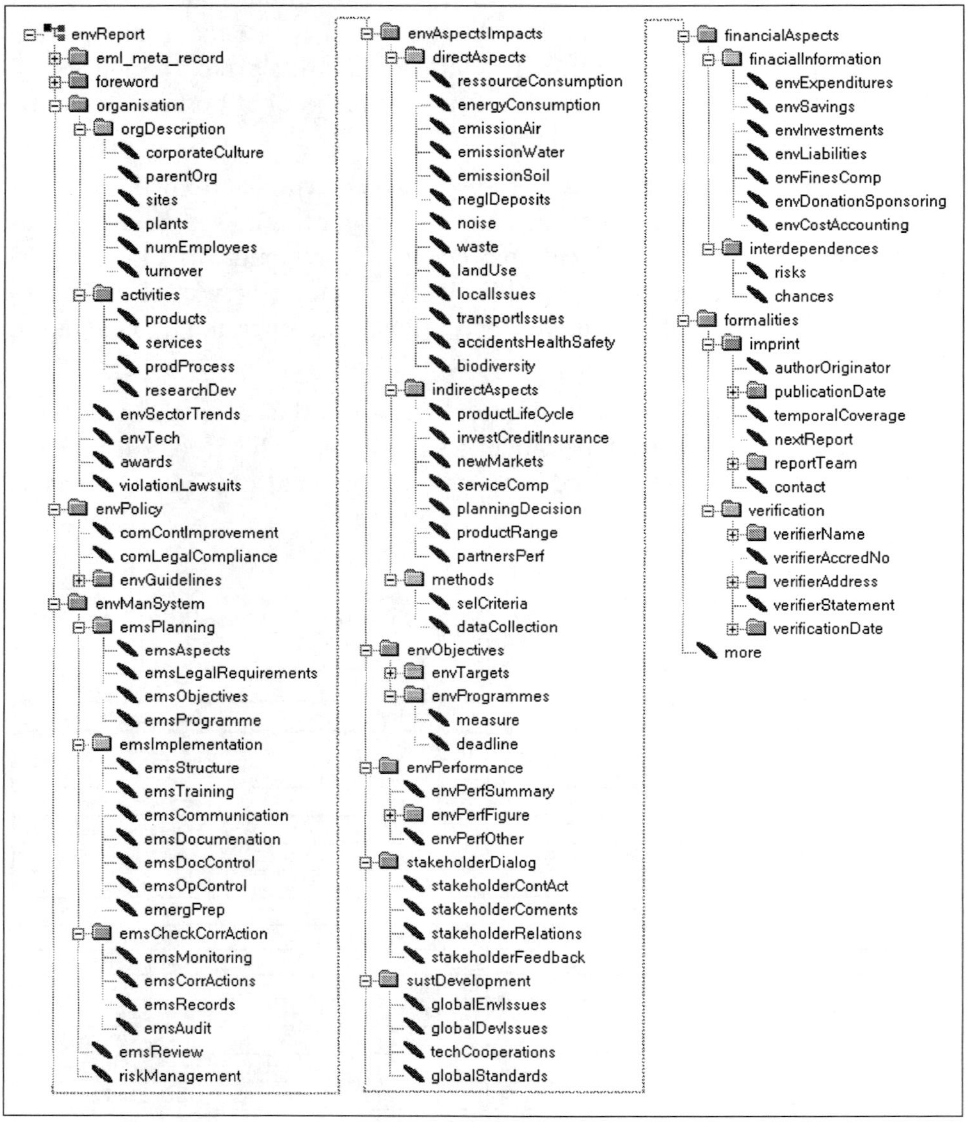

- *Implementation of the document type model (step 5)*: Finally, the document type model was implemented; that is, noted according to XML and transformed into a DTD, and documentation was prepared.

Employing an XML-based DTD offers an impressive array of benefits, improves a company's information management, supports its reporting workflow, allocates its resources efficiently, exactly meeting requirements proposed by emerging guidelines, and helps to communicate with its target groups in a meaningful way; that is, facilitating stakeholder dialogue, interactivity, feedback possibilities and tailor-made reports. In total, on the basis of an XML-based DTD, companies are enabled to provide integrated and customized environmental reports, prepared by machine processing and generated in an automated manner.

ICT Architecture

Reaping the media-specific benefits that the Internet and XML may offer requires an appropriate ICT architecture, suitable to operate XML-based DTDs and appropriate to provide single-source multiple media publishing. For that reason, a three-tier Web application is proposed:

- The *basic data layer* contains several sources where DTDs, stylesheets, user profiles and a number of other XML documents are stored. These sources include relevant data, metadata and thesauri. The data layer is managed through a database server.
- The *application layer* contains different services and applications to generate and distribute reports in an automated manner by machine processing. This complex layer is used as a data integrator responsible for system management and is accessed through an application server.
- The *presentation layer* represents an interactive user interface that is used for submitting users' information needs as well as for presenting reports. The presentation layer provides easy access via a standard Internet browser, for example Netscape Navigator or Microsoft Internet Explorer.

The procedure of an Internet-based environmental reporting system is depicted as follows (Figure 13):

(1) A certain stakeholder representing a report user (client) looks for environmental information using a common browser. Thus, he or she submits his/her information needs and probably specifies his/her preferences, perhaps including a choice of preferred distribution channel, medium and presentation style. His or her submission initiates the report's generation.

(2) The Web server forwards the inquiry to the application server where the application logic is implemented. Then, the application server transforms

Figure 13. XML-based Web application for Internet-based environmental reporting

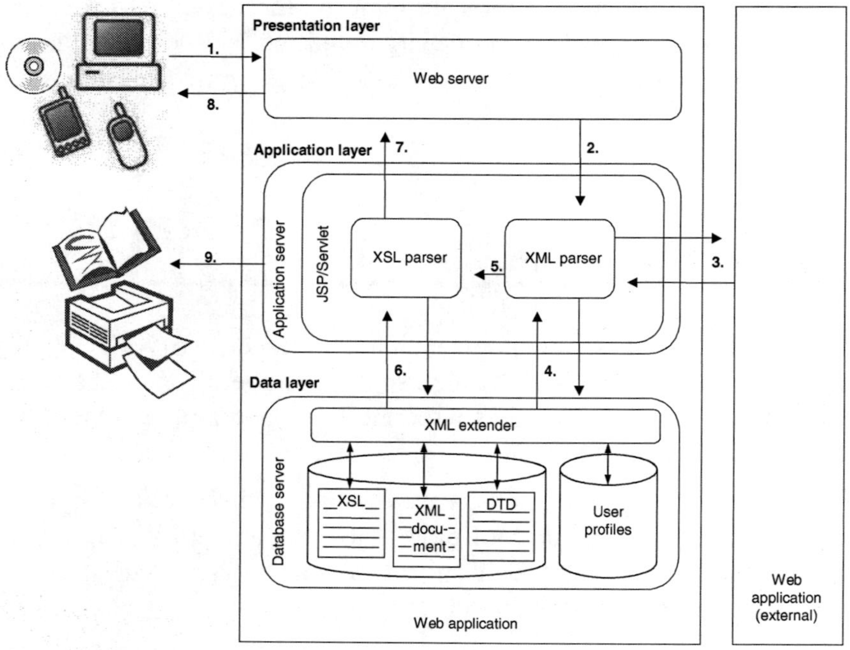

the inquiry submitted, and analyzes the parameters (contents, layout, media, guideline, user identification, etc.).

(3) Within the application server, an XML parser calls for requested XML data either externally from other Web applications or

(4) internally from the basic data layer. The interface between application server and database server is performed through an XML extender. This XML extender is responsible for storing and extracting XML documents by or from databases or other sources.

(5) The extracted data again are arranged through an XML parser. Next, the XML parser consolidates the data to a compound document that is valid according to the underlying DTD. Then, the XML document is forwarded to an XSL parser. Using XSL (eXtensible Stylesheet Language) goes one step beyond. XSL (and its three parts, i.e., XSL Transformations, XML Path Language and XSL Formatting Objects) enables one to modify the structure of an XML document, and also to extract certain contents. Consequently, XSL can create different views of a single report when prepared as an XML document.

(6) This XSL parser connects the prepared XML document with an XSL stylesheet exactly meeting the user's preferences, which are stored in user

profiles in a database within the database server. The XSL parser applies all stylesheet instructions onto the XML document.

(7) The result is the requested report that is forwarded to the Web server and

(8) then submitted to the user's client via the WWW. When using a suitable set of XSL stylesheets, reports can be generated and made available on any media, according to personal preferences.

(9) Instead of (7) and (8), reports could also be published in a CD ROM and then sent to users via mail, or alternatively submitted as a print version via fax.

In order to present efficiently an environmental report prepared as an XML document smartly, Cascading Stylesheets (CSS) might be used analogous to HTML documents. Except for a few extensions, however, CSS can only change representation, that is, layout and style of elements, while the contents and structure of the underlying document remain consistent. Now, customized environmental reports are possible without any need to change the underlying XML document (environmental report). Several components can be extracted, consolidated according to a certain structure and then presented in a tailored manner that exactly meets the user's specific information needs or the requirements proposed by certain emerging guidelines.

For demonstration purposes, we developed two XSL stylesheets (Figure 14): The stylesheet on the left may be called "plain" because all components of the XML-based report are presented as flat text without any layout features. Such a plain presentation might be suitable for benchmarking a report's pure substance. The stylesheet on the right demonstrates how certain contents can be extracted from the same underlying XML-based report, and how these contents might be arranged and presented according to certain user preferences in an automated fashion.

Taken together, the framework describes a comprehensive and fully ICT-based reporting approach in a broader sense, including its variety of added value features. Due to its fully supported underlying ICT infrastructure, an Internet-based reporting system of this kind provides a set of important contents, different media, corresponding distribution principles and various presentation styles.

The ICT architecture discussed above has been implemented in a software prototype as a practical application. At the heart of its ICT architecture lies Cocoon, a Java-based, modular structured, open source publishing software (Apache, 2003), able to perform XML-based DTDs, and suitable to provide individualized or even personalized environmental reports. Users just need to submit personal information, for example name and address. The system can be considered an adaptable environmental reporting system even providing personalized reports, truly able to accomplish one-to-one-communication on the fly. In

Figure 14. Different views of an underlying XML-based environmental report through specific XSL stylesheets

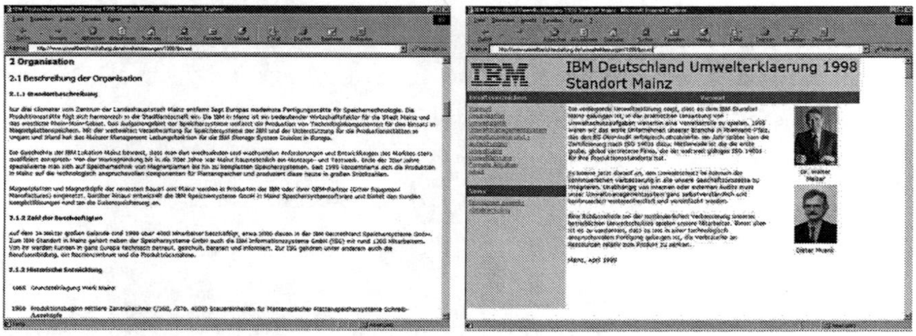

sum, companies are in a position to make progress in customization step by step, starting with stereotyping and next moving towards an individualized or personalized environmental reporting system.

The reason why we have employed Cocoon lies – among other advantages – in its powerful and sophisticated application capabilities. The modular application components could be arranged flexibly, serially grouped in so-called pipelines where different reports are then created dynamically on the basis of an XML-based DTD, thus exactly meeting each user's individual needs. At present, this customized environmental reporting system is implemented as a prototype, but soon it will be implemented in a number of German SMEs. Those may be regarded as pioneers in the field of corporate environmental reporting, at least in terms of customization and using the Internet for environmental reporting properly.

Numerous target groups are no longer satisfied solely with reports on print media or mere electronic duplicates. Professional use in the financial community, for example investors, financial analysts, investment consultants, brokers, private and institutional investors, banks, and insurance companies as well as ranking or rating organizations need updated and fine-tuned reports, preferably online and prepared for machine processing without any need to capture the data in an electronic form once again. This makes good business and environmental sense for two main reasons: environmental reporting is becoming increasingly relevant for decision making[12]; and responding to multiple inquiries that a variety of stakeholder groups are directing to companies is very time consuming and costly (Axelrod, 2000). Rather than endure these procedures, companies are recognizing the value in having a readily available tool for providing the information needed. Pioneering companies will implement Internet-based applications in the near future. Verie Sandborg, Baxter International's manager of environmental health and safety requirements regards a good environmental or sustainability report as excellent source material to use when responding to formalized requests for environmental or sustainability information (Axelrod, 2000, p. 5).

Many of the questions asked are already answered in comprehensive reports. However, it would be helpful to have a fully Internet-based reporting system: users could extract the information they need from a publishing database, and create an automatically generated customized report themselves; that is, users generate their own "reports à la carte," merely selecting keywords, clicking on preferences on a menu or choosing a certain guideline – perhaps creating a sustainability report in accordance with the GRI guidelines at one's fingertips[13].

Conclusions

DiPiazza and Eccles (2002, p. 127), two experts in the field of corporate reporting, state that "corporate information, in all its growing quantity and complexity can be – and in reality must be – communicated more effectively with the use of new technology. Reported information needs to break away from the constraints of paper-based formats." For some companies, Internet use for advanced environmental reporting might seem to be a nice extra or just a buzzword in comparison to orthodox practice and the traditional environmental reporting focused on print media. The unique capabilities and benefits of Internet-based reporting, however, elevate it beyond the status of a mere buzzword. Internet technologies and services employed with XML and incorporated into a Web content management system can do more than offer new channels for report distribution or presentation.

The WWW is a service for distributing and presenting reports, including hypermedia features, online information and global access around the clock. Furthermore, information management can be improved in various ways: environmental data are captured from different data sources, combined despite different data formats, analyzed for decision making, professionally mastered and hypermedia-featured, tailored according to specific information needs and certain guidelines, distributed and presented, for example via e-mail, cross media, fax, or ordinary mail.

Furthermore, the content and design of reports will be transformed: online availability, downloads, additional environmental documents, interactivity, feedback opportunities, contact details, automatic order forms, environmental electronic forums, hyperlinks, graphically designed Web sites, navigation, search engines, Web rides, regular updates, and site promotion are some of the form and content capabilities that are already implemented to a certain extent.

All in all, the Internet is considered a "reporting facilitator". Sensing that traditional environmental reporting might have its limits, more companies are considering improving their reporting practice and increasing the use of reports in general. On improving environmental reporting, Volkswagen (2003) makes the point: "Glossy brochures which are not real are worthless. A classic glossy brochure makes little sense in this context. What is required here is to harness modern, flexible and cost-effective information technologies and channels – means which are also within the reach of small and medium-sized companies, and not just the global players. The Internet provides numerous possibilities along these lines." With this in mind, one major challenge seems to be using the Internet properly. Internet-based reporting supports companies in moving away from traditional environmental reporting practice towards more advanced sustainability reporting.

The latter is a powerful means for those companies that have already been publishing environmental, financial, and social reports for a long time and for those with experience using the Internet professionally for their business activities. For companies new to such Internet-based reporting, substantial initial costs and problems may be incurred, for example to put in place the data capture, data storage, metadata management, data analysis, and decision support which are seen as basic ICT prerequisites. Moreover, to establish a workflow will result in at least some initial costs. However, many companies no longer see managing sustainability reporting as an extra cost or burden on hard-pressed management, as from a long-term perspective, the attainable benefits may exceed the costs by far. Thus, it is recommended here that companies weigh the costs and benefits of such advanced sustainability reporting approaches against the target groups' information needs and the companies' resource capabilities to meet such needs.

The goal of this chapter has been to shed more light on moving away from early environmental reporting stages towards sustainability reporting, bringing to the surface tacit opportunities using the Internet and the benefits of its associated technologies as a reporting backbone for companies' underlying ICT infrastructure. Such a forward-looking approach may be a harbinger for a groundbreaking shift in the field, but at a minimum it will lead to progress in terms of reporting along three dimensions:

- Companies' workflow could be performed more efficiently, supporting all the core processes from automated preparation and streamlined administration towards fast distribution and appropriate presentation. Internet-based reporting can also facilitate the teamwork of different departments involved in text editing and other procedures, both internally and externally when co-operating with suppliers, intermediaries and rating or ranking institutions.
- The scope of the reports' contents could be expanded gradually, integrating economic, environmental and social issues according to companies' capabilities and communication strategies, but also to meet stakeholder needs. The typical evolution would move from an environmental report towards a fully integrated sustainability report, very often in line with the triple bottom line approach.

- Companies could improve their communication on environmental and sustainability issues, moving away from simple monologue and merely providing information towards an intensified stakeholder dialogue, user interactivity, information on demand, and thus developing from "one size fits all" publications on print media towards customized or even personalized reports available on different media.

Acknowledgments

The author thanks Therese Bracher and Daniela Hofstetter, EMPA (Switzerland), for their kind support and motivating assistance. Further, the author is very thankful to the editors, Lorenz Hilty, EMPA (Switzerland), Eberhard K. Seifert, Wuppertal Institute (Germany), and Réne Treibert, Hochschule Niederrhein (Germany), for their patience and benevolence. Special thanks to Jorge Marx Gómez, Otto-von-Guericke-Universität Magdeburg (Germany), and Jan Brosowski, University of Kaiserslautern (Germany), for fruitful discussions. Last, but not least, the author expresses his warmest thanks to Christoph Bey, Groupe Sup de Co La Rochelle (France), and Thomas Ruddy, EMPA (Switzerland), for their valuable help in linguistic matters and proofreading.

References

Adams, R., Houldin, M., & Slomp, S. (1999). Towards a generally accepted framework for environmental reporting. In M. Bennett & P. James (Eds.), *Sustainable measures. Evaluation and reporting of environmental and social performance* (pp. 314-329). Sheffield, UK: Greenleaf Publishing.

AEG. (2000). *AEG Grünbuch 2000: mit Umwelterklärungen der Werke in Rothenburg ob der Tauber, Nürnberg und Kassel.* Nürnberg, Germany: AEG Hausgeräte.

Andrews, O. (2002). Getting started on sustainability reporting. *Environmental Quality Management, 2*(Spring), 3-11.

Apache. (2003). Apache Cocoon. Retrieved June 24, 2003: *http://cocoon.apache.org.*

Arndt, H.-K., & Günther, O. (eds.). (2000). *Environmental markup language (EML).* First workshop, Berlin. Marburg, Germany: Metropolis.

Axelrod, R.A. (2000). Brave new words: The financial value of environmental communications. *Environmental Quality Management, 9*(4), 1-11.

Azzone, G., Brophy, M., Noci, G., Welford, R., & Young, W. (1997). A stakeholders' view of environmental reporting. *Long Range Planning, 30*(5), 699-709.

Badische Stahlwerke. (2000). *Umwelterklärung 2000 gemäß Artikel 5 der Verordnung (EWG) Nr. 1836/93 und DIN EN ISO 14001.* Kehl, Germany: Badische Stahlwerke.

Bayerische Landesbank. (1999) *Umweltbericht 1999. 3. Ökobilanz.* München, Germany: Bayerische Landesbank.

Beiersdorf. (1996). *Environmental protection/safety. Annual report 1996.* Hamburg, Germany: Beiersdorf.

Berkeley, S. (2000). Corporate reputation and the Internet. Environmental Data Services. Retrieved March 5, 2003: *http://www.endsdirectory.com/articles/index.cfm?action=dir12.*

Blumberg, J., Korsvold, A, & Blum, G. (2000). *Environmental performance and shareholder value.* World Business Council for Sustainable Development (WBCSD). Retrieved June 13, 2001: *http://www.wbcsd.org.*

Brophy, M., & Starkey, R. (1996). Environmental reporting. In R. Welford (Ed.), *Corporate environmental management. Systems and strategies* (pp. 177-198). London, UK: Earthscan.

Butner, S. (1996). Using the Internet for environmental benchmarking. Retrieved February 8, 2002: *www.seattle.batelle.org/p2online/eshweb.htm,* © 1996. Originally prepared for: *Seattle Daily Journal of Commerce,* environmental supplement, last update 1996-08-03).

Charter, M. (1998). Electronic environmental reporting (EER). The Centre for Sustainable Design. Surrey (UK). Retrieved February 7, 2000: *http://www.csfd.org.uk/eer/indey.htm.*

Cherry. (1998). *Umwelterklärung 1998 gemäß EG-Öko-Audit-Verordnung für die Werke Auerbach und Wolfsbach.* Auerbach, Germany: Cherry.

Clausen, J., Loew, T., Klaffke, K., Raupach, M., & Schoenheit, I. (2001). *The INEM sustainability reporting guide – A manual on practical and convincing communication for future-oriented companies.* Hamburg, Germany: International Network for Environmental Management (INEM). Retrieved March 22: *http://www.inem.org/free_downloads.*

Commission of the European Communities (COM). (2001). *Green paper. Promoting a European framework for corporate social responsibility.* 366 final, Brussels, Belgium.

Commission of the European Communities (COM). (2002). *Communication from the commission concerning corporate social responsibility: A business contribution to sustainable development.* 347 final, Brussels, Belgium.

Corporate Social Responsibility (CSR) Europe. (2000). *Communicating corporate social responsibility. Transparency, reporting and accountability. Recommendations for CSR reporting.* Brussels, Belgium: CSR Europe.

Daimler Benz. (1997). *Daimler-Benz Umweltbericht 1997.* Stuttgart, Germany: Daimler-Benz.

Deloitte Touche Tohmatsu International (DTTI), International Institute for Sustainable Development (IISD), SustainAbility Ltd. (1993). *Coming clean - Corporate environmental reporting, opening up for sustainable development.* London, UK: DTTI.

DiPiazza, S.A., & Eccles, R.G. (2002). *Building corporate trust. The future of corporate reporting.* New York, USA: John Wiley & Sons.

Dresdner Bank. (2000). *Nachhaltiges Handeln für Umwelt und Gesellschaft.* Bericht 1999 der Dresdner Bank AG. Frankfurt am Main, Germany: Dresdner Bank.

Dutch Association of Investors for Sustainable Development (VBDO). (1998). *Environmental information for investors.* Culemborg, The Netherlands: VBDO.

Edwards, D., Andersen Consulting. (1998). *The link between company environmental and financial performance.* London, UK: Earthscan.

Elkington, J., & Priddey, C. (1997, May/June). The CER report. Next: The paperless report. *Tomorrow,* 52-56.

EPCOR. (1998). *Voluntary action plan progress report 1998.* Edmonton, Canada: EPCOR, Environmental Affairs and Sustainable Development.

EPCOR. (1997). *Voluntary action plan progress report 1997.* Edmonton, Canada: EPCOR, Environmental Affairs and Sustainable Development.

Ernst & Young, KPMG, PricewaterhouseCoopers, House of Mandag Morgen. (1999). *The Copenhagen Charter. A management guide to stakeholder reporting.* Copenhagen, Denmark: Mandag Morgen.

European Committee for Standardization (CEN). (1999). *EN ISO 14031. Environmental performance evaluation. Guidelines.* Brussels, Belgium: CEN.

European Communities (EC). (2001). Regulation (EC) No. 761/2001 of the European Parliament and of the Council of 19 March 2001 allowing voluntary participation by organizations in a Community eco-management and audit scheme (EMAS). *Official Journal of the European Communities,* L 114.

Federal Environmental Agency. (2002). *Global voluntary corporate environmental reporting. The corporate register directory*. Berlin, Germany: Federal Environmental Agency, Section "Environmental Economic and Social Issues".

Fédération des Experts Comptables Européens (FEE). (2002). *FEE discussion paper providing assurance on sustainability reports.* Brussels, Belgium: FEE.

Fichter, K. (1998). *Umweltkommunikation und Wettbewerbsfähigkeit. Wettbewerbstheorien im Lichte empirischer Ergebnisse zur Umweltberichterstattung von Unternehmen.* Marburg, Germany: Metropolis.

future e.V., Institute for Ecological Economy Research (IÖW). (1994). *Environmental reports – environmental statements. Guidelines on preparation and distribution.* Osnabrück, Germany: future e.V.

Gassen, J. (2001). Internetbasierte deutsche Jahresabschlusspublizität. Eine experimentelle Analyse der HTML- vs. PDF-Entscheidung. *Die Betriebswirtschaft, 61*(4), 409-426.

German Institute for Standardization e.V. (DIN). (1997). DIN 33922. *Environmental reports for the public*. Berlin, Germany: Beuth.

Global Reporting Initiative (GRI). (2000). Sustainability reporting guidelines on economic, environmental, and social performance. Retrieved February 5, 2002: *http://www.globalreporting.org*.

Global Reporting Initiative (GRI). (2002). Sustainability reporting guidelines. Retrieved October 15, 2002: *http://www.globalreporting.org*.

Gröner, S. (2000). *Umweltberichterstattung für eine nachhaltige Entwicklung – Eine theoretische und empirische analyse*. Aachen, Germany: Shaker.

Heidelberg. (2000). *Umweltbericht 1999/2000. Umwelt, Gesundheit, Sicherheit.* Heidelberg, Germany: Heidelberger-Druckmaschinen.

Henkel. (2000). *Henkel environmental communication 5.* Düsseldorf, Germany: Henkel (CD-ROM).

Henseler, J., Isenmann, R., & Müller-Merbach, H. (2004). *Internetbasierte Geschäftsberichterstattung. Stand und Entwicklungstendenzen.* Berlin, Germany: Erich Schmidt.

Herremans, I.M., Welsh, C., Kane, D., & Bott, R. (1999). How an environmental report can help a company 'learn' about its own environmental performance. *Business Strategy and the Environment, 6*(4), 155-169.

Hoechst. (1996). *Progress Report 1996. Umwelt, Sicherheit, Gesundheit. Daten und Fakten.* Frankfurt am Main, Germany: 3rd edition, Hoechst (CD-ROM).

Isenmann, R., & Lenz, C. (2001). Customized corporate environmental reporting by Internet-based push- and pull-technologies. *Eco-Management and Auditing, 8*(2), 100-110.

Isenmann, R., & Lenz, C. (2002). Internet use for corporate environmental reporting: Current challenges – technical benefits – practical guidance. *Business Strategy and the Environment, 11*(3), 181-202.

Isenmann, R., Lenz, C., & Müller-Merbach, H. (2001). Betriebliche Umweltberichterstattung im Internet. Der aktuelle Stand für Deutschland. *Praxis der Wirtschaftsinformatik, 38*(218), 97-107.

Isenmann, R., Lenz, C., & Müller-Merbach, H. (2002, September 25-27). The future of corporate environmental communication. Trends, contents, media, technologies. In W. Pillmann & K. Tochtermann (Eds.), *Environmental communication in the information society.* Proceedings of the 16th conference "Informatics for environmental protection," Vienna, Austria. Part 1 and 2 (pp. 234-241). Vienna, Austria: International Society for Environmental Protection.

Isenmann, R., Lenz, C., Reitz, C., & Müller-Merbach, H. (2001, September 19-21). Nachhaltigkeitsberichterstattung. Internet als Medium zur Integration der Geschäfts- und Umweltberichterstattung von Unternehmen. In H.U. Buhl, A. Huther & B. Reitwiesner (Eds.), *Information Age economy. Innovations, methods and applications for electronic commerce. 5th International Conference Wirtschaftsinformatik 2001/3rd Conference Information Systems in Finance 2001, Augsburg* (pp. 817-830). Heidelberg, Germany: Physica.

Jones, K., Alabaster, T., & Hetherington, K. (1999). Internet-based environmental reporting. Current trends. *Greener Management International, 26*(Summer), 69-90.

Jones, K., & Walton, J. (1999). Internet-based environmental reporting. Key components. In M. Bennett & P. James (Eds.), *Sustainable measures. Evaluation and reporting of environmental and social performance* (pp. 412-425). Sheffield, UK: Greenleaf Publishing.

Kaptein, M., & Wempe, J. (1999). *Sustainability management: Balancing and integrating economic, social and environmental responsibilities.* Management report no. 51-1999. Erasmus Universiteit Rotterdam, The Netherlands.

Kerkhoven, J., & Nelson, S.B. (1994). Electronic environmental reporting. The Internet and corporate environmental accountability. Retrieved January 11, 2000: *http://www.communicopia.bc.ca/library/emar&WWW.cfm.*

Kiernan, M.J. (2001). Eco-value, sustainability, and shareholder value: Driving environmental performance to the bottom line. *Environmental Quality Management, 11*(4), 1-12.

Klaffke, K., & Krick, T. (2003). *Informationsoffenheit von Unternehmen. Die Nachhaltigkeitsberichterstattung der DAX 100 Unternehmen.* imug Arbeitspapier 12/2003. Hannover, Germany: imug Institut für Markt-Umwelt-Gesellschaft.

Kolk, A. (1999). The Internet as a green management tool. *Harvard Business Review, 6*(3), 307-316.

Kolk, A., Walhain, S., & van de Wateringen, S. (2001). Environmental reporting by the Fortune Global 250: Exploring the influence of nationality and sector. *Business Strategy and the Environment, 10*(1), 15-28.

KPMG. (1999). KPMG international survey of environmental reporting 1999. KPMG: University of Amsterdam. Retrieved December 23, 2002: *http://www.wimm.nl/publications/kpmg1999.pdf.*

KPMG. (2000). *Beyond the numbers: How leading organizations are linking values with value to gain competitive advantage.* KPMG's Assurance & Advisory Services Center (AASC). KPMG, Switzerland. Available at: *http://www.kpmg.ca/en/services/audit/beyondthenumbers.html.*

KPMG. (2002). *KPMG International survey of corporate sustainability reporting 2002.* KPMG: University of Amsterdam. Retrieved December 23, 2002: *http://www.wimm.nl/publications/KPMG2002.pdf.*

Krut, R., & Moretz, A. (2000). The state of global environmental reporting: Lessons from the global 100. *Corporate Environmental Strategy, 7*(1), 85-91.

Lange, C., Ahsen von, A., & Daldrup, H. (2001). *Umweltschutzreporting. Umwelterklärungen und – berichte als Module eines Reportingsystems.* München, Germany: Oldenbourg.

Larsen, L.B. (2000). Strategic implication of environmental reporting. *Corporate Environmental Strategy, 7*(3), 276-287.

Laudon, K.C., & Laudon, J.P. (2000). *Management information systems. Organization and technology in the networked enterprise* (6th ed.). Upper Saddle River, NJ, USA: Prentice Hall.

Lenz, C. (2003). *Empfängerorientierte Unternehmenskommunikation – Einsatz der Internet-Technologie am Beispiel der Umweltberichterstattung.* Köln, Germany: Eul.

Lenz, C., Isenmann, R., & Reitz, C. (2001, May 10-11). Zielgruppenorientierte umweltbericht-erstattung von unternehmen mit XML. In K. Tochtermann & W.-F. Riekert (Eds.), *Neue Methoden für das Wissensmanagement im Umweltbereich. 4. Workshop Hypermedia im Umweltschutz/3. Workshop Environmental Markup Language, 2001, Ulm* (pp. 57-69). Marburg, Germany: Metropolis.

Line, M., Hawley, H., & Krut, R. (2002). The development of global environmental and social reporting. *Corporate Environmental Strategy, 9*(1), 69-78.

Lippman, S. (2001). Supply chain environmental management. *Environmental Quality Management, 11*(2), 11-14.

Lober, D.J. (1997). What makes environmental reports effective: Current trends in corporate reporting. *Corporate Environmental Strategy, 4*(2), 15-24.

MacLean, R., & Gottfrid, R. (2000). Corporate environmental reports: Stuck management processes hold back real progress. *Corporate Environmental Strategy, 7*(3), 244-255.

Marshall, S.R., & Brown, D. (2003). Corporate environmental reporting: What's in a metric? *Business Strategy and the Environment, 12*(2), 87-106.

Marx Gómez, J., & Rautenstrauch, C. (eds.). (2001). *Von der Ökobilanzierung bis zur automatisierten Umweltberichterstattung mit Stoffstrommanagementsystemen – Eine Fallstudie*. Aachen, Germany: Shaker.

Merck. (1999). *Komposition der Elemente. Pharma, Labor und Spezialchemie*. Darmstadt: Merck (CD-ROM).

Merrick, J., & Crookshanks, C. (2001). Report on a survey of environmental reporting costs and benefits. Tempe, UK Department of Environment, Food, and Rural Affairs (DEFRA). Retrieved August 19, 2002: *http://www.defra.gov.uk/environment/envrp/environ/environ.pdf*.

Mesterharm, M. (2001). *Integrierte Umweltkommunikation von Unternehmen. Theoretische Grundlagen und empirische Analyse der Umweltkomunikation am Beispiel der Automobilindustrie*. Marburg, Germany: Metropolis.

Miele. (1999). *Umwelterklärung Werkstandort Gütersloh 1999*. Gütersloh, Germany: Miele.

Moore, M.A. (2003). Through the eye of a needle: The importance of portals to environmental information management. *Environmental Quality Management, 13*(1), 55-66.

Morhardt, E.J. (2002). *Clean, green, and read all over. Ten rules for effective corporate environmental and sustainability reporting*. Milwaukee, USA: ASQ Quality Press.

Morley Fund Management. (2001). *Corporate governance and voting policy 2001*. London, UK: Morley Fund Management.

Müller, K., de Frutos, J., Schüssler, K.-U., Haarbosch, H., & Randel, M. (1996). *Eco-efficiency and financial analysis*. Basel, Switzerland: European Federation of Financial Analysts Society.

Ollier, A. (1996, March 27). *Corporate environmental reporting on the Internet. Environmental issues in visual communications design.* Workshop proceedings. London, UK.

RheinLand Versicherungen. (1997). *Umweltbericht 1996.* Neuss, Germany: RheinLand Versicherungen.

Schaltegger, S., & Figge, F. (1997). *Umwelt und Shareholder Value.* WWZ-Studie/Bank Sarasin & Cie, Investment Research. Basel, Switzerland: WWZ Forum der Universität Basel.

Schoop, E., & Gersdorf, R. (2001). Content Management für Single Source Multiple Media and Multiple Usage Publishing. *Wirtschaftswissenschaftliches Studium, 30*(7), 991-998.

Schraml, T. (1997). *Operationalisierung der ökologieorientierten Berichterstattung aus Sicht des Informationsmanagements - Konzeption eines Vorgehensmodells zur formalisierten Explikation von Dokumentstrukturmodellen im Rahmen der Umweltkommunikation von Unternehmen.* Dissertation thesis, Technical University Dresden, Germany.

Schulz, T.M. (1995). *Ökologieorientierte Berichterstattung von Unternehmen. Ökologieorientierte Berichterstattung in Geschäfts- und Umweltberichten unter Berücksichtigung der Informationsbedürfnisse der Stakeholder, untersucht in der europäischen Chemieindustrie.* Dissertation thesis, University of St. Gallen, Switzerland.

Scott, P., & Jackson, R. (2002). Environmental, social and sustainability reporting on the Web: Best practices. *Corporate Environmental Strategy, 9*(2), 193-202.

Shepherd, K., Abkowitz, M., & Cohen, M.A. (2001). Online corporate environmental reporting: Improvements and innovation to enhance stakeholder value. *Corporate Environmental Strategy, 8*(4), 307-315.

Skillius, Å., & Wennberg, U. (1998). *Continuity, credibility and comparability. Key challenges for corporate environmental performance measurement and communication.* The International Institute for Industrial Environmental Economics at Lund University, Sweden.

SocialFunds (Socially responsible investing information concerning corporations, mutual funds, and more). (2000). Investors prod CEO's to adopt new reporting standards. Retrieved December 16, 2000: *http://socialfunds.com/news/article.*

Spencer-Cooke, A. (1995). Engaging stakeholders: The next challenge in corporate environmental reporting. *IÖW/VÖW-Informationsdienst, 10*(3-4), 4-5.

Steven, M., Schwarz, E., & Letmathe, P. (1997). *Umweltberichterstattung und Umwelterklärung nach der EG-Öko-Audit-Verordnung. Grundlagen, Methoden und Anwendungen.* Berlin, Germany: Springer.

SustainAbility Ltd. (2002). *Virtual sustainability.* London, UK: Beacon Press.

SustainAbility Ltd., United Nations Environmental Programme (UNEP), Technology, Industry and Economics Division. (1999). *Engaging stakeholders 1999. The Internet reporting report.* London, UK: Beacon Press.

Swissair. (1997). *Der dritte Umweltbericht 1995/1996. Flying the globe with the world in mind.* Zürich, Switzerland: Swissair (CD-ROM).

The Association of Chartered Certified Accountants (ACCA). (1997). *Guide to environment and energy reporting and accounting 1997.* London, UK: ACCA.

The Association of Chartered Certified Accountants (ACCA). (1998). *Making values count: Contemporary experience in social and ethical accounting, auditing, and reporting.* London, UK: The Certified Accountants Educational Trust.

The Association of Chartered Certified Accountants (ACCA). (2001). *Environmental, social and sustainability reporting on the World Wide Web: A guide to best practice.* London, UK: The Certified Accountants Educational Trust.

The Association of Chartered Certified Accountants (ACCA). (2003). *The big picture: How the environment influences corporate profit.* London, UK: ACCA.

The Canadian Institute of Chartered Accountants (CICA). (1994). *Reporting on environmental reporting.* Carried out in association with Canadian Standards Association, Financial Executives Institute Canada and International Institute for Sustainable Development (IISD). Toronto, Canada: CICA.

Unilever. (2000). *Unilever environmental performance 2000. How we care for the environment.* London, UK: Unilever (Digidisc).

United Nations Environment Programme Industry and Environment (UNEP), Sustainability Ltd. (1994). *Company environmental reporting. A measure of the progress of business and industry towards sustainable development.* Technical Report 24. Paris, France: UNEP.

van Dalen, M. (1997). *Company environmental reporting. Conditions for the optimal information structure of environmental reports.* Dissertation thesis. University of Humberside, UK, and Zeeland Polytechnic Flushing, The Netherlands.

Volkswagen, A.G. (2003). Mobility and responsibility. Improving social performance reporting. Retrieved April 4, 2003: *http://www.vw-ag.de/english/defaultIE.html.*

Vollmer, S.A.M. (1995). *EG-Öko-Audit-Verordnung Umwelterklärung: Anforderungen, Hintergründe, Gestaltungsoptionen.* Berlin, Germany: Springer.

Weil, W.B., & Winter-Watson, B. (2002). The Internet and sustainability reporting. Improving communication with stakeholders. In J. Park & N. Rome (Eds.), *The ecology of the new economy. Sustainable transformation of global information, communications and electronic industries* (pp. 85-97). Sheffield, UK: Greenleaf.

Wheeler, D., & Elkington, J. (2001). The end of the corporate environmental report? Or the advent of cybernetic sustainability reporting and communication. *Business Strategy and the Environment, 10*(1), 1-14.

World Business Council for Sustainable Development (WBCSD). (2003). *Sustainable development reporting. Striking the balance.* Geneva, Switzerland: WBCSD.

Endnotes

1 As an attempt of a definition, corporate environmental reports are regarded as the core instruments within environmental communication, usually addressing a wide range of target groups, often produced as single documents and issued for a certain period of time (Fichter, 1998, p. 44; Herremans et al., 1999, p. 158). The whole variety of tools used by companies for communicating environmental issues is outlined by DTTI, IISD and SustainAbility (1993, pp. 17-19), UNEP and SustainAbility (1994, pp. 10-11; 21), CICA (1994, pp. 40-44), and Brophy and Starkey (1996). Moreover, Mesterharm (2001, pp. 549; 555-565) provides a comprehensive classification for environmental communication instruments. He considers such a report as the primary and leading vehicle and thus calls it the pivotal instrument of environmental communication because of its unique claim to credibility and the reliance external stakeholders ascribe to it, containing quantitative data as well as qualitative. Companies use these reports for disclosing their environmental performance, often including the following topics: top management statement, management policy and system as well as input-output-inventory of environmental impacts of production processes and products. See for example UNEP and SustainAbility (1994, p. 11) or Lober (1997, p. 15). Due to its voluntary status in most countries and

its lack of generally accepted standards, there are several different methods of environmental reporting currently in use, for example: compliance based reporting, toxic release inventory based reporting, eco-balance reporting, performance based reporting, product focused reporting, environmental and social reporting, and sustainability reporting.

2 The Internet is used as a catch phrase for a set of information and communication technologies and services (Laudon & Laudon, 2000). Basic Internet technologies include client-server-architecture, technical protocols resp. standard interfaces (TCP/IP) and hypermedia. These technologies provide certain Internet services such as WWW, e-mail and markup languages suitable for advanced Internet use like XML and its XML-based applications such as eXtensible Business Reporting Language (XBRL) and Environmental Markup Language (EML) that are both developed for progressing in the field of reporting.

3 XML is a promising formatting language that provides a standardised, platform-independent format, to be used in many ways for structuring data and documents. Used for environmental reporting, it may be appropriate to understand XML as a collective term, summarising a range of technologies associated in this context. For an overview in the field of environmental reporting see Arndt and Günther (2000).

4 It is one of the early stated goals that environmental reporting will develop towards sustainability reporting, or at least that sustainability issues should be an integral part of it. Cf. DTTI, IISD and SustainAbility (1993, p. 1).

5 The three developments highlighted here are the essence of a comprehensive analysis carried out by Isenmann, Lenz and Müller-Merbach (2002).

6 See Endnote 1.

7 PDF is a document format, primarily used for reproducing hard copy reports and other documents on the Internet. A report stored as PDF file retains design, layout and formatting features and thus has exactly the same appearance as the underlying hard copy document. Although PDF is an offline-document format that could be downloaded, such a file can also incorporate some interactive features of a Web site, for example hyperlinks. These opportunities have made PDF the format of popular choice for electronically distributing reports although produced with a clear print focus. PDF can be opened, viewed and printed via Acrobat Reader, a freely available software tool. Miele's 1999 environmental statement as well as Cherry's 1998 environmental statement clearly demonstrate that PDFs incorporating well-designed hyperlinks could be in fact a suitable and cost-saving alternative, particularly for small and medium sized companies.

8 Gassen (2001) observed a really interesting phenomenon: Due to increasing Internet use in the field of financial reporting, he analysed impacts that

reports' data format will have on user-friendliness and quality assessment. More precisely, he tested whether a report should be provided exclusively offline as PDF file or if it would be more useful disclosing reports' content online via HTML. Maybe surprisingly, the results strongly demonstrate that HTML was clearly preferred, for example in terms of time needed to answer certain questions, smaller data transfer, correctness of data users are searching and usability. Perhaps, the findings are in contrast to insights of the early stages of environmental reporting when PDF was thought of as a fairly proper and cost-saving format used for environmental reports available on the Internet. Further, for companies starting with a paper based report – as many still do – producing PDFs can be a first step to provide reports on the Internet because this could be performed with little effort without reengineering the reporting workflow.

[9] See Henkel's variety of instruments, including special interest articles, CD-ROM, site reports, open house events, sustainability ratings, reports, direct dialogue, Internet platform, consumer information, press releases and other vehicles relevant within this field: Retrieved March 13, 2003, *http://www.she.henkel.com/com/html/content/main_05-01.htm.*

[10] Just visit BP's Web site on "environmental and social" <*http://www.bp.com/environ_social/index.asp#*> and then leading to the data desk: <*http://www.bp.com/datadesk02/selections.asp*>. Retrieved January 18, 2003. Closely related to the above, but in the field of financial reporting, Software AG offers several features to provide tailored views on its online financial report; visit <*http://213.68.23.41/de/index.htm*>. Retrieved January 18, 2003.

[11] Web mining is an evaluation procedure supported through software analysing Internet protocols, cookies and other footprints while surfing or browsing a company's Web sites. It gathers information on how many users have visited a reporting Web site, who they are, where they are from, which Web sites they have read or which are preferred ones.

[12] The increasingly affecting nature of environmental reports as a source for the financial community is described by Edwards and Andersen Consulting (1998), Müller et al. (1996), and more recently by Axelrod (2000) and Klaffke and Krick (2003). The fact that analysts scrutinise these reports as carefully as they currently analyse its financial counterparts is sometimes called the "greening of investor relations". See also: <*http://www.sustainable-investment.org*>, an Internet platform that provides a wide range of information on the market for sustainable investment.

[13] Crucial steps towards an automated reporting system based on the Internet have already been taken, including frameworks, proper sustainability-DTD, and ICT applications. See Isenmann et al. (2001), Lenz (2003), and Marx Gómez and Rautenstrauch (2001).

Chapter XIII

Web Portals: A Tool for Environmental Management

Martin Kreeb, University of Hohenheim, Germany

Werner Schulz, University of Hohenheim, Germany

Christof Voßeler, University of Hohenheim, Germany

Helmut Krcmar, Technical University Munich, Germany

Annette Rudel, Technical University Berlin, Germany

Abstract

*Ecoradar (*www.ecoradar.org / www.oekoradar.de*) is the name of an innovative Internet portal that sets out to use the simplest and most persuasive means to motivate others to implement sustainable management in those enterprises that have so far taken little or no interest in this subject. This major project, in which over 80 German enterprises and institutions participated, is part of the new funding focus "Integrated Environmental Protection – Instruments for Sustainable Business Management" set by the German Federal Ministry of Education and Research. The primary task of the portal is the creation of an environmental management community. The purpose of this article is to show the structure and elements of the ecoradar community. Both the creation of a "culture of trust" among the participating enterprises and the* *strategy of successful integration of the joint project partners are of specific interest. In the following, the content models are presented and the article examines the ability of the ecoradar community to develop, share and use the available knowledge by using the tools of knowledge management. Finally, the authors describe the technology used to create the portal.*

Construction of Ecoradar Knowledge Community

A great variety of research papers have been published in the field of environmental management during the last 20 years. The problem, however, has persisted: conversion of this knowledge into enterprise practice. The development target of the ecoradar portal is to reduce the information costs of those SME enterprises interested in environmental management. In order to achieve this target, a strategic community concept of the third generation has been developed in order to build a knowledge community in the SME sector (Kreeb et al., 2002).

The main emphasis of the ecoradar community is on the knowledge field and the service and project areas. The community started as a project community. For a start, ecoradar, as a classic research project, measures success by certain criteria focusing on timeframe and milestones (Bullinger, 2002). An additional feature is the use of a virtual project team (scientists, consultants, entrepreneurs). A form of virtual cooperation has been implemented by establishing a specific editorship- and tele-cooperation system. These project communities represent the preliminary stage on the way to a knowledge community. Ecoradar is a knowledge network stretched beyond the limits of individual universities and enterprises.

Wenger and Snyder (2000) describe a knowledge community as a "flexible organizational unit, beyond official organizational or informal units. The community is motivated by the common interest of the members in the field of knowledge. Participation is voluntary. The motivation to participate is a positive cost/benefit relation." (Wenger & Snyder, 2000)

The collective benefit is categorized by Rheingold (1994, 2000) using the following three dimensions:

- social use, identification by a common goal
- knowledge capital, use of knowledge from various sources
- community feeling, system of real contacts and experience backgrounds

The ecoradar community understands itself as community of interests, with the following features defined by Hagel and Armstrong (1997):

- focus and emphasis on a specific interest
- the ability to integrate contents and communication
- the use of information, supplied by the members
- access to competing providers

The major task of the community developers is the professional relations management among the individual community members. The goal of ecoradar relation management is to integrate over 100 participants in the community process. This means that anonymous co-workers are transformed into active community members. The socio-economic group-dynamic processes together with technological organizational processes have absolute priority. It could be summarized as: Who makes what with whom for what purpose?

Knowledge Management in the Ecoradar Community

An expert set of 21 different research institutions is involved in the joint project. The expert set has the function of editing the relevant knowledge of the "community environment" so that enterprises can transfer this expert knowledge into practical environment-oriented management. The knowledge management model of ecoradar supports the creation of knowledge within the enterprise on the basis of external knowledge in the spirit of an ontological knowledge spiral. The expert knowledge supports the acquisition of external knowledge and the development of one's own knowledge. Current knowledge distribution is supported both by a specifically designed telecooperation system as well as by the portal (Boehmann & Krcmar, 1999) itself. That telecooperation-model and the portal are regularly updated by the experts and support knowledge preservation (Kriwald & Haasis, 2001) in enterprises. In the later course of the project it has to be assessed by the experts whether an ontology-based knowledge evaluation can be implemented. This evaluation research in co-operation with enterprise practice and with the help of empirical methods has to ensure that the quality criteria pursued by ecoradar such as environmental discharge, target group orientation and in particular suitability for practical use (often referred to as "SME relevance") are actually respected and implemented. The evaluation of enterprise practice is performed by the practice community.

Table 1. Knowledge warehouse vs. knowledge network (Wallert, 2002)

Criteria	Knowledge Warehouse	Knowledge Network
Philosophy	Externalization of knowledge	Direct communication, Reference to human experts
Range of application	➢ structured problem areas ➢ given goal ➢ known relevance of information ➢ Consequences of the decision foreseeable ➢ re-usable solutions	➢ unstructured problem areas ➢ goal not given ➢ unknown interdependencies ➢ Consequences of the decision unforeseeable ➢ limited reusability of solutions
Artificial Intelligence	High (CMS)	Low
Knowledge-requirements	Rules and methods	Not exactly specifiable
Moment of knowledge division	At the beginning of the knowledge process	On demand
Method of displaying knowledge	Structured knowledge	Reference to knowledge carriers as well as presentations of expert's assessment
Knowledge transfer	Knowledge conveyed by knowledge carrier (experts)	Bilateral negotiating of the modalities for the sharing of knowledge
Role of IT	Storage and processing of knowledge	Support of the information process and communication process
Access to knowledge	Information retrieval & data mining	Creating contact and communication with knowledge carrier

Ecoradar's development team confirms the experience of Davenport and Prusak (1998), that knowledge can only be created in the brains of knowledge carriers. Ecoradar's knowledge carriers are scientific experts and entrepreneurs, who cooperate within the community process. The primary focus is on the externalization of the expert's knowledge. Know-how is transferred in an external information system (knowledge warehouse, Content Management System CMS). Externalization of knowledge (Nonaka & Takeuchi, 1995) is especially suitable for standardizable knowledge (standards, laws, etc.). The recent experience of the ecoradar research project has shown that direct communication in a knowledge network is the best way to convey the expert's knowledge and experience.

Ecoradar Practice Community

Representatives of the joint project's target group, enterprises in Germany, have already given it broad approval in its start-up phase. Some 40 enterprises employing an estimated one million members of staff have made the decision to support production and development of the prototype. The development of so-called "eco-radar" screens is to be carried out in 18 workshops, hand in hand with business representatives and numerous experts. The organization of the high-calibre working groups has been taken on by Europe's largest business-led environmental initiative, the German Environmental Management Association (BAUM e.V.), Hamburg. In addition, in summer 2001 a representative written survey was conducted in around 9,000 enterprises. The survey results reflect the state of the art in the field of sustainable management in German enterprises. These results are integrated in the ecoradar development process in order to enable enterprises to identify relevant technical, political and economic risks – as well as market opportunities – in the field of sustainability and environment much earlier than their competitors.

Content Model

The ecoradar system portal consists of eight screens that can be used as an ensemble – or individually if preferred – to scan a company profile (Company Radar – "micro-level") or the wider economic setting (Macro Radar – "macro-level"). Company Radar is a system component that can be accessed from any ecoradar screen, enabling users to systematically record and evaluate their company's environmental data, policy and goals. Macro Radar, a similar system component that can be accessed from any ecoradar screen, enables users to record and evaluate the macro-level on the basis of the latest research – such as global, national and regional environmental data and environmental goals.

Within the project ecoradar the Internet portal is being created as an environmental service. First, it is essential to embed information, references and checklists that have been already part of the ecoradar framework and former designs. In addition to these functions, the final version will be able to accommodate all interested parties by providing a virtual community. Further, it will also identify possibilities for cooperation among all participants. Finally, it is created to enable the integration of environmental management in business processes.

The first step is the creation of a user-friendly layout of the portal's Web sites. The essential features are a clear graphical structure, easy handling and direct access to services available within short download times.

Figure 1. Ecoradar portal screenshot

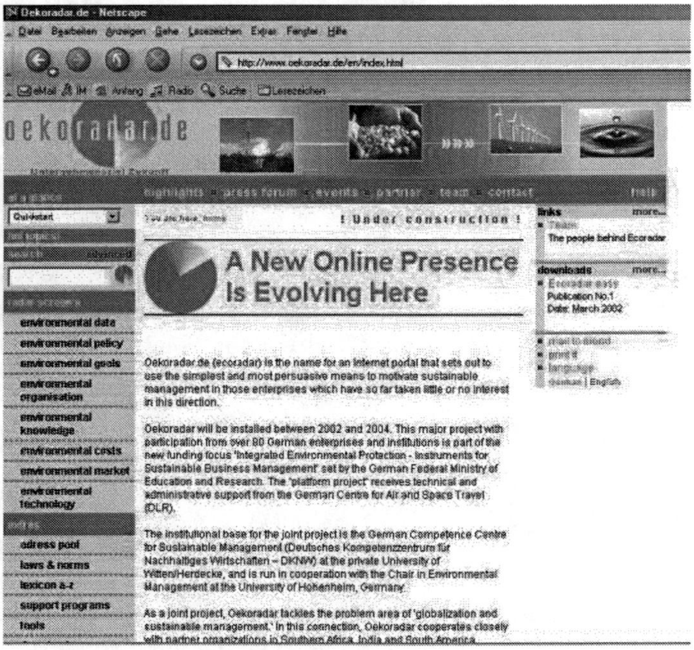

Portal Structure

Reflecting the development of a micro-macro link, that is, a link between a company and its surroundings, each of the following eight screens has been selected as a theme-oriented platform for supporting services and information to business and industry. The micro-macro link is represented in each screen by the company and the macro radar.

Environmental Data

Environmental data are generally regarded as the "oxygen" of environmental policy. Regional, national and global environmental data provide a key basis on which companies can take action. Wherever the environmental situation is monitored and observed, wherever citizens are surveyed for their subjective experience of environmental problems, this can provide impetus for action in environmental policy. Basic company environmental data, for example, might be figures relating to energy, water, wastewater, waste, emissions and hazardous substances. Carbon dioxide emissions would be one example of key global environmental data.

Environmental Policy

Approaches for Action Toward Sustainable Management

Future environmental standards imposed on enterprises are moulded partly by their own environmental policies, but also by national governments and party programs. For example, national environmental policy approaches for action form an important basis for the future use of "command-and-control" instruments. In Germany, for instance, the ideas of the coalition parties, the opposition and the independent parties at the national, federal state and municipal levels are not the only matters of importance. Considerable influence is exerted on future environmental policy by the policy-making bodies of the European Union and numerous other international organizations.

Environmental Goals

Principles for Action Toward Sustainable Management

While environmental data represent a significant basis on which to take environmental policy action, environmental goals provide principles for action that, for their part, form the basis for the future application of environment policy instruments. Society should come together and use environment quality objectives to define core elements of environment policy action, working towards sustainable management in the years to come. A company's own environmental targets, in contrast, are an element of the company's internal early detection system. Basically these should be geared to continuous improvement of environmental performance.

Environmental Organization

An effective environmental early detection system can only be incorporated successfully within the enterprise once an efficient organization is in place for the structure and processes of environmental performance. Then, and only then, is it possible to perform the target-performance comparisons that are necessary for early detection. Another important factor is to work closely with public environmental authorities and associations: environmental authorities are the pivotal interface between the letter of the law and its enforcement. Enterprises that maintain good contacts with environmental authorities have swift access to information on new requirements according to environmental legislation. Associations are seen as powerful environmental policy actors and can pass on to their corporate members targeted advance information on environmental performance, picked up during the course of their lobbying.

Environmental Knowledge Management

Environmental know-how, both inside and outside a company, is a central element of environmental early detection. A cornerstone for knowledge transfer in the environmental sphere is formed by institutions such as the German Federal Environmental Agency, the Federal Agency for Nature Conservation, the Federal German Foundation for the Environment, and the International Transfer Centre for Environmental Technology. Likewise the media, as environment policy opinion-formers, play an important role in early detection.

Environmental Costs

Monitoring and assessment of environmental costs in the widest sense (calculation of a company's pollution control costs, anticipation of external costs and the costs of neglecting environmental aspects, identification of potential cost reductions) is a permanent task within early detection. In particular, deducting – at least mentally – the costs of environmental degradation (today's external costs – tomorrow's operating costs) is a strategic element of eco-controlling.

Environmental Market

Environmental protection has developed into a significant economic factor over the past 30 years. In the year 1997 only, German private and public sector spending on environmental protection was around DM 65,000 million. Studies predict that the market for environmental technology and environmentally friendly products will continue to grow internationally in the coming years. Admittedly Germany still has a high market share in this area. However, other industrial nations – notably the USA, Canada and Great Britain – have developed strategies for gaining targeted access to new markets and supporting exports of environmental technology by their suppliers.

Environmental Technology

Technical indicators play an important role in the early detection process. In particular, specialist trade fairs and exhibitions not only create new contacts and stabilize business relationships but also provide advance information on technical innovations. Delphi surveys are increasingly conducted as part of this technology foresight process, and these can serve to guide future strategic orientation.

Content Structure

Besides the recording and evaluation of a company's environmental data, policy and goals, *Company Radar* offers further information and instruments as management tools in each screen. *Company Radar* of the screen "environmental organization" offers such information as management tools to successfully organize an internal environmental project, to successfully integrate a system of environmental indicators into business operations or how to organize an environmental management system according to ISO 14000ff or EMAS.

Macro Radar focuses on the external surroundings of the company. In the *Macro Radar part* of "Environmental Data," relevant environmental data from the local, regional, national, European and worldwide levels is provided. The screen "Environmental Organization" offers all-important information about institutions and organizations of the private and public sectors in the fields of business and environment from the local up to the world-wide level.

Ecoradar is the result of a wealth of research that has been collected over at last two decades. There are copious research findings under all eight of the subheadings, along with case studies and applications tested in practice. Some parts of the ecoradar system rely heavily on the latest environmental performance standards. The sequence of "Environmental Data – Environmental Policy – Environmental Goals – Environmental Organization – Environmental Knowledge" largely follows the thread of the European Union Eco-Management and Audit Scheme (EMAS) and ISO 14001. The integration of the ecoradar screens "Environmental Costs," "Environmental Market" and "Environmental Technology" in the overall system is largely attributable to the experience reported by companies and reflects the fact that there is a recurring demand for this kind of information in business practice.

Four-Point Menu for Company Radar

Ecoradar will use the Internet to provide structured communication of the latest expertise on sustainable management in a way that assists decision making and is comprehensible and relevant to enterprises. A four-point menu – which once again is integrated into all ecoradar screens – will make this task easier for companies.

1. *Getting Started.* The "Getting Started" menu shows companies the fundamental points they should take into account.
2. *Stumbling Blocks.* The "Stumbling Blocks" menu shows how common mistakes can be avoided.
3. *Checklists.* The "Checklists" contain guidelines for action that can be used interactively.
4. *Benchmarks.* The "Benchmarks" allow comparisons with other enterprises by "looking over their shoulder".

"Ecoradar Extras"

The eight screens above are complemented by the so-called "ecoradar extras". Users are offered structured information within the "extras" found in Table 2.

Table 2. "Ecoradar Extras"

'Oekoradar Extras'	
➢ Environmental Laws	➢ Environmental Standards
➢ Environmental Financing Programs	➢ Environmental Software
➢ Tools and Downloads	➢ Training
➢ Address Pool	➢ Policy Programs of Political Parties
➢ Glossary	➢ www highlights

Information Technology (IT)

IT research should contribute to ensuring that ecoradar actually fulfils the quality criteria it has set itself, namely coherence and effectiveness, capacity for integration, clarity and, in particular, user-friendliness. The ecoradar system must measure up to the latest developments in IT so that it can do full justice to its future-oriented role. Intelligent solutions must be developed for three fields in particular:

- *Ecoradar as a workable tool.* The concern here is to create interactive, creative opportunities for the user (examples: automatic generation of indexes on the basis of a personal database; form-filling assistance; checklist programs). The success of the ecoradar system may well critically depend on the level of convenience built into the system architecture.
- *Integrating ecoradar into existing business processes.* The better environmental performance is integrated into typical business processes, the greater the prospects of success for sustainable management.
- *Uploading ecoradar technology onto the Internet.* The core parts of the ecoradar system are supposed to be placed on the Internet as soon as possible (no later than one year into the project) and continually updated, so that the feedback coming from users can be integrated reasonably quickly into the current research and development process. Ecoradar forms an ideal foundation for an Internet portal for sustainable management and can be seen as the seed from which such a portal may grow.

Internet Strategy

The concept of a Web portal has proven useful in handling the overwhelming amount of data available on the Internet. A portal can structure the information and is able to display the content in a user-friendly layout. This is the basis for effective research by the business community. A portal is a universal and comfortable system to access applications, content and services focused on a specific topic.

Portals can be labelled as Web-based, multimedia-style and accessible via standard Internet-browsers:

- *task-oriented:* adaptable regarding the tasks of users or customers
- *categorized:* content and services structured by categories

- *personalized:* individually designed to achieve 1:1 relationships with users/ customers.

Internal and External Aspects of Portal

The original concept of portals (i.e., Yahoo, Lycos, Excite, ...) was focussed on the private, individual Internet user. The idea of the portal is now increasingly focussing on individual companies. This is called an "Enterprise Information Portal" (EIP). An EIP is focused both on internal users (employees and management) and external parties (customers, suppliers and other stakeholders of the company).

The internal focus of the portal has increasingly been on knowledge management and the supply of software applications (i.e., inventory management, Production Planning System PPS, sales).

The external focus has in addition functions for transactions such as e-commerce, e-procurement, e-logistics and supply chain management. The internal interface is sometimes referred to as "Workplace," while the external side is called "Marketplace" (see SAP AG, mySAP.com). The themes of a portal such as applications, content and services can be designed to meet the needs of a specific geographical region or enterprise, and the themes can further be selected to cover the requirements of a specific task or problem. It is also possible to mix a focus of a specific subject and a specific enterprise.

Workplace and Marketplace Functions

The basic idea of ecoradar is the combination of "Company Radar" and "Macro Radar". This is the ideal basis to create a theme-related portal with a public/ external side ("Marketplace") to supply content and services for all companies and individuals interested in "Sustainable Management" and an internal side ("Workplace") to supply the enterprise with functions for "Environmental Management" with both strategic and operational tasks. Figure 2 illustrates this Internet-based dual approach.

The key innovation is the consistent use of all available "Internet technologies". The grand idea of sustainable management will substantially benefit from this transition towards an "Internet economy".

Figure 2. EIP-workplace "environmental management"

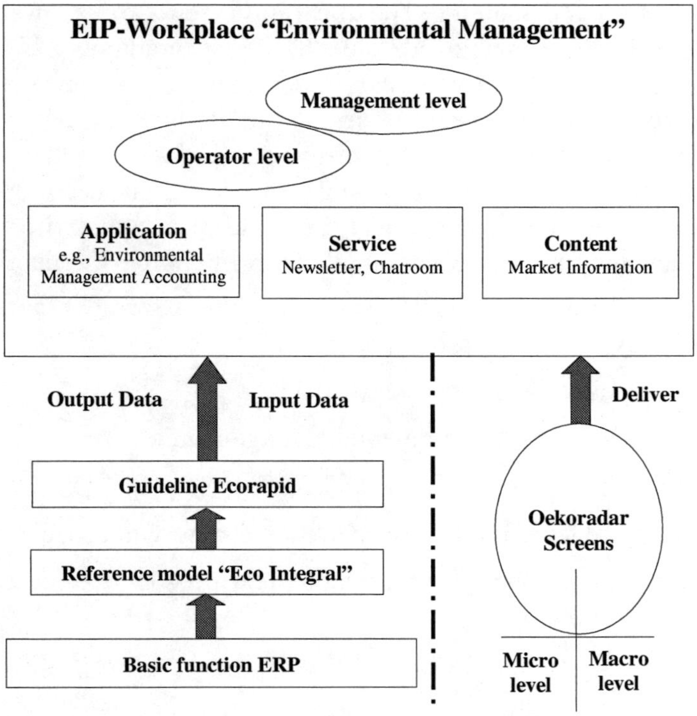

Creation of Internet Platform for Environmental Management: "Workplace"-Architecture

One of the important trends in enterprise data processing is the introduction of so-called "Enterprise Information Portals" (EIP). As described above, every individual employee (from the operator to top manager) is offered customized information, applications and services via a common, open-platform Internet browser. Besides these operational functions, various functions in knowledge management are also increasingly offered now. The final goal of the development of a portal based on ecoradar is the concept and consecutive design of a workplace (following the concept of an EIP) that offers all information, applications and services necessary for the tasks encountered in environmental management.

In addition to ecoradar, the project "ECO-Rapid" is an important basis for this development. Both projects cooperate with one another. There is an active exchange of results and planning. The illustration seen above shows roughly the workplace architecture envisioned on the basis of ecoradar and "ECO-Rapid": Creation of Web-based, open, dynamic access to all relevant resources of sustainable management for enterprises and individuals. The bundling of all relevant resources concerning sustainability on one Webpage is the primary goal of this public portal. The task of this portal is to cover all the needs of enterprises and individuals for information about the topic of sustainability. There is a substantial demand for that kind of bundled information in Germany.

The following topics are possible and some are already integrated in the presented framework of the prototype ecoradar:

- current and historic environmental data
- knowledge base for environmental management and
- environmental technology
- environmental laws, intelligent checklists for individual use
- ecological market (purchase of ecological products for enterprises and private households)
- ecologic investments
- list of ecologic business consultants
- specific literature

The portal offers three main functions:

1. Passive, regularly updated information for research
2. Interactive communication among users, assuming that there is a demand for exchange of specific subjects via chat-rooms, interactive message-boards, exchange of knowledge and experiences
3. Transactions, products and services. The portal can be upgraded for electronic procurement of environmentally friendly products and services.

The module for supply of information can already be almost completely covered by ecoradar. The only module still required would be a content management system to provide a regular flow of information at reasonable costs. The module for transactions could be started with partner companies and then be gradually expanded.

Editorial System & Telecooperation System

The design of the portal requires the development of a technological infrastructure. The community that is providing the environmental information needs a system for editing and telecooperation. Careful design of a sustainable project has to ensure the possibility of fast and easy upgrades. It is also necessary to introduce the portal to the business community as quickly as possible. Therefore the technology platform will be developed in two versions: The first version should be available within 12 months. This approach of iterative prototyping and learning-by-doing will provide constant input by users that can be integrated in the development process. These valuable data will also contribute to the development of a business model for the portal ecoradar.

References

Böhmann, T., & Krcmar, H. (1999). Werkzeuge für das Wissensmanagement. In C.H. Antoni & T. Sommerlatte (Eds.), *Spezialreport Wissensmanagement - Wie Deutsche Firmen ihr Wissen Profitabel Machen.* Düsseldorf.

Bullinger, H.-J., Baumann, T., Fröschle, N., Mack, O., Trunzer, T., & Wallert, J. (2002). *Business Communities: Professionelles Beziehungsmanagement von Kunden, Mitarbeitern und B2B-partnern im Internet.* Bonn: Galileo Press.

Hagel, J., & Armstrong, A.G. (1997). *Net gain. Profit im netz: Märkte Erobern mit Virtuellen Communities.* Wiesbaden: Gabler Verlag.

Kimble, C., Hildreth, P., & Wiright, P. (2001). Communities of practice: Going virtual. *Knowledge Management and Business Model Innovation* (ch. 13). Hershey, PA: Idea Group Publishing.

Kraft, A., Pitsch, S., & Vetter, M. (2000). Agent-driven online business in virtual communities. *Proceedings of the 33rd Hawaii International Conference on System Sciences,* Maui, Hawaii.

Krcmar, H. (ed.), & Scheide, W. (2000). *Informationssysteme für das Umweltmanagement: Das Referenzmodell ECO-Integral.* München and Wien: Oldenbourg-Verlag.

Kreeb, M. (2002). Strategisches Risikomanagement durch Webbasierte Umweltinformationssysteme. In P.M. Pastors/PIKS (Eds.), *Risiken des*

Unternehmens - Vorbeugen und Meistern. München: Reiner Hampp Verlag.

Kreeb, M., Schulz, W., Gutterer, B., Krcmar H., Burschel, C., & Rudel, A. (2002, September 25-27). Implementing an environmental management Web-portal. In W. Pillmann & K. Tochtermann (Eds.), *Environmental communication in the information society, Proceedings of the 16th Conference "Informatics for Environmental Protection".* International Society for Environmental Protection, Vienna, 254-261.

Kriwald, T., & Haasis, H. (2001). Betriebliches Wissensmanagement in Produktion und Umweltschutz. In H. Haasis & T. Kriwald (Eds.), *Wissensmanagement in Produktion und Umweltschut.* Berlin and Heidelberg: Springer Verlag.

Nonaka, I., & Takeuchi, H. (1995). *The knowledge creating company. How Japanese companies create the dynamics of innovation.* Oxford University Press.

Rheingold, H. (1994). *Virtuelle Gemeinschaft. Soziale Beziehungen im Zeitalters des Computers.* Bonn.: Addison-Wesley.

Schulz, W.F. (2002). Oekoradar.de * Auf Dem Weg Zum Nachhaltigen Wirtschaften. In R. Böcker & A. Sandhage-Hofmann (Eds.), *Globale Klimaerwärmung und Ernährungssicherung* (p. 34). Hohenheimer Umwelttagung. Ostfildern: Verlag Günter Heimbach.

Waltert, J. (2001). *Elektronische Kommunikationsforen als Element des Wissensmanagement. Eine Fallstudie bei Genossenschaftlichen Filialbanken.* Dissertation Informationswissenschaft, Universität Konstanz.

Wenger, E., & Snyder, W.M. (2000, January/February). Communities of practise. The organizational frontier. *Harvard Business Review.*

Chapter XIV

From "Industrial Symbiosis" to "Sustainability Networks"

Alfred Posch, Karl-Franzens-University Graz, Austria

Abstract

Industrial recycling networks are very effective in minimizing impact on the environment by building up closed loops of material and energy use within the industrial system. These interorganizational recycling activities among various industries can be a starting point for "sustainability networks," that is, systems of voluntary, but organized cooperation among different stakeholders with the common target of the sustainable development of society within a certain region. To work well, an overall vision of the sustainability network needs to be clearly defined and then translated into strategies and strategic objectives. These in turn need to be transformed into operational targets that can be measured by a comprehensive set of environmental, social and economic indicators. This procedure is quite similar to the balanced scorecard approach of Kaplan/Norton, which is considered as an appropriate management information system not only for industry but also for sustainability networks. As part of inter- and transdisciplinary research and educational projects at the University of Graz the concept of sustainability networks is being implemented for the first time in the Eisenerz region, an abandoned iron-ore mining area in Austria.

Introduction

In the last few decades many industrial organizations have implemented an environmental management system (EMS) to comply with international standards, such as ISO 14000 and EMAS regulations. In addition to these intraorganizational activities the concept of "industrial symbiosis," emphasizing similarities between natural and industrial ecosystems, has emerged. The fact that a natural ecosystem tends to recycle all materials biologically, using only energy from the sun to "drive" the system, is used as a metaphor for industrial systems (Ayres & Ayres, 1996). The main idea of this attractive concept is to design industrial systems in a way that the by-products ("waste") produced by one company are used as a raw material by another company. The aim is to minimize industries' impact on the environment by building closed loops of material and energy use within the industrial system. The best-documented example here is Kalundborg in Denmark, but the industrial recycling network in Styria, Austria, has also become a well-known case in the field of industrial symbiosis (Strebel, 2002). While in Europe the main focus lies on the waste exchange relationships among existing companies within a certain area (Schwarz, 1994; Strebel, 2000; Wallner, 1999), overseas the construction of so-called eco-industrial parks is considered the most effective way to implement the concept (Chertow, 1998). Whatever the case, the protection of the environment as the ultimate goal is achieved through collaboration and inter-company partnering. The totality of the firms involved and the recycling-oriented collaborative relationships between them is often represented in diagrams with vectors for each waste flow.

Characteristic for recycling networks is the participation of several different industries, since this makes a higher variety of processes available for potential recycling activities. Except for those industries where highly organized markets for recycling residuals are already used, such as in waste paper or scrap iron, recycling within a single industry is not usually inter- but intraorganizational.

Figure 1. Part of the recycling-network Styria (Posch et al., 1998, pp. 220-221)

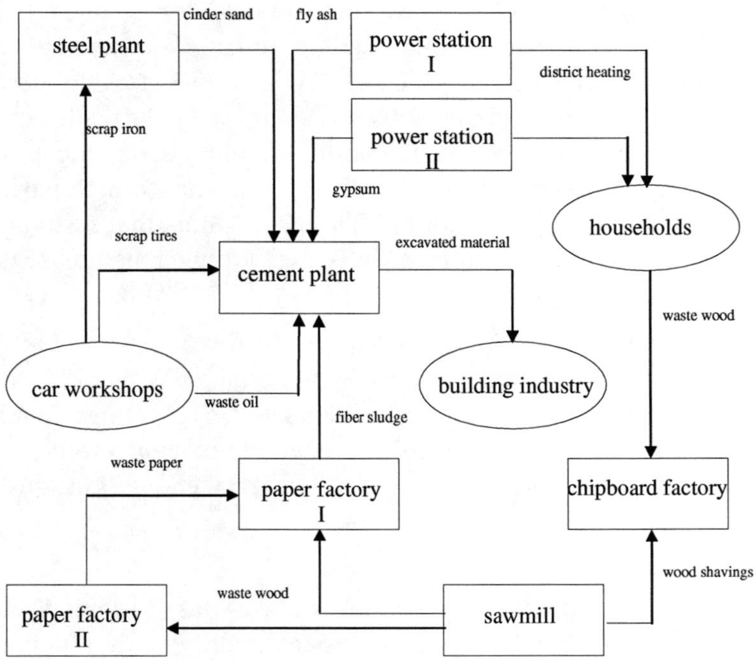

Sustainability Networks

The aim of this chapter is to show how these interorganizational recycling activities among various industries can be used as starting point for sustainability networks. For this the currently rather narrow view of recycling cooperation between industries needs to be broadened to include the following:

- Firstly, environmental protection is more than the recycling of material. In fact, recycling is an end-of-pipe-activity and therefore counts only as a second best solution. It does not aim to avoid or reduce the negative outcome of production processes at the origin, but only tries to reduce the negative impact on the environment by reusing the existing by-products. In contrast, Clean Production aims to modify the production processes at a more fundamental level so that no production waste will be produced at all. Or Design for the Environment, a product-oriented approach, suggests dematerializing goods while still retaining their capacity to function.

- Secondly, sustainability is more than environmental protection. According to the famous Brundtland Report of the World Commission on Environment and Development, sustainable development is a "development that meets the needs of the present without compromising the ability of future generations to meet their own needs" (WCED, 1987). Among the many attempts at more precise definitions (Perman, 1997), the triple bottom line approach stands out: here sustainability implies economic prosperity, environmental quality and social justice – an element which business has largely overlooked (Ulrich, 2001). "Those who think that sustainability is only a matter of pollution control are missing the bigger picture" (Elkington, 1999).
- Thirdly, sustainable development requires the involvement of all actors – not only industry. A major step was undertaken with the move from intraorganizational environmental management to recycling networks. The next necessary step is the move from recycling networks to the so-called sustainability networks integrating all relevant stakeholders in a sustainable regional development.

This leads us to the definition of sustainability networks as "systems of voluntary but organized cooperation among different stakeholders with the common target of sustainable development of society within a certain region". A very important term in this definition is "stakeholders". They are defined here as "persons or groups of persons who pursue interests in the context of the regional development or who are affected positively or negatively by the activity under investigation". This definition differs considerably from the original version of the Stanford Research Institute, according to which stakeholders are defined as "those groups without whose support the organization would cease to exist". It is much closer to the extended definition of Freeman, whereby "any group or individual who can affect or is affected by the achievement of the organization's objectives" can be called a stakeholder (Freeman, 1984). However, it needs to be noted that the definition used here does not refer to any single organization, but rather to the development of the whole region. Also the question arises whether the term "persons or group of persons, whose interests are hurt" also includes future generations, whose possibilities to meet their own needs may be compromised by the respective project. This generates a link to the definition of sustainability by the WCED, but obviously also leads to the question as to who, if anyone, would be able to represent them in the sustainability network. In fact, it does not seem to make a lot of sense to include future generations in the definition of stakeholders, since their interests are already implicitly protected by the overall objective of the sustainability network.

Membership in a sustainability network is voluntary. Obviously compulsory membership would be highly counterproductive. But why might private persons or groups, companies or even public or governmental organizations take part in a sustainability network? In general there are two possible motives for membership:

- On the one hand, there can simply be economic reasons whenever activities within the sustainability network also lead to profits. In fact, interorganizational recycling activities among the companies in a recycling network are a good example of environmentally and economically advantageous behavior. Recycling networks such as those in Styria would never have developed if there had not been clear economic advantages for the firms involved, for example lower prices for recycled materials than for raw materials or cheaper/safer disposal of by-products.
- On the other hand, it cannot be denied that economic, environmental and social win-win-win situations for all stakeholders do not always exist. Hence, the objective of sustainable development does need to be a normative one. In terms of Kant's categorical imperative it becomes obvious that caring for future well-being is an ethical obligation for the whole of society. That we need to act responsibly towards our descendants is clear, but the extent of this responsibility is still a matter of discussion.

Although, in practice, the exchange of by-products for recycling purposes may still count as the most important activity within these sustainability networks, the field of potential cooperation is in fact much larger. For example, common R&D activities leading to environmentally oriented innovation, continuous improvement, and common knowledge management could all be established. Moreover, infrastructure might be shared, such as in the case of common sewage plants or car-sharing activities. To initiate such cooperation among stakeholders and to promote cooperative activity over time, the management of a sustainability network needs to be supported by an adequate management information system (MIS).

Management Information Systems for Sustainability Networks

The management information system for a sustainability network has to be able to cope with the specific objectives of the individual stakeholders involved, as well as to comply simultaneously with the overall vision of the network. Hence,

Figure 2. Objectives of a sustainability network

the starting point for developing a management information system has to be the definition of a vision that is shared by all members of the sustainability network. While the core mission of an organization is usually strongly determined by the respective business field and historical development of the company, achieving consensus on objectives of a sustainability-network is much more difficult, as the experience and attitudes of the persons involved may differ considerably. But the network's vision is the most important basis from which the objectives of the network are to be derived. A prerequisite for defining the network's vision is information about the status quo, for example about the environmental impact of the region's activities or the social situation of the inhabitants.

In order to find out the contribution of the specific network to the environmental issues an input-output balance needs to be provided, at best supported by a series of database-compatible checklists. In general the checklists refer to material and energy flows of the network's members. The more detailed checklists may also contain quality-oriented data fields about solid waste production, sewage production and treatment, gaseous emissions and highly toxic substances or dangerous processes (see issues above). As any information system is only as good as the data input, it is essential to check data quality even in this early phase. The consistency, plausibility, completeness and immediacy of the data need be ensured. For example, time periods referred to need to be consistent, the sewage BOD figure (which reflects only easily degradable compounds of the organic pollutants) needs to be lower than the COD figure (this represents all organic pollutants in the wastewater). But the most relevant key figure that indicates the quality of the input-output analysis is still the quantitative difference between the input- and output-flows.

For strategic environmental management in industry there are several tools available to help focus information gathering activities on the most relevant issues, such as the eco-portfolio developed by Sturm/Mueller. Here, on the basis of given ecological problem areas – from problems relating to primary energy consumption or treatment of dangerous waste or even up to ozone depletion in the atmosphere – this portfolio helps to identify issues in terms of socioeconomic/ public priority and company contribution – or in our case, the contribution of the network. The higher the socioeconomic priority and the greater the network's contribution, the higher the relevance of the issue for the sustainability network.

It is worth mentioning that the eco-portfolio focuses almost exclusively on external threats or internal weaknesses. However, the management of sustainability networks entails more than mere identification of legal restrictions or the high costs of end-of-pipe-technologies. Building sustainability strategy rather means turning threats into opportunities and weaknesses into strengths as far as possible. Hence, for defining goals and creating strategies of the network it seems to be highly advantageous to undertake something like sustainability-oriented SWOT analysis, in order to promote proactive sustainability strategies. In general, it is the totality of the institutions and persons involved which needs to be taken into consideration when trying to clarify and translate the network's vision and mission into concrete strategies and specific strategic objectives. Traditional company objectives emphasize revenue, costs, cash flow or profitability, whereas those of sustainability networks contain not only monetary but also technical-physical measures like energy consumption or waste production, plus further more complex objectives such as the justice of the income distribution, which do not lend themselves to easy quantification at all.

Furthermore, these strategic objectives must be translated into a sufficient number of relevant and understandable targets, which then need to be communicated throughout the whole network. The individual activities of all members ought to be focused on the network's objectives and targets. It is obvious that participating companies need to gain profitability, at least to remain competitive in the long term. The compatibility of economic and non-economic goals in a competitive setting has long been a subject of discussion in the literature (Müller-Christ, 2000). Only in the case where a company has expressed interest in sustainability and has therefore set itself not only economic but also environmental and social objectives to achieve does it make sense for the company to play an active role within a sustainability network. As there is a high probability that there are dependencies between economic and environmental or social objectives in whatever manner and direction, the management system of the sustainability network must not be separated from the traditional core business strategies and management systems of the participating companies. Good correspondence between individual and network objectives is essential, since it provides a basic prerequisite for cooperation.

The most critical success factor in developing a management information system is the definition of a comprehensive set of suitable performance measures or indicators. These should closely refer to targets, and thus provide a framework for continual environmental, social and economic evaluation of the activities within the network. While several highly aggregated environmental indicators have been developed to aid continuous monitoring of environmental performance, such methods remain unsatisfactory for two main reasons:

- Firstly, the aggregation of different environmental impacts leads to an immense loss of information. The aggregation algorithm tends to misrepresent the degree of accuracy that can be achieved in practice. There is a definite danger that those basing their decisions on the indicators used may be acting in partial ignorance or at least on the basis of unfounded faith.
- Secondly, all environmental evaluation models imply that the value and target system is known, when in fact each evaluation ultimately depends on the unification of factual information with the value or target system. Hence, it makes a great difference whether the evaluation corresponds to the value system of a national or even international community (macro level) or to the target system of a small region with specific conditions and peculiarities. But the management system of a sustainability network certainly needs to refer to the network's own target system.

Hence, an approach for creating and monitoring a well-defined system of disaggregated or low aggregated indicators is followed here.

Certainly the choice of indicators for the environmental, social and economic performance evaluation strongly depends on the nature and scale of the sustainability network and the stakeholders involved. Nevertheless, it is crucial that the set of indicators is not a mere collection of piecemeal measures but should rather be a linked series of critical indicators that are internally consistent and related to the overall vision of sustainable development. In terms of the management approach of Kaplan/Norton, this could be seen as a form of "Sustainability Balanced Scorecard" (Kaplan & Norton, 1996).

The set of sustainability performance indicators of a whole network is the basis for the performance indicators of its members. In this way, the network's objectives and targets are cascaded down to local units of responsibility, allowing them to work coherently towards the strategic goals of the sustainability network. It is thus crucial to combine environmental, social and economic performance measures in a way that provides decision makers with an appropriate set of measures. In the future, both benchmarking within the network, and benchmarking among networks, will also help to incorporate existing best practice and to verify that the proposed targets do indeed assess network sustainability.

Figure 3. Example of a sustainability balanced scorecard

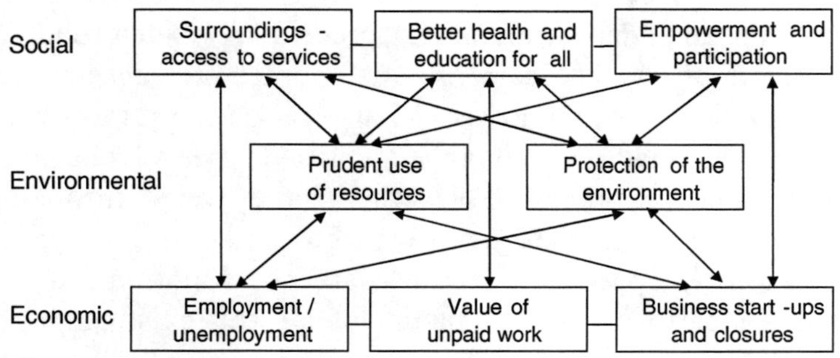

Case of Sustainability Network Eisenerz

The Eisenerz region, located in a mountainous area in the middle of Austria, was once considered to be the biggest iron-ore deposit in Europe. Hence, the region was not only shaped by the gigantic surface mining area, the so-called Erzberg, it was also heavily influenced by iron-ore mining in terms of its social, economic, ecological and cultural impact over the last centuries. While mining boomed during the period of the two World Wars and post-war reconstruction, it declined steadily over the last few decades – and with it the social and cultural standing of the Eisenerz region. Now, the region is known as an example of a region with immense structural problems. The loss of thousands of jobs has led not only to a decline in the number of inhabitants of the region, as a consequence of migration the average age of the remaining population has also risen considerably. At more than 30%, the percentage of pensioners in Eisenerz is the highest in the whole province of Styria.

Be that as it may, in terms of Schumpeter's "creative destruction" the crisis of the Eisenerz region can also be considered as a chance for innovation and reorientation – hopefully towards sustainable development. A conversion from mining to different economic fields such as tourism based on a regional capability profile and an updating of the regional vision and identity has to take place. Hence, to us the moment seemed optimal for implementation of the concept of "sustainability networks". This was carried out in the form of an interdisciplinary research project sponsored by the Federal Ministry of Sciences as part of its Austrian Cultural Landscape Research program. Experts of following disciplines were involved: ecology, archaeology, mining history, folklore/art history, socio-economics, sociology and geology. The region's relevant stakeholders and their places in the intended development process were identified first. The participation of these stakeholders provided for greater acceptance of the proposed project ideas and initiatives and also raised the probability of their implementation. The relations among the identified types of stakeholders also needed to be examined, in order to assess whether they were either complementary or competitive, and whether they were of a short-, medium or long-term orientation. As a next step we organized a "Market of Opportunities" workshop in Eisenerz in order to clarify the nature of already existing projects and initiatives, to generate new ideas and to specify the region's strategic goals. Any initiative, irrespective of its current state of development, and any stakeholder was welcome to present ideas, interests and objectives. As a result of this intense interaction among and with the stakeholders the interdisciplinary project team was able to define the strategic goals for the Eisenerz region with respect to the development of sustainability (see Table 1).

For each of the strategic goals the interdisciplinary project team defined a set of targets with measurable indicators. For example the goal g_4 (competitiveness) consists of targets such as profitability, capital requirements, capital structure, financial resources, available subsidies, liquidity, and market attractiveness. Most of the economic targets can be measured with well known financial indicators; however, the measurement of others is much more difficult. Defining recreational value, for example, is no simple task since it involves assessing the existing variety of natural and cultural elements, the naturalness of the landscape in terms of its recreational quality and the components in the region promoting social interaction. In any case it was the business of the specific experts of the research team to define the best possible set of measures and indicators for each goal.

As there was no information concerning the relative importance of the goals, available priorities had to be set. For this, preference profiles of the interdisciplinary expert group and of the regional stakeholders were drawn up. The expert group proceeded as follows: During a two-day workshop the team gathered arguments related to each goal in isolation, just to make each discipline familiar with the peculiarities of criteria from other disciplines. Inter-goal comparison was avoided. The half-matrix method was then applied to determine the ordinal importance of each goal, based on the number of times it was selected. It is most remarkable that the relative importance of the goals was not a result of voting, but of unanimous expert decision-making arrived at on the basis of discussing the arguments presented.

In addition, opinion polls were carried out in order to obtain stakeholder preference profiles. A random sample of around 300 inhabitants (from the total

Table 1. Strategic goals for the Eisenerz region

g_1	➤ Consideration of mining as part of the regional identity
g_2	➤ Preservation of important monuments and settlements
g_3	➤ Preservation of culturally important sites (sites of origin of various legends)
g_4	➤ Competitiveness of the proposed entrepreneurial or public project
g_5	➤ Employment opportunities for present and future generations
g_6	➤ Sustainable use of resources (such as energy, water, wood or mineral oil)
g_7	➤ Citizens' participation in the decision process concerning the future of the region
g_8	➤ Future availability of mineral (e.g., iron ore) and natural (e.g., ground water) resources
g_9	➤ Natural risk potential in connection with the proposed project (e.g., avalanches or morays)
g_{10}	➤ Preservation or enhancement of the recreational value of the region
g_{11}	➤ Preservation of the regional peculiarities (natural, architectural phenomena, etc.)
g_{12}	➤ Preservation of animal and plant variety
g_{13}	➤ Accessibility of archeological mining monuments for the public
g_{14}	➤ Scientific investigation of archeological mining monuments in the region

population of 11,200), a sample of 65 students aged between 14 and 18 years and the CEOs of all companies with more than two employees were all surveyed. A major factor of interest in the analysis was the rank correlation between the different preference profiles. The statistical analysis shows, however, that no correlation exists between the preference profiles of the three groups of stakeholders on the one hand, namely households, youth and businesses, and the preference profiles of the expert group on the other hand (assuming an error probability of 1%). However, all three groups of stakeholders were positively correlated with one another (Katter et al., 2000).

The results of this investigation show how important it is to be aware that preferences can differ considerably among experts and various groups of stakeholders. Future project steps will therefore certainly be strongly characterized by transdisciplinarity. Close cooperation between scientific experts of different disciplines is no longer sufficient. In addition, very intense interaction between experts and stakeholders in the region must take place. In fact such an approach is to provide a new research paradigm at our university. In the case of

Figure 4: Preference profiles of experts and stakeholders in the case of Eisenerz

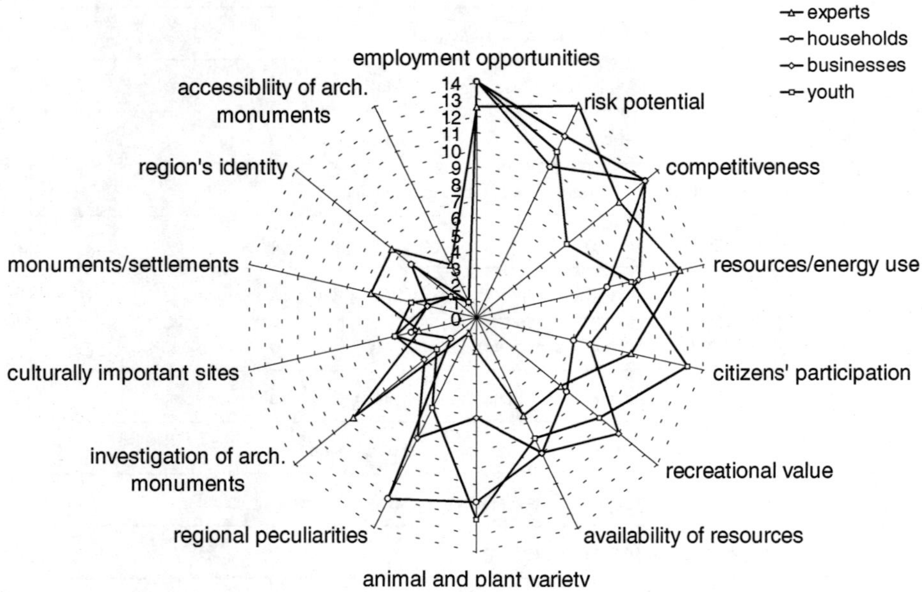

Eisenerz, courses are planned at the University of Graz where the university teachers and students accompany projects and initiatives of the region in order to support their implementation in a way that the region's vision of ecological, economic and social sustainable development is implemented. Here we will apply the case study approach of R. Scholz from the Swiss Federal Institute of Technology in Zurich (Scholz & Tietje, 2002), a well-established research and training model that combines training, research and action in the defined case study region. In this upcoming follow-up-project, again part of the Austrian Cultural Landscape Research program, and again sponsored by the Federal Ministry of Sciences, close cooperation among departments of the University in Graz and the regional stakeholders in Eisenerz will be established. About 30 to 40 students of "Environmental System Sciences," an interdisciplinary course unique in central Europe, will work in the region together with their teachers for two semesters. In a mutual learning process between science and society the sustainability network Eisenerz is to be consolidated in order to bring the region close to sustainable development, and to provide a model of best practice.

References

Ayres, R.U., & Ayres, L. (1996). *Industrial ecology – Towards closing the material cycle*. Cheltenham, UK: Edward Elgar.

Chertow, M. (1998). Eco-industrial park model reconsidered. *Industrial Ecology 1998, 2*(3), 8-10.

Daly, H. (1996). *Beyond growth: The economics of sustainable development.* Boston, MA: Beacon Press.

Elkington, J. (1999). *Cannibals with forks – The triple bottom line of 21st century business.* Oxford: Capstone.

Freeman, R.E. (1984). *Strategic management: A stakeholder approach.* Marshfield, MA: Pitman Publishing.

Göbel, E. (1995). Der Stakeholderansatz im Dienste der Strategischen Früherkennung. *Zeitschrift für Planung, 6*(1).

Kaplan, R.S., & Norton, D.P (1996). *The balanced scorecard: Translating strategy into action.* Boston, MA: Harvard Business School Press.

Katter, R. et al. (2000). *Perspektiven zur Gestaltung und Nutzung von Bergbaufolgelandschaften.* Endbericht, Leitschwerpunkt Kulturlandschaftsforschung: Modul MU7 Bergbaufolgelandschaften, Graz: Joanneum Research.

Müller-Christ, G. (2001). *Umweltmanagement.* München: Vahlen.

Perman, R. (1997). *Natural resource and environmental economics.* London, New York: Addison Wesley Longman.

Posch, A., Schwarz, E., Steiner, G., Strebel, H., & Vorbach, S. (1998). Das Verwertungsnetz Obersteiermark und Sein Potential. In H. Strebel & E. Schwarz (Eds.), *Kreislauforientierte Unternehmenskooperationen: Stoffstrommanagement Durch Innovative Verwertungsnetze* (pp. 211-221). Wien: Oldenbourg.

Scholz, R., & Tietje, O. (2002). Embedded case study methods. *Integrating quantitative and qualitative knowledge.* London: Thousand Oaks.

Schwarz, E.J. (1994). *Unternehmensnetzwerke im Recycling-bereich.* Wiesbaden: Gabler.

Strebel, H. (2000). Industrial recycling networks: Redesign of industrial systems. *Helsinki Symposium on Industrial Ecology and Material Flows,* 294-300. Retrieved January 10, 2003: *http://www.jyu.fi/helsie.*

Strebel, H. (2002). Möglichkeiten und Grenzen Nachhaltiger Wirtschaft im Unternehmen. In F. Keuper (Ed.), *Produktion und Controlling* (pp. 105-125, 295). Wiesbaden: DUV.

Sturm, A., & Müller, K. (2000). *Eco-controlling – A tool to implement value based environmental management.* Retrieved April 22, 2002: *www.ellipson.com.*

Ulrich, P. (2001). *Politik der "Nachhaltigkeit" und Ihre Ethischen Grundlagen.* St. Gallen: Ethikgruppe im Grossen Rat des Kt. St. Gallens, 3. Workshop 23.1.2001, 1.

Wallner, H.P. (1999). Towards sustainable development of industry: Networking, complexity and eco-clusters. *Journal of Cleaner Production, 7,* 49-58.

World Commission on Environment and Development. (1987). *Our common future.* Oxford University Press.

Chapter XV

Information Systems for Co-Operative Procurement of Organic Food as a Basis for Decentralised Eco-Villages

Stefan Naumann, University of Applied Sciences Trier, Germany

Abstract

In this chapter we describe the "eFood-Coop" software system that supports an eco-community in ordering, purchasing and delivering organic products such as food, clean construction material and so forth. In addition, offering services and hiring or lending goods such as tools and so forth can be supported. Besides presenting products, the software supports communication and co-operation among the members/consumers. This promotes a sustainable economy locally and makes it possible to order organic food at wholesale (which requires collecting single orders to exceed the minimum order quantities required to obtain wholesale sales units). Thus, it is one essential contribution to a decentralised eco-village structure, where several hundred people consider themselves as inhabitants of a virtual village. This village is spread over a limited area with a diameter of about 20-30 miles. The local restriction is necessary because otherwise material flows would be too extensive and maintaining social bindings would be more difficult.

Introduction

In the space of environmentally friendly products and services, organically produced food is an essential contribution to sustainable development (World Commission, 1987), especially if it is produced and sold within the same region. Food-coops are groups that purchase organic food in a self-organised, co-operative manner.

Organic Food

There are different ways to sell and buy organic food (see e.g., Kreuzer, 1996, for selling by electronic means (Nachtmann, 2002)):

- purchasing from an organic farm (e.g., a farm-shop) directly,
- farmers' markets,
- green box schemes (food delivery service),
- natural food shops,
- supermarkets with a product range in organic food,
- Internet grocery portals,
- wholesalers,
- producer/consumer communities, and
- food-coops.

The last way means to procure regional organic food by having consumers organise the buy-side on their own in a co-operative (BAG, 2000). A food-coop is characterised by:

- a group of people interested in (co-operatively) buying regional organic food,

- a number of suppliers and producers of organic food (regional farms, wholesalers), and
- a transaction process, which is completely self-organised within the group and encompasses the whole supply chain from producer to consumer.

If a food-coop wants to purchase at wholesale, it is necessary to collect and to adapt all requests for items of a sales unit, because a private person normally does not want to buy for example 20 items of 500g noodles. Following BAG (2000), we can distinguish three main types of food-coops:

1. A rural food-coop, typically consisting of 10-30 member households. The rural situation causes longer transportation distances.
2. An urban food-coop with more than 50 (or even 100 households). Here members are often students.
3. Food-coops with a shop for the members. This may sometimes be open for non-members, too, but the latter have to pay higher prices.

From a sustainable point of view, we identify several advantages of a food-coop organisation:

- promotes organic farming;
- lowers environmental impacts;
- supports groups in acting together to achieve goals of sustainability;
- need for transportation is reduced because most of the groceries are produced and/or distributed within the region; and
- supports direct communication between producers and consumers and enforces useful side effects such as car sharing/transport sharing or product improvements in the sense of e-support/e-services (see for example, Fichter, 2001).

When a food-coop community uses information technology (IT) to support procurement and transactions, we can consider them to be a virtual/decentralised community (Rheingold, 2000; Schubert, 2000) with ecological interests (Hummel & Lechner, 2000).

But, especially in rural coops the distance between the group members makes co-operation and communication more difficult. Here, electronic means are useful for supplementing and substituting direct contacts and communication. However, transportation of goods by car is still necessary.

Problem Scope

In our project context we can identify the following problems in purchasing organic food:

1. *Organisation of food-coops:* Especially rural food-coops have problems organising communication, and therefore the transaction phases such as ordering, optimising bundles and so forth are difficult to handle.
2. *Food retailing via the Internet:* Many B2C Internet portals dedicated to selling food have closed their doors because of problems with logistics and trust.

The first point is related to the distances encountered in rural regions. As common purchasing requires communicating collectively, which is a substantial obstacle.

Our observations result from experiences we made as a member of a food-coop in a rural region in Rhineland-Palatinate, Germany. Before using the "eFood-Coop" software system (Naumann, 2001), the catalogue with organic products was handed around among members of the community. Hence, it was time-consuming (sometimes taking several weeks) to collect orders and then to purchase the products from wholesalers. In addition, optimising the sales units to reach the minimum order quantities was rather difficult.

Considering the second point, we can observe that several Web portals for purchasing food closed down (e.g., in Germany Tegut, Spar, and LeShop). The main problems in Internet retail with food are, firstly, that the delivery process is complicated because the consumer has to be at home (or can make available a safe and even cool place), and secondly, that the customers often want to see the groceries (especially vegetables and meat) before buying them.

We tried to solve both problems with our eFood-Coop approach for procurement of food.

Decentralised Eco-Villages

Our information system for procurement could be extended to a software package that facilitates the procurement and exchange of sustainable everyday life requirements (Naumann, 2001). These requirements consist of organic product purchasing for example as well as communication, social contacts among the members and so forth. We call this structure a "decentralised eco-village": This idea stands for a community of about 200 households who are organised into an eco-village community (GEN, 2002), but live spread over a (limited) region. The households try to share an ecological and social lifestyle. A similar approach, the "Pinekernel Network," is described in Alexander (2002).

For the evaluation of our project we refer to an actual existing food-coop located in Rhineland-Palatinate, Germany. The group consists of about 60 members in 25 households. It has been ordering organic food since 1993, and using electronic means for that ordering since 2001. They want to extend their network into a decentralised eco-village.

Organisation of the Chapter

Our contribution is organised as follows: First we describe the organisation and procurement process of an existing food-coop without using any electronic solution and derive certain requirements for an information and transaction system that makes electronic co-shopping possible. After that we provide some details of the system we have implemented. We conclude with a short discussion of our approach and give an outlook to future work.

Case Study Food-Coop

Before introducing our eFood-Coop software solution, let us take a closer look at the organisation of food-coops and their procurement process.

Organisation of a Food-Coop

In a food-coop we find different business partners and different roles. We can identify three major participants within the procurement process: The food-coop members (the consumers), the ordering co-ordinator(s) and the involved suppliers (regional farms and wholesalers).

Food-Coop Members

Food-coop members are consumers who have joined the self-organised procurement community. They are interested in purchasing organic food and want to act co-operatively.

Ordering Co-ordinators

Tasks of the ordering co-ordination are:

- Organising and supervising the complete procurement process from receiving product information to billing as described in Figure 1;
- Contacting manufacturers of organic food and wholesalers; and
- Collecting general information about organic agriculture and organic products (organic agriculture associations, processing, relevant political factors, etc.) as well as information referring directly to the products, for example cooking recipes or related life-cycle assessments.

Self-organisation of a food-coop implies that the ordering co-ordinators are also community members. Ideally the co-ordinators alternate among the group too over time. However, often the ordering team consists of the same people (BAG, 2000).

Suppliers and Producers

The suppliers of a food-coop can be regional farms, organic food wholesalers or other manufacturers/dealers of groceries produced in an environmentally friendly way. Unfortunately, the relationship between wholesalers, natural food shops and food-coops is somewhat problematical. Because natural food shops may consider a food-coop a competitor (due to the fact that coops can sell the articles to members at a reduced price), a lot of wholesalers are not willing to deliver coops. However, some wholesalers do deliver, and many farms are particularly interested in closer customer relationships, which are given in the relation to a community like a food-coop.

Figure 1. Overview of procurement process

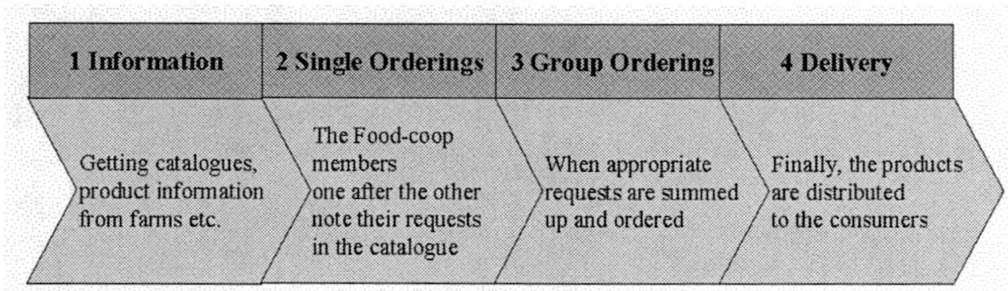

Procurement Process within the Food-Coop

Before introduction of the software in our case the food-coop ordering transactions were handled as described below:

1. The organic wholesaler and the producers sent their printed catalogues to the ordering co-ordinators.
2. The catalogue was handed around the community and each coop member marked the articles s/he requested. Furthermore s/he added a note whether s/he wanted the sales units completely or only some items of it (e.g., four packets of a 12 packet sales unit of 500g noodles).
3. When all the members had finished choosing from the catalogue, the requests were summed up by the ordering co-ordinator. Because the members could give additional information to partial orders such as "at least" and "at most", s/he was able to decide which sales units could be ordered from the wholesaler. "At least" meant that they wanted the requested quantity or more (up to the minimum order quantity of the sales unit) if not enough other members were interested in fulfilling the bundles; "at most" meant a maximum delivery of the requested item. In case of requests from other members that were insufficient to exceed the minimum order quantity, it was possible that the member would not get any package.
4. After compilation of all requested sales units, the order was sent to the wholesaler or farmers who delivered the order to a central point (normally to a member of the food-coop). If the delivered quantity differed from the ordered quantity, another step similar to step 3 was necessary. Then the delivered items had to be packaged according to the individual orders and the members had to pick up their packages.
5. In the last step, invoices were sent to members referring to the actual delivery.

The description illustrates the principles of the food-coop procurement process. This practice was successful, but had some disadvantages: it was time-consuming, co-ordination of the fulfillment of bundles was elaborate, and procurement from more than one supplier was hard to manage within the food-coop.

E-Food-Coop System

In order to solve the problems described in the last chapter and in the introduction, we simplified the procurement process and developed a system to support the main steps of the procurement process described in the last chapter. The system supports the food-coop members in communication and co-operation to fulfill wholesale sales unit requirements and is able to recognise fulfilled bundles. We implemented the system as a distributed application in Java. For co-operatively purchasing together, the users can download the catalogue with products and are able to order concurrently. They can also see the orders of all other coop members.

For showing products in the catalogues we encountered the problem that the suppliers do not use common formats. For our task it would be helpful to have standard catalogue formats, either like BMEcat (BME, 2002) or xCBL (Commerce One, 2002). Also common (electronic) classification systems, for example like eCl@ss (IW, 2002), which are used in industrial settings, would be desirable. For our application the proprietary bnn-format (BNN, 2000) (which is limited to the organic food trade) had to be processed and read in. In addition, small farms or companies do not often provide an electronic catalogue file, so it has to be created by the ordering co-ordinators.

The decision to set up a distributed application and to discard the Web interface was made because the former would give us more programming flexibility and data security. In addition, the system offers the feature to order offline, as all data from the database server are replicated locally.

With computer-assisted procurement we can distinguish among the following steps:

1. The wholesalers and producers have to send their product catalogues together with additional information such as country of origin and so forth to the food-coop.
2. The ordering co-ordinators have to convert the product data to fit the internal database scheme and have to input them into the database.

Figure 2. Former procurement compared to electronic solution

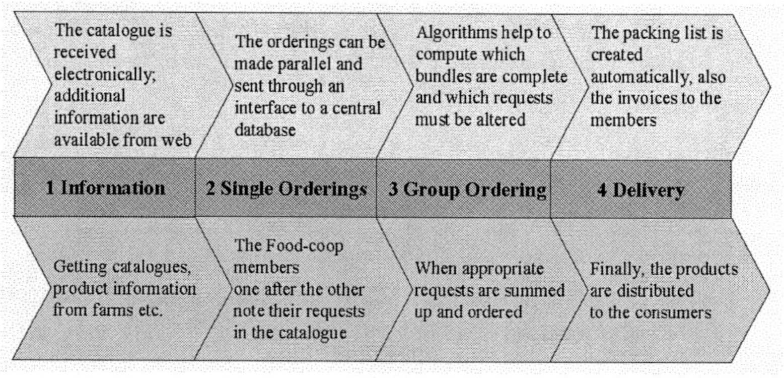

3. For each supplier a deadline has to be fixed. Up to this deadline all members can send requests, note comments and negotiate about the common procurement.
4. After the deadline, the requested quantities have to be combined by the ordering co-ordinator. Since there is flexibility within the requests by "at least" and "at most," it is easier to decide whether a requested article will be ordered or not. The co-ordinator is assisted by the software that includes special algorithms to check for bundles that are not fulfilled. The system can propose the co-ordinator requests that have to be modified.
5. After ordering and delivery, the articles have to be prepacked. In order to support this process, the software can print out a list of all requests, sorted by articles and consumers. If the delivery differs from the order – what sometimes happens for example due to bad harvests – step 4 has to be repeated until the allocation of the delivery to the consumers is completed.

Figure 2 shows the extension of the former procurement process with the electronic solution.

Communication and Co-Operation Process

At first, coop-members want to know which deadlines are coming up next. The GUI window in Figure 3 gives an overview of the suppliers and the planned procurement deadlines.

Articles currently offered are shown by the form "Complete Catalogue" (Figure 4). Here all suppliers and all product groups are visible. Members are

Figure 3. General survey over the next supplier deadlines (translated)

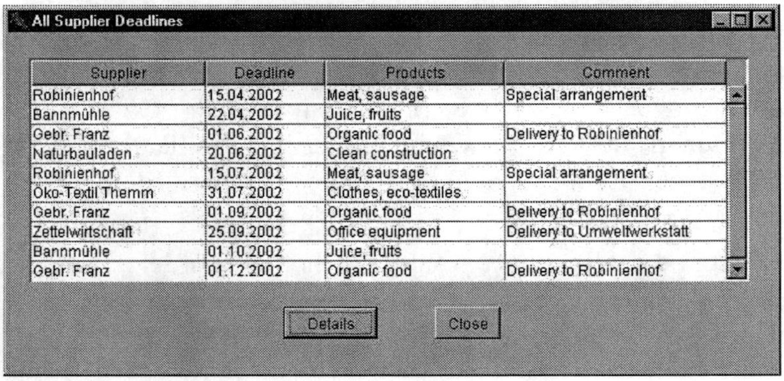

Supplier	Deadline	Products	Comment
Robinienhof	15.04.2002	Meat, sausage	Special arrangement
Bannmühle	22.04.2002	Juice, fruits	
Gebr. Franz	01.06.2002	Organic food	Delivery to Robinienhof
Naturbauladen	20.06.2002	Clean construction	
Robinienhof	15.07.2002	Meat, sausage	Special arrangement
Öko-Textil Themm	31.07.2002	Clothes, eco-textiles	
Gebr. Franz	01.09.2002	Organic food	Delivery to Robinienhof
Zettelwirtschaft	25.09.2002	Office equipment	Delivery to Umweltwerkstatt
Bannmühle	01.10.2002	Juice, fruits	
Gebr. Franz	01.12.2002	Organic food	Delivery to Robinienhof

Figure 4. Survey of the complete catalogue with additional information on current orders

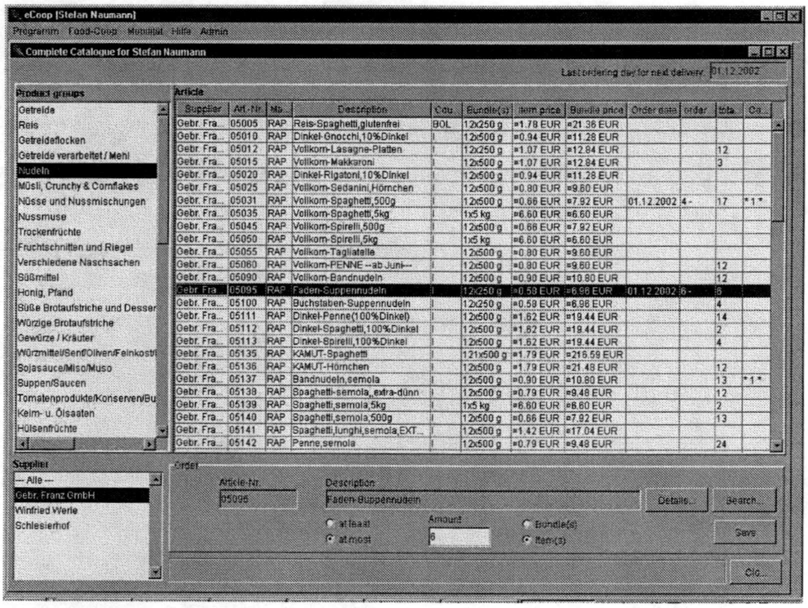

able to choose between a product group – which contains all offered products – and the articles of a special supplier. In this form the consumers can also make their requests and can see how many items of a bundle have been requested by the other consumers (column "total ordered").

To reinforce communication among the participants, it is possible to give comments. We can classify these comments into two groups: comments directly referring to the product (such as additional information, recipes) and comments that concern the current order (such as requests to fulfill, to deliver, etc.).

For instance if one person wants to order six items of a sales unit of rice containing 12 items, and another person wants to have six of 12 items from another sort of rice and both requests are "at most," it is not possible to order from a wholesaler. However if the persons communicate their flexibility through the comment option in the application, they may decide to order the same article (in this case the same sort of rice) and the bundle may be fulfilled.

The system supports procurement from multiple suppliers. Food-coop members can see all suppliers, all product groups and their own orders. Additionally the total requested quantity of a product is shown, and they can see if there are any comments to a particular article.

Figure 5. Details of a selected article (comments can be chosen to be valid only for one ordering or to have an unlimited validity)

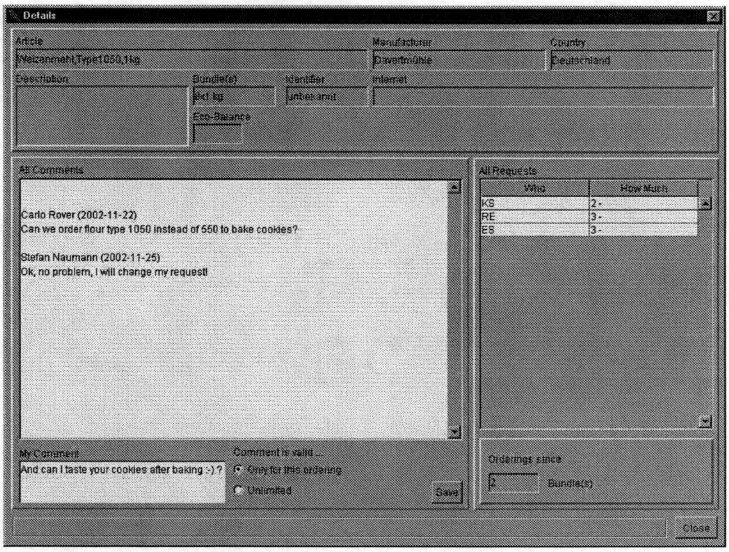

With the button "Details" the consumer can get more information about the selected article (Figure 5). Information about country of origin (an important attribute to calculate a product's life cycle assessment) and the manufacturer is available, and they can see all comments and which food-coop members have requested the selected article. This information reinforces the members' co-operation to attain the minimum order quantities of wholesale bundles and reinforces communication among the community members generally.

After having ordered, the consumers can view their own requests with a corresponding mask "My orders and comments". The window shows the requests and the resulting orders of a consumer, as well as the sales units where the minimum order quantity is currently being met and fits the requests, or where a modification must be expected.

Optimising Order Requests

After uploading all user requests to the database server has been finished and after the deadline is passed, the ordering co-ordinator is able to look to see whether the minimum order quantities have been reached. He or she is supported by the form shown in Figure 6. The optimisation is divided into two parts:

Figure 6. Mask that supports the ordering co-ordinator(s)

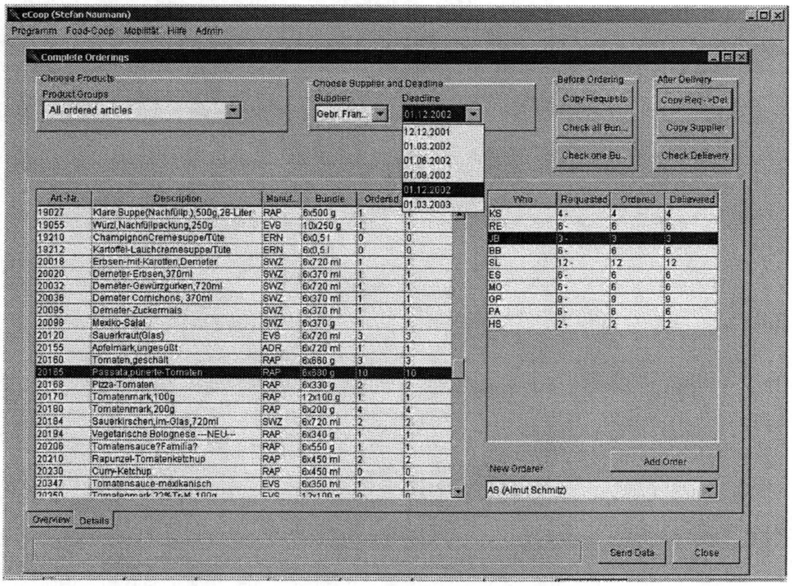

- The requests have to be summed up to complete sales units – considering the added "at least" and "at most" notes – and then sent as one order to the supplier.
- After delivery, the delivered sales units have to be compared to the order. If necessary, the allocation of products to the customers has to be adapted.

Generally we distinguish between "requested" (which means the user requests for (items of) sales units) and "in fact" (which describes the actual number of parts ordered from wholesale after optimisation). The ordering co-ordinator is authorised to change the "in-fact" ordering, but not the "requested" ordering. At any time, he or she can start an algorithm to compute which of the sales units are complete and which are not.

Technical Architecture

We implemented the software using the programming language Java to provide secure Internet transactions and to be platform-independent. The data are stored locally in files (serialised objects); we run a relational database on the server (using Java classes to wrap objects to relational tables). Figure 7 shows the

Figure 7. Distributed architecture between suppliers, consumers and provider

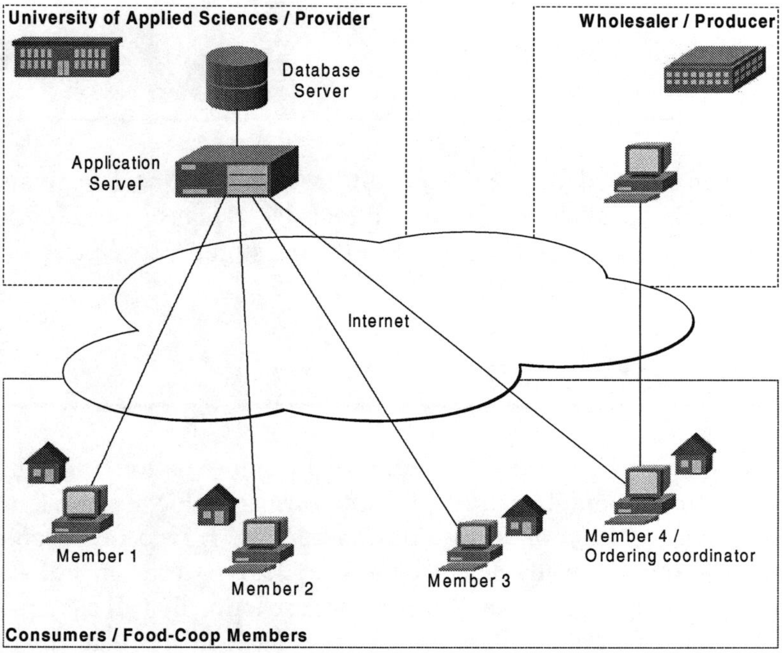

distributed architecture. Using a classic three-layer architecture, we have a client, a server application and a database.

Client

The client is used by the food-coop members and has to display data and product information, to collect user data (requests, orders and comments) and to communicate with the server. In addition, it checks bundles for whether they are fulfilled and performs bundle optimisation, because every member has to be able to act as the ordering co-ordinator to satisfy our self-organised business model.

Server

The server serves as middleware between the clients and the database, wrapping objects from the clients into relational database tables. We use a servlet engine to run the servlets (server-side Java programs). They receive and send datastreams from/to the clients. If necessary, for example if the data have to be stored in the database, the servlets wrap the incoming objects to relational statements. The server can also give an overview of users who are currently online.

Database

We use the open source database PostgresSQL 7.1 to store the data persistently and centrally and to ensure data safety and security. Because other food-coops may use other database vendors, we do not use stored procedures or other features that are database dependent.

Locally Stored Data

Because one part of the electronic solution is to allow offline ordering, it is necessary to store the complete procurement information locally, especially the product catalogue and the ordering information. We solved this problem by generating files containing all relevant data. The files are stored on the local hard disc. To avoid update anomalies aside from the restriction that all customers can change only their own orders, all database tables have an alternate key besides the primary key. Therefore, data integrity is ensured (Schäfer, 2002).

Summary and Conclusions

Our described software system "eFood-Coop" can meet several requirements associated with (co-operative) online procurement of (organic) food.

Generally, food-coops can cope with problems of environmental impacts of food production and the lack of trust in the anonymous food industry, because organically produced food is healthier and contains fewer harmful substances than industrial food. In addition, regional farms are less anonymous than agricultural factories. Existing trust within the food-coop community supports the trust in community-procured groceries.

But co-operative procurement – especially of perishable products such as food – requires a high degree of communication and co-ordination. Since this is not easy to manage in rural regions, these problems can be solved by our application, which assists in the whole procurement process.

With the new software system concurrent ordering is possible. Thus, more people can participate in the food-coop system. After using it for the first time

Figure 8. Overview over all offered rides of one member, supplemented with comments

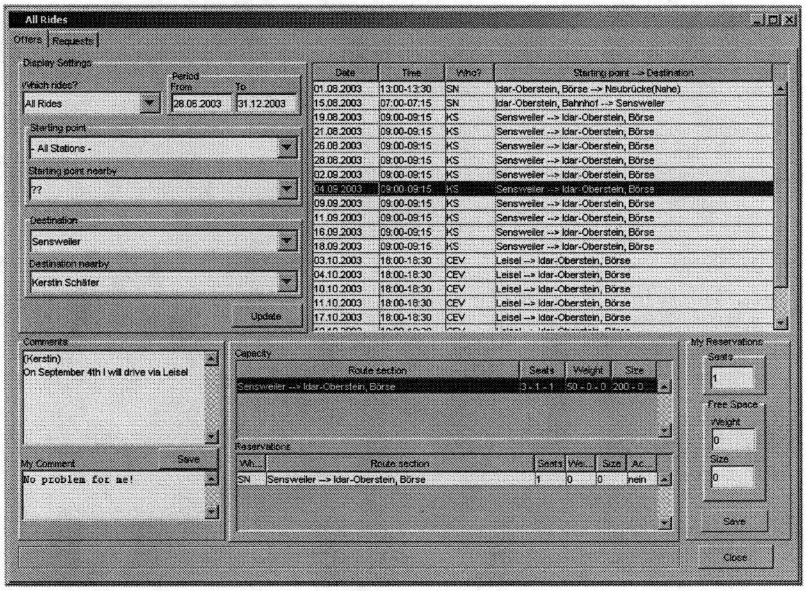

in December 2001 in our test coop, more new consumers wanted to order organic food through the eFood-Coop software and turnover was trebled. Ordering and fulfilling bundles are also easier, since an algorithm computes which sales units are complete.

A major problem is the electronic data exchange between software and suppliers. The small and medium-sized businesses and farms we have in mind rarely use ERP-systems or utilise standard electronic catalogue formats and classification systems. Here the interaction can be improved, for example with delivery notes that can be electronically processed.

A sensible extension is to increase the products offered by adding non-food articles and services which can be lent or exchanged, which constitutes a local exchange trading system (LETS, e.g., Hoffmann, 1998). Thus, we have a virtual regional shop for organic products and environmentally friendly services that support a virtual community in a sustainable lifestyle we call "decentralised eco-village". This community subsists in a limited area and is able to reduce various environmental impacts by means of environmentally friendly procurement.

The next step we plan is the integration of an information system that supports shared rides and car sharing. Thus an agency for arranged lifts can be created within the food-coop. The corresponding application "eMobil-Coop" was released into the eFood-coop software in the spring of 2003. The main points are:

- to give an overview over all offered rides within the group,
- to make available special views, for example, all rides to an event (for example the distribution of the food delivery), and
- to show personalised links to public transportation facilities such as bus and train.

Figure 8 shows an example of all rides offered by one person. We distinguish here between regular (e.g., rides to work) and individual rides (e.g., to a cultural event).

One advantage of this mobility-coop is – aside from the reduction of environmental impacts – the opportunity to communicate directly among our members and thus to improve co-operation beyond the software.

References

Alexander, G. (2002): *eGaia. Growing a peaceful, sustainable Earth through communications.* Norfolk: Lighthouse Books.

Bundesarbeitsgemeinschaft (BAG) der Lebensmittelkooperativen (ed.). (2000). *Das Food-Coop Handbuch.* Bochum: Eigenverlag.

Bundesverband Materialwirtschaft, Einkauf und Logistik (BME). (2002). BMEcat 1.2. Retrieved June 7, 2004 at: *http://www.bmecat.org/.*

Bundesverbände Naturkost Naturwaren (BNN). (2002). BNN-Schnittstelle Version 3, 12.04.2002. Retrieved June 7, 2004 at: *http://www.n-bnn.de/seiten/service/bnn_schnitt_ fs.htm.*

Commerce One. (2002). xCBL 3.0. Retrieved June 7, 2004 at: *http://www.xcbl.org/.*

Fichter, K. (2001). Sustainable business strategies in the Internet economy. In L.M. Hilty & P.W. Gilgen (Eds.), *Sustainability in the Information Society, Proceedings of the 15th International Symposium Informatics for Environment Protection,* Zurich 2001. Marburg: Metropolis Verlag.

Global Ecovillage Network (GEN). Retrieved June 7, 2004 at: *http://www.gaia.org.*

Hilty, L.M., & Gilgen, P.W. (Eds.) (2001). Sustainability in the information society. *Proceedings of the 15th International Symposium Informatics for Environment Protection*, Zurich 2001. Marburg: Metropolis Verlag.

Hoffmann, G. (1998). *Tausche Marmelade gegen Steuererklärung. Ganz Ohne Geld - Die Praxis der Tauschringe und Talentbörsen.* München.

Hummel, J., & Lechner, U. (2000). Ökologische Konsumentengemeinschaften. In U. Schneidewind, G. Steingräber, & A. Truscheit (Eds.), *Nachhaltige Informationsgesellschaft. Analyse und Gestaltungsempfehlungen aus Management - und institutioneller Sicht.* Marburg: Metropolis Verlag.

Institut der deutschen Wirtschaft Köln (IW). (2002). eCl@ss 4.0. Retrieved June 7, 2004 at: *http://www.eclass.de/.*

Kreuzer, K. (1996). *Bio-vermarktung. Vermarktung für Lebensmittel aus Ökologischer Erzeugung.* Darmstadt: Pala-Verlag.

Nachtmann, M. (2002). *Electronic Commerce im Naturkosthandel. Vermarktung ökologisch erzeugter Lebensmittel im Internet.* Darmstadt: Deutscher Universitätsverlag.

Naumann, S. (2001). eFood-Coops: Elektronische Unterstützung von Bestellgemeinschaften für Lebensmittel als Baustein eines virtuellen ökologischen Dorfes. In M. Engelien & J. Homann (Eds.), *Virtuelle Organisation und Neue Medien.* Lohmar/Köln: Josef Eul Verlag.

Naumann, S. (2002). Supporting regional sustainable development by IT-assisted communication and co-operation. In W. Pillmann & K. Tochtermann (Eds.), *Environmental communication in the information society. Proceedings of the 16th conference "Informatics for Environmental Protection".* International Society for Environmental Protection, Vienna.

Rheingold, H. (2000). *The Virtual Community.* MA: MIT-Press.

Schäfer, K. (2002). *Entwicklung eines Java-frameworks zur Unterstützung von Mobilitätsanforderungen im Ländlichen Raum Unter Besonderer Berücksichtung von Kooperativen und Ressourcenschonenden Aspekten.* Master's Thesis, University of Applied Sciences Trier, Location Birkenfeld.

Schubert, P. (2000). *Virtuelle Transaktionsgemeinschaften im Electronic Commerce* (2nd ed.). Lohmar/Köln: Josef Eul Verlag.

World Commission on Environment and Development (ed.). (1987). *Our common future.* World Commission on Environment and Development, Oxford: Oxford Paperbacks.

Chapter XVI

ORISS: A Web-Based Carpooling System

Simon Giesecke, RWTH Aachen University, Germany

Gerriet Reents, Carl von Ossietzky University, Germany

Abstract

In this chapter, we present the Web-based carpooling system ORISS, which was initially developed by a student project group at University of Oldenburg. It is currently being deployed at Carl von Ossietzky University of Oldenburg with support of the DBU (Federal German Foundation for the Environment). We describe the role of carpools in traffic, particularly in commuter traffic, and show perspectives of an increased usage of carpools. A significant impact on the eco-balance of the university can be expected. We explain how Internet technologies and geographic information systems can be used for the arrangement of carpools, and show advantages over traditional methods of carpooling. The concrete architecture of ORISS and the algorithms used are outlined. We conclude the chapter by describing the circumstances of deployment and propose possible future extensions of the system.

Introduction

In this chapter we describe the Web-based carpooling system ORISS (Oldenburg RIdeSharing System). The system was initially developed by a student project group at the Department of Computer Science of Carl von Ossietzky University of Oldenburg. Following the initial development phase, ORISS was extended by several student theses.

This chapter is structured as follows: First, the fundamental problem of arranging carpools is outlined and the use of Internet technologies to solve this problem is explained. The second subsection deals with the social and environmental effects of carpooling, while the subsection "A classification of carpooling" gives an overview of different types of carpooling. The subsection entitled "Project goals and circumstances of development" describes our intention in offering the proposed solution. Next the particular circumstances of developing ORISS are described.

Afterwards, we describe the implementation on the basis of the system architecture, the user interface and the algorithms used. Finally, we give an overview of the additional work that has been done in the context of ORISS and a preview regarding the deployment of ORISS at Carl von Ossietzky University of Oldenburg.

Fundamentals

Problem to be Solved

There are several reasons demanding the arrangement of carpools: On the one hand, substituting one multi-person carpool ride for several one-person private car rides is sensible for ecological reasons, since a reduction in environmental pollution can be expected. In certain cases, even the substitution of a carpool ride for a ride using public transportation may be ecologically beneficial.

On the other hand, considering purely pragmatic reasons, it may be said that due to overstressing of the public road infrastructure, which arises particularly during rush hour traffic, building a carpool is directly associated with individual benefits.

Happily, commuter traffic—from and to offices, and similar traffic from/to campuses in particular—can bring about a great traffic reduction if carpools spread. One reason is that these types of traffic show many opportunities for bundling movements from or to nearby locations. It is therefore not only most desirable but also most beneficial to support the arrangement of carpools in such contexts.

Considering the situation at a university, it may be noted that the field "traffic" amounts for a large share of the eco-balance. A study conducted at the University of Osnabrück (Viebahn et al., 1999) showed the field "traffic" amounts for a share of 32% of the total energy consumption (representing the input side of the eco-balance) and for a 31% share of the carbon dioxide emissions (output side). The University of Osnabrück and the University of Oldenburg are very similar with respect to their structure and connection to traffic infrastructure.

However, several studies (Jantzen & Böhmer, 1998; Viebahn et al., 1999; US DOT, 1997) indicate that the road users at universities do not make full use of the available potential for establishing carpools: Taking the situation at the University of Oldenburg as an example, 21% of the students commute using their own car; an additional 5% make use of a carpool counting both drivers and fellow passengers; and 65% travel by bike. In the case of the employees, 42% commute using their own car, and an additional 4% arrange carpools.

The reasons that most car drivers do not set up carpools include shortcomings of the available means of communication, such as difficulties in finding suitable carpool participants: In a study in Germany (Reinkober, 1994, 3.2.3), 26.1% of the participants stated not knowing about potential fellow passengers being a reason for not using a carpool. An additional 37.5% stated they saw no possibility for arranging a carpool.

The system we have developed seeks to provide a solution starting at this part of the problem. By using the Internet as the communication medium, it becomes possible to support the arrangement of carpools even on short notice, while providing a flexible service at minimum cost. However until now this possibility has not been adequately utilized. In the course of the student project group, previous Internet systems aiming at supporting the carpool arrangement task were evaluated. We found that the existing systems provided little more than an electronic counterpart of traditional blackboards or file-card boxes, which are known to be used to support the arrangement of carpools at universities or similar institutions. Many offline services are reimplemented 1:1 as online services, but this is clearly not innovative and usually provides no additional value to the users. These systems are suited to support the arrangement of long-term carpools or carpools for long-distance travel, such as weekend home rides or holiday trips. Due to the inadequate spatial and temporal resolution of these systems, however, they are not suited for supporting the arrangement of carpools requiring more flexibility. Since the possibilities of the Internet remained unexploited by the existing services, we saw a need to develop a better carpooling system. The situation has not changed substantially since we conducted the study.

Unless information technology is used, it is only practical to set up long-term carpools with permanent participants. Our system does not aim at replacing such carpools completely. On the contrary, our system makes it possible to recognize existing offline carpools in its assignment process, and to fill any remaining seats not occupied by permanent participants.

We call a carpooling system dynamic if it allows arranging carpools on short notice with participants not personally known to each other and handles exact location coordinates. The first implementation of such a system known to us was the Seattle Smart Traveler project (US DOT, 1997), which was put into practice in the mid-1990s in the state of Washington (USA). One precondition for implementing a system in urban areas was the availability of a geographic information system (GIS) and suitable cartographic data.

In Germany a dynamic carpooling system called M21 (*http://www.m21zentrale.de/*) was implemented by DaimlerChrysler AG and the Ministry of Environment and Traffic of the state of Baden-Württemberg starting in 1999. The functions provided by M21 and those implemented in ORISS overlap in certain fields. M21, however, is embedded in a different overall concept and aims to optimize management of car fleets of large company sites. Currently, it is only used by a few departments of DaimlerChrysler in Baden-Württemberg. M21 shows deficiencies over ORISS with respect to its carpooling component in that it does not allow for a detailed a priori specification of characteristics of potential carpooling partners. Neither does it allow for a posteriori personal judgment of an actual carpool ride. ORISS provides a more flexible specification of temporal and spatial parameters of a ride. In general, our system aims more at supporting individual users.

Recently a new carpooling system called PTV RideShare was released by PTV AG. It also shares some properties with ORISS, but lacks – to our knowledge – coordinated assignment; that is, it does not prevent overbooking of a carpool or multiple placement of the same requesting user into several carpools; nor does it allow personal judgment of fellow passengers.

Social and Environmental Effects of Carpooling

Carpooling directly leads to a reduction in energy consumption and emission of exhaust fumes and noise, since for every former single car driver participating in a carpool her single ride is no longer necessary.

Considering a relatively well-enclosed target area like the campus of the University of Oldenburg, this leads to the conclusion that an increase in carpooling reduces the necessary size of parking areas on the university campus, which already shows a high degree of soil surface sealing. On a long-term basis, the possibility of unsealing currently existing parking areas can be realistically expected.

As a result of the assessment of the Seattle Smart Traveler (US DOT, 1997), it was established that an Internet-based carpooling system appeals to a group of people that is different from the group of participants of traditionally arranged carpools. It can thus be expected that ORISS has the potential to attract new users of carpooling.

Considering the University of Oldenburg again, under the assumption that 10% of the current single car drivers would participate in carpools arranged by ORISS, a reduction of the road kilometers traveled per year of 3.6 million kilometers could result. This number was determined on the basis of the road kilometers traveled on average by each member of the University per year as stated in Jantzen and Böhmer (1998).

As a further social advantage, it may be noted that carpooling increases the social interaction of the participants and may introduce new acquaintances to the system users. Carpooling reduces the travel costs of each participant, which is particularly important for students who cannot afford owning a car on their own.

The deployment of a Web-based carpooling system combines ecological, economic and social advantages for its users and society. By demonstrating a positive correlation between these dimensions, the environmental awareness of the system's users can be increased.

Classification of Carpooling

The necessity of arranging carpools – the process is also called ride-matching – to reduce traffic was initially recognized in the USA. The focus was primarily on carpools in urban areas, and especially in commuter traffic. The infrastructure created to support such carpools can also be used for other types of carpools to a great extent. There are several types of carpools, which are usually distinguished from one another:

- *Traditional ride-matching:* Traditional ride-matching means the long-term arrangement of standing carpools through manual or computer-aided matching of participants.
- *Casual carpooling:* Casual carpooling – also instant carpooling – identifies a form of arranging carpools on park-and-ride parking areas, which is performed without prior consultation often on a daily basis. This form of carpooling can indeed be observed in certain areas in the USA. In several larger US cities there are so-called HOV lanes (High Occupant Vehicle lanes), which are reserved for cars occupied by at least two to four persons

during rush hours. To be able to make use of these circumstances, such informal carpools are formed.

One problem with this kind of carpooling is, of course, that there is no guarantee a carpool can be established every day (cf. US DOT, 1997). This poses a problem for someone without a car at her disposal for the rest of the ride.

- *Dynamic ride-matching:* Dynamic ride-matching – also real-time ride-matching – is the variant of carpooling we want to support. It may be regarded as a formalization of the casual carpooling phenomenon, because there is no need for long-term arrangements.

There have been Internet-based approaches to this problem, and other ideas for solving it have been conceived of: One scenario required the participant to make a phone call to a call center on the evening before the planned ride, and to convey the parameters of the ride. The call center operated a matching program, called the participant back a short time later, and transmitted the parameters of the arranged carpool.

Project Goals and Circumstances of Development

The central goal of the student project group was to develop a Web-based carpooling system capable of filling the technological gap described above. In fulfilling this goal the project group could make use of the ride-matching algorithms resulting from current research in the Environmental Informatics group at University of Oldenburg (see Reents, 2002, and subsection "Assignment algorithms").

We identified the following requirements as fundamental for the design of a Web-based carpooling system:

1. The user interface should be simple to use and task-oriented.
2. The specification of ride properties should be as flexible as possible, particularly with respect to the spatial and temporal resolution.
3. The system should offer coordinated carpool assignment; that is, a user's decision whether she accepts an assignment must be known to the system in order to prohibit multiple assignments.
4. The users should be supported in planning the routes necessary to pick up fellow passengers.
5. Individual preferences of the users regarding their fellow passengers should be taken into account when matching carpool participants.

6. The data input and the matching process should be chronologically separated; the matching should be fixed chronologically close to the ride time.
7. The users should be notified using a medium of their choice when important events in the matching process occur.
8. The system should be able to provide information of alternative travel possibilities in case a carpool cannot be established.
9. The system should provide scalability with respect to the number of users.

Student Project Group

The initial development of ORISS was performed by a student project group [whose 11 members were the authors of the project report (Burchardt et al., 2001)] between October 2000 and December 2001 under supervision of Dr. Ute Vogel and Gerriet Reents. Such project groups constitute an optional element of the Diploma program in computing science at the University of Oldenburg, for which its members receive 24 ECTS credit points.

The project group started with a seminar phase, during which every member prepared and carried out a lecture or a workshop. The goals of this phase were:

- to gain an overview of the state of the art with respect to the automated arrangement of carpools, and
- to learn about several technologies which could be used in designing and implementing the system.

In the second phase preliminary decisions regarding the technologies to be used were made, on the basis of which a pilot study was done. This document was used to develop a requirements definition, which listed functional and nonfunctional requirements in detail, described expected usage scenarios and defined a fundamental system architecture in a preliminary manner.

This phase was followed by a design phase during which a detailed object-oriented system architecture was constructed and documented. On this basis the implementation of the system was created, which involved recurring adaptations of the system architecture. The system architecture and implementation are described in detail in the following section. The project group was concluded by an integration phase in which the components of the system were put together, errors were corrected and the system and user documentation was completed.

Figure 1. System architecture

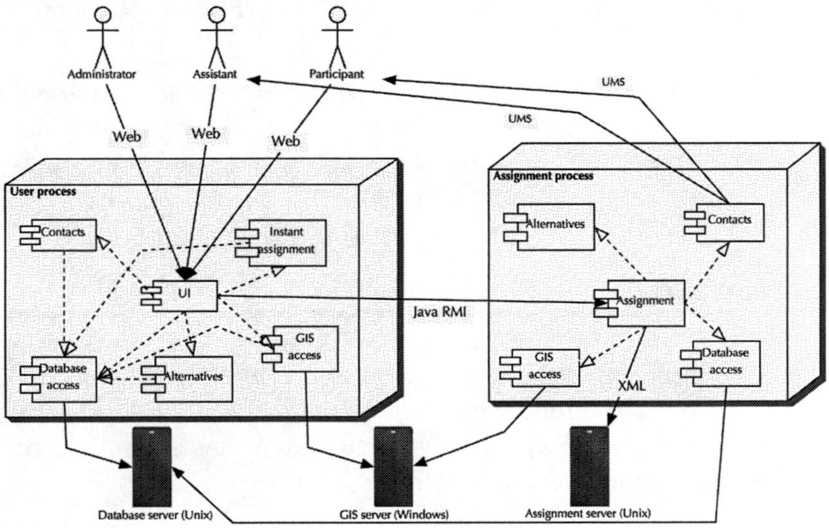

ORISS Software System

System Architecture

Figure 1 depicts the basic system architecture schematically. The nodes (shown as cuboids in the diagram) represent the two main processes of the system that may run on physically different computers: the user and the assignment process. Three other processes are involved in the system, namely a database server, a GIS server and the assignment server. These are depicted differently, as they were not created as part of the project.

The main parts of the system are implemented in the Java 2 language, running on Java 2 SDK 1.3.1 or newer. The user process is run in a servlet container implementing Java Servlet Specification 2.2 and JavaServer Pages 1.1. We use the reference implementation of these specifications, Apache Jakarta Tomcat. Both user and assignment process are run on a Linux system.

The assignment server was developed by Gerriet Reents as part of his forthcoming dissertation. The GIS server we used is MapServer by Map&Guide/PTV. At the time of system design it was only available for Microsoft Windows NT, and thus needs to be run on a separate physical or virtual machine. It provides a COM (Component Object Model) interface, which is difficult to access directly from Java applications. For this reason we developed a proxy written in C++ which is deployed on the same machine as the GIS server. It is accessed by a simple TCP/IP protocol from the user and assignment processes. The GIS proxy was omitted from the diagram for simplicity. The communication between user and assignment processes is performed through the Java RMI (Remote Method Invocation) protocol.

Most of the software we used is available as open source. This excludes the GIS server, for which an open source solution is currently unthinkable. The reason for this is the restricted availability of cartographic data, which in any case would need to be licensed on a proprietary basis.

User Interface

The users are expected to use the services provided by ORISS by means of any Web browser. To use the functions of the system a personal log-in – after an initial registration – is necessary. The system distinguishes three classes of users who are offered different sets of functions:

Figure 2. Input form for a new car pool offer

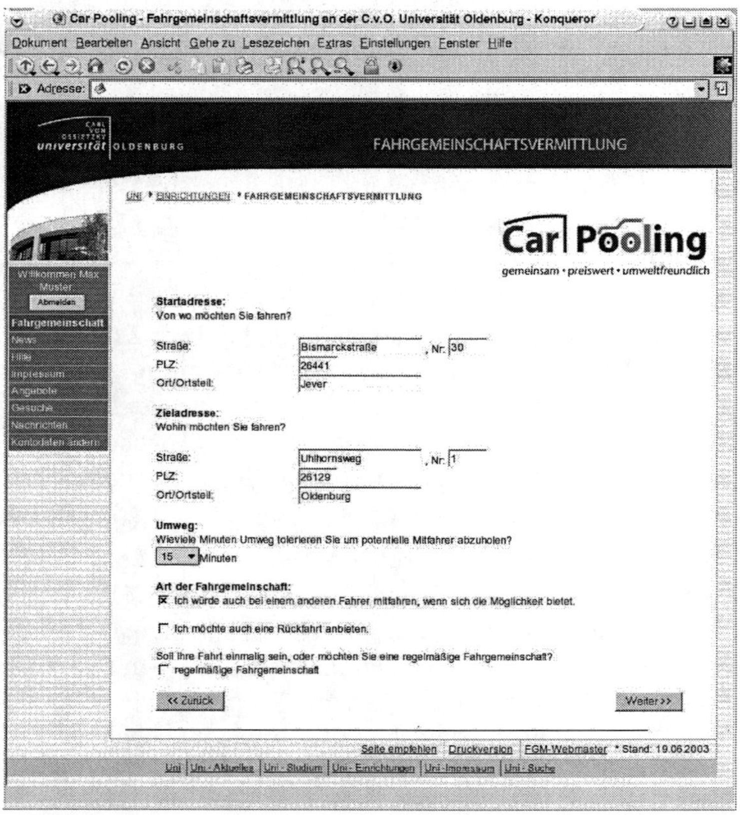

- *Participants:* A (potential) participant in a carpool uses the system for requesting or offering seats in carpools.
- *Assistants:* Assistants are system operators who are able to assist users in using the system. They may also act as telephone operators who act as a proxy and allow the use of the system by people (permanently or temporarily) without Internet access.
- *Administrators:* Administrators manage the system. They are allowed to change global system settings and modify the system help.

The user interface provides a participant with the opportunity:

- to offer carpools as driver of a car, or to request seats in carpools as a fellow passenger,
- to read messages sent by the system or other users, and to send messages to other users herself,
- to modify her personal system preferences, in particular specify preferred and supplemental ways of contact.

A typical part of an input form is shown in Figure 2. This particular input form is used to create a new offer for seats in a carpool. The system is currently only available in a German version as depicted. After a request or offer has been entered, it is passed over to the assignment process. This process periodically calls the assignment server, which tries to find a globally optimal match of requests and offers forming sets of carpool participants or, in short, carpools. Details regarding the exact interpretation of what constitutes "globally" optimal are given in the next section. The participants of each carpool are sent a message via their preferred contact medium, which conveys the contact data of their fellow passengers, a description of the car to be used (brand, color, class and registration number), and a proposed route containing all pickup points (Figure 3).

Since we wanted to provide as much flexibility as possible with respect to specifying desirable fellow passengers, it is possible to make preferences regarding their smoking habits, sex and age. After a carpool ride has taken place, every participant can judge her fellow passengers, which is taken into account in future carpool assignments. Every judgment is, however, only registered for one pair of participants and is only visible to the participant who entered it.

In any attempt to arrange carpools it is of course essential to specify the parameters regarding the ride most accurately. We distinguish first of all between single and periodic carpools. Periodic carpools are handled specifically in that the assignment process tries to find regular fellow passengers, which seldom change, provided the pair of participants is not judged negatively by either party.

Figure 3. Example of a result of the assignment process

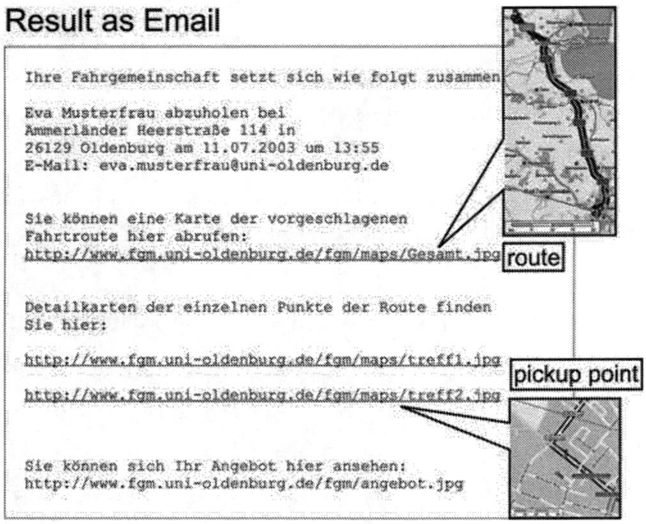

When entering a request for a seat in a carpool, it is possible to specify multiple alternative pickup locations. This feature is thought to make it possible to use well-known locations, especially car parks at expressway entrances, as pickup locations for multiple passengers. This enables a more flexible matching of carpools and increases the convenience for drivers. It is thus well suited for attracting more people to participate in the carpooling system.

Finally, it is possible to enter a combined offer and request for the same ride. This is meant for people who have a car at their disposal, but do not necessarily want or need to use it and thus would be willing to participate in a carpool as a fellow passenger. If there is a surplus in available drivers, such an item is handled as a request.

Assignment Algorithms

One important part of ORISS is the solution of the assignment problem itself, that is, the matching of requests and offers. This is performed by an assignment server as depicted in Figure 1. A sophisticated assignment algorithm was necessary to achieve the goals of ORISS. On the one hand, environmental issues were taken into account; that is, carpools are formed in a way minimizing the total distance traveled by all rides known to the system, counting both the carpools arranged and the remaining single rides. On the other hand, preferences of the users had to be satisfied in a convenient way. To achieve this, the users were able to specify their ride preferences using several constraints, including detour tolerance, via locations and alternate starting points.

A formal optimization model incorporates all these properties using mixed integer programming (MIP) as the formalism. This model is related to the traveling salesman problem (Lawler et al., 1985) and vehicle routing problems like pickup and delivery problems with time windows and capacities (Golden & Assad, 1988), but also entails aspects specific to the carpool assignment problem. The optimization goal is expressed as the objective function in the MIP, which consists of two parts: one for minimizing the total distance and the other for taking mutual judgments into account. All other characteristics of the assignment problem are modeled as constraints of the mixed integer program.

This formal model of the problem is descriptive; that is, it defines the result an assignment algorithm has to deliver. We consider three aims central to designing the algorithm:

- performance permitting application in practice,
- good solution quality,
- ability to work under online conditions.

By online conditions we mean that the assignment problem is not known completely when the algorithm starts work, but instead changes with every user interaction. Nevertheless, ORISS has to make decisions based on intermediate results. These decisions are taken into account by the further optimization process.

An online algorithm should be able to find a feasible solution of the assignment problem within given temporal limits, for example approximately in 30 minutes. Only a heuristic approach can thus be used for realistically scaled problems. Calculating the exact solution of the assignment problem within the given temporal limits cannot be guaranteed because of the algorithmic complexity. Two heuristics were developed whose performance makes it possible to meet the temporal limits. However, an exact solution algorithm was nevertheless developed to assure the quality of these heuristics. By comparing heuristic solutions to the exact solutions we are able to ensure that the loss of solution quality caused by heuristic approaches remains in foreseeable and acceptable bounds.

The first heuristic method is based on a greedy principle, and assigns each request to the carpool currently considered most favorable according to the objective function, beginning with the request, which fits into the fewest carpools. The individual carpools with given participants are calculated optimally; that is, the path of each carpool is as short as possible. This is particularly important, because members of a carpool could easily notice any detour in a route proposed by ORISS. Globally suboptimal solutions would, however, usually remain unnoticed. A second (meta-)heuristic approach based on tabu search (Glover & Laguna, 1997) was implemented. It is divided into a constructive part, working similarly to the greedy heuristics, and the actual tabu search part, pursuing a neighborhood based search strategy.

Both heuristics can be used in the online assignment process since they are able to process modifications of the problem by new or withdrawn requests as well as the fixation of assignments. The exact algorithm we developed performs a decomposition of the original problem definition to reduce the structural complexity of the problem. The principle of set partitioning with column generation is used as the solution technique (see Desrosiers et al., 1984 for example).

Measurements based on artificial, but realistic benchmarks showed that performance and solution quality fulfill the requirements for deployment at the University of Oldenburg.

Figure 4. ORISS welcome page

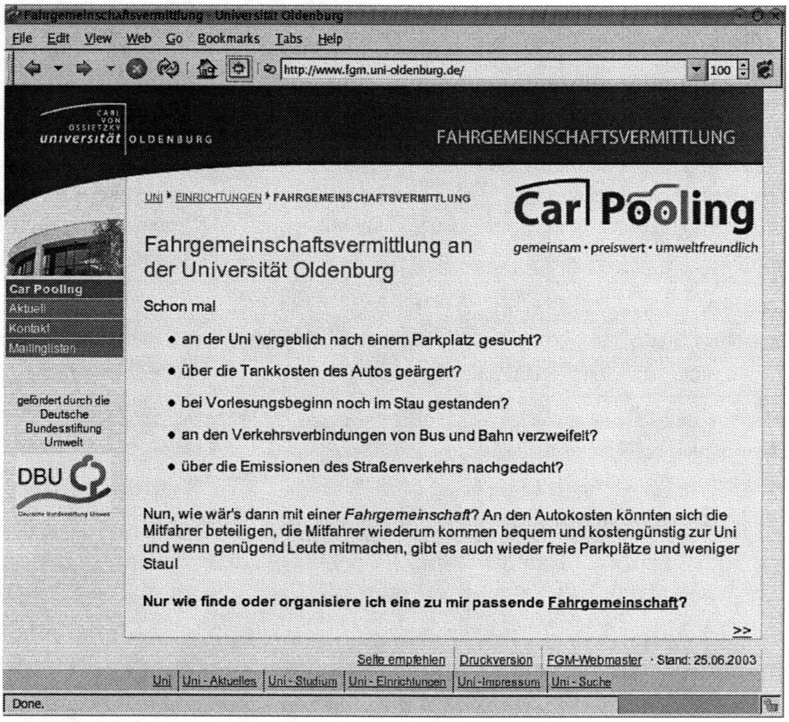

Current Project Status

At the end of the student project group a usable and fundamentally deployable system was available which just had not been exposed to practical use. During and after the project group, further work was done on the system in the form of Diploma theses and individual student projects. These projects dealt with:

- the advancement of heuristic and exact carpool assignment algorithms,
- the ergonomics of the user interface on the basis of the ISO 9241 standard,
- the visualization of inventorial and assignment information, and
- the generation of automatic test scenarios for the assignment and user processes.

After the project group ended, a pilot phase was drafted by a group headed by Prof. Dr. Michael Sonnenschein and Prof. Dr. Thomas Raabe, which would put ORISS into practical use at the University of Oldenburg. Finally, this project was realized with financial support of the Federal German Foundation for the Environment (Deutsche Bundesstiftung Umwelt). The pilot phase will last for 16 months during which the employees and students of the University of Oldenburg will have the opportunity to use the system. After preparatory measures, which are currently being conducted (adaptation to corporate design, technical installation, promotion), the test service started in October 2003. Information about the test service can be found at *http://www.fgm.uni-oldenburg.de/*, but is currently only available in German.

During the pilot phase the system will be adopted to the expectations of its users on the basis of their experiences and the ergonomic study previously conducted, and remaining errors shall be corrected. The Institute for Business Administration and Education will conduct accompanying research to study how well the system meets the requirements of the users, and to perform an analysis of its outreach. In the case of a successful pilot phase, the ongoing operation of the carpooling system for at least three years is guaranteed through financial means of the University administration and the student board.

The system was awarded an acknowledgment in connection with the Oldenburg Environmental Protection Prize 2002 by the city of Oldenburg. In 2003 the project was awarded the Environmental Informatics Prize 2003 for Students by the Technical Committee "Informatics for Environmental Protection" of the German Informatics Society.

Future Work

In the future, the system may be extended to a mobility control center. To some extent it is already possible to provide the user with information about alternative means of travel in case a carpool cannot be arranged. However, the integration of data about public transportation systems or the coupling with similar, already existing information systems still has to be implemented. In addition, it is worth studying how cooperation with a car sharing supplier could improve the usefulness of a carpooling system: In case there are multiple requests for a similar route, but none of the potential participants has a car at her disposal, a shared car may be automatically reserved.

Currently, monetary considerations are not considered at all in the system. It is thus not possible to charge the users for the use of the system. In the current deployment at the University this is not necessary, and for legal reasons not possible, but in principle the system could be deployed for other user groups or for general use, which could make it necessary to take such aspects into account. Integration with a car sharing service would certainly require support for charging individual costs to the system users.

As a consequence, the participants of a carpool have to take care of reimbursing the driver themselves. It is possible, however, as the pilot phase will definitely show, that the users would welcome having a system to manage these costs, which is conceivable for several reasons: It would increase convenience, since then no payment in the car would be necessary; the driver could be sure of getting paid; and all participants could be definitely informed about the costs in advance.

In the current system version, notification of users by using an externally provided UMS (Unified Messaging System) mechanism is possible via various media; that is, multichannel push subscriptions are available. Access in a pull mode is currently only possible by using a desktop Web browser. It is planned to additionally provide access via a WAP interface or similar access method, which can be used from mobile phones.

One problem of the current version of the system is that a request or offer must be entered a couple of hours before the ride will take place to ensure that the assignment happens in time. In cases in which the time between data input and the time of the ride is smaller than a certain threshold, the system should offer an instantaneous assignment of a carpool and discard the request, whenever it is not possible to arrange a carpool at the time of data input.

ORISS Project Participants

Initial student project group members: Henning Burchardt, Hauke Duden, Lars Ebert, Simon Giesecke, Marco Helmers, Thilo Manske, Sebastian Mittelstädt, Andreas Möller, Oliver Robbe, Axel Steinbach, Jesko Strala (2001); individual student projects: Ina Wentzlaff, Hüseyin Beter, Holger Höwener, Torben Christian Sliwka (2002), Jan Friedrich, Simone Grewatsch (2003); Diploma theses: Michael Winkler (2001), Axel Giertz, Thorsten Meyer (2002), Henning Burchardt (2003). Current staff members, partially funded by DBU: Michael Sonnenschein, Thomas Raabe, Tanja Hüsken, Jörg Hammermeister, Gerriet Reents, Ute Vogel, Jens Finke, Jesko Strala, Fabian Grüning.

References

Burchardt, H. et al. (2001). *Abschlussbericht der Projektgruppe WWW-basierte Vermittlung von Fahrgemeinschaften.* Tech. Rep. Fachbereich Informatik, Carl von Ossietzky Universität Oldenburg.

Desrosiers, J., Soumis, F., & Desrochers, M. (1984). Routing with time windows by column generation. *Networks, 14,* 545-565.

Glover, F., & Laguna, M. (1997). *Tabu Search.* Dordrecht: Kluwer Academic.

Golden, B., & Assad, A. (eds.). (1988). *Vehicle routing: Methods and studies.* Elsevier Science Publishers.

Jantzen, J., & Böhmer, N. (1998). *Ökobilanz der Carl von Ossietzky Universität Oldenburg: Teilbereich Verkehr.* Tech. Rep. Lehrstuhl für Allgemeine BWL, Unternehmensführung und Betriebliche Umweltpolitik der Universität Oldenburg.

Lawler, E.L., Lenstra, J.K., Kan, A.H.G.R., & Shmoys, D.B. (1985). *The traveling salesman problem.* New York: John Wiley & Sons.

Reents, G. (2002). Carpooling in commuter traffic aided by an Internet communication platform. In K.T.W. Pillmann (Ed.), *Environmental communication in the information society: The 16th International Symposium Informatics for Environmental Protection,* Marburg: Metropolis, pp. 494-501.

Reinkober, N. (1994). *Fahrgemeinschaften und Mobilitätszentrale: Bestandteile eines zukunftsorientierten Öffentlichen Personennahverkehrs.* Bielefeld: Erich Schmidt Verlag.

United States Department of Transportation (US DOT). (1997). *Assessment of the Seattle Smart Traveler.*

Viebahn, Huischen, & Matthies. (1999). Die Verkehrsbilanz der Universität Osnabrück: Ermittlung der Umweltbelastungen durch die Pendler und den internen Verkehr. *Umweltwissenschaften und Schadstoff-Forschung, 11*(3), 167-175.

Chapter XVII

Citizen-Centered Environmental Information Dissemination via Multiple Information Channels

Thomas Rose, FIT, Germany

Gertraud Peinel, FIT, Germany

Kostas Karatzas, IT Environmental Consultant, Greece

Per Henrik Johansen, Norgit AS, Norway

Jon Erik Lindberg, Norgit AS, Norway

Abstract

Citizens call for timely and high-quality environmental information for reasons of awareness and personal well-being. Only an informed citizen will be in the position to participate in urban environment decision making and planning. This interest recommends an easy-to-understand and easy-to-access presentation of such up-to-date information. Rather than presenting raw data in an extensive fashion, one ought to engineer customizable information services that can be tailored to individual user groups, be it for reasons of content or be it for reasons of citizen's ease of access. APNEE has designed information services that draw upon various information channels, such as mobile technologies, interactive portals for the Internet, as well as street panels for municipality usage scenarios. In a nutshell, the APNEE system promotes user-friendly information management and dissemination services via multiple information channels, effectively combining information content and service providing schemes. This dissemination platform can be applied not only to the environmental sector but also in multiple information domains. Based on the APNEE approach, environmental information turns into an attractive product (electronic information service).

Introduction

Citizens are getting more and more concerned to be aware of the environmental terms of their everyday life and the environmental pressures that they are exposed to. They request for adequate levels of environmental information service quality, in order to play a crucial role in relevant decision-making and planning, be it at an individual or community level. This is well reflected in one of the five top priorities of the sixth environment action program of the European Community (CEC, 2001), which involves the empowerment of people as private citizens and the attempt to change their perception of environmental issues. Their effective involvement in decision-making presupposes that full definitions and an understanding of environmental problems as well as certain ways of resolution and contribution are provided. Therefore, environmental information, including indicators and maps, can serve as a driver in this direction. Some proposed actions include the improvement of public accessibility to this kind of information and the preparation of new user-friendly toolkits for information perception that will change one's environmental behavior. Systems for more efficient gathering, modelling and forecasting of environmental information is another noteworthy action of the EU programme that thus reinforces the need for designing new citizen-centered information services.

This chapter reports on a citizen-centered approach for the dissemination of information on air quality in APNEE (Bøhler et al., 2001). APNEE deliberately promotes an active stance for the dissemination of information in order to reach the citizen in a variety of individual circumstances by utilizing a set of telecommunication technologies. In addition, the provision of individualized presentations of environmental information has proven crucial for reaching the citizen. This chapter discusses the needs for the customization of information in the environmental domain. Based upon these customization needs, a dissemination platform will be presented that allows one to customize the kind of information, the textual and visual presentation, and the access channel of transfer.

Citizen-Centered Environmental Information Systems (EIS)

The need of citizen-centered information dissemination in the environmental sector is a concept that is continuously gaining support, not only because of the increased interest in the environment but also due to the recognition of the environmental information as a valuable asset towards a sustainable urban planning. This need has already been pointed out in a survey conducted in order to reveal aspects, requirements and perspectives on improvement of environmental information concerning an EIS for London: *London Environment Online* (Haklay, 2000). The citizen-centered design can be seen as the approach to the development of interactive systems that mainly aims to make all available environmental information usable and accessible, regardless of the type of the information channel. The primary design principles of this kind of design can be characterized by:

- dedicated awareness of the potential users' requirements,
- significant efforts to design as simply as possible,
- the use of existing standards and technologies,
- user-oriented control and freedom of navigation, and
- prevention of errors and provision of error recovery.

In the London Environment Online study it was concluded that the public should not be treated as a one-piece monolithic body, but that the multiple identities and profiles of each individual user should be considered carefully. Most users view environmental information as a set of interconnected matters of their daily lives, express interests in various directions and consider environment as a cumulative picture. In addition, a review of the existing public EIS demonstrated the lack of plurality in the design of such systems (Haklay, 2002). The amount of available environmental information has increased rapidly during the last years, while it is stored on different platforms and in different formats, and organized according to various constructing schemes and models. Another survey suggested that providing air quality (AQ) information and data on their own is insufficient, while most responders revealed a high degree of concern on possible health impacts of air pollution and wished to learn more about ways of helping to reduce poor AQ circumstances (Beaumont et al., 1999). From the above surveys, a demand of localized and regional environmental information was recognized. Most users stressed the need for simplified language, so as to eliminate the possibilities of misunderstandings and inconsistent interpretation. In similar studies, the obvious preference for processed data and interpreted information has been stressed (EPA, 1998). Meta-information, that type of information that can be seen as an indicator pointing to another piece of information or data source in the form of maps or air quality indexes provides attractive ways of information packaging, visualization and presentation and it is thus suggested that it should be implemented in the public EIS design.

Toward Multi-Access Environmental Information Systems

Several directives and regulations have been devised to improve levels of comfort and other conditions for quality of life. But any imposition on people has been proven to fail rather consistently. People will only change their behaviour if they can grasp the junction between individual behaviour and their levels of comfort. Citizens require more information regarding the quality of the environment they live in, and as they become more aware of environmental issues, this desire continues to rise, thus raising the volume of information requests. The question arises of how to design and implement citizen-centered information services, since the level of sensitivity corresponds proportionally to the quality of information services and the ease of use from a user's point of view. To meet such levels of quality, information services have to have higher levels of user friendliness and pro-activity of services.

In APNEE, citizens can access the air quality information system through different information channels: In the World Wide Web, a GIS-based interface founded in the concept of smart maps (Peinel/Rose, 2001) guides the user to relevant air quality information at various levels of granularity. In the mobile world, SMS is used for active dissemination of early warning enabled by subscriber services for concerned citizens, for example endangered people living in or approaching polluted regions. WAP-based services provide more sophisticated information in terms of presentation, content, and navigation. In city environments, street panels serve as public broadcasting means to inform citizens on forecasted trends. Voice servers provide information by phone, as well as e-mail is used for active notifications. In the future, also enhanced SMS as well as PDA will provide additional mobile interfaces.

APNEE studies the feasibility of these different broadcasting methods and evaluates them with regard to acceptance, potential impact on citizen behaviour, future markets for online environmental information services for city authorities, as well as telecommunication service providers and other entrepreneurs in the information society.

Mobile technologies are not intended to replace Internet technologies (European Commission, 2002). Moreover, we foresee that mobile technologies and Internet technologies will be used complementarily depending on the location or individual interest of customers. One example of a mobile customer using several dissemination channels based on his or her location might be:

- get a short information by GSM SMS (early warning – push technology),
- look for further information on the WAP while being mobile, and finally
- look at home for detailed information with the PC on the Web.

Besides being mobile, this technology would also allow to serve different scales of interests. For example, athletes who want to know which time of day is better for their sports activity, or parents with children suffering from pseudo-croup planning to take a walk. This special customer group might require more detailed or specialized information than others.

APNEE Approach

APNEE transmits information on air quality to selected citizens in urban regions in a customized fashion. Customization refers to the tailoring and processing of information content, such as warnings or recommendations for further action with respect to the user group registered, to the technical capabilities of the end-user devices targeted, and of course to the geographic location. Two dimensions for the improvement of information services are conjectured: Firstly, sophisticated means for information visualization are required to elevate the user-friendliness of the information encounter. Rather than presenting raw data from some environmental management systems, a new interaction metaphor for navigation and access in information spaces is employed. Special attention has been devoted to means for visualizing data in a cartographic stance and for providing interactivity amid exploration. Secondly, information services have had to mature from a passive delivery task towards a pro-active, customizable

Figure 1. APNEE dissemination platform

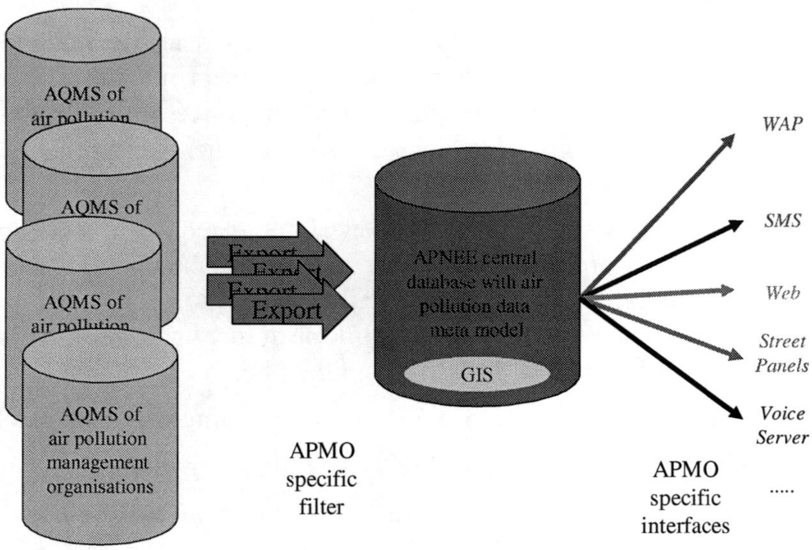

service that orchestrates data for a specific purpose and employs appropriate information modality whilst reaching citizens that might have even subscribed to specific profiles.

The APNEE solution is based on one common central system allowing new users' sites as well as new interface providers to easily connect to the system.

The beauty of this approach is the ease of connecting new air pollution management organizations (APMO) to the APNEE system by building only an export filter to the APNEE central database (Figure 1). That is, APNEE provides in principle the dissemination core, that is, broker platform, employing several communication channels to be used by content providers, in our case information on air quality and levels of comfort.

While the mobile interfaces have to be implemented with respect to the telecommunication providers involved in APNEE, the Web solution as well as the subscription service is based on one common platform, open source and freeware for all user sites. Separation of layout and content allows easy adaptation to new user sites reflecting their individual corporate identity as well as of course language and country specific issues.

Mobile access and street panels for new user sites are also easily connectable to the database, but individual technical architectures and modules of telecommunication providers require a little more effort for implementation.

Based on this open approach new components can be connected. "New" components include and will be tested in the follow-up project APNEE-TU:

Figure 2. APNEE service portfolio

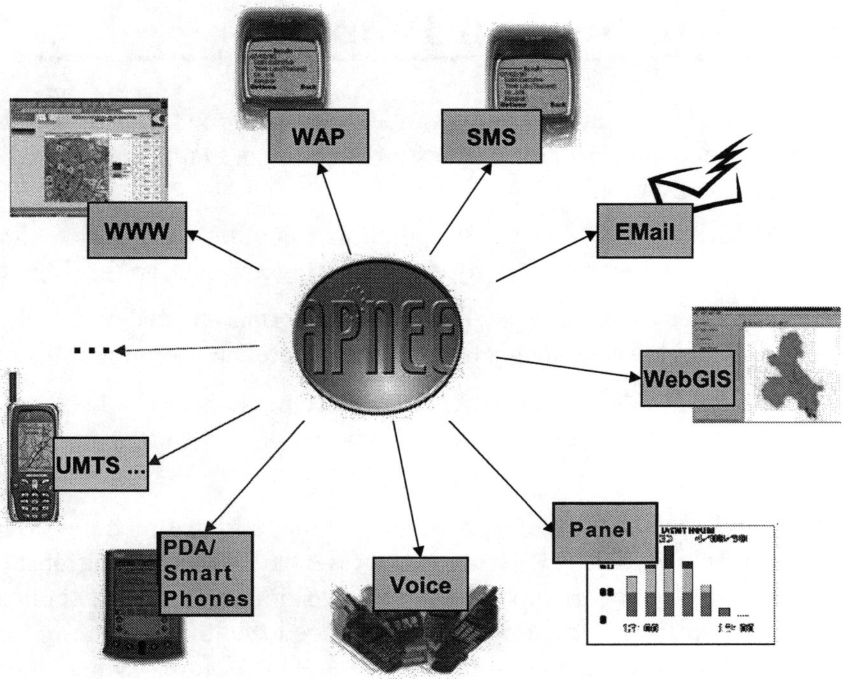

- Additional user sites with data sources provided by regional data providers (selected regions in Germany, Oslo in Norway, Canary Islands and Andalusia in Spain, Thessaloniki in Greece),
- Alternative types of data to cover new information domains, such as pollens,
- Emerging devices and communication channels, such as PDA (Personal Digital Assistant) connected via GPRS as well as smart phones with GPRS and UMTS.

Transferring the Look and Feel of APNEE-Like Information Portals to Other Application Domains

The spectrum of information channels materialized in the frame of APNEE make the portal an ideal platform for various information domains that call for multi-channel information applications.

One major advantage of APNEE is the combination of pull and push techniques, where the latter is essential for any early warning application (cf. Figure 3):

- *Pull services:* interested persons request information on demand, information will be returned on this request immediately by sending information.
- *Push services:* "push" content to interested persons who subscribe to such a service on timely or event-specific basis.

APNEE push services are directly adaptable to other application domains calling for early warning, which by their nature represent emergency situations: floods, earthquakes, fires, and tornado warnings. In addition, commercial applications, for example traffic information or personalized health information, can be served. An APNEE application example is depicted in Figure 4, where the APNEE regional server and the supporting multi-access information system developed for one of the city application domains (here Athens) are visualized.

The use of open source software for the Web, as dictated by a strategic decision within the APNEE consortium, is evident in Figure 4. This decision strengthened

Figure 3. APNEE push and pull services

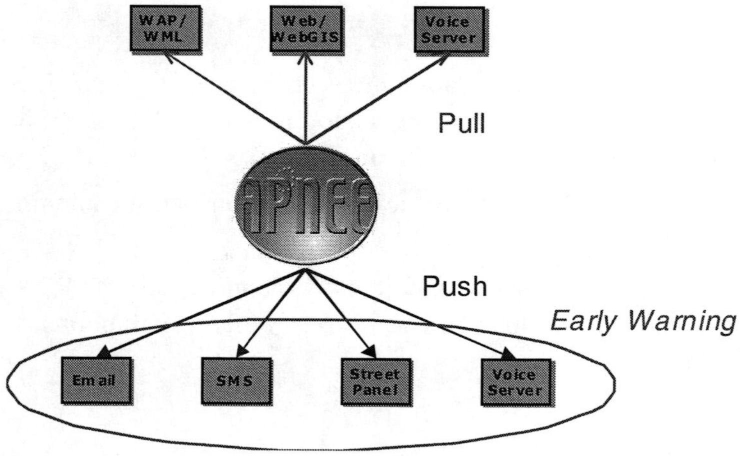

Figure 4. Apnee Athens regional server application

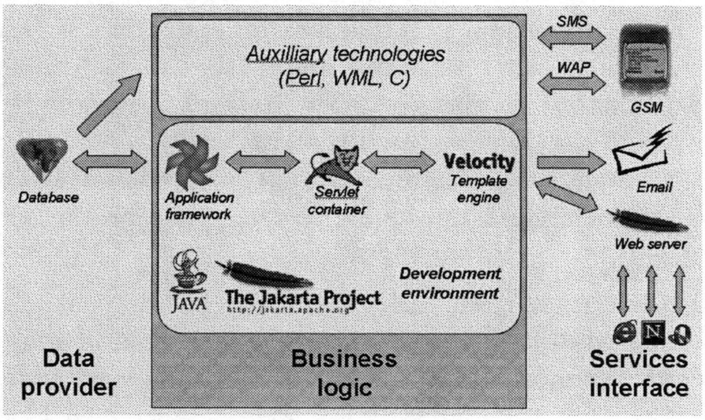

the Apnee approach with the necessary flexibility, modularity and independence from commercial software, without jeopardizing its functionality. The Apnee system can be combined with any existing EIS and blends smoothly with future modules to be developed per site.

Cartographic Visualization

The use of a GIS for presenting environmental information content and providing environmental information services is expected to be beneficial, as it allows the citizens to:

1. navigate in the information domain on the basis of individual needs and interests, and
2. have a better insight and understanding of the content of the information provided.

It has already been stated that the use of Web-based GIS can enhance public democratic involvement (Kingston et al., 2000). In addition, major emphasis has been put on ease of use and customizability. Cartographic visualization allows citizens to access information in an intuitive way, and map layers allow a customization of information content as well as presentation, an approach resulting in a high level of user acceptance.

When presenting the average citizen with scientific data, it is important to make the information understandable and easily available. This is most important when presenting pollution forecasts, which may have an impact on the daily routines of a citizen. Tufte (1983) shows how the understanding of scientific data and their meaning are greatly enhanced through careful adoption of graphics. The graphics must encourage data comparison, present the data at different levels of detail, avoid data distortion, and so forth. Most of these issues might be accomplished by static graphic presentation alone, but the use of direct manipulation and interactive query tools has proven highly instrumental when travelling in such not easily understood information spaces as represented by APNEE (Shneiderman, 1994).

This, along with the fact that APNEE will disseminate geographical information to the citizen, makes a well-designed GIS map a natural incarnation of the user interface. Also, the support of a GIS for reaching the end user has been implemented with success in other EU funded projects, such as IRENIE (IRENIE) and GeoNet 4D (Peinel & Rose, 2001). The APNEE system is built upon several components based on a sound programming methodology (Nichols, 2000). The model consists of a database and GIS system (GRASS) along with well-defined methods to access the data.

The advantage of this design is that the APNEE system easily adapts to new ways of information visualization. If a new push technology is invented or has to be employed, a new "view" might easily be added to the existing APNEE umbrella of different dissemination techniques. Therefore, the APNEE system is highly (re-) configurable and scalable. Following this requirement, the map server has been built in a modular fashion with an open environment conforming to the OpenGIS standard in order to incorporate alternative browsing styles if necessary. OpenGIS is defined as "the ability to *share heterogeneous geodata and geoprocessing resources* transparently in a networked environment". The OpenGIS consortium has specified several standards for the implementation of a standardized and flexible exchange of geographical information. A decision was made to use the OpenGIS® Web Map Server Interfaces Implementation Specification (OpenGIS, 2000) as a starting point for the GIS Internet communication.

The WebGIS interface enables the user to access air pollution information through maps. The main idea is that the server side provides all GIS functionalities and the client, for instance a Java applet, simply displays the map as an image. The communication between applet and GIS is done according to the Open GIS specifications.

Two different WebGIS interfaces are provided by APNEE:

1. A simple HTML interface providing enough functionality to give a fast overview. It is easy to load and print while the screen only shows a simple map with a specific theme. That means the user cannot modify the content

Figure 5. Screenshot of the APNEE *WebGIS interface prototype*

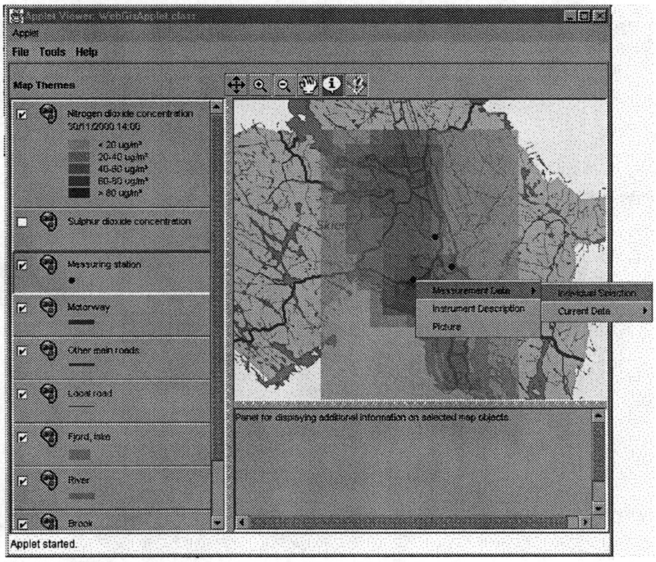

of a layer dependent on the needs and cannot carry out any specific queries on the database.

2. An advanced Java applet with direct manipulation features, and data mining and dynamic queries applied to the currently selected map layers.

The system administration generates predefined maps by using a map generation tool. This tool offers the possibility to generate maps containing different layers, and to define the drawing features for each layer, such as shape, size, and color of the signature. Additionally there is an option to specify whether and how the user can modify the layer content, and which information should be shown if the layer objects are defined as sensitive areas.

Since objects on a layer can be sensitive areas, maps become reactive as smart maps (Peinel & Rose, 2001). Whenever the mouse enters such a region, a little information about this map object is shown and a flipped icon of the mouse cursor indicates that additional information on this object is available. Clicking on such a sensitive region pops up a menu with related information topics. A selection of one of these hierarchical ordered topics displays the requested information in a Web window. This enables a somehow strolling on a map and discovering information by chance.

As stated by Evans et al. (1999), the prospects for the delivery of GIS-centered environmental information applications across the Web are excellent, and the response of the public seems promising given the newness of the field. In terms of public response, it seems highly likely that democratic apathy can be reduced by presenting rapidly developed but well informed views to those in power.

Conclusions

The APNEE system promotes user-friendly information management and dissemination via multiple information channels. Based on such high quality dissemination services, environmental information can turn into an attractive product once perceived and provided as indicators for emerging interests of citizens toward levels of comfort.

In a *technology stance,* APNEE provides an information service platform to disseminate information spatially and temporarily varying information, successfully tested for air quality information in urban environments. Individual citizen needs are met by APNEE's multi-access information services. Yet, the question arises how to implement this kind of service from a technology point of view. Technology standards are still missing to offer SMS or WAP services at a European scale. Moreover, they seem to be tailored to individual service providers; that is, each bulk broadcasting of SMS messages requires individual interfaces for each provider. WAP has a higher degree of interface compatibility, yet each interface has to be tested on a huge set of phones. WAP also comes with a higher cultural affinity, that is, services well established in one country might have a lower acceptance in other countries. Unfortunately, language carries also a significant impact on the design of services once devices with a small resolution are targeted.

In a *business stance,* APNEE implements an electronic supply chain of environmental content from certified sources, over commercial content service providers, to customers. This cross-business chain has proven crucial for the success of APNEE. Commercial content providers seek new content opportunities and are eager to provide quality assured information. Environmental institutions provide quality assured content, but not in an attractive form. Here it is where two business opportunities meet in the clouds of public-private partnerships.

In an *information society stance,* APNEE is a first step towards e-environment that is intended to offer environmental information as a professional business service towards the citizen while it provides the first pan-European reference for harmonizing environmental information provided towards the citizens, thus producing a considerable momentum for a commonly accepted way of defining and using air quality indicators. Future extensions will be explored to establish information of the environment as attractive service that reaches the citizen and is based on an economical sustainable basis.

APNEE has started as an RTD measure with support from the European Commission and is now starting further field trials in the course of APNEE-TU (APNEE Take-Up) as take-up measure. The APNEE information service platform will be extended in APNEE-TU to new mobile devices (PDAs and smart phones based on GPRS and UMTS) as well as new regions (in Germany, Norway and Greece) and additional information services (levels of comfort, pollen, UV index).

References

APNEE. (1999). Air pollution network for early warning and on-line information exchange in Europe, IST-1999-11517 project. Retrieved August 18, 2003: *http://www.apnee.org/.*

Beaumont, R., Hamilton, R.S., Machin, N., Perks, J., & Williams, I.D. (1999). Social awareness of air quality information, *The Science of the Total Environment, 235,* 319-329.

Bøhler, T., Karatzas, K., Peinel, G., Rose, T., & San Jose, R. (2002). Providing multi-modal access to environmental data — Customisable information services for disseminating air quality information in APNEE. *Computers, Environment and Urban Systems, 26*(1), 39-61.

Card, S.K, Mackinley, J.D, & Shneiderman, B. (1999). *Readings in information visualization: Using vision to think.* Morgan Kaufmann Publishers.

CEC (Commission of the European Communities). (2001). COM(2001)31, final. Retrieved August 18, 2003: *http://europa.eu.int/eurlex/en/com/pdf/2001/en_501PC0031.pdf.*

EPA. (1998). Environmental data and information: Interim findings from an EPA customer survey. Retrieved August 18, 2003: *http://www.epa.gov/eq/ceisdocs/phase3c.pdf.*

European Commission. (2002). *Digital content for global mobile services, eContent.* Office for Official Publications of the European Communities, Belgium. Retrieved August 18, 2003: *http://www.cordis.lu/econtent/studies/stud_mobile.htm.*

Evans, A., Kingston, R., Carver, S., & Turton, I. (1999). *Web-based GIS used to enhance public democratic involvement.* Retrieved August 18, 2003: *http://www.geog.leeds.ac.uk/papers/99-1/.*

GRASS [The GRASS GIS Home Page]. Retrieved August 18, 2003: *http://www.geog.uni-hannover.de/grass/index.html*.

Haklay, M. (2000). *London environment online-user requirements study – Final Report*. Centre for Advanced Spatial Analysis, University College London. Retrieved August 18, 2003: *http://www.casa.ucl.ac.uk/leosurvey.pdf*.

Haklay, M. (2002). Public access to environmental information: Past, present and future. *Computers, Environment and Urban Systems 27*(2), 163-180.

IRENIE: Improved Reporting of Environmental Information using EIONET, Environmental Telematics Project, Contract Number EN 4002. Retrieved August 18, 2003: *http://www.nilu.no/irenie/*.

Karatzas, K., & Moussiopoulos N. (2000). Urban air quality management and information systems in Europe: Legal framework and information access. *Journal of Environmental Assessment Policy and Management 2*(2), 263-272.

Kingston, R., Carver, S., Evans, A., & Turton, I. (2000). Web-based public participation geographical information systems: An aid to local environmental decision-making. *Computers, Environment and Urban Systems, 24*(2), 109-125.

Kuhn, Th. (1996). *The structure of scientific revolutions* (3rd ed.). University of Chicago Press.

Nichols, B. (2000, March). Evolution of programming methodology, Part II. *BYTE Magazine*.

Chapter XVIII

Accessing Public Sector Environmental Data and Information: Development and Demonstration of a National Portal

Chris Jarvis, Environment Agency, UK

John Kupiec, Environment Agency, UK

Abstract

This chapter highlights the importance that the Environment Agency places on the provision of information and the key part it plays in achieving environmental goals, an importance that is recognised in a range of national, European and international laws and agreements. The Agency is seeking to ensure that it meets the "letter" and, importantly, the spirit of all relevant legislation. To this end, our vision is environmental information freely available to all – quickly and easily, where and when people want it, and in a format to meet particular needs. The opportunities that present themselves in today's "Information Age" are exciting and the potential to lever environmental benefit is great. The Agency's track record in this field is already considerable, with five years' experience of providing key environmental datasets through "What's in Your Backyard?" – a GIS, Internet based national portal (www.environment-agency.gov.uk). This system has been developed and extended to include a pollution inventory, flood plain maps, landfill sites and a range of other data layers. Members of the public can find information from a national level, right down to their local environment: locating areas of interest by postcode or place name, displaying data to a chosen scale, formulating individual queries on the datasets, gaining background on information of interest, and downloading data for their own use off-line. The key components in establishing such services are people, data and technical infrastructure. The Environment Agency's National Centre for Environmental Data & Surveillance has developed a conceptual architecture within which these components can be effectively managed and brought to bear on the processes of delivering timely data and information products. This is a challenging task within large administrations where data collection, management and storage are widely distributed both geographically and organisationally. Experience to date has shown the approach to be flexible, reliable and scalable. We have also developed our understanding of why people want information and how they want to access it – and importantly why some people do not see the relevance of environmental information to them. We have therefore formulated a strategy to improve the flexibility and response of the services we provide. This strategy also includes developing highly tailored information services that feed off the same base datasets. The Agency has recently piloted just such a service aimed at residential house purchasers. This is an e-business service accessible by solicitors over the Internet, with individually tailored environmental reports generated and delivered in real time. There is the potential to develop similar tailored services wherever environmental information is, or should be, a key part of business activities and decisions. Future development will therefore not solely be making more information available in an electronic format. Information must be made relevant to particular needs at particular times. Citizens must be made aware of the wider environmental impacts of their consumer choices and the implications to themselves and others. They must also understand the real effect of the environment on their daily lives and why it is in their interest to be interested.

Introduction

The Environment Agency (the Agency) is the leading public organisation for protecting and improving the environment in England and Wales. Its duties include regulating industry, maintaining flood defences and water resources, and improving wildlife habitats. The Agency also monitors the environment, and makes the information collected widely available.

This chapter highlights the importance that the Agency places on the provision of environmental information and the key part it plays in achieving environmental goals. The necessity of ensuring that the public has up-to-date environmental information is essential as their power and influence help to achieve sustained environmental improvements. Operating openly is also essential in maintaining the credibility of our regulatory functions, and in enabling fully informed decision-making by regulatory bodies and the public alike.

The Agency's track record in information provision is considerable, as highlighted by its experience in providing key environmental datasets through "What's in Your Backyard?" – a GIS, internet based national portal (*www.environment-agency.gov.uk*). Our vision for the future is a much wider range of environmental information freely available to all – quickly and easily, where and when people want it, and in formats designed to meet particular needs. This will form the basis for the Agency, other public bodies, business and the general public, being well equipped to make better decisions for the environment. Exciting opportunities for achieving this vision present themselves in today's "Information Age" and the potential to lever environmental benefit is great.

Agency's Policy Framework

The importance of information provision is recognised in a wide range of national and European legislation, and in international agreements, including Public Register laws, the UK Freedom of Information Act and the UN-ECE Convention on "Access to Information, Public Participation in Decision Making and Access to Justice in environmental Matters" (the "Aarhus" Convention).

The interaction between these and other laws result in some complex issues surrounding information provision. These include balancing requirements to make information available against respect for commercial, personal and other confidentiality, and applying rules on charging and cost recovery in light of copyright and other intellectual property rights. The right policy decisions are vital in meeting all the various legal requirements in a way that enacts the "spirit" of the legislation.

Intellectual Property Rights

The Agency seeks to make information as freely and as widely available as possible. To meet this aim we have developed a framework for applying intellectual property rights and for recovering costs in some instances. The elements of this framework have been specifically designed to ensure that there is no significant barrier in accessing information, whilst maximising the effectiveness of the resources at our disposal.

The Agency operates a cost recovery "charging for information" scheme for the reactive supply of information upon request. This scheme is based on the premise that, within reason, all the information we provide is accessible in one form or another without charge. Only when we are asked to supply information that we have already made "reasonably available" to the public (e.g., via the Internet, public registers, reports and libraries), will we recover the extra costs involved in answering that specific request.

The Agency's Intellectual Property Rights when supplying information are set out in a "Standard Notice" that accompanies all information we supply. These conditions allow for greater use of information than that required by statute: they allow for information to be used for personal and internal business use, and for copies of information to be distributed as long as no charge is applied. However, in some instances, environmental information has a commercial value over and above that of its use for internal business purposes, and commercial suppliers market services for re-packaging and passing on information. Where we consider that the commercial use is in accordance with our aims and goals, we "licence" activities, recover royalties - and most importantly allow our information to reach wider audiences.

Tailored Information Services

There is also potential for public authorities such as the Agency to develop their own "tailored" information services and products that give added value to certain customers who choose to pay to access information in ways particular to their needs. An example of this is the recognised need from people involved in property transactions for key environmental information to be provided in a tailored way to inform their purchase decisions. In the UK Government guidance indicates that such products and services should be priced to achieve full cost recovery or, where there is an element of competition with the private sector, the market price, in the interests of fair competition.

To ensure that such developments do not compromise access to information, the Agency is seeking to develop such services based upon data sets that are also generally accessible to the public without charge. This clarifies that the customer is choosing to pay for an "added-value" service rather than being charged for the information itself.

Pro-Active Information Supply

New legislation is increasingly focussing on pro-active information supply to complement reactive supply on request. In the UK, one of the requirements of the Freedom of Information Act is a clear duty to pro-actively provide information through the adoption and maintenance of a "Publication Scheme" to cover all the information and data that a Public Authority makes available. As well as paper reports and publications, Publication Schemes includes databases, public registers, functional initiatives, technical guidance and educational material.

Certain information included in the Publication Scheme may have a "reasonable" charge attached (e.g., for publications or tailored information products). In contrast, there are expected to be very severe restrictions on abilities to charge outside of the scheme. Therefore the Act will effectively compel public authorities to pro-actively make information of interest to the public available by enforcing the alternative of giving away any information not included on demand without charge.

Given such considerations it is essential that public authorities make as much information available as possible in an electronic form. In meeting this need, the Agency is introducing "Electronic Document and Records Management" throughout its range of operations. This will result in a step change in access to information, as not only data, summaries and reports, but individual documents can then be provided via the Internet. This approach opens up the possibility of providing not only access to information, but to enable full and effective public participation in decision making – as envisaged by the Aarhus Convention.

To maximise the potential for disclosure of information, the Agency is also categorising all the information it holds in terms of accessibility. Where policy and legal checks confirm that the information in a category will always be released upon demand, it is also defined as suitable for pro-active release.

Establishing Information Services

The key components in establishing information services are people, data and technical infrastructure. The Environment Agency's National Centre for Environmental Data & Surveillance (NCEDS) has developed a conceptual architecture within which these components can be effectively managed and brought to bear on the processes of delivering timely data and information products. This is a challenging task within large administrations where data collection, management and storage are widely distributed both geographically and organisationally. However, experience to date has shown the approach to be flexible, reliable and scalable.

EDMS

The first requirement to deliver an information service is to assemble the necessary data from various distributed corporate sources. NCEDS have developed the "Environmental Data Management System" (EDMS), which has the capacity to extract, transfer, reformat and integrate distributed data into a single spatially-enabled database. This integrated data source can then provide the basis for Web-enabled data and information services. The key features of the EDMS are that:

- distributed data stored in various systems are integrated to a single consolidated source
- it reformats textual grid references to spatial data
- base data are automatically and regularly refreshed to maintain data currency

A great advantage of this system is that source data remain in host systems serving primary business purposes and are owned and maintained locally. Ideally, the data extracts would not have to be made, but as the source data reside in a number of legacy systems that are not due for redevelopment, it is necessary to make extracts.

Once data have been gathered, they can be further processed into information, interpreted and given context, for example by relating pollution emission loads to potential health effects. Therefore the same datasets can be presented in ways meaningful to a range of different user requirements. This includes "extra" use of the data internally (mapping, statistics, incorporation into reports and analysis for anomalies), or for a range of external reporting and service requirements. This concept is outlined in Figure 1.

A National Portal: "What's In Your Backyard?"

The EDMS has provided the capability to support "What's in Your BackYard?" (WIYBY) through which the Agency has provided access to corporate environmental datasets for the last four years. This integrated GIS, Internet based national portal is based on three dedicated NT Web servers running various html pages, a SQL server and a Map Objects geographic application to display mapped data. It has been developed and extended to include a pollution inventory, flood plain maps, landfill sites and a range of other data layers.

Members of the public can find information from a national level, right down to their local environment: locating areas of interest by postcode or place name, displaying data to a chosen scale, formulating individual queries on the datasets, gaining background on information of interest, and downloading data for their own use off-line.

Figure 1. Current information provision

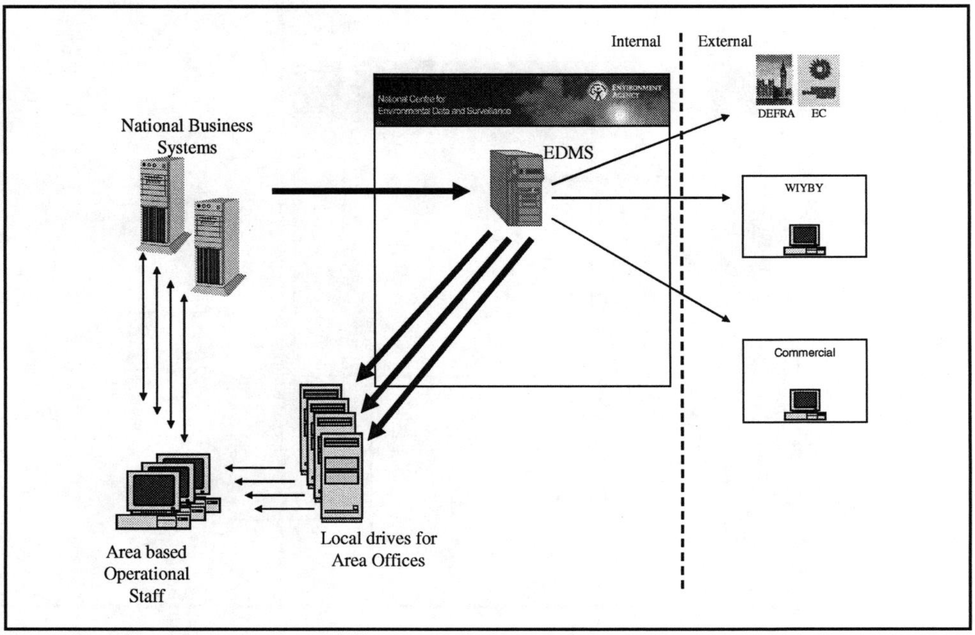

Future Integrated Services

The approach taken in Figure 1 has been highly successful to date. However, some issues have highlighted the need to examine a new approach for future development. One of these issues is the existing need to transfer very large volumes of data from the National Centre via an internal Wide Area Network to numerous servers local to the 26 Area offices. This is time consuming, expensive and becoming increasingly difficult to accommodate as the volume of data required in an electronic format increases. This approach also introduces added complexity in data management as distributed copies of data need to controlled and refreshed to ensure integrity. In addition, the current WIYBY is based on a fairly "inflexible" application that makes the accommodation of new data layers increasingly difficult and re-engineering into different tailored information services difficult and expensive.

A new approach has therefore been established through the delivery of a "Property Search" Information Service to support the decision-making process of purchasing a property. This service is generating and delivering tailored environmental reports directly to solicitors in real time. The system for delivering this is based upon Web map server technology as outlined in Figure 2. The

Figure 2. Future information provision

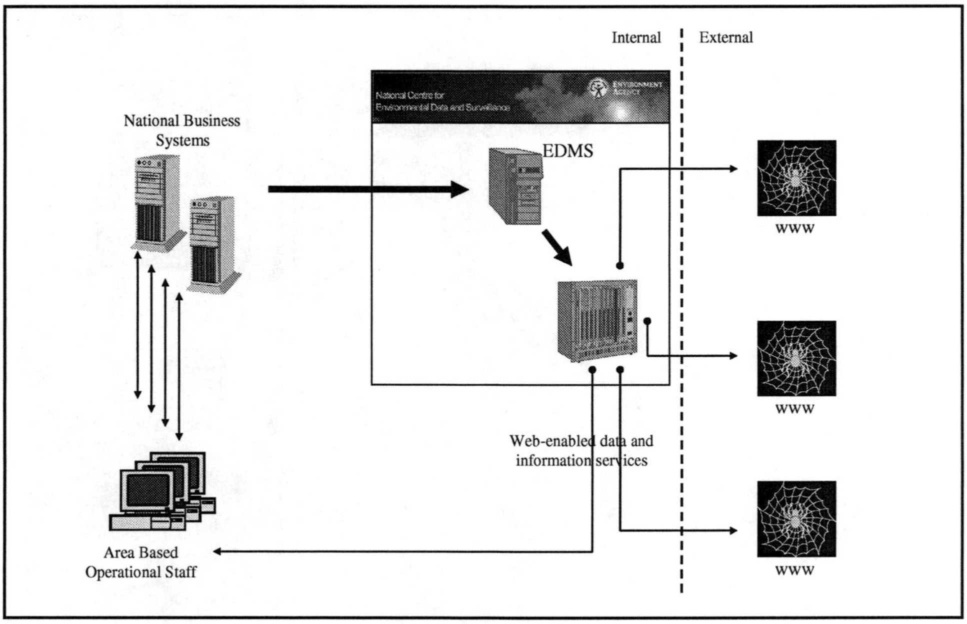

Figure 3. Vision for the future

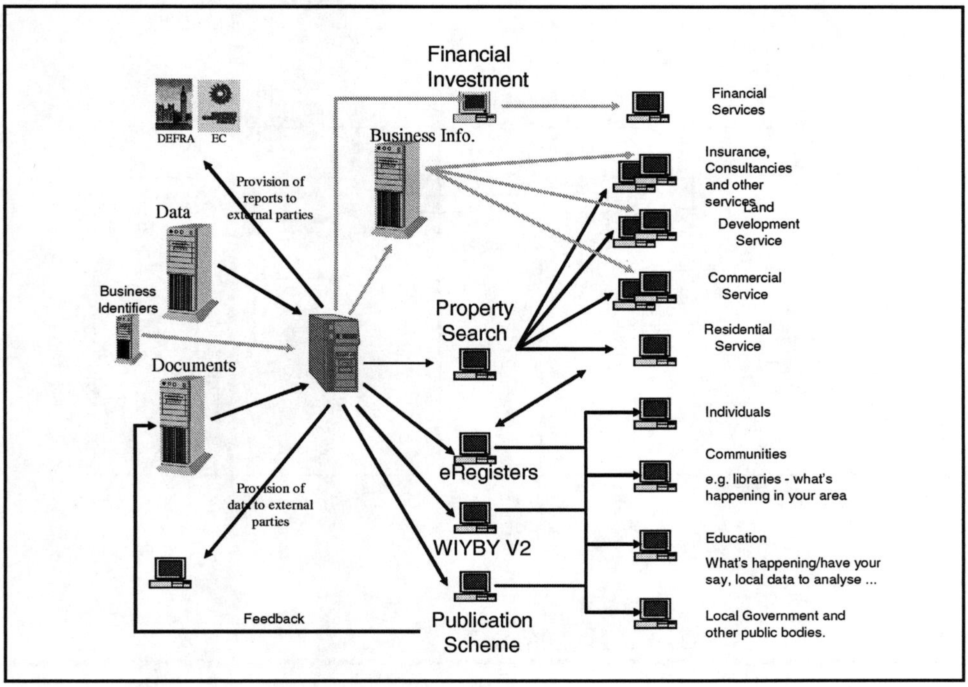

immediate advantage in this approach is the removal of the need for copying data to local servers. This is replaced by a single copy of the data being held centrally and operational staff accessing this central resource via an intranet and/or the Internet.

The other main advantage is a very flexible system that can provide the basis for a range of general and tailored information services. The vision for the future is outlined in Figure 3, where the same system components are used to meet a range of identified user requirements.

Figure 4 illustrates the major system components of the Property Search Web service in more detail. A browser client (MS Internet Explorer 5.0 or higher) connects to the Web site on Box 2. Postcode references are translated in X, Y grid coordinates using Quick Address Pro-web. X, Y coordinates are passed to ArcIMS on Box 2 and ArcSDE locates coordinates on the spatial database (ORACLE). A map of the location is generated and passed back to the client. The user confirms the correct location and requests a report to be generated. The confirmed coordinates are passed back to Box 1 and ArcIMS, ArcSDE and ORACLE work together to perform a 0.5 km search around the coordinates for all EA data in the spatial data store. The results of the search are passed to the publishing framework (cocoon) where a .pdf file is generated and returned to the client. A copy of the pdf file is retained on Box 1.

Figure 4. Schematic overview

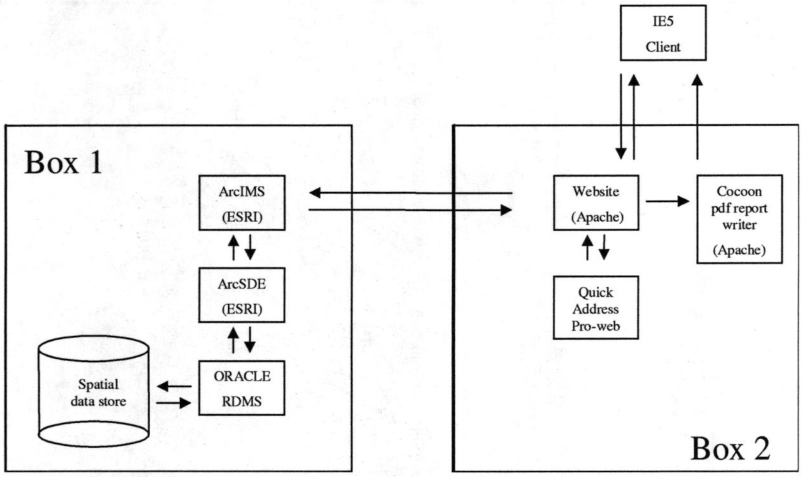

Making Information Relevant

Technical infrastructure and developments in electronic information supply are of little use without a thorough understanding of why people want information and how they want to access it. If the concept is that the environment is of importance and relevance to all, it is important to appreciate some people do not currently see the relevance of environmental information to them. This is essential if goals are to be achieved.

One method of engagement is to encourage public participation in the decision making of regulatory bodies. The importance of information is paramount in the Agency's regulatory role. As part of its statutory obligations in permitting potentially polluting activities, for example in waste management and industrial processes, the Agency is required to consult widely on its decision making. Part of this requirement is the maintenance of "Public Registers" of relevant information – applications for permits, consultation responses, permit details and requirements, subsequent monitoring information and any enforcement action taken.

In practice, the success of these registers in providing public access to the decision making processes is limited. The registers are mainly paper based and now run to some 10 million documents. The registers are located at the 26 Agency Area offices, but are still relatively remote from communities impacted by decisions, and not generally conducive to general public access (see plate 1).

Plate 1. A typical public register

Finally, existing requirements to advertise permits in newspapers has limited use in raising community awareness of rights to participate in the consultation regarding the decision on granting the permit.

The Agency, in implementing Electronic Document Management throughout its operations, now has the opportunity to facilitate real and effective "environmental democracy" through electronic access. As another facet of an integrated approach, "live" information relating to decisions still yet to be made would be "flagged" in real time on a geographic basis over the Internet. Many opportunities would stem from this, including, for example, electronic open forums to enable members of the public to exchange views and hear responses in an open manner – akin to that experienced at a public meeting.

Achieving this aim would result in environmental decision making being fully informed by the people such decisions will affect, and enable the Agency to further its aims of operating openly and transparently. This will further the credibility and support for our regulatory functions.

Summary

The Agency's experience to date in providing electronic access to environmental information has provided the knowledge upon which a range of integrated information services can be developed. This integrated approach, in "feeding" off the same base data sets and being built upon flexible applications, is both efficient and effective in providing ready access to information for a wide range of user requirements.

Future development must be concerned with more than solely making ever more information available in an electronic format. Information must be made relevant to particular needs at particular times, as in the case of the "Property Search" example, which encourages informed decision making by people in their normal lives. Citizens must be made aware of the wider environmental impacts of their consumer choices and the implications to themselves and others. They must also understand the real effect of the environment on their daily lives and why it is in their interest to be interested.

References

Convention on Access to Information, Public Participation in Decision Making and Access to Justice in Environmental Matters; United Nations Economic Commission for Europe, Fourth Ministerial Conference "Environment for Europe," Aarhus, Denmark, 23-25 June 1998.

Freedom of Information Act 2000, Chapter 36; The Stationary Office Limited.

Section III

Risk Management

Chapter XIX

The Integration of Safety, Environmental and Quality Management Systems

Werner Strauß, Kisters AG, Germany

Klaus-Dieter Herrmann, Kisters AG, Germany

Christoph Roenick, Kisters AG, Germany

Abstract

This chapter will show how the demands on safety, environmental and quality management systems and their implementation into IT solutions have changed over the years and how such systems may appear in the future. Tangible business processes from the areas of occupational health and safety and environmental protection are described and a solution shown as to how these can be dealt with in a task-related way. Furthermore, there will be shown the connection between these business processes and the relevant legislation and the special benefits pertaining to legal security. Following this we describe how the linking of IT systems mentioned with scientific management systems with the primary processes of the company can be arranged. We also provide a look at the benefits arising from using such systems. The chapter concludes with a critical look at the future distribution and use of such integrated, process-oriented and legally based management systems. This chapter is particularly directed to companies that have set the carrying out of the material-related legal requirements and cost reduction through thought-out product use as a corporate objective. The concept of a networked corporate occupational health and safety and environmental protection information system and its implementation as a standard product will be introduced. Core components include basic data maintenance, modules for supporting decentralised specialised tasks and an efficient reporting system used at all locations and linked to an intranet.

Development of Corporate Environmental Information Systems in the Last 10 Years

At the beginning of the nineties IT began its entry into the workplaces of the safety and environmental protection departments.

In these departments existing tasks such as the saving of dangerous substance-related data in database systems, the administering of directives of safety-relevant systems and the handling and organisation of the drop currents were depicted and supported with electronic data processing systems.

The multitude of solutions that consequently arose on the market resulted in increased pressure on the program users to create integrated systems to reduce the high spending on parallel data entry and data maintenance and to do away with the irritation caused by data inconsistencies.

The demands on the IT environment also grew however with the arrival of integrated systems with, for instance, more demands on the hardware platform utilised and the operating and administration systems as well as on the training of personnel to use these systems.

Manufacturer expenditure increased almost exponentially in order to meet the existing demands in all areas of application with a single management system and to continue with this in accordance with the legal requirements. Around the end of the nineties it became clear that the amount spent on obtaining the operational data that were necessary for operating such systems was too high and that it was necessary to connect these systems with scientific management systems as well as with process-controlling systems.

Thus integrated turnkey systems were demanded with material flow analyses, connection to commercial systems and process control engineering, and linked to the respective relevant legislation, so that laws and decrees had to be stored.

The application of Internet technology represents a new opportunity in this context to link all levels of a company to these systems and to participate in the results. It therefore represents an opportunity to make available efficiently and promptly various views of data and results prepared by media and related to interests.

Conversion into an Integrated Corporate Environmental Information System

Requirements on a Corporate Environmental Information System in Industry and Commerce

The requirements essentially derive from environmental legislation. Some essential requirements are derived from the wealth of regulations. The handling of dangerous materials obliges company management and representatives to provide suitable organisation forms, processes and work material:

- Dangerous materials register in accordance with §16 Dangerous Materials Regulation and TRGS 222
- Operating instructions in accordance with §20 Dangerous Materials Regulation and TRGS 555
- Work area analyses and control measures in accordance with the Dangerous Materials Regulation and TRGS 402/TRGS 403
- Waste management certificates, accompanying certificates and acceptance certificates (regulation on utilisation and removal certificates)
- Waste balance and waste management concepts (regulation on waste management concepts and waste balance [AbfKoBiV])
- Administration of plant approvals and tests
- Annual report of the dangerous goods representative (dangerous goods regulation road)
- Reports in accordance with environmental statistics law and so forth

In order to weigh the benefit of products used in accordance with the regulations against their risks and resulting costs the purchasers and group-buying department are responsible for product choice and the resulting acknowledged risks and costs incurred by storage, transport, application and waste management:

- Protective equipment (suction, filter, gloves, decontamination, etc.)
- Measurements and medical checkups
- Safety fittings, for instance, for warehouses with water-polluting substances
- Sewage charges and waste disposal costs
- Reduction of accident risks and damages to image, and so forth

A variety of obligations and duties arise from these requirements and are set down within the framework of an environmental protection and occupational health and safety system in accordance for example with ISO14001 or EMAS regulation. The following business processes, which are to be supported by a corporate environmental information system, result in the area of occupational health and safety and environmental protection from the work instructions:

- Documentation on the dangerous materials in the workplace (safety data sheets, dangerous materials register, etc.)
- Drawing up of operating instructions and instructing of employees
- Drawing up of waste analyses based on the waste disposal processes of waste that requires monitoring
- Drawing up of a waste management concept
- Drawing up of transport papers for the transport of dangerous goods
- Annual report of the dangerous goods representative
- Registering and analysis of workplace accidents
- Accident reports to the trade associations
- Provision of relevant and widely available legal information

The business processes in the area of occupational health and safety and environmental protection are marginal processes within the value-added chain. These processes are not therefore coupled to the core processes. There are nevertheless several points of contact. Possible points which, depending on the company, have different weightings are:

- *A system for processing transportation in companies:* communication of information relating to dangerous goods (classification of dangerous goods, labelling, equipping, disposal instructions, exchange of storage lists for testing dangerous goods)

- *Purchasing:* provision of information on dangerous goods/safety data sheets (evaluation of products, procurement of replacement material)
- *Research and development:* research into materials
- *Product recycling:* waste disposal information on materials
- *Material management:* quantities of used products
- *Operator obligations at the plants:* dangerous materials information results in certain obligations

It frequently becomes apparent at a second glance that the views in these systems, for example of a material, differ from the safety and environmental protection view and that therefore the saved information is frequently not redundant and also only has limited use in corporate environmental information system. Integrating a corporate environmental information system into such a system is therefore not absolutely necessary. A corporate environmental information system should also however offer a way to exchange information with these systems using interfaces.

The basis for the fulfilling of the documentation obligations and the minimisation of product-related risks and costs is an information alliance that reaches across

Figure 1. Requirements from information management in order to carry out material-related legal regulations

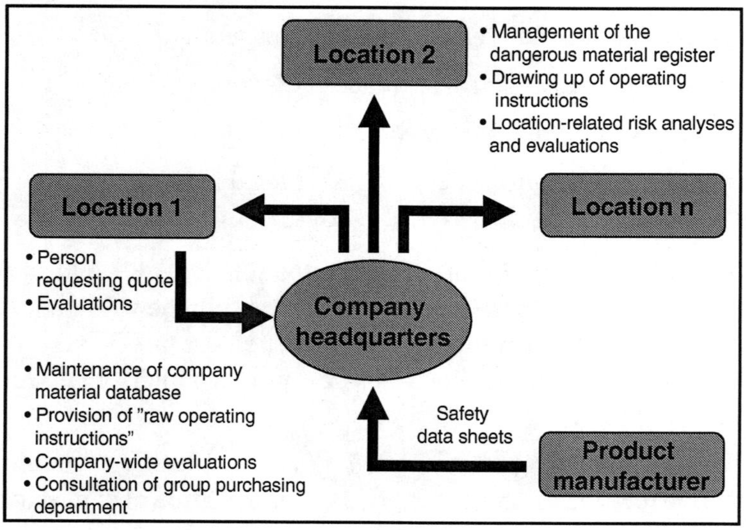

the company. This must make the relevant product information and reports available with assured quality (relevant and up-to-date, complete, consistent).

Concept and Complete Architecture of a Comprehensive Corporate Environmental Information System

Corporate occupational health and safety and environmental protection systems cover a wide spectrum of process support and documentation creation. The complexity of the data processing support, which results in a high degree of spending on training and high hurdles of acceptance, is generally a serious disadvantage. In the corporate environment there are however numerous types of users who, firstly, do not have the specialist background and knowledge of the process and who, secondly, require nowhere near all the functions. Examples of this are the specialist worker or master craftsperson who needs to update his or her dangerous materials register, the works manager who needs to submit a waste analysis, and the lab technician, the group purchasing department or the fire brigade who need rapid access to specific material information. In order to meet this need in a user-friendly way, the complex function structure in the classical client-server environment is to be expanded by so-called "specialist assistants" (Figure 2).

Figure 2. Expansion of the system architecture of corporate environmental protection and occupational health and safety information systems through intranet-based specialist assistants

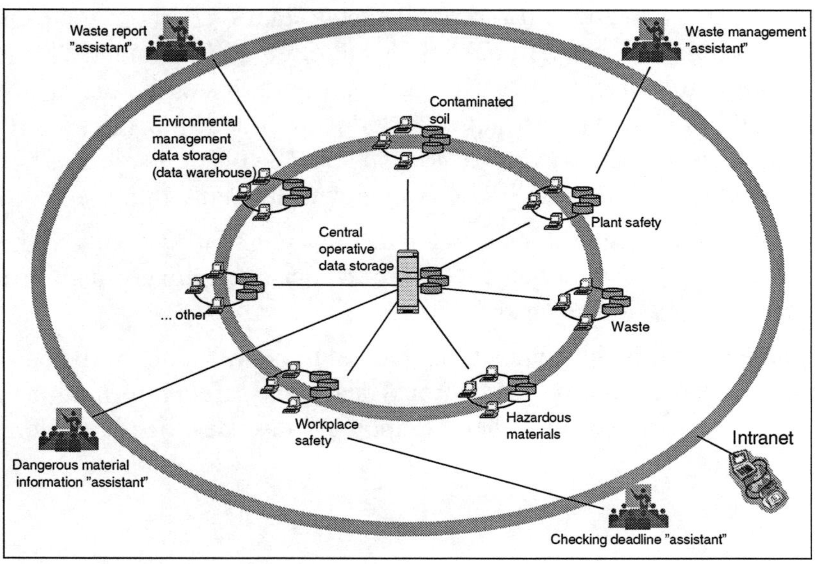

Specialist assistants provide intuitive access via an intranet and browser to waste analyses, risk analyses, operating instructions, information on materials, legal information, and so forth. Another aspect is the use of specialist assistants to maintain movement data such as dangerous material registers, waste declaration, plant audits and so forth. In so doing the operating area in question of the corporate environmental protection and occupational health and safety information system becomes redundant and implemented as a simple and easy to operate intranet application.

A corresponding system concept and its implementation using standard products are introduced below. The architecture of the system supports centrally organised, cost-effective and professional maintenance of basic data, the execution support at the various individual company locations and an intranet-based company-wide reporting system.

Central Maintenance of Basic Data Using Example of Material Data Management

The offered solution that is introduced below is based on the use of existing and market-tested software components. The product family of the dangerous material information system (IGS) and of the corporate environmental information system WAUplus are at the centre of this. All components cooperate, but can also be used separately depending on the requirements of the customer and can gradually be expanded into a comprehensive solution for corporate environmental protection and occupational health and safety management. This results in a flexible and scalable system, which can be adjusted to the size of the company. All components can be used individually. In addition, this system is not dependent on the use of existing ERP systems. The offered solution however offers connection to the usual ERP systems with its many interfaces.

Figure 3 shows the central material data management system architecture including the system components IGS-check/*net for company-wide research into product information using an intranet.

The exchange agent is the connection channel to components of the corporate environmental protection and occupational health and safety information system WAUplus (Chapter 3). The other components are described in Herrmann (1998).

Figure 3. Central material data management IGS system architecture

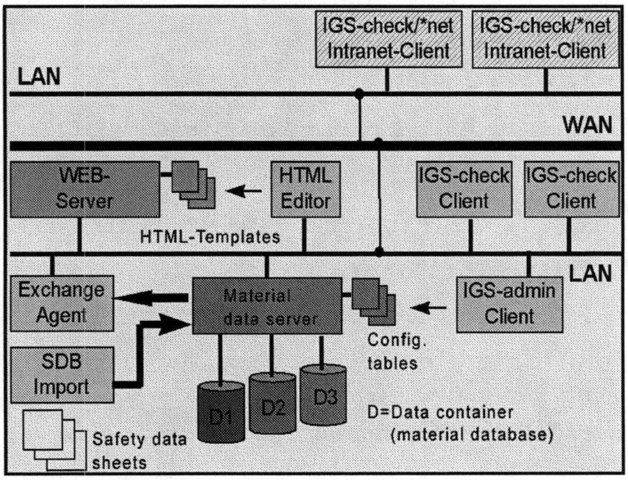

Components of Decentralised Execution Support of Corporate Environmental Protection and Occupational Health and Safety

WAUplus has been on the market as a corporate environmental protection and occupational health and safety management system since 1993 and is used by more than 100 customers in many industry sectors. The system optimises the work of the ultimate unit of responsibility and supports the uniform and lawful implementation of the legal directives in the different divisions:

- Corporate occupational health and safety
- Dangerous materials management
- Dangerous goods management
- Waste management
- Corporate accident affairs

At the centre of WAUplus and its task support are the laws and regulations concerning environmental protection and occupational health and safety. The ongoing changes and extensions to the legal regulations are taken into account in the form of regular updates to the software so as to ensure legal security in corporate environmental protection and occupational health and safety.

The system simplifies routine activities, gives structure to the data distributed in companies and therefore creates the necessary transparency and the benefit in many areas:

- Automatic drawing up of the legally prescribed reports for the authorities
- Increased efficiency through reduced outlays on time and personnel
- Reduced expenditure on maintenance as a result of integrated data stocks
- Creation of specific views for users, superiors and the management
- Improved controlling on the basis of evaluations of any data connections

The entire information requirement in corporate environmental protection and occupational health and safety can be consistently administered: corporate structure and safety-relevant information on the location, adaptation to the size of the premises and the ultimate unit of responsibility, the dangerous materials and the quantities of them used. The integrating of information and evaluations is also provided in the internal reporting system. The area of application is rounded off with the ascertaining of and protection against risk, field of work analyses in accordance with TRGS 402/403 and the administering of measurement data in the field of work as well as plant data and process data.

The WAUplus corporate environmental protection and occupational health and safety system supports the most important documentation duties listed in Chapter 1 using corresponding specialist modules. The basic data that span various fields such as corporate structure, catalogues, symbols, addresses, material data, material-related operating instructions and so forth are administered in the same way by a central base system.

The dangerous material module (GF) provides information on all dangerous products and material preparations used in the company with up to 350 features. Updating immediately after creation of the safety data sheet is in familiar terms. The company's own phrases and the commercial standard catalogues (BDI/CED) can be used, scanned-in safety data sheets can be adopted and external material databases can be connected.

The dangerous goods management module completely determines the organisational and technical measures for the implementation of any dangerous goods transport using all traffic carriers and in accordance with classification data, application of the small-volumes regulation and packaging regulations, markings, requirements for loading, vehicles, drivers and transport papers.

Checklists facilitate control, and discrepancies are displayed in infringement chains, therefore avoiding any fines. Data on the transport processes are provided for tables, analyses and statistics. The central legislation database and updating for the target date are constantly maintained.

Figure 4. System architecture of the corporate environmental protection and occupational health and safety system

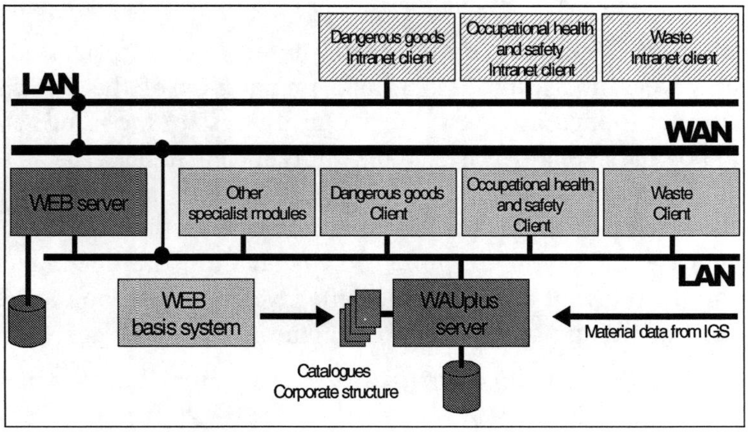

The waste management module (AR) supports both the observance of the legal requirements of the cycle management law and waste law as well as the ecological and economic optimisation of waste management within the company. Generators, points of occurrence, collection points, storage places, waste catalogues and company addresses are administered centrally. Waste processes (delivery tickets, accompanying certificates and dock receipts), storage books, assigned volumes, costs and proceeds can be recorded and evaluated according to waste. The creation and administering of waste certificates is completely supported. Waste analyses and waste management concepts can be called up from the system in their respective current status.

Corporate waste processing is used for recording and processing all accident data that are necessary for reporting to the trade associations. The basis is the form for BG reporting. Furthermore, comprehensive statistical evaluations can be implemented for the accident procedure in the workplace.

Provision of Environmental Law Information

The company can implement environmental protection measures efficiently and effectively if corresponding legal information, for example environmental law and labour law, are made available across the company via Internet-based information systems. In the past the knowledge pertaining to legal information and the obligation to take measures was as a rule communicated in "system-incompatible" media, for example, as a guideline or action instruction on paper or verbally between users. Since that time it has been recognised that Internet-based legal information systems are an ideal technological medium, firstly, for surmounting the rift between information and data procurement and, secondly, for accessing information for the relevant positions or the interested public at large.

The efficient and effective use of Internet-based legal information systems requires, however, intense processing and preparation of the information in advance, in order to increase the value and usefulness of the information. The associated knowledge engineering increasingly means intense discussion with data processing-based communication media for those in charge of the legal departments in the companies and administrative departments. In the field of environmental law it is, for example, no longer only the documentation of environmentally relevant facts but also the exchange of knowledge that is becoming an expanding part of internal structures.

The legal information module is based on the original Internet-based legal information system H.I.R.N. that was developed at FAW. It consists of a variety of characteristics that have been implemented as an environmental law information system in large companies like Deutsche Bahn AG and DaimlerChrysler AG. The module meets the three requirements that are of central importance for modern companies against the background of an integrated company-wide document stock with opportunities for specification of specialist views and opportunities for knowledge transfer:

- the unlimited accessing of general and specific environmental law information,
- the generation of specialist views of the range of information,
- the practical capacity of the information to be supplemented by individual experience when implementing requirements connected with environmental law.

Company-Wide Reporting

The expandable location-wide or company-wide evaluations are of particular importance. These are prepared with standard MS Office components in such a way that they are retrievable via the Web server by an intranet client. Tables 1 and 2 show typical evaluations.

Summary and Outlook

The intranet as an integration platform enables a new quality of information management in corporate occupational health and safety and environmental

Table 1. Evaluation of dangerous material registers for the intranet

Number of places of occurrence per material [Evaluation of all organisational units]				
Place key	**Product**	**No. Of Places**	**D.-Masse / kg**	**D.-Vol / m³**
*	**Benzol**	6	1'368.00	8.10
*	**Cold purifier 30**	5	850.00	0.50
*	**Hydrofluoric acid**	4	112.00	0.02
*	**ATMOSIT 12673A**	4	400.00	0.00
*	**Hydrochloric acid (30%)**	3	200.00	0.01
*	**Sterifix**	2	22.00	0.10
*	**Acetone**	1	100.00	0.00
*	**Ethanol**	1	80.00	0.00
	TOTAL		**3'132.00**	**8.73**

Table 2. Waste analysis with portrayal in intranet

Waste analysis: Waste volumes per				
Place of occurrence	**Generator number**	**LAGA number**	**LAGA**	**Volume in t**
1	E1130602A	125 01	Content of	5.00
1	E1130602A	172 01	Wood wrappings	5.00
1	E1130602A	353 26	Mercury/mercury-containing remains. Mercury vapour discharge lamps	0.25
1	E1130602A	542 09	Solid operating material contaminated with grease and oil	6.60
1	E1130602A	544 02	Drill and abrasive emulsions and emulsion blends	113.70
1	E1130602A	555 03	Varnish and dye sludge	27.00
2	E112345	172 01	Wood wrappings, wood waste	2.50
2	E112345	353 26	Mercury/mercury-containing remains. Mercury vapour discharge lamps	0.18

protection. This applies exactly when one manages to organise the available information oriented towards the ultimate unit of responsibility and problems. It is only then that the end user with his or her specific specialist tasks can be reached in a targeted way. The classic corporate environmental information systems in client-server architecture can be further used for gaining information and supporting processes but can be expanded today by a flexible and Web-compatible reporting system. The advantage is that the end user no longer inevitably has to involve him or herself with the complexity of an entire system but instead profits from the supply of information tailored to his or her responsibilities.

This is reflected by a trend according to which companies are using complete integrated systems less often. It is because, firstly, these systems require considerable investment in their procurement and operation and, secondly, the tasks of corporate environmental protection as well as occupational health and safety do not represent core processes in the company. That is the reason why today these tasks must be fulfilled with a minimum of employee involvement, which often makes the usage of comprehensive solutions in companies impossible. Even in large companies the processing is often carried out only with regard to location and increasingly aggregation only takes place via the reporting system.

In addition to this, environmental protection and occupational health and safety in companies play a less important role compared with, for example, five years ago due to declining public interest. This also slows down investments in comprehensive, corporate environmental information systems in productive areas. On the other hand, the good value of corporate public relations work combined with eco-marketing is playing an ever more important role.

There had been an inevitable tendency to a decline in the number of software providers over the last few years. Only those providers who can offer flexible solutions that are scalable and can be expanded in steps as well as adapted from the single-console system to the multi-console system and who offer the opportunities of the intranet as a comprehensive support for the end user will have a chance. Only in this way will the complexity be manageable.

The costs and benefits also tally with such systems and the employees of the safety departments are prepared to "give themselves up" to such systems.

References

Herrmann, K.D. (1998). Stoffinformations-betreiberzentren. In H.W. Borries, J. Brandt, R. Demuth et al. (Eds.), *ECOINFORMA '98, 8,* 49-66. Wien: Umweltbundesamt.

Tochtermann, K., Roenick, Ch., & Klingler, G. (2000). Intranet-basiertes management von umweltrechtsinformationen mit H.I.R.N., Conference Vol. 12. *Internationales Symposium Informatik fü den Umweltschutz.* Bonn, Marburg: Metropolis-Verlag.

Chapter XX

Support of Integrated Management Systems by the Use of In-Plant Information, Management and Monitoring Systems

Stefan Bräker, Institute of Environmental Management Consultancy, Germany

Abstract

For many organisations the present status of integration of management systems raises the question where the development goes and whether there are not further new approaches to be pursued in the next years. Due to different perceptions of the term integration and in conflict for the right approach to the system, numerous parallel systems developed in the past. The following contribution describes the targets of different types of management systems and points out strategies and structural approaches of integration. In a second step the possibilities of ICT-supported solutions are resumed exemplarily. ICT-supported information, management and monitoring systems as components will take a central role in integration of management systems and have to be developed for further requirements.

Introduction

A management system comprises all activities for planning a business policy and introducing it into an organisation. It is as well an instrument for systematic and targeted corporate management and as for the overall operational monitoring system, it helps to fulfil all obligations to exercise the proper care. The advantage of an integrated management system is in the utilisation of synergistic effects resulting from the combination of joint management structures and processes for the production of goods and services.

Thus far it has not been possible to implement operationally a clear and concise description of an integrated management system. Due to different perceptions of the term integration and a conflict over the right approach to the system, numerous parallel systems have developed, which are to be integrated in the future.

In connection with the provision of data referring to in-plant regulations of processes and procedures, as well as to operational data of different origins in ICT-supported management, information and monitoring systems, the question of the structure of integrated management systems under a new point of view comes more and more to the fore. This contribution shows the structural approaches of integration and points out possible ICT-supported solutions as examples.

Development of Management Systems and their Standardisation

A short review on the historical development of the different management systems shows how requirements to organisations, and thus to management as well, have changed over the course of recent decades (Figure 1).

In the following, a short survey of both current and planned requirements of standards and regulations is given, which have to be considered in connection with the combination of multifunctional operational information and management systems.

Quality Management

In the beginning, quality checks at the end of production were at the fore of the quality system. Soon it became clear that such systems would pay for themselves

Figure 1. Evolution of management systems since the '50s

Period	Purpose
'50s	Compliance with technical standards, suitability for use
'60s	Compliance with specifications, suitability for defined purposes of use
'70s	Fitness for use, fulfillment of customer requests as agreed
'80s	Fulfillment of customer requests and requirements, introduction of quality management systems (DIN EN ISO 9000 ff)
'90s	Fulfillment of requirements of different groups of requirements and minimisation of legal liability; introduction of environmental (EMAS/ EN ISO 14001) and occupational safety and health management systems (OHSAS 18001)
since 2000	Continual improvement of customer-referred processes, postulation of a safety and risk management system and an energy management system as part of the overall operational monitoring system

soon, because they could recognise and save expenditures for refinishing. With the standards series EN ISO 9000 pp, management was respected as a vital factor affecting quality. Quality since then has become a factor that can be actively controlled and designed. EN ISO 9000:2000 among others allows a process orientation. Such process oriented representation corresponds to the modern microeconomic perception of value added processes and the focussing on management and core skills.

Environmental Management

Then, in the '60s and '70s, there was initially a concentration on the mere technical aspects of environmental protection at the end of production (end-of-pipe philosophy). In connection with the duties for notification regarding the operational organisation (Bundes-Immissionsschutzgesetz federal ambient pollution control act; § 52a BImSchG), the reversal of the burden of proof (§ 6 UmweltHG environmental liability act; 1990) and the EMAS regulation (*e*nvironmental *m*anagement and *a*udit *s*cheme) coming into force (1993), the operational organisation of environmental protection and the management system came in Europe and Germany considerably stronger to the fore. In particular, with the new emphasis on liability risks and the liability for organisational faults enshrined in § 130 OwiG regulatory offences act and in § 831 BGB civil law code company managers were urged to organise management systems and to supervise and control environmental aspects and effects of operational activities for economic reasons as well as for self-interested ones.

With the EMAS regulation coming into force in 1993, a basis for the implementation and structure of an environmental management system was given, which was directly applicable law in the member states of the European Union as an EC Regulation.

Since 1996 organisations can make use of the international standard EN ISO 14001 for environmental management systems as a basis for the certification of an environmental management system. The requirements of the so-called PDCA-principle are inherent in EN ISO 14001. This principle consists of the elements planning (*P*lan), implementation and performance (*D*o), checking and corrective measures (*C*heck) and management review (*A*ct), which are relevant to all management processes. The PDCA structure today is one of the fundamental structures for the development of any management system.

Occupational Safety and Health Management

Today not only compliance with legal requirements is in the fore, but also the implementation of an occupational safety and health management system. The intention is to implement occupational safety and health in all operational processes and to achieve target-oriented improvement processes in occupational safety and health. In Germany, according to the guideline for occupational safety and health management systems (Bundesarbeitsministerium, 1999) of the Bundes-Arbeitsministerium BMA (Federal Department of Employment), an occupational safety and health management system consists mainly of specific directing elements (work policy and strategy) and an appropriate organisation of implementation and procedures. The core of the occupational safety and health management system is procedures to determine, analyse and, if necessary, modify operational processes with the target of a consistent prevention and a further improvement as well as a following evaluation of the results by the management. The British Standard OHSAS 18001 has in application to the standard structure of the EN ISO 14001 founded a world wide accepted basis for such a management system.

Safety Management

With the amendment of the Störfall-VO (ordinance on hazardous incidents) in April 2000, the regulations for the fulfillment of the safety requirements as well as for the prevention and limitation of the effects of hazardous incidents at safety relevant plants, which until then had been restricted to documented procedures, were essentially extended in German law. For the first time a safety management system for companies with extended liabilities was regulated by law and its introduction was scheduled (Paeger & Niehoff, 2000).

The requirements for a safety management system given in Annex III of the Störfall-VO define this as part of the overall monitoring system. The processes and procedures for the prevention of hazardous incidents and the continual improvement of incident prevention including the related communication are included.

Energy Management

Regarding the eco-tax and the partial exemption from it, German legislators are considering making the existence of an implemented and working energy management system enough of a reason for being exempted from the tax. The establishment and implementation of an energy management system is performed according to general rules for management systems. The intention is to save energy, which can be achieved most intensively and effectively by a management system. According to the EG-regulation 2003/87/EG for a system of emission trading of green house gases the requirements for an implementation of an energy management are additional promoted.

Approaches and Strategies for the Integration of Management Systems

Present Integration Strategies

It is uncontested that a company or an organisation does not want and is not able to implement and maintain several self-contained management systems. Therefore, attempts at integrated management systems are abound, whose common denominator is the merging of the regulations and data within the network.

In practice, numerous prejudices and disappointments have become apparent in connection with the setting up of integrated management systems. An analysis of the reasons shows two boundary conditions, which have thus far prevented their successful implementation (Sprenger, 2000):

1. The demand for integration developed with intensified conditions of competition and a high cost-push prevented. The development of constructive solutions and implementation processes was not given.
2. Integration became a struggle between the different staffs which are responsible for management systems within an organisation. Confrontation and the insistence on standard-bound system elements instead of opening

and searching for amicable efficient solutions are encountered often in everyday life.

But there is no alternative to integration for two reasons:

1. With shareholders claiming that management, or in some cases the executive board, it is supposed to implement a sustainable monitoring system for the control and early warning for all developments endangering the persistence of the company in German law (§ 91, Abs. 2 KonTraG (Corporate Sector Supervision and Transparency Act)). Hereby, the course was set to the integration of different sub-management systems and to the harmonisation and optimisation of business and monitoring processes. Additionally there is the intention for corporate risk minimisation and limitation of liability in German law (§ 831 BGB, § 130 OWiG) together with the striving for an increase in efficiency through improvement of operational procedures and for consistent company profits.
2. With the amendment of the standards series EN ISO 9000 ff to version 2000 many companies will for the first time be forced to decide on the structure and content of their existing management systems. For reasons of organisation and liability, company management will no longer be able to afford implementing a management system by reorganisation that disregards the requirements of environmental, occupational safety and health protection and in which the respective procedures are organised in numerous subsystems.

All this results in the fact that the in-plant information, management and monitoring systems of processes and procedures as well as of relevant data (production, quality, environmental, health and safety, and financial data) have to be intensively considered.

Today the integration of management systems has to comprise the following expectations (Pichler & Wildburger, 1999):

- the system is supposed to become slimmer and easier to care for
- double work and double stress are supposed to be avoided
- discrepancies and target conflicts are supposed to become apparent earlier
- competencies and responsibilities are supposed to be definite and clear
- external contact and communication are supposed to be harmonised
- the monitoring system is supposed to be effective and transparent

Integration Strategies

The different integration strategies of management systems are discussed controversially in the field. In the end, these strategies reveal how different conceptions exists to what integration means. Under the collective name integrated management system different integration strategies are nowadays worked out in practice. One method of integrating different management systems is by means of the similarity theorem between the system elements, and another is by means of integrating management systems with operational processes.

Element Based Integration Strategy

The element based approach describes a strategy that was practiced in the beginning, when the first environmental management systems were to be integrated with existing regulations (mostly the quality management system). As quality management systems according to EN ISO 9000 ff. were already in use in many companies at that time, in the simplest case the environmental management system or its special requirements were included in the existing documentation as a separate chapter or kept as a parallel independent manual (Sprenger, 2000). Often the 21st element in a quality management system, environmental protection and occupational safety and health management, was simply attached to the other 20 elements of the system. The right sorting of elements and their quality rating were intensely discussed, but seldom were constructive solutions worked out. Sometimes the systems were mixed so badly that they became unrecognisable (Sprenger, 2000).

During the implementation and performance it was soon discovered that a lining-up of the different subsystems, that is, keeping two or more systems on all operational levels, was hardly acceptable. Problems in communication among the creators of the systems and discrepancies in regulations became obvious.

Also in everyday operation the management systems with element-based integration soon proved impracticable. The employee ultimately addressed by the system seldom thinks in the form of elements. Handling remains difficult, if not impossible. In combination with high pressure for competitive success, this approach was pre-programmed for failure.

The summation of different subsystems with the element approach to integration is no solution, because the management system of an organisation as corporate monitoring and checking system is indivisible and therefore all requirements to the organisation have to converge in one management system.

System Based Integration Strategy

The questions of communities of the different systems and of a common demand for regulations, for example for audit systems, arose early out of the discussion concerning the combination of elements of a management system.

What the systems have in common can be summarised by the "good management practices" mentioned in the EMAS regulation. These say that the operational activities have to be:

- systematically planned,
- implemented,
- controlled, and
- the reaching of targets is controlled, as well as
- a continual improvement is pursued.

So, for example, certain elements show up in all systems likewise, for example:

- strategy creation and targeting,
- PDCA-principle,
- continual improvement, and
- audits and reviews for the system checking.

Therefore, checking and control is of substantial importance to help avoid parallel spheres by integration and a merging of the flows of information. For system based integration, the regulations common to all management systems are combined; only the specific regulations of the individual systems remain discrete (Figure 2).

Accordingly this is a matter of combining individual sub-management systems and their integration into a comprehensive corporate management system. These experiences were picked up in EN ISO 14001 "Environmental Management Systems" as a younger subsystem. System comprehensive elements, such as targeting, audits and so forth are pulled out and defined as generally valid for all management areas. In principle, all of the other above-mentioned subsystems such as safety and energy management, finance and personnel management can be integrated step by step over the interface of the similarity of all management systems. This is a matter of conformance of management philosophy and structure of the subsystems with those of the integrated management system.

This integration strategy avoids a double definition of the same system elements. In this way inconsistencies are avoided and the system is developed on a higher

Figure 2. Further development of the element based management system

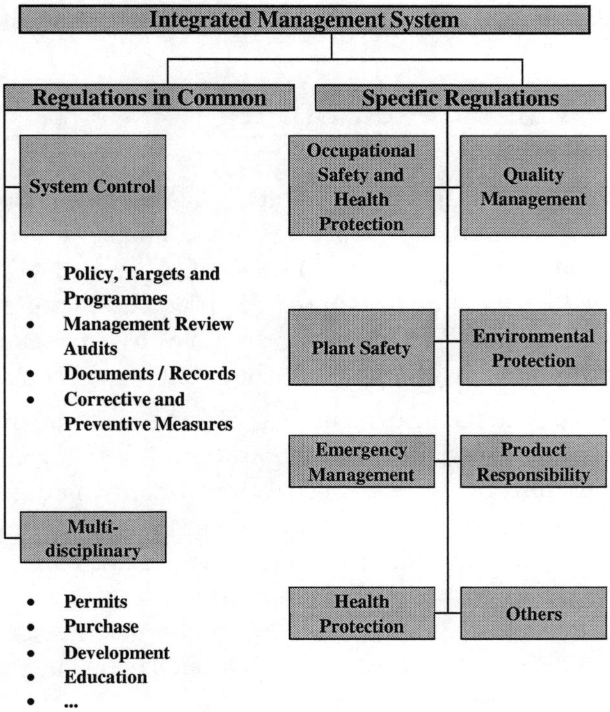

level. Developing on existing systems brings with it advantages in time and a greater acceptance by employees (Pichler & Wildburger, 1999). In spite of the systems showing basically different areas of regulation, targeting and weighting, we discovered a whole series of things in common (Figure 3).

Figure 3. Integration strategy for a safety management system with PDCA-structure following EN ISO 14001

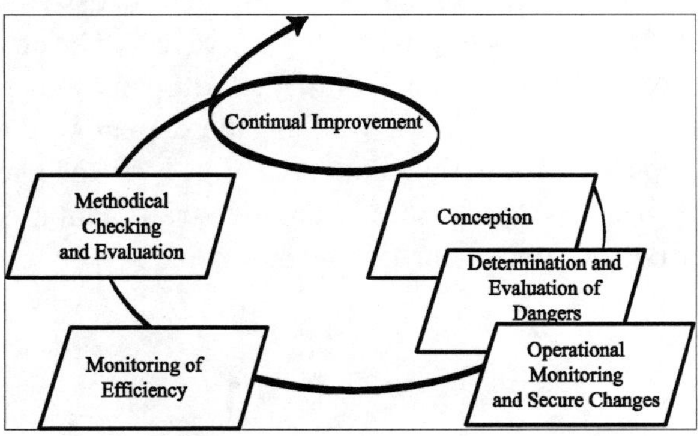

The disadvantage of this integration strategy is that in spite of all search for community, one fact has been disregarded so far, namely that the management systems basically have different areas of regulation, targeting and weighting.

Process Based Integration Strategy

Recently a process oriented integration strategy has become popular that keeps close to the current value creating processes of a company. Process orientation means organisation around processes instead of around functions (Meuche, 2000). Correspondingly the responsibility for process functions is no longer associated with functions. That makes it possible to implement subsystems appropriately and to implement a functional horizontal integration.

It is not possible to ignore specific regulations because operational processes are made the source of considerations and requirements and they are allocated to these processes. Initially on the level of concrete work instructions the thematic regulations were partially combined with core processes. Core processes are manufacturing processes, development and so forth; management processes, on the other side, are strategy creation, the target system, the agreement on targets, communication and so forth. Furthermore, support processes such as purchase regulations, personnel development, real estate management, supply and disposal, and so forth have to be defined.

In connection with its implementation this process oriented approach needs an additional process based provision of information, which the conventional element oriented management systems often do not provide because of their lack of user orientation.

For the implementation there are two strategies in application (Meuche, 2000):

1. The activities are brought together step by step from the smallest unit to activities, partial processes, and eventually to core, support and management processes. The disadvantage of this approach is that it is connected with a great amount of data and a high time expenditure.
2. The operational core, management and support processes are identified first and then concretised as required. Here there has to be an analysis first as to which core processes exist within the company and how are they classified. The classification on the other side depends on the company strategy, the type of production and orders as well as the production programme. Typical core processes of an industrial plant are for example development, distribution, and provision of service.

The conversion to an integrated process oriented management system has to be implemented in several steps:

1. ascertainment of the processes
2. evaluation of the processes
3. definition of targets and parameters
4. identification of requirements
5. evaluation of requirements
6. derivation of tasks and integration to the processes
7. checking for effectiveness

After ascertainment and evaluation of the processes, the respective relevant requirements have to be linked to the processes (Figure 4). Requirements result from legal provisions (occupational safety and health protection, environmental protection, product liability, criminal law), official requirements (e.g., secondary provisions in notices of approval), standard specifications (e.g., EN ISO 9001 ff., EN ISO 14001 ff.), customers' requests (ISO 16949:2002 - Quality Management Systems: Automotive) or internal requirements (company and concern guidelines).

Figure 4. Integration strategy of process integration

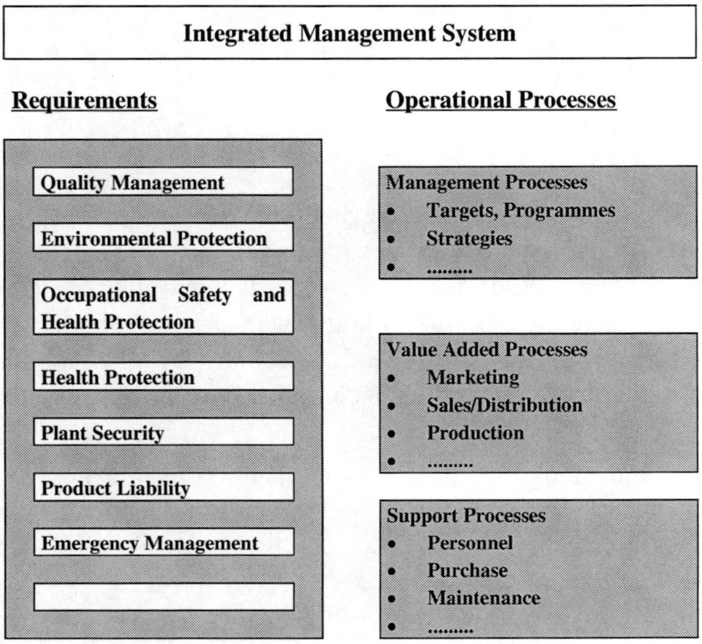

For operational practice this means checking and designing individual instruments of the management system such as instructions, forms, check lists for their multidimensional usability. So for example the regulations for the instruction of new employees can be integrated into a joint instruction in which the subjects' environment and employee protection are treated in common.

In the implementation of the process structures it worked satisfactorily to provide so-called function assignment diagrams. Additionally the documentation of the processes has to be recorded. Then from the superior targets (company targets, department targets) process targets for the individual processes are derived. In this way, one has to make sure the grade of attainment of superior targets is immediately influenced by the grade of attainment of the process targets.

For the evaluation the allocation to the core elements of process oriented management systems have to be regarded. These comprise:

1. *Processes*
   - core processes
   - management processes
   - support processes
2. *Requirements*
   - laws, standards
   - customers' requests
   - company targets
3. *Good Management Practices*
   - PDCA principle
   - continual improvement

The process oriented approach means a methodical ascertainment and handling of the processes implemented within an organisation as well as the interactions among these processes. Wherever this has already been determined or achieved (e.g., with the conversion of the Quality Management System to EN ISO 9001:2000), increased efforts for coordination still exist. On the other hand discrepancies can be cleared up at once and do not appear as contradicting postulations in the different statements.

A further development of the process based system-spreading approach is in the utilisation of synergy effects by the integration of joint system elements and the adaptation of the system to basic processes for the production of goods and services.

Therefore nowadays process management in combination with the system-spreading integration of systems is favoured as the most promising way to manage the numerous requirements practically. Thus the processes build the basic structure of the company, which is linked to the external and internal requirements and regularly adjusted. The good management practices of the PDCA circle and of continual improvement are effective for all elements.

Application of ICT-Supported Information, Management and Monitoring Systems as Components of Integrated Management Systems

The operational experiences obtained with management systems show that the regulations provided there are needed for various requirements within the organisation and that many user groups within the organisation revert to flow regulations, data and applicable documents under different aspects.

In connection with the integration of the various areas of organisation management these various requirements are being increasingly supported in a reasonable way by computer-supported information, management and monitoring systems.

So computer-aided information systems are successfully applied in the following company departments:

1. *Application in Company Documentation:* ICT-supported "manuals," which always reflect up-to-date documents, such as system regulations and process control as well as work instructions and up-to-date catalogues of laws, are available to all employees at their workplaces. In particular, the advantages are in the document control (constant topicality of regulations and low efforts for revision). Thus, for example new process regulations, flow regulations, and work instructions can be laid down in such a way that a receipt has to be confirmed by the user at the local computer workplaces as soon as s/he accesses it for the first time. Furthermore, links in the text provide ways to refer directly to the respective documents relevant to the department or workplace as well as to the applicable documents and records.
2. *Application at In-plant Monitoring and Controlling:* In most companies, measured data and records for different areas and targets are required for the purpose of checking and control. Thus, for example, in the environmental field for the control of the continual improvement often

specific key indicators have to be developed, which in most cases are more significant than the absolute consumption figures. Using ICT-supported management systems in an integrated management system, these data can be applied to a multifunctional use and be evaluated in many different partial aspects. Another field of application is in the control of environmental relevant monitoring measurements. Here clear specifications regarding the tolerable range of variation, for example of pollution data or sewage disposal and so forth can be given. In connection with environmental controlling, it then becomes possible to recognise trends early, thus enabling the company to intervene in these processes promptly and to take corrective measures.

3. *Application at Audits:* Furthermore, an ICT-supported "manual" with respective system regulations offers advantages for audits. The specific flow regulations for individual job and function holders can be checked by means of function allocation charts. Thus, matrices can be developed from the function allocation charts, and methodically queried at defined intervals within the frame of a three-year audit cycle. Furthermore, the results of the audits and their grade of fulfilment can be fed into a direct statistical evaluation over defined evaluation scales.
4. *Application in Checking Measures:* For regular controls and checking in connection with the monitoring of dates (e.g., issuing of inspection instructions, arranging of expert opinions or expert examinations as well as preventive maintenance measures) ICT-supported management systems offer essential advantages for the support of the integrated management system. In the ICT system a time schedule can be laid down for these control periods and later retrieved punctually at the respective point in time. This practice is often applied in large companies especially because there daily checks by internal and external employees or service providers have to be performed and an ICT-supported management grants an effective controlling here.
5. *Application in Purchasing:* In purchasing, ICT-supported material management is in use in many large companies. From the environmental point of view, it is particularly relevant that the products used in the ICT system are released by quality management, environmental management and occupational safety and health management (dangerous goods). In this way it can be avoided that individual parts of the company continue ordering materials for which a substitution is already decided by the head of the department materials administration. Another essential advantage is in the warehouse management and controls, where an ICT-supported provision of information can avoid that those storage areas are not appropriately used (e.g., by storing materials illegitimately together or by exceeding maximal storage amounts, etc.).

6. *Application in Public Relations:* ICT-supported information systems are of special importance for public relations and reporting as well. Many companies nowadays do not only keep their environmental reports and environmental statements in the company's intranet, but also present them on their homepage, which makes them available to a greater clientele.

But for all these advantages, it has to be mentioned that some operational processes and documentation still cannot be managed by ICT-supported information retrieval. In particular the job specifications and appointment documents and so forth that have to be kept between the companies and the representatives are to be mentioned.

Outlook

For many organisations the present status of integration of management systems raises the question as to where developments are going and whether there are not other new approaches to be pursued in the next three years. In this connection it can be said that process orientation is becoming integrated into current standards and management conceptions more and more. For this reason it may take on a position that is fundamental as good management practices, the principle of the continual improvement or the PDCA structure. Which way will be pursued in individual cases depends very much on the requirements and possibilities of the respective company/organisation. A combination of process management and the system-spreading integration of systems will probably be the most reasonable way.

The fact is that integration has to take place both in content (coordination with quality, safety, environmental protection and finances) and in structure (company-comprehensive as well as social). ICT-supported information, management and monitoring systems as components of an integrated management system will take on a central role in this process, for the documents created and data entered must be suitable for different applications and evaluation purposes within the company. This will require further development.

References

Bundesarbeitsministerium. (1999). Arbeitsschutzmanagementsystem. Eckpunkte des BMA, der Obersten Arbeitsschutzbehörden der Bundesländer, der

Träger der Gesetzlichen Unfallversicherung und der Sozialpartner zur Entwicklung und Bewertung von Konzepten für Arbeitsschutzmanagementsysteme. *Bundesarbeitsblatt, 2,* 43- 46.

Directive 2003/87/EC of the European Parliament and of the Council establishing a scheme for greenhouse gas emissions allowance trading within the Community and amending Council Directive 96/61/EC.

EMAS - Regulation (EC) No. 761/2001 allowing voluntary participation by organisations in a Community eco-management and audit scheme.

EN ISO 19011:2002 - Guidelines for quality and/or environmental management systems auditing.

EN ISO 14001:1996 - Environmental management systems, specification with guideance for use.

EN ISO 9000:2000 - Quality management systems - Fundmentals and Vocabulary.

EN ISO 9001:2000 - Quality management systems - Requirements.

Hessische Landesanstalt für Umwelt. (1997). Leitfaden Integrierte Managementsysteme. *HfLU-Schriftenreihe Umweltplanung, Arbeits- und Umweltschutz, 240.* Wiesbaden.

ISO 16949:2002 - Quality Management Systems: Automotive.

Meuche, Th. (2000). Prozessorientierung beim IMS. *ForUm, 1*(1), 8-10.

OHSAS 18001 - Occupational Health and Safety Assessment Series.

Paeger, J., & Niehoff, A. (2000). Die neue Störfall-Verordnung. Sicherheitsmanagementsystem gefordert. *ForUM, 1*(1), 58 – 61.

Pichler, A., & Wildburger, J. (1999). Integration ist der Schlüssel. *Beratende Ingenieure, H 5,* 66-69. Springer.

Sprenger, F. (2000). Integration – Ende der Nabelschau. *ForUm, 1*(1), 6-8.

Chapter XXI

Remote Monitoring of Nuclear Power Plants in Baden-Württemberg, Germany

Walter Hürster, T-Systems GEI GmbH, Germany

Klaus Bieber, T-Systems GEI GmbH, Germany

Bruno Klahn, T-Systems GEI GmbH, Germany

Reinhard Micheler, T-Systems GEI GmbH, Germany

Thomas Wilbois, T-Systems GEI GmbH, Germany

Roland Obrecht, Ministry of Environment & Transport, Stuttgart, Germany

Fritz Schmidt, IKE, University of Stuttgart, Germany

Abstract

The technical implementation of a new remote monitoring system for nuclear power plants is described in this chapter as an example of a modern environmental monitoring and surveillance system. The concept, the architectural design and the user interface of this system had to meet extremely high demands. Fulfilling the imposed requirements, a system solution was developed which is suitable not only for environmental monitoring but also for hazard management and early warning systems. The pilot installation of this system has successfully passed the operational test phase and has been in full operation since August 2001.

Introduction

The Ministry of Environment and Transport in Baden-Württemberg, Germany, operates a system for the Remote Monitoring of Nuclear Power Plants (RM/NPP) in its role as a supervisory authority for nuclear facilities. This system is used to monitor the operation of the nuclear power plants in the Federal State of Baden-Württemberg (Obrigheim KWO, Philippsburg KKP I and II and Neckarwestheim GKN I and II) and those close to the border (Fessenheim, France and Leibstadt, Switzerland) (Figure 1).

The RM/NPP is a complex measuring and information system which records and monitors approximately 20 million data sets per day. The actual operational state of the nuclear facilities including their emissions into air and water, together with the radioactive emissions into the environment are automatically recorded around the clock independently of the operator of the nuclear power plant. In addition, the RM/NPP system continuously surveys the meteorological data at the sites and also receives data from external measuring networks.

Figure 1. Location of the nuclear power plants

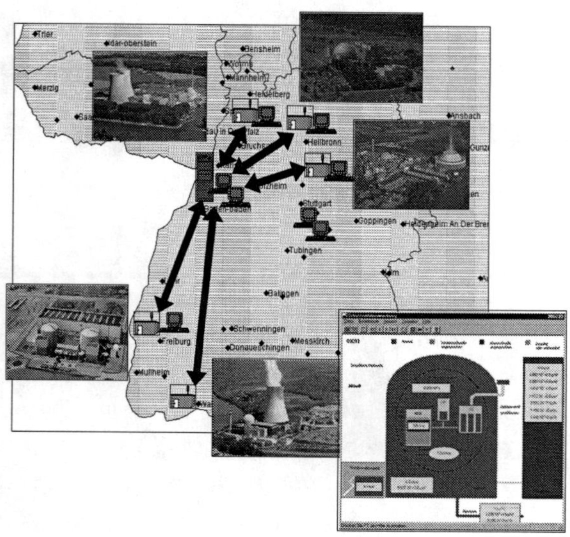

This not only provides a basis for monitoring the operator's compliance with legal provisions, but also enables effective action to be taken in case of an incident or accident.

Therefore, the RM/NPP provides numerous possibilities to visualize the data and to check them against threshold values and protection objectives. In the case of a radioactive leak, potentially affected areas can be determined at an early stage by a transport calculation and protective measures can be adopted by the ministry in cooperation with the authorities responsible for civil protection.

Data Sources

One feature of the system is the duality and independence of the main data sources: emission data at the nuclear power plants and the radiological emissions into the environment are measured at the same time.

Measurements in the Nuclear Power Plants

The following measured quantities are mainly transferred to the RM/NPP system by the Baden-Württemberg nuclear power plants:

- Emissions into the atmosphere with the activity concentrations and emission rates of inert gases, aerosols and iodine.
- Emissions into waste water with activity concentrations and waste water output.
- Operating parameters of the facilities with neutron flux, pressure in the safety tanks, voltage applied to conductor lines, the positions of control and safety valves.
- Measured quantities within the reactor building with relevance for the radiation protection such as the dose rate and activity concentrations in various sections of the facility.
- Meteorological data such as wind speed, wind direction and air temperature at various altitudes, precipitation rate and radiation balance.

Measurements in the Local Vicinity of the Reactor Sites

Emission measuring stations surround the nuclear power plant either in ring form or in semi-circular form (Figure 2). These emission measuring rings or semi-rings

Figure 2. Measuring stations surrounding the nuclear power plant of Obrigheim

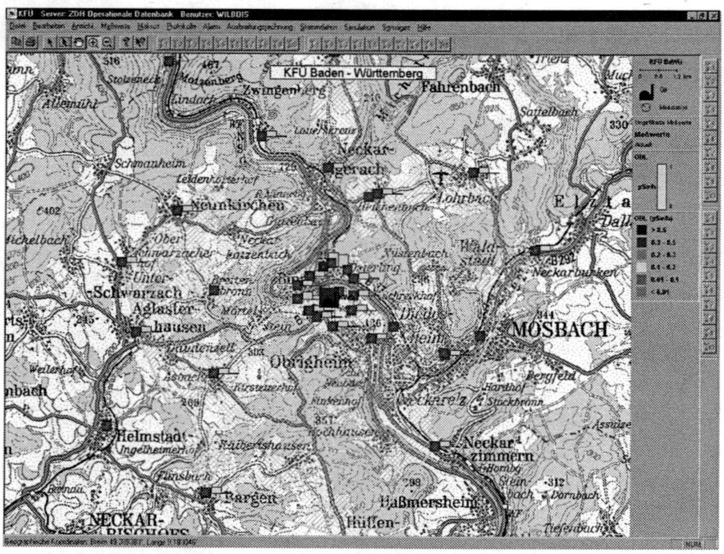

have been set up in accordance with the requirements of civil protection. The inner measuring ring (1 km) is normally equipped with measuring huts. The central measuring ring (4-10 km) exists in the form of measuring points on public buildings. The outer ring (max. 25 km) consists of measuring stations from the Federal Office for Radiation Protection (BfS, Bundesamt für Strahlenschutz), which are integrated in the RM/NPP.

All stations measure continuously the local Gamma dose rate. One station in each of the emission measuring rings is additionally equipped with devices for determining alpha and beta activity concentrations of aerosols and airborne iodine activities. Each of the emission arcs, which monitor the foreign power plants close to the border, also has one fully equipped measuring station, which records not only the local dose rate but also meteorological data for the German Meteorological Service (DWD, Deutscher Wetterdienst), apart from a continuous determination of individual nuclides in aerosols. In addition to the meteorological data from the power plant locations, the regional observation and forecast data from the German Meteorological Service are also processed in the RM/NPP.

Concept, Design, Technology and Realization of the System

The structure of the system was conceived in form of a client/server architecture with the following components (Figure 3):

- Communication Server (CS)
- Central Database (CDB)
- Application Server (AS)
- Dispersion Modelled Transport Calculation (DMTC)
- PC based User Interface (Clients)
- Integrated Information System (based on HTML)

All important components of the control centre, measuring data recording and networking are organized in a redundant manner. The central data storage is hosted on a computer cluster, which is additionally provided with an emergency power supply. The database servers are equipped with a commercial database system. Standard PCs are used as clients, enabling the RM/NPP data to be accessed and visualized with the assistance of GIS functions (Geographical Information System). The RM/NPP client software provides standardized

Figure 3. System concept and design – structure of the system

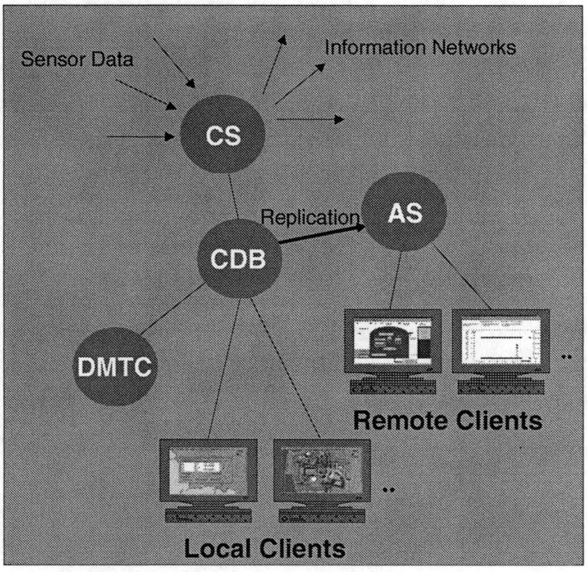

export interfaces to office and graphical applications. In order to support the information of the public, the RM/NPP system can also be accessed via WWW browser technology without any need for RM/NPP client software. The local networks (LAN) installed in the individual locations are connected by routers via redundant wide area networks (WAN).

Fulfilling the high demands and requirements imposed, the system solution provides:

- A modern graphical user interface with GIS functions
- Diagnosis and forecast calculations of radiological pollution in the case of incidents (DMTC)
- The automatic setting off of the alarm when threshold values are exceeded
- High availability and reliability of the central server and data transfer routes
- Economical operation with few personnel
- Good and long-term maintainability by using standard technologies
- Supporting public relations work by means of Videotext and the Internet

Airborne Transport of Radioactive Nuclides

In case of a nuclear incident, a service called "Dispersion Modelled Transport Calculation" (DMTC) is initiated automatically. The transport calculations provided by this service are based on complex mathematical models (diagnostic windfield, Lagrange particle transport, advanced dose calculations), which calculate the expected radiation exposure in the near vicinity of the discharge location. The current meteorological situation, the form of the terrain and measured values from the RM/NPP system are taken into account. For prognostic purposes, it is also possible to utilize the forecast data from the German Meteorological Service (DWD). The results of DMTC are visualized for the user with the assistance of GIS functions.

The varying concentrations of radioactivity are displayed in the form of isodose lines or isodose areas on a map as the case may be (Figure 4). This provides the user with an important decision-making tool as it is easy to detect whether, and if so to which extent, certain towns or areas are affected by an event. This facilitates taking immediate protective measures.

Figure 4. Results of a DMTC visualized in the form of isodose areas

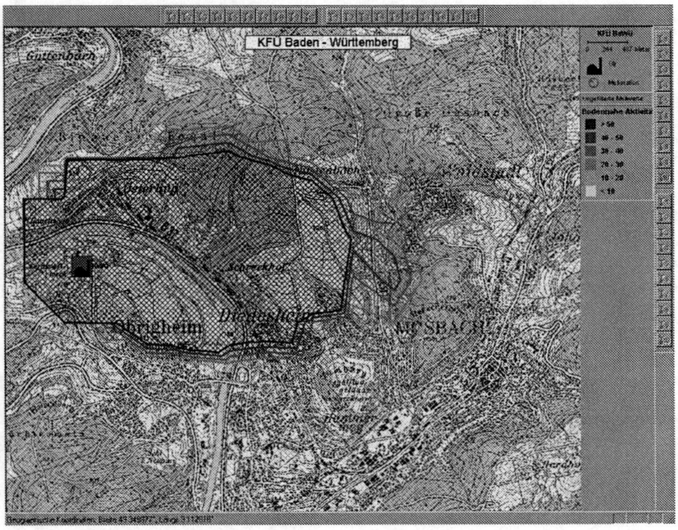

Additional Features

Apart from the results of the DMTC, additional information can be overlaid onto a computer generated map, enabling a more accurate assessment of an incident, for example:

- Wind vector fields for varying heights
- Precipitation fields
- Helicopter flight paths and the results from measuring flights
- Positions of measuring vehicles
- Water levels
- Additional measured values from stationary and mobile measuring stations (Figure 5)

Extremely high demands are placed on the user interfaces in order to guarantee a secure and simple operation of a very complex system such as the remote monitoring system for nuclear reactors. Due to the ergonomic design, consequent use of graphical and geographical visualization and operating technologies from the GIS environment, the RM/NPP system can be operated by the user in a simple and safe manner.

Figure 5. Emission data from Obrigheim and local Gamma dose rates

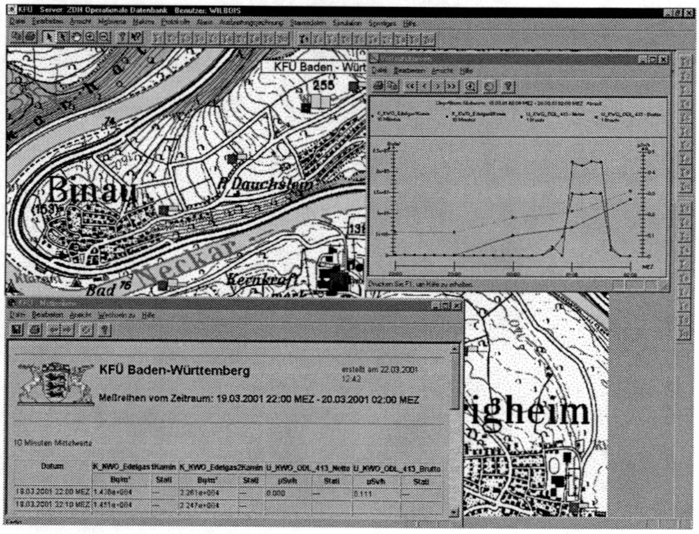

Conclusions

The new remote monitoring of nuclear reactors enables the supervisory authorities to meet their obligations under atomic legislation in a safe and economical manner. The extended possibilities of evaluating and visualizing measured data and parameters of the power plant stations, together with the complex models for the transport calculations, simplify the assessment of an incident by the supervisory authority and the Regional Administrations responsible for civil protection.

Acknowledgments

The system described above was contracted to T-Systems by the Federal State of Baden-Württemberg, Ministry of Environment and Transport, as a turnkey system, with the integrated service "DMTC" provided by the Institut für Kernergetik und Energiesysteme (Institute for Nuclear Energetics and Energy systems) of the University of Stuttgart (IKE). The research work related with the development and integration of the DMTC was supported by the Ministry of Environment and Transport within the framework "Environmental Information System" Baden-Württemberg. The underlying program modules of the DMTC were taken from the library of the OECD Nuclear Energy Agency.

References

Bieber, K. (1999). Die Technische Realisierung der Neuen Kernreaktorfernüberwachung Baden-Württemberg. In C. Dade & B. Schulz (Eds.), *Management von Umweltinformationen in Vernetzten Umgebungen.* Marburg: Metropolis Verlag.

Bieber, K., Hürster, W., & Klahn, B. (2001). Umweltinformation und Gefahrenmanagement bei der Überwachung des Betriebs von Kernkraftwerken. In R. Treibert (Ed.), *Betriebliche Informationssysteme fü Umwelt, Qualität und Sicherheit.* GI-Workshop, Wuppertal. Marburg: Metropolis Verlag.

Hürster, W., & Hetzel, M. (1997). GIS in Modernen Gefahrenüberwachungssystemen. *Geo-Informationssysteme, 5,* 21-24.

Klahn, B., & Bieber, K. (1998). Eine Moderne Benutzeroberfläche für ein System zur Kernreaktor-Fernüberwachung. In W.F. Riekert & K. Tochtermann (Eds.), *Hypermedia im Umweltschutz, 1st Workshop, Ulm 1998.* Marburg: Metropolis Verlag.

Obrecht, R., et al. (2002). Erneuerte Kernreaktorfernüberwachung in Badenwürttemberg. In R. Mayer-Föll, A. Keitel & W. Geiger (Eds.), *UIS Badenwüttemberg, Projekt AJA Phase III.* Forschungszentrum Karlsruhe, Wissenschaftliche Berichte FZKA 6777.

Schmidt, F., Kopetzky, R., Grohmann, A., & Obrecht, R. (2001). *Entwicklung einer Ontologie fü die Einbindung von Simulationsdiensten in die Kernreaktor-Fernüerwachung (KFÜ) Baden-Wüttemberg.* Paper presented at the Fourth GI-Workshop, Hypermedia im Umweltschutz, Ulm, Mai.

Weigele, M. (1997). *Berechnung der Nassen Deposition von Spurenstoffen im Rahmen des Notfallschutzes.* Dissertation. Universität Stuttgart, IKE report No. 4-146.

Chapter XXII

Development of a Decision Support Tool for Technological Risk Management with Remote Sensing and GIS

Nektarios Chrysoulakis,
Foundation for Research & Technology - Hellas, Greece

Poulicos Prastacos,
Foundation for Research & Technology - Hellas, Greece

Constantinos Cartalis, University of Athens, Greece

Abstract

In this study, a GIS based decision support tool is proposed for the support of technological risk management by integrating moderate and high spatial resolution satellite imagery with in-situ vector data. The Advanced Very High Resolution Radiometer (AVHRR) on board the NOAA satellites has been used for the detection of fire as well as for the detection and monitoring of plumes caused by major technological accidents. The Thematic Mapper (TM) on board the Landsat satellite has been used for the depiction of the urban areas and the main road network as well as for the estimation of the spatial distribution of vegetation in the study area. A major technological accident scenario was developed for the broader area of Athens (Greece) in order to present the functionality of the GIS tool for the support of decision making during the crisis, as well as for the assessment of the accident's impact on the natural and human environment.

Introduction

Major technological accidents comprise great danger to the environment and public health. A number of accidents have taken place in recent years with serious costs in terms of human life as well as with considerable – and in many cases irreversible – damage to the natural environment. In many cases toxic substances or released airborne material develop into plumes which may reach high concentrations at ground level and pose dangers to the human and natural environment. Damages may thus occur both as an immediate and direct consequence of the accident, and subsequently during propagation and dispersion of the resulting plume. Exhaustive consideration is usually given to the immediate ground-level effects in close vicinity to the installation; however, it should be mentioned that in several cases, only limited effort was given to examining the impacts of the plume in the wider geographic area during the course of the hours or days following the accident. Technological accidents can be characterized by a number of different events and processes, including spillage or sudden release of materials, fire, or explosion. Airborne releases usually develop in plumes, which can thereafter be monitored either due to their optical depth or their temperature difference from the ambient air. The emission of toxic gases and formation of carbon particles which can carry toxic material absorbed onto their surface as well as obscuring vision both present hazards in a fire situation.

A number of experiments (Atkinson et al., 1994; Bartelds et al., 1993; Cozzani et al., 1996; Davie & Nolan, 1993; Grant & Drysdale, 1994; Lang, 1993; Marliere, 1996; Martins & Borrego, 1994; Martins et al., 1996; Miles & Cox 1994; Porter et al., 1996) involving fires in warehouses and awareness of the hazards of plumes in a fire situation have been oriented towards the definition of the properties and of the amount of the plume particulates generated by different materials, including pesticides, under varying fire conditions. Various numerical models and software packages have been developed for the simulation of the conditions and the process of technological accidents (Andronopoulos et al., 1994; Cleaver et al., 1995; Hanna et al., 1993; Khan & Abbasi, 1999; Kukkonen et al., 1994; Webber et al., 1993).

In this study, the design and implementation of a technological risk management decision support tool (DST) is presented. It is based on the detection and space-time monitoring of the produced plumes by integrating moderate and high spatial resolution satellite imagery with vector data in a GIS platform capable of supporting technological risk management. A major technological accident scenario for the broader area of Athens was developed by adjusting Advanced Very High Resolution Radiometer (AVHRR) images that were acquired during the massive explosion in a fireworks factory in Enschede (The Netherlands) on May 13, 2000. This scenario was used to present the functionality of the developed DST for the support of decision making during the crisis, as well as for the assessment of the accident's impact on the natural and human environment.

Fire and Plume Detection Methodology

The methodology for the detection of fires caused by major technological accidents with the use of AVHRR imagery has been presented in a past study (Chrysoulakis & Cartalis, 2000). The detection algorithm has the advantages of multispectral analysis and provides valuable results for the detection of fires caused by technological accidents. In practice, the pseudochannel image of brightness temperature difference between AVHRR channels 3 (3.55 - 3.93 μm) and 4 (10.5 - 11.3 μm) is created and filtered for clouds by applying a cloud-masking algorithm which is based on the combination of AVHRR channels 1 (0.58 - 0.68 μm) and 5 (11.5 - 12.5 μm). In this filtered image, pixels with brightness values greater than an experimental derived temperature threshold correspond to fires produced by major technological accidents. The fire detection algorithm has been programmed as a stand-alone application for the automatic detection of fires caused by major technological accidents with use of AVHRR imagery (Chrysoulakis & Cartalis, 2003a).

The methodology for the automatic detection and monitoring of plumes caused by major technological accidents with the use of AVHRR multispectral imagery has also been presented in a previous study (Chrysoulakis & Cartalis, 2003b). A two-dimensional feature space image is used in order to discriminate pixels that contain plumes from those that may contain clouds or the underlying surface. The two-dimensional feature space is generated by combining AVHRR channels 1, 2 (0.72-1.10 μm) and 5.

Both methodologies have been evaluated on the basis of past technological accidents (Thessaloniki, February 24, 1986; Lyon, June 2, 1987; Genoa, April 13, 1991; Enschede, May 13, 2000). AVHRR images acquired over the broader area of the Netherlands on May 13, 2000 (14.44 UTC and 17.20 UTC) were used for the development of a major technological accident scenario in this study. This date refers to the massive explosion in a fireworks factory in the town of Enschede. The fire was detected by applying the aforementioned fire detection algorithm to the AVHRR images; whereas, in order to simplify the scenario, AVHRR channel 2 images were used for monitoring the plumes.

Design and Application of a GIS Based Tool for Support of Technological Risk Management

The main factors that need to be covered in the course of preparing an emergency plan for major industrial accidents range from the definition of land use/cover and the potentially exposed population to the rate and direction of propagation of the plume. Satellite data are the main information source in the proposed system. The fire and plume detection algorithms are applied to AVHRR imagery. If both results are positive (this means that an industrial fire and a plume have been detected in the same area), the system will classify the corresponded pixels as "potential incident pixels". Since the AVHRR images are geometrically corrected, the coordination of these pixels is automatically stored in the system. The areas in which a technological accident is most likely to occur (industrial installations, warehouses of toxic substances, offshore installations, petroleum products storage sites, ports, airports, etc.) were mapped with the use of high spatial resolution satellite imagery (Landsat TM) in combination with other sources of information (CORINE land cover data, land use maps, etc.). These areas were classified as "possible areas of occurrence". Therefore, the developed DST examines whether the detected "potential incident pixels" are located within any possible area of occurrence. A positive result will verify the occurrence of a technological accident and will comprise an "alarm" for the system. This alarm sets off the plume monitoring modules as well as the modules used by the system for the estimation of the population at risk. The latter combine the high spatial resolution satellite derived information (urban areas, road network) with in-situ derived vector data (spatial distribution of population in the vicinity of the incident).

About half of the population of Greece is concentrated in Athens. A lot of refineries, chemical industries and warehouses are located in the broader region of Athens and especially within the industrial zone of "Thriasio Pedio," about 15 km NW from the centre of the city. For the application of the proposed GIS tool, taking into account that the prevailing winds in the area of concern are from the N – NW directions, a major technological accident scenario for a refinery installation at Thriasio Pedio was generated. In the past, similar accidents took place in this area (i.e., Petrola refinery, February 1, 1992), but for the application of the GIS tool in this study, real plumes depicted on AVHRR imagery were needed. For this reason, the available AVHRR data of May 13, 2000, were used (major technological accident in Enschede). Rectangular portions (50x30 km), around the pixels corresponded to plumes, and were extracted from these AVHRR images and adjusted to the broader area of Athens. High spatial resolution satellite imagery and in-situ vector data have been also used. More specifically, for the development and implementation of the scenario the following data were integrated:

(a) *NOAA/AVHRR images (May 13, 2000, at 14.44 UTC and 17.20 UTC).* The fire detection algorithm was applied to these images in order to detect the pixels corresponding to the accident site in Enschede. Since pixels corresponding to the fire caused by this accident were detected, AVHRR images were adjusted to the area of Athens by adapting these pixels to the position of the refinery at the Thriasio Pedio. A transverse Mercator projection was applied (Projection System: Hellenic Geodetic Reference System 87 - HGRS87; Reference Ellipsoid: GRS80). Figure 1 presents the position of the plume at 14.44 and 17.20 UTC (AVHRR channel 2).

(b) *Landsat TM image (April 26, 1994).* Ground Control Points (GCPs) were used for the geometric correction of this image and for its projection to the HGRS87 system. The TM image was used for the depiction of urban areas and of the main road network, as well as for the depiction of the industrial zones in combination with land use maps. It was also used for the estimation of the state of the environment in the area of concern.

(c) *CORINE Land Cover data and land use maps.* These data were used in combination with Landsat TM imagery for the depiction of areas in which a technological accident is most likely to occur (possible areas of occurrence).

(d) *30m contours were used for the production of a Digital Elevation Model (DEM) for the broader area of Athens.* This DEM is used to feed the dispersion models with topographic information, as well as to produce 3D views of the landscape with the combined use of Landsat TM imagery.

(e) *Vectors of the main and secondary road networks for the broader area of Athens.* The integration of these vectors with the Landsat TM image has the potential to support either the development of emergency plans for the area of concern, or the decision making during the crisis mitigation phase.

Figure 1. AVHRR channel 2 images presenting the position of the plume at 14.44 UTC (left) and at 17.20 UTC (right), according to the technological accident scenario

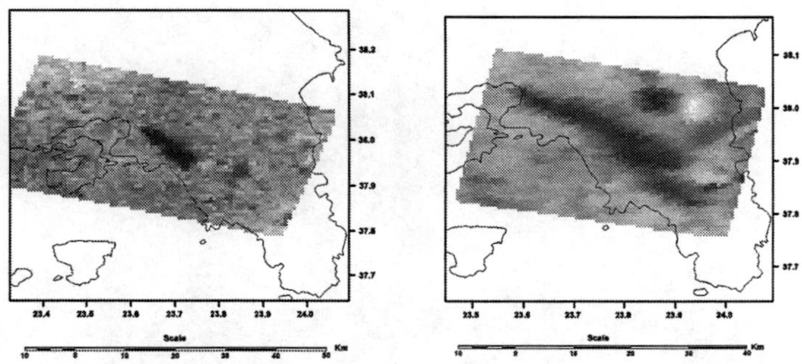

(f) *Vectors of the spatial distribution of population for the broader area of Athens.* These vectors were used by the GIS tool in order to support the decision making during the crisis mitigation phase, especially regarding the evacuation of urban areas to avoid plumes. The system has the capability to combine these vectors with the satellite derived information in order to estimate the population at risk.

Results

The red polygons correspond to the possible areas of occurrence in Figure 2. These areas have been superimposed on a pseudocoloured composition (RGB: 3-2-1) of TM channels 1, 2 and 3. The DST examines whether the detected "potential incident pixels" are located within any possible area of occurrence. According to the scenario used in this study, the area represented by the detected "potential incident pixels" (yellow polygon) is located within a possible area of occurrence.

Figure 3 presents the physical and artificial characteristics of the area located around the accident site. Three sources of information have been used: a) NOAA/AVHRR imagery for the detection of the exact position of the technological accident (yellow polygon); b) Landsat TM imagery for the monitoring of the area located around the accident site; c) vectors of the main and secondary road network. This type of visualization is used in the developed GIS tool to inform about the accessibility of the area of interest, as well as to depict the

Figure 2. TM pseudocoloured image (The possible areas of technological accident occurrence and the scenario accident's site have been superimposed.)

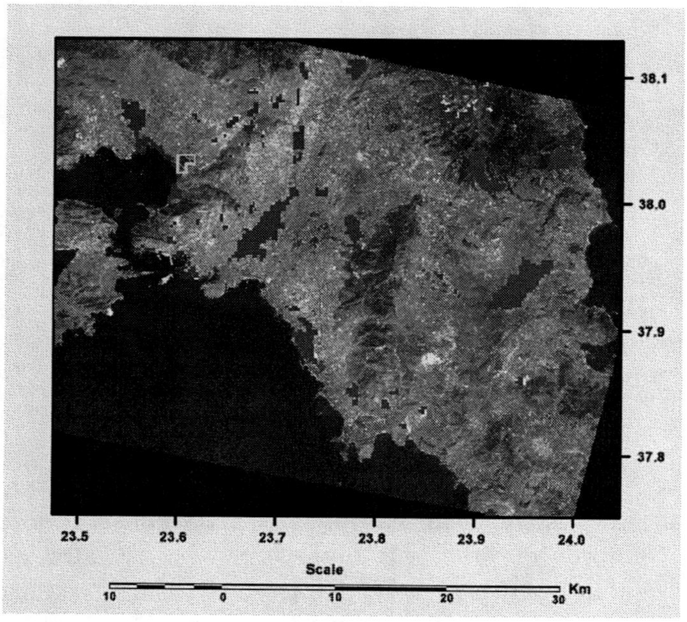

artificial characteristics, which may be used during the crisis mitigation phase (i.e., airports).

Figure 4 presents a product of the "monitoring module" of the proposed DST. The selected GIS layers present: (a) the urban areas (Landsat TM pseudocoloured image 3-2-1); (b) the spatial distribution of vegetation, in green tones (Landsat TM, NDVI); (c) the position of the accident site, within the red polygon (from NOAA/AVHRR channels 3 and 4); (d) the position of the plume at 14.44 UTC, within the black polygon (from NOAA/AVHRR channel 2); (e) the position of the plume at 17.20 UTC, within the blue polygon (from NOAA/AVHRR channel 2).

This product may be used for the monitoring of urban and natural disaster areas as well as for the location of areas where high ground level concentrations of toxic substances are expected. It can be also used for the estimation of the horizontal propagation velocity of the produced plume. For the scenario used in this study, the analysis of this product indicated that the mean plume propagation velocity along the main propagation direction (NW to SE) was about 3.5 Km/h, whereas its mean diffusion velocity in a perpendicular direction was about 0.8 Km/h. Therefore, this product has the potential to offer valuable information to the decision making authorities, either during the crisis mitigation phase, or during

Figure 3. Physical and artificial characteristics of the area located around the accident site are presented (The road network has been superimposed.)

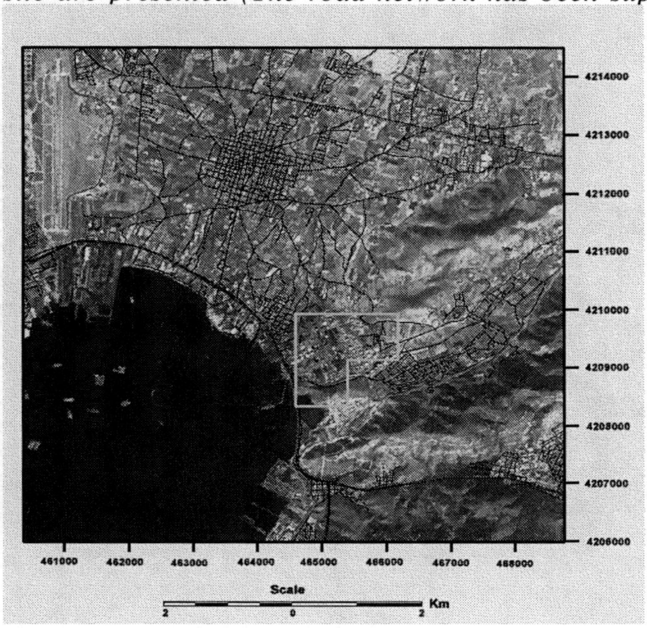

a post-crisis assessment. However, for the estimation of the population at risk during the propagation of the toxic plume, the spatial distribution of population was needed.

Figure 5 presents the final product of the "population distribution module" of the GIS tool. The selected GIS layers present: (a) the position of the accident site (within the yellow polygon); (b) the spatial distribution of population between 5 and 10 Km (blue circles) from the accident site; (c) the position of the plume at 14.44 UTC (green polygon); (d) the position of the plume at 17.20 UTC (red polygon); (e) the urban web and the physical and artificial characteristics of the broader area. The population distribution module has been designed for the automatic estimation of the population at risk. In terms of the scenario used in this study, the number of potentially affected inhabitants at the area within a circle centred at the accident site with 5 km radius was found to be at the order of magnitude of 15,000 persons, whereas the number of potentially affected inhabitants at the area between 5 and 10 Km from the accident site was found to be at the order of magnitude of 300,000 persons. Therefore, the integration of the spatial distribution of population with moderate spatial resolution satellite data has the potential to estimate the population at risk during the dispersion of a toxic plume, as well as to support (in combination with other elements of the proposed

Figure 4. Integration of Landsat, NOAA, CORINE and in-situ data for the monitoring of the urban areas, of the spatial distribution of vegetation, of the position of the accident site, of the position of the produced plume at 14.44 and 17.20 UTC

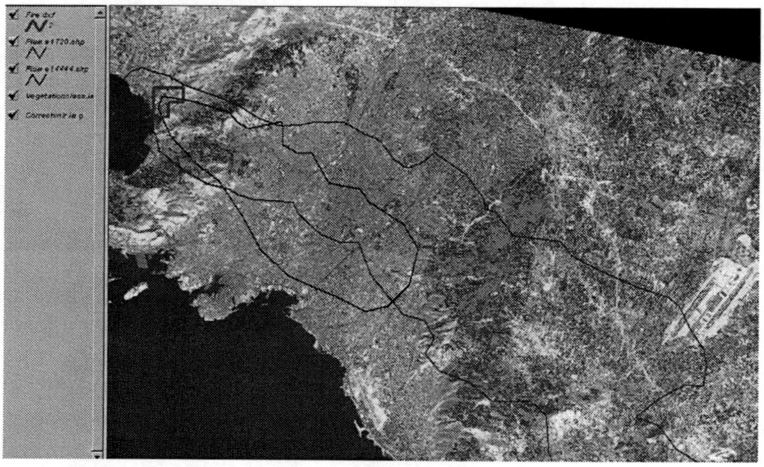

Figure 5. Estimation of population at risk during the propagation of toxic plumes over the city of Athens

DST such as the road network) the decision making regarding evacuation of the disaster area.

Conclusions

In this study, a GIS based tool was designed for the support of technological risk management. It has the advantages of the detection and space-time monitoring of the plumes by integrating moderate and high spatial resolution satellite imagery with vector data in order to estimate the population at risk during an emergency, as well as to support the assessment of the impacts of these plumes on the local environment. A major technological accident scenario was developed to present the functionality of the GIS based tool for the support of decision making during a crisis, as well as for the support of the assessment of the accident's impact on the natural and human environments.

During the crisis phase, the proposed tool has the potential:

(a) to support dispersion models and to verify their results;

(b) to describe and map the characteristics of the natural environment and the population, thereby providing a means to assess the environmental and health impacts of the plume;

(c) to help identify at-risk populations and environments which may need special protection;

(d) to support the coordination among involved parties as well as the decision making regarding the evacuation of urban areas to avoid plumes.

During the post-crisis assessment phase, it has the potential:

(a) to thematically map disaster areas;

(b) to support the assessment of the impacts on the local (anthropogenic and natural) environments;

(c) to help design and plan follow-up strategies to deal with the consequences of accidents.

The main advantage of the proposed DST is its wide area coverage with very good spatial and temporal resolution. The main disadvantages are:

(a) It is able to detect the technological accidents that cause fires and/or explosions, whereas incidents such as the release of dangerous substances cannot be detected.

(b) The observation of a given area with the use of AVHRR is not accomplished on a continuous basis, because NOAA are polar orbiting satellites.

References

Andronopoulos, S., Bartzis, J.G., Würtz, J., & Asimakopoulos, D. (1994). Modelling the effects of obstacles on the dispersion of denser than air gases. *Journal of Hazardous Materials, 37,* 327-352.

Atkinson, G.T., & Jagger, S.F. (1994). Plume seeding mechanisms in warehouse fires. In S.T. Cole & P.J. Wicks (Eds.), *Industrial Fires II Workshop Proceedings.* Report EUR 15967 EN, European Commission.

Bartelds, H., Smit, E., & Molag, M. (1993). Emissions from medium scale fires of chemicals. In S.T. Cole & P.J. Wicks (Eds.), *Industrial Fires Workshop Proceedings.* Report EUR 15340 EN, European Commission.

Chrysoulakis, N., & Cartalis, C. (2000). A new approach for the detection of industrial accidents, using NOAA/AVHRR imagery. *International Journal of Remote Sensing, 21,* 1743-1748.

Chrysoulakis, N., & Cartalis, C. (2003a). TAD - A new satellite images analysis software tool for the detection of major fires caused by technological accidents. *International Journal of Remote Sensing, 24,* 1259-1271.

Chrysoulakis, N., & Cartalis, C. (2003b). A new algorithm for the detection of plumes caused by industrial accidents, on the basis of NOAA/AVHRR imagery. *International Journal of Remote Sensing, 24,* 3353-3367.

Cleaver, R.P., Cooper, M.G., & Halford, A.R. (1995). Further model development of a model for dense gas dispersion over real terrain. *Journal of Hazardous Materials, 40,* 85-108.

Cozzani, V., Amendola, A., & Zanelli, S. (1996). Hazardous substances formed as a consequence of industrial fires. In S.T. Cole & P.J. Wicks (Eds.), *Industrial Fires III Workshop Proceedings.* Report EUR 17477 EN, European Commission.

Davie, F.M., & Nolan, P.F. (1993). Combustion of chemical substances and the impact on the environment of the fire products. Particle characterisation. In S.T. Cole & P.J. Wicks (Eds.), *Industrial Fires Workshop Proceedings.* Report EUR 15340 EN, European Commission.

Grant, G., & Drysdale, D. (1994). Flame spread modelling and fire growth in warehouses. In S.T. Cole & P.J. Wicks (Eds.), *Industrial Fires II Workshop Proceedings.* Report EUR 15967 EN, European Commission.

Hanna, S.R., Chang, J., & Strimaitis D.G. (1993). Hazardous gas model evaluation with field observations. *Atmospheric Environment, 27A,* 2265-2285.

Khan, F.I., & Abbasi, S.A. (1999). MAXCRED - A new software package for rapid risk assessment in chemical process industries. *Environmental Modelling & Software, 14,* 11-25.

Kukkonen, J., Kulmala, M., Nikmo, J., Vesala, T., Webber, D.M., & Wren, T. (1994). The homogeneous equilibrium approximation in models of aerosol cloud dispersion. *Atmospheric Environment, 28,* 2763-2776.

Lang, D. (1993). Development of a methodology for the prediction of the formation of toxic species in warehouse fires. In S.T. Cole & P.J. Wicks (Eds.), *Industrial Fires Workshop Proceedings.* Report EUR 15340 EN, European Commission.

Marliere, F. (1996). Acute toxicity of smoke: Study of gaseous interactions. In S.T. Cole & P.J. Wicks (Eds.), *Industrial Fires III Workshop Proceedings.* Report EUR 17477 EN, European Commission.

Martins, J.M., & Borrego, C. (1994). Simulation of the atmospheric dispersion of gases and aerosols. In S.T. Cole & P.J. Wicks (Eds.), *Industrial Fires II Workshop Proceedings.* Report EUR 15967 EN, European Commission.

Martins, J.M., Borrego, C., Holdin, A., & Mejean, P. (1996). Comparison of the real scale, wind tunnel and numerical model results of atmospheric dispersion in the vicinity of a building. In S.T. Cole & P.J. Wicks (Eds.), *Industrial Fires III Workshop Proceedings.* Report EUR 17477 EN, European Commission.

Miles, S.D., & Cox, G. (1994). Transient computational fluid dynamics model to predict fire product emissions from warehouses. In S.T. Cole & P.J. Wicks (Eds.), *Industrial Fires II Workshop Proceedings.* Report EUR 15967 EN, European Commission.

Porter, S.R., Hall, D.J., & Carruthers, D.J. (1996). Physical and computer modelling of dispersion of toxic smoke from warehouse fires. In S.T. Cole & P.J. Wicks (Eds.), *Industrial Fires III Workshop Proceedings.* Report EUR 17477 EN, European Commission.

Webber, D.M., Jones, S. J., & Martin, D. (1993). A model of the motion of a heavy gas cloud released on a uniform slope. *Journal of Hazardous Materials, 33,* 101-122.

About the Editors

Lorenz M. Hilty received his degree in Computer Science and his PhD from Hamburg University. As a postdoc, he worked in the field of environmental information processing with Prof. Dr. H. C. Binswanger at the University of St. Gallen, Institute for Economy and the Environment, and with Prof. Dr. Dr. F. J. Radermacher at the Research Institute for Applied Knowledge Processing (FAW) in Ulm, Section for Environmental Information Systems. His habilitation (postdoctoral thesis) on "Environ-mental Information Processing – Contributions of Informatics to Sustainable Develop-ment" was accepted by the Computer Science Department of Hamburg University in 1997. Dr. Hilty has published more than 70 scientific articles and books on environmental and social aspects of Computing. At present, he is the head of the Technology and Society Laboratory at the Swiss Federal Laboratories for Materials Testing and Research (EMPA), professor for Information Systems at the University of Applied Sciences Northwestern Switzerland (FHSO) and lecturer at several Swiss universities.

Eberhard K. Seifert studied economics and social sciences, history and philosophy at the Cologne, Hamburg, and Wuppertal universities where he was awarded a PhD in economics on the genesis and development of industrial working times (1985). After research and teaching at these universities and the Hamburg Institute for Social Research on socio-economic and bioeconomic subjects, he co-designed in 1992/93 the program for the new working group on "New Models of Wealth" at the Wuppertal Institute for Climate, Environment and Energy where he has been working since 1993. Dr. Seifert changed the Environment Department and worked with the new director, Prof. P. Bartelmus, on new measures of "wealth" on the macro as well as the micro level. In particular he worked on green accounting serving among others as for example co-author of the Club-of-Rome Report "Taking Nature into Account" and as a member of the scientific council of the Environmental Ministry for the implementation of green accounting in the federal statistical office system. Recently he was co-editor with Bartelmus of the reader "Green Accounting"/Ashgate-UK 2003. Dr. Seifert is involved in corresponding activities at the ISO TC 207 process on Environmental Management standards ISO 14000-series several national DIN. International functions include "Environmental Performance Evaluation" (ISO 14031), Environmental communication forthcoming ISO 14063 and "Climate Change" ISO 14064.

René H. Treibert was born in 1960. He studied mathematics and economics at the Bergische University Wuppertal. From 1985 until 1988, he was a scientist at the Department of Safety Technology of the Battelle-Institut Europe in Frankfurt/Main. In 1989, he earned a doctoral degree in Safety Engineering at the Bergische University Wuppertal under the supervision of Prof. Dr. Sylvius Hartwig. From 1989 until 1994, he worked at the Department of Information Technology for Environment at PSI AG, Berlin, as a leader of various projects in Waste Management. From 1994 until 2002, he led the Department of Application Systems at the public utility company of Düsseldorf. In 2003, he was appointed to Honorarprofessor at the Department of Safety Engineering of the Bergische University Wuppertal. Since 2003, he has been a professor of Business Informatics in the Department of Economics at Niederrhein University of Applied Sciences.

About the Authors

Klaus Bieber was born in 1966 in Bavaria, Germany, and studied electrical engineering at the University of Karlsruhe. He started working with T-Systems in 1992 as a software developer. Since 1998, he has been head of the project group "Measuring Networks and Environmental Information Systems" at T-Systems in Ulm, Germany. His area of responsibility includes the development of decision support systems in the context of safety, such as early warning systems and remote monitoring systems.

Stefan Bräker was born in 1960 in Leverkusen, Germany. He studied geography, geology and geoecology at the University of Cologne, Germany, promoted to assessor at the Ministry of Economics of North Rhine Westfalia, Germany, and graduated from the University of Tübingen, Germany. From 1988-1993, he operated as assessor at the authority of geological survey of North Rhine Westfalia at Krefeld. Since 1993, he has been a senior consultant at the environmental management consultancy of the Dr. Werner Wohlfarth Institute. As consultant, he aids industrial customers und the authorities with all kinds of complex environmental solutions and is expert on permit procedures and environmental protection. He is specialized in integrated management systems and due diligences of company organisation structures and legal compliance. In addition to consulting activities he operates as external auditor. His profession includes environmental and safety and health audits at different industrial sectors of various size, from handicraft enterprises to large concerns such as nuclear power plants, automotive and railway fabrication, metal production and aircraft maintenance. He lectures on legal certainty, management systems, management by delegation, emission trading and so forth at different further education institutes.

Constantinos Cartalis is assistant professor at the University of Athens, Greece, Department of Physics. He holds a BSc in physics from the University of Athens, an MSc in aerospace engineering, an MSc in atmospheric science and a PhD in atmospheric physics with an emphasis in remote sensing from the University of Michigan (USA). He has been specializing in the use of image processing techniques for the analysis of satellite images of various types. He has worked as an expert for the European Union on earth observation matters with relevant participation in specialised thematic co-operation groups and in the pathfinder and design and implementation steering committees of the Centre for Earth Observation. He has been involved in R&D projects funded by the EU, the Ministry of Environment Physical Planning and Public Works, the Ministry of Education and others. Dr. Cartalis has published several articles in journals on the use of earth observation for environmental applications.

Nektarios Chrysoulakis is a researcher at the Foundation for Research & Technology - Hellas (Greece), Institute of Applied and Computational Mathematics. He holds a BSc in physics, an MSc in environmental physics and a PhD in remote sensing from the University of Athens. Dr. Chrysoulakis has been involved in R&D projects funded by the EU, the General Secretariat of Research and Technology of Greece, the Ministry of Environment Physical Planning and Public Works, the Ministry of Education and others. He has considerable experience in the area of remote sensing and his main research interests include radiative transfer and surface fluxes, digital image processing, DEM development and 3D visualizations, atmospheric and microclimatic physics, environmental monitoring and change detection.

Aldo de Moor works as an assistant professor in the Department of Information Systems and Management of Tilburg University, The Netherlands. He holds a PhD in information management from this university and has been a visiting researcher at the University of Guelph, Canada, and the University of Technology in Sydney. His research interests include the evolution of virtual communities, communicative action theories, user participation in systems development, normative system specification methods and the impact of ICT on society. Projects in which he has participated include the development of the GRASS environmental argumentation support system, an electronic journal, a business negotiation support system, and various virtual community development projects.

Stefan Enzler was born in 1969 and has studies economics and social science at the University of Augsburg in Germany. He has spend eight years in the areas of managerial research and consultancy. His main topics of interest include flow management, environmental management systems including management information systems and integrated management systems. For the last six years, he has focused on the field of flow management and flow cost accounting. He has been an expert speaker at several international symposia and diverse universities. He has projects with several co-operation partners of the Institute for Management and the Environment among others: Freudenberg Haushaltsprodukte Augsburg KG (Augsburg, Germany), Dr. Grandel GmbH (Augsburg, Germany), Carl Zeiss Foundation (Oberkochen, Germany), and Lucent Technologies GmbH (Augsburg, Germany). Since 1995, he has been a partner of the Institute for Management and the Environment (Germany), which functions as a mediator between the scientific and practical worlds.

Rolf Frischknecht studied civil engineering at the Swiss Federal Institute of Technology (ETH), Zurich, Switzerland. From 1990-1997, he worked for the Department of Energy Technology at ETH Zurich on methodology, data collection and data management for life cycle inventories of energy systems and was responsible for the development of the first version of an Internet-based LCA database. He wrote his PhD on life cycle inventory analysis and decision making. Since 1998, he has led a consulting company on life cycle assessment and material flow analysis and works for multinational companies as well as for national and local authorities. He is project leader of the E ecoinvent 2000 project, teaches LCA at ETH Zürich and is a member of the editorial board of the *International Journal of LCA*.

Simon Giesecke was born in 1980. In 1997, he received the youth prize of the Eduard Rhein Foundation for Radio, Television and Information Technology. From 1998-2003, he studied informatics and mathematics at Carl von Ossietzky University of Oldenburg. He was supported by a scholarship of the German National Academic Foundation. In 2003, he completed his diploma with a thesis on "Clone-based Reengineering for Java on the Eclipse Platform" under Prof. Dr. Wilhelm Hasselbring. In October 2003, he began his doctorate studies under Prof. Dr.-Ing. Manfred Nagl in the graduate school "Software for Communication Systems" at RWTH Aachen funded by the German Research Foundation (DFG).

Paul W. Gilgen was born 1945 in Berne/Switzerland and studied chemistry, physics and mathematics (as well as human sciences) at the University of Berne. He earned a licentiate degree (Msc). His first industrial experience was in the

Research and Development Department of a Dutch printing ink manufacturer. He spent 10 years in the Research and Development Department of a Swiss company involved in the development and worldwide distribution of electrochemical analytical instruments – the instruments are used particularly for the trace and ultra-trace analyses favoured in environmental and process analysis. From 1987, he has been an assistant vice president, head of the corporate ecology team in the corporate staff of Alusuisse-Lonza multinational group of companies. Since 1996, he has been head of the Ecology Department (in the meantime renamed to Technology Cooperation) at Swiss Federal Laboratories for Materials Testing and Research. Since 1990, he has been a lecturer at the University of Zurich in the academic MBA courses. He is a founding member and deputy chairman in Ecoinvent steering committee (Ecoinvent is the most comprehensive and worldwide-leading LCI/LCA database).

Hans-Dietrich Haasis was born in 1958. He studied industrial engineering, graduated and was promoted to professor at the University of Karlsruhe. In 1994, he was appointed to professor at the University of Bremen. From 1986-1994, he was leader of the research group "System Analysis: Energy, Environment, Industrial Production" at the Institute of Business Administration and Industrial Production. The subject of his postdoctoral lecture qualification is: "Planning and Control of Low Emission to Run Industrial Production Systems." He gave lectures at the Ecole Nationale Supérieur de Pétrole et des Moteurs, Paris Rueil-Malmaison and at the University of Eichstätt-Ingolstadt. Since 1997, he has been a professor for the Chair of Business Administration, Production Management and Industrial Economics. From 1998-2001, he was dean of the Department of Economics. Since December 2001, he has been director of the Institute of Shipping Economics and Logistics (Germany).

Jan Hedemann is director of Software Development at IFU Hamburg GmbH in Germany. He graduated in computer science from the University of Hamburg, Germany. Since 1993, he has been responsible for the ongoing development of the LCA and material flow management software Umberto. As a project leader, Hedemann has managed various software projects, such as the technical implementation of the Ecoinvent 2000 database for the Swiss Centre for Life Cycle Inventories. Other projects targeted at an integration of Umberto into existing corporate IT environments. In a research project he developed the interface between SAP R/3 and Umberto, described in this publication.

Klaus-Dieter Herrmann studied electrical technology and did his PhD in this field. He has acquired special knowledge in environment informatics, in particular information systems for dangerous goods/GIS. Furthermore, he has gained detailed knowledge in environment safety law and quality assurance law, as well as in ISO 9001 quality management. He is a K3 product manager. Since 1999 he has been product and project manager with Kisters AG in Aachen, Germany.

Roland Hischier is working as a project manager at the Swiss Federal Laboratories for Materials Testing and Research (EMPA). He has a degree as "Nat. Sc. ETH" from the Department of Environmental Sciences at ETH Zürich, Switzerland. His research is focussed on questions in the area of life cycle assessment (LCA) and environmental information systems. At the moment, he is a local project leader for the project "Ecoinvent 2000" – a project together with other institutes from the ETH domain that aims to establish a publicly accessible Swiss national LCI (life cycle inventory) database.

Catherine Houstis received her BS and MS in electrical engineering and her PhD in computer science (Purdue University, USA). She was an assistant and associate professor for the Electrical and Computer Engineering Department of University of South Carolina, an associate professor with the Electrical Engineering Department of Purdue University, and an associate professor and full professor with the Computer Science Department of University of Crete, Greece. Currently, she is a full professor with the Computer & Communications Engineering Department of University of Thessaly, Greece. She is also head of the Distributed Systems Laboratory at the Institute of Computer Science – FORTH.

Walter Hürster was born 1947 in Schmieheim, Germany, and studied physics at the University of Freiburg. He was attracted to nuclear physics and the physics of elementary particle at higher energies. After his research work at the Swiss Institute for Nuclear Research (formerly SIN, now PSI), he changed to the field of computer science and the executive management of application projects, such as radar-based air surveillance systems (national and international), air traffic/nautical control and information systems (national and international), safety critical avionics systems, early warning/public warning, risk and emergency management systems, simulation systems, remote monitoring of nuclear power plants and radiation protection. His current position is principal consultant embedded services and information management, with specific emphasis on the subject of environmental information systems, early warning and risk management systems.

Ralf Isenmann lectures on economics, business administration and industrial engineering at the Technical University of Kaiserslautern, Germany, and has also background in applied computer science and industrial ecology. He is a senior researcher with the Department of Business Information Systems and Operations Research (BiOR), head: Prof. Dr. Heiner Müller-Merbach, and executive manager of several research projects focussed on using ICT – especially the Internet and associated technologies such as XML – for corporate reporting. Before, he worked as research fellow at the Department of Philosophy and then as project manager at an interdisciplinary research program. He published more than 40 refereed contributions, in particular in the fields of Internet-based corporate reporting, environmental informatics and industrial ecology.

Chris Jarvis has worked with national public organizations in the field of environmental information provision for more than 10 years. Initially producing "State of the Environment" reports, he has moved to be responsible for ensuring that the Environment Agency of England and Wales is an open and transparent organisation that values the provision of information in raising environmental awareness. He manages the agency's commercial "Property Search Service," which provides relevant and timely environmental information for house buyers in a format that specifically meets their needs (*www.environment-agency.gov.uk/propertysearch)*. He is currently leading on a number of new initiatives for the agency, which includes the electronic provision of licensing information to engage the public in environmental decision making, and a joint project with the UN on transfer of capability in electronic environmental information provision to eastern Europe.

Per Henrik Johansen works at Interconsult Norgit AS (Norway) as a systems developer. The main focus is on open standards and open source software mainly in the GIS area. He got his education in informatics at Ostfold Regional College and the Norwegian University of Science and Technology, specializing in HCI. Prior to working at Interconsult Norgit, Per Henrik was a project manager and group leader at Statistics Norway and was working on both domestic and international projects, and was a member of the Statistical Open Source Consortium.

Gunnar Jürgens was born in 1970. He studied environmental engineering at the Technical University of Berlin, Germany. From 1997-2002, he was scientist and leader of the Environmental Management Group at the Fraunhofer Institute for Industrial Engineering in Stuttgart, Germany. His main areas of scientific work include: applied science in the context of supporting the effective handling of environmental information in environmental management systems. In 2002, he earned a doctoral degree at the University of Stuttgart. Since 2003, he has been an environmental manager for product development at Continental Teves in Frankfurt, Germany.

Kostas Karatzas is a research leader at the Laboratory of Heat Transfer and Environmental Engineering, the Department of Mechanical Engineering, Aristotle University of Thessaloniki (AUTh), Greece, heading the group of Environmental Informatics and is an adjunct assistant professor with the Department of Engineering and Management of Energy Resources at AUTh. He holds a diploma and a doctor degree in mechanical engineering from AUTh. He works mainly in the field of integrated software system applications, focusing primarily on urban air quality management and information issues, multimedia information content tools, and e-content engineering applications. He is the author and co-author of more than 80 refereed and non-refereed scientific publications, has served as a reviewer for international peer-review journals, as a scientific committee member for international conferences and has participated in several national and international research projects.

Bruno Klahn was born 1947 in Winsen (Luhe), Germany, and studied mathematics and physics at the Technical University of Clausthal and at the University of Göttingen. His special attention was attracted by quantum chemistry, mathematical physics, and the structures of organic molecules and their determination by quantum chemical computational methods. After his research work at the University of Göttingen and the University of Delaware (USA), he changed to the field of computer science and the management of IT application projects, such as air traffic control systems, public warning, radar based surveillance, remote monitoring of nuclear power plants and radiation protection, e-government, and traffic management. His current position is head of a department that realizes, introduces, and maintains customer specific IT systems, especially in the public sector. The currently most important projects are remote monitoring of nuclear power plants, electronic land register, and event management traffic.

Rolf Kleef works at AIDEnvironment (The Netherlands), a non-profit consultancy organization in natural resource management, and specializes in virtual communities, collaborative environments, knowledge management networks and platforms. He works for environmental and development organizations, ranging from government departments to civil society organizations. A key aspect in his work is creating stimulating online environments to support collaboration and discussion between stakeholders. He holds an MSc in computer science and has been keen to link practical experiences in Internet-enabled communication processes around policy-making and learning to theories of collaborative communities and organizational development.

Helmut Krcmar has held the chair for Information Systems with the Department of Informatics, Technische Universität München (TUM), Germany, since 2002. He is also a member of the faculty of the TUM Business School. He received his MBA and PhD in business administration from the University of Saarbrücken. At the Institute for Information Systems, University Saarbrücken, he worked as researcher and management consultant with Prof. Dr. H.C. Mult, A.-W. Scheer, then as post doctoral fellow at the IBM Los Angeles Scientific Center, as assistant professor of Information Systems at the Leonard Stern Graduate School of Business, New York University, and as assistant professor of Information Systems at Baruch College, City University of New York. From 1987-2002, he held the chair for Information Systems at Hohenheim University, Stuttgart, Germany, where he also served as dean of the Faculty of Business, Economics and Social Sciences from 2000-2002. His research interests include information and knowledge management, IT-enabled value Webs, service management, computer supported cooperative work (CSCW) and information systems in health care and e-government.

Martin Kreeb studied economics and business administration, specializing in environmental economics and management, at the Universities of Stuttgart/Hohenheim, St. Gallen and Witten/Herdecke. He is one of the founders of the Competence Center for Sustainable Management (dknw) at the Witten/Herdecke University funded by the Deutsche Bundesstiftung Umwelt (DBU), Osnabrück. Currently he is working as managing director of the research project "www.ecoradar.org" at the German Competence Center for Sustainable Management (dknw), at Witten/Herdecke University and at Hohenheim University. His main interests are environmental performance evaluation, computer supported environmental information systems and environmental cost management.

Torsten Kriwald was born in 1972. He studied economics and business administration at the University of Bremen, Germany. From 1997-2001, he was a scientist and lecturer at the chair of Business Administration, Production Management and Industrial Engineering, University of Bremen, Germany. Since 2002, he has been project manager at the Institute of Shipping Economics and Logistics in Bremen, Germany. His main areas of scientific work include: knowledge management, logistics systems, process and production integrated environmental protection and sustainable development.

Michael Kuhndt studied chemical engineering, environmental management and policy in Germany, Sweden and the US. In 1997, he worked as a research assistant for General Motors developing and applying environmental information for decision support. In 1998-1999, he worked for the European Commission on linking environmental information demand and supply in industry and science. Currently he is a senior consultant within the "Eco-Efficiency and Sustainable Enterprise Team" at the Wuppertal Institute and director of Triple Innova. He is a member of the Centre of Environmental Science, Leiden University, Germany, the Global Reporting Initiative, the Factor 10 Innovation Network and member of the European Eco-Efficiency Network launched by the WBCSD and the European Partners for the Environment. Since 1999, he has been a consultant at United Nations Environment Programs. At the present he is a project manager in the field of information technology (e-commerce and e-work) and sustainable development, the assessment of product value chains and the design of sectoral sustainability indicator set based on multistakeholder approaches.

John Kupiec has a background in environmental research – specifically in forestry and remote sensing, gaining an MSc (Aberdeen) and a PhD (Wales). Since leaving academic research work, John has worked for the Scottish Natural Heritage (government agency for nature conservation in Scotland) as a research and advisory officer (1994-1998). Since 1998, John has worked for the Environment Agency (UK and Wales) in the field of data/GIS/computer sciences applied to environmental issues.

Spyros Lalis received his diploma in computer engineering and a PhD in technical sciences from the Swiss Federal Institute of Technology Zurich (ETHZ) (1989 and 1994, respectively). From 1989-1994, he was research assistant at the Institute of Computer Systems of the Swiss Federal Institute of Technology Zurich (ETHZ). From 1997-1999, he was a visiting assistant professor with the Computer Science Department of the University of Crete. Since 1997, he has been a research associate at the Institute for Computer Science of the Foundation for Research and Technology Hellas (FORTH). Since 2000, he has been an assistant professor at the Computer and Communications Engineering Department of the University of Thessaly.

Jon Erik Lindberg works at Interconsult Norgit AS (Norway) as an advisor and project coordinator. He has a degree in social sciences from the University of Bergen, Norway. For several years he worked as an advisor in Statistics Norway, gaining experience from several statistical fields. He was also engaged in statistical cooperation at Nordic and European levels. From 1997 he has been engaged in Interconsult Norgit AS as a project coordinator and is responsible for marketing, research and development activities towards central and local government administrations. He is also an expert on demography and population projections and works as a consultant towards planning authorities in several local governments.

Reinhard Micheler was born in 1958 in Bavaria, Germany, and studied technical informatics in Ulm. From 1983-1988, he worked at Dornier as a software developer for environmental information and monitoring systems. From 1988-1997, he was project manager for the first renewal of the remote monitoring systems for nuclear power plants (Federal States of Baden-Württemberg and Rheinland-Pfalz). He was also responsible for a feasibility study for remote monitoring systems for the state of Hungary. Since 1997, he has been working as a project manager with T-Systems in the field of monitoring systems for nuclear power plants and administration systems for public clients and authorities.

Andreas Möller majored in computer science and is an expert in material flow management. He developed the concept of material flow networks and played an important role in the Umberto software development at ifu Hamburg GmbH. He further researched on the incorporation of cost accounting systems in material flow management (material flow-based cost accounting), interface requirements for environmental information systems and integration of material flow management software into enterprise resource planning (ERP) systems. He currently leads the Department of Environmental Informatics at the University of Lüneburg, Germany.

Peter Müller-Beilschmidt studied computer science at the University of Erlangen-Nürnberg, Germany, and the University of Hamburg, Germany. His specialization is in environmental informatics. In 1994, he joined the Umberto software development team at IFU Hamburg GmbH. Later, Müller-Beilschmidt became head of sales and marketing at IFU. In this role, he focuses on life cycle assessment (LCA) studies and material flow management implementation projects for customers from producing industries. His interest is developing new international markets for environmental information systems and he has lectured repeatedly on industrial ecology topics in Asia and South America.

Stefan Naumann was born 1969 in Lower Saxony, Germany, and studied computer science in Kaiserslautern and Saarbrücken. During his study he founded an office for environmental affairs called “Umweltwerkstatt” and started several projects for environmental protection. Since 1998, he has worked as a member of the scientific staff at the University of Applied Sciences Trier (Location Umwelt-Campus Birkenfeld), the Institute for Software Systems in Business, Environment and Administration. He is engaged in several NGOs, especially in the "Bund für Umwelt- und Naturschutz Deutschland," the German branch of "Friends of Earth". He is member of a "food-coop" for common procurement of organic food since 1993 and, in 2001, started the project titled "Decentralized Eco-village" in the region where he lives. His research interests are sustainable development in conjunction with online communities and the environmental and social impacts of information technology.

Roland Obrecht was born 1956 in Stuttgart, Germany, and studied chemistry in Munich, Bavaria. Starting his work in 1986 for the Bavarian Environmental Protection Agency in the field of radiation protection and radiological environmental protection, he was involved in the development of IMIS – the German Integrated Radioactivity Information and Decision Support System. In 1991, he changed to the Ministry of Environment and Transport (Federal State of Baden-Württemberg), being engaged for radiation protection, environmental radiation protection, supervision of the emissions from nuclear power plants, the telemetric monitoring system for nuclear power plants (KFÜ Baden-Württemberg) and emergency management for nuclear power plants. He is member of several working groups for radiation protection, such as the German-French and German-Swiss Commission for the safety and security of nuclear power plants.

Bernd Page holds degrees in applied informatics from the Technical University (TU) of Berlin, Germany, and from Stanford University, USA. Prof. Page was employed as a scientific associate in the Environmental Information System Group at the German Federal Environmental Agency in Berlin before he was appointed professor for Applied Informatics with the Computer Science Department at the University of Hamburg (Germany), where he is doing research and teaching in the field of computer simulation and environmental informatics.

Gertraud Peinel received her MS in business computing (Applied Mathematics and Economy) from the University of Ulm in 1993. She joined the Research Institute for Applied Knowledge Processing (FAW) at the University of Ulm, Germany, in 1993 and worked as project manager in the department of business processes and telematics of FAW. Her fields of expertise include system architectures, Internet technologies and implementations as well as information navigation. She was working on projects in the domain of electronic trade networks, system interoperability, and integrated data and flow management in heterogeneous system environments. She was also project manager on behalf of the FAW for several projects for the EC as well as national funded projects. Since January 2003 she works for FIT (Fraunhofer Institute for Applied Information Technology), Schloss Birlinghoven, Germany, in the research group on business process management and co-ordination of marketing and sales projects. She also manages the EC projects APNEE-TU and Env-e-City on behalf of FIT.

Roland Pfennig was born 1961 in Heilbronn, Germany, and studied forestry science in Freiburg i. Brsg, Germany. Since 1990, he works as an IT consultant and since 1989 he is engaged in the "Naturschutzbund Deutschland (NABU)". In 2001, he worked as a member of Green IT GmbH, Konstanz, Germany, in the "Eco Rapid" project, being responsible for the realization of flow cost accounting with the SAP BW (Business Information Warehouse). His research interests are sustainable development in conjunction with reference models and business intelligence.

Marios Pitikakis received his BSc in mathematics and BSc in computer science from University of Crete, Greece (1996 and 2000, respectively). Currently he is senior software engineer and research assistant at the Distributed Systems Lab of the Institute of Computer Science – FORTH, Greece.

Alfred Posch has been a university assistant for the Institute of Innovation and Environmental Management at the School of Economics and Social Sciences of the Karl-Franzens-University of Graz since 1996. He spent eight years working in the food industry. He earned a master's degree in business administration and in business education, and a PhD in business administration. His current research fields are: sustainable development, environmental management and information systems, intercompany partnering and networking in industry.

Poulicos Prastacos is director of research in the Regional Analysis Division of the Institute of Applied and Computational Mathematics of Researcher in Foundation for Research and Technology - Hellas, Greece. He holds a PhD in transportation systems and regional planning, University of Illinois, Urbana-Champaign (1981), a Master of Science in construction management, University of Illinois (1976), and a BS in civil engineering, Columbia University (1975). His main research interests include GIS applications for transportation, environment, regional planning; statistical, geographic and environmental databases; Web GIS and applications on the Internet; development of land use, transportation, and regional economic models; and implementation of decision support systems. In the past he was associate professor at Stanford University, California, and a senior planner at the Association of Bay Area Governments in Oakland, in charge of the design and development of forecasting models for the San Francisco Bay Area. He has collaborated with many organizations in Europe and the USA on the development of environmental and statistical databases, design of transportation and economic forecasting models, linking models with GIS databases and implementing methods for impact assessment. He has published more than 30 scientific papers in the areas of transportation modelling, mathematical models, integration of GIS tools in decision support, and environmental information systems.

Gerriet Reents was born in 1972. From 1992-1998, he studied informatics at Carl von Ossietzky University of Oldenburg. In 1993, he was awarded "prize-winner" of the 11th "Bundeswettbewerb Informatik" of the German Informatics Society (GI). He completed his diploma thesis on "Effizienzsteigerung bei der verteilten Thor-Netz-Simulation" in 1996. Since 1998, he has been working on his dissertation on carpool assignment algorithms advised by Prof. Dr. Michael Sonnenschein at the Environmental Informatics Group at the Carl von Ossietzky University of Oldenburg.

Christoph Roenick is a certified engineer in economic engineering with an emphasis in business management, mechanical engineering and environment technology. He has acquired special knowledge in environment safety technology management, environment information systems in the field of public administration and industry, information systems for dangerous goods and energy data management systems. Since 1999, he has been sales and marketing manager with Kisters AG in Aachen, Germany, with a focus on environmental informatics.

Dirk Rohdemann holds a degree in business administration of the University of Siegen, Germany. Before joining SAP in 1996, he was consultant for environmental management systems. At SAP, Dirk Rohdemann worked in environment, health & safety as well as recipe management with different responsibilities. Since beginning of 2003, he has been a manager in a SAP's Strategic Research and Development, Germany.

Thomas Rose received his diploma in computer science from the University of Dortmund (1985), and a doctoral degree in computer science from the University of Passau (1991). From 1990-1993, he was a research associate with the Department of Computer Science at the University of Toronto, Ontario, Canada. From October 1993 until recently, he has been a senior researcher with the

Research Institute for Applied Knowledge Processing (FAW) at the University of Ulm, Germany. Rose was head of the Department of Business Processes and Telematics. Particular emphasis has been put on applications of information and communication management technologies and services to optimize current service and business processes and eventually to design new services for businesses and the citizen. At FAW, Rose has been managing several projects for industrial sponsors and publicly funded research projects. He has been project coordinator of APNEE as well as APNEE-TU and served as technical coordinator for a number of projects. Recently, Rose has moved to FIT (Fraunhofer Institute for Applied Information Technology), Schloss Birlinghoven, Germany. He is head of the research group on business.

Annette Rudel studied law and media at the Universities of Freiburg, Düsseldorf, and the Technical University of Berlin (TU), Germany. She focused on knowledge management, Web communities and environmental management. Since 1998, she has worked on research projects with the Universities of Witten/Herdecke and Hohenheim. Currently she is working as a research fellow for the NWD-Institute, Stuttgart and Berlin.

Wolfgang Scheide is managing director of Green IT GmbH, Germany, a company specialized not only in tracing and tracking material flows but also developing solutions for industrial enterprises. In addition to the commercial activities, he continues to be involved as a researcher in several research projects. In both areas, he is particularly interested in finding a balanced mix of flow methods, IT tools and communication instruments to solve issues related to efficient and environmentally sound material use. He teaches on a regular basis eco-management at the University of Applied Sciences Constance (Department of Information Systems). He was awarded a PhD from the University of Hohenheim in Stuttgart (1988), where he also worked as a research and teaching associate at the Institute of Business Administration (Department of Information Systems) and at the Institute of Farm Management (Department of Computer Applications and Business Management). His dissertation empirically analyzed the information management in the German food industry.

Fritz Schmidt was born in 1941 in Heilbronn, Germany. He studied physics and nuclear engineering in Stuttgart and during an 18-month visit at Oak Ridge National Laboratory. He got his PhD in engineering (1970) and became a professor for simulation of complex systems in 2001. He is head of the Department for Knowledge Engineering and Numerics of the IKE (Germany). He is responsible for teaching in the field of simulation of complex technical systems. He has contributed numerous papers in nuclear physics and engineering, numerical methods in nuclear engineering, reactor safety and development of integral information systems. In 1998, he and his team specialized on distributed systems and developed new technologies to support model based interpretations of data available in large online database systems. These systems include nuclear monitoring systems, monitoring systems for large buildings and e-learning systems.

Mario Schmidt is professor of Environmental Management at the University of Applied Science in Pforzheim, Germany, and director of the Institute of Applied Sciences IAF. Since 1985, he has worked in the fields of radioecology, emission control and climate change, environmental management systems and life cycle assessment (LCA). In 1989 and 1990, he joined the ministry of environment of the state of Hamburg. Afterwards he built up a new department at ifeu-Institute for Energy and Environmental Research Heidelberg focussed on ecological material flow analysis and management systems. He was responsible for numerous studies in behalf of the German government and many companies. He has written and edited some books about material flow analysis and environmental management

Bernd Schmitt was born in 1970. He studied landscape ecology at the Technical University (TH) of Karlsruhe, Germany, and ecology at the University of Burgundy in Dijon, France. He received his diploma in 1998. Schmitt worked as scientific assistant at the Institute for Energy and Environmental Research (ifeu) in Heidelberg, Germany, and at the Fraunhofer Institute for Systems and Innovation Research (ISI) in Karlsruhe, Germany. Since 1999, he has worked for SAP AG in Walldorf, Germany, in the areas environment, health & safety (EH&S) and product lifecycle management (PLM).

Uwe Schneidewind was born in 1966 in Cologne, Germany. From 1986-1991, he studied business administration at the University Cologne (D) and HEC, Paris. From 1991-1992, he was a strategic consultant in environmental management at Roland Berger & Partner, Düsseldorf. From 1993-1997, he was a research assistant at the Institute for Economy and the Environment (IWO-HSG) at University of St. Gall (PhD- and Habilitation thesis on strategic environmental management issues). Since 1998, Schneidewind has been a full professor for Production Management and the Environment at the University of Oldenburg, Germany. His research interests include: e-organization in business and society.

Werner Schulz studied economics at the Technical University of Berlin. In 1985, he earned a doctorate in economics. Between 1985-1999, he served *inter*

alia as director of the "Environmental Economics and Social Issues" unit at the Federal Environmental Agency. Since 1999, he has held the rank of full professor of Environmental Management at the University of Stuttgart/Hohenheim and worked as director of the German Competence Center for Sustainable Management, Witten/Herdecke University. He is the head of the research project *www.ecoradar.org* funded by the German Federal Ministry of Education and Research. His specializations include: sustainable and environmental management and policy advice.

Werner Strauß is a certified engineer in physical technology with an emphasis in metallurgy and metal physics. In addition he has studied nuclear power plant technology, reactor physics and radiation protection. He has acquired special knowledge as an engineering specialist for industrial safety, a commissioner of pollution control and as a commissioner of radiation protection and transportation systems. He is a certified auditor for ISO 9001. Since 1999, he has been product manager with Kisters AG in Aachen, Germany, with a focus on business and environmental protection information systems.

Markus Strobel studied business economics at the University of Augsburg, Germany. In 1992, he, together with Prof. Wagner, founded the imu augsburg, which is a research and consulting institute in the field of management and ecology. Since 1990, he has managed several projects for multinational companies (Ciba, Novartis, etc.) as well as for national and local authorities. He is the project manager of the major and well-known project eco-effizienz (www.eco-effizienz.de). His PhD is about flow management and flow cost accounting. In addition to teaching at the Management Center of the University of Augsburg, he also is a speaker at international conferences and author of several books and articles.

Volker Türk, MSc, studied land resources management at the University Giessen, Germany, and environmental management and policy at the International Institute for Industrial Environmental Economics in Lund, Sweden. Currently working as consultant in the Eco-Efficiency and Sustainable Enterprises Team at the Wuppertal Institute for Climate, Environment and Energy, Germany, his focus area is the sustainability assessment of new technologies. He has worked extensively on information and communication technologies and their applications, ranging from the assessment and improvement of products, life-cycle wide analysis of e-business applications to sectoral analysis. Nanotechnology, as new emerging technology, has developed a subsequent area of expertise. A second competence field are tools and concepts for a sustainable development in enterprises, ranging from performance evaluation, capacity building to management approaches.

George V. Vasilakis received his diploma in computer engineering and informatics from the University of Patras, Greece, and an MSc in advanced computing from the Imperial College of London (1999 and 2000, respectively). Currently he is a software engineer and research assistant at the Distributed Systems Lab of the Institute of Computer Science – FORTH.

Emmanuel Vavalis received his BSc in mathematics from Aristotelian University of Thessaloniki, an MSc and PhD in numerical analysis from Brunel University, UK, and Aristotelian University of Thessaloniki, respectively. He was an assistant professor with the Computer Science Department of Purdue University, USA, and an assistant professor with the Mathematics Department of the University of Crete, Greece. Currently, he is associate professor with the Mathematics Department of University of Crete, Greece. He was a researcher at the Institute of Applied & Computational Mathematics - FORTH and currently he is a researcher at the Institute of Computer Science - FORTH.

Christof Voßeler studied environmental engineering at the Technical University of Berlin, Germany. Between 1997-2001, he worked in the field of environmental management in the frame of development co-operation for the Deutsche Gesellschaft für Technische Zusammenarbeit (GTZ, German Corporation for International Cooperation) GmbH and as program manager for the Internationale Weiterbildung und Entwicklung gGmbH (InWent). He developed tools for environmental and chemicals management and managed several international projects in Southern Africa and South-East Asia. Since 2001, he has been a researcher at the Institute for Environmental Management of the University of Hohenheim. Voßeler works within the project "*www.oekoradar.de*". His main research topic is sustainable technology management.

Justus von Geibler studied forest sciences and environmental management and policy in Germany and Sweden. In 1997, he worked as public relations assistant for waste management in a governmental administration. From 1997-1999, he was a research and teaching assistant at the University Göttingen with focus on the development and use of different analytical tools for forest measurement and management. Since October 2000, he is working at the Eco-efficiency and Sustainable Enterprise Group in the fields of concept and tools for sustainable business development, sustainability evaluation of new technologies (information and communication technologies, biotechnologies), sectoral approaches to sustainable development as well as for International Networking.

Thomas Wilbois was born 1965 in Mandern / Germany and studied physics at the University of Mainz. His special attention was attracted by theoretical nuclear physics, especially in the investigation of electromagnetic and strong interactions in few body systems. After his research work at the universities of Mainz and Hannover and various international collaborations, he changed to the field of computer science and the management of IT application projects. His main fields are object relational databases and software designs for servers. As a Project Manager he is responsible for development, introduction, and maintenance of customer specific IT systems, especially in the public sector. The currently most important project is the Remote Monitoring of Nuclear Power Plants.

Volker Wohlgemuth was born in 1966. He studied computer science at the universities of Hamburg, Germany, and Christchurch, New Zealand (1991-1997). In 1997, he earned his degree as dipl. Informatiker from the University of Hamburg. Since 1997, he has worked as a research assistant with the Department of Computer Science, Social and Applied Oriented Unit, University of Hamburg as well as senior environmental software developer at the ifu Hamburg GmbH. His research interest lies in the field of modelling and simulating environmental business systems.

Index

D

E